BANKING AND BANKING DEVELOPMENTS

BANK FAILURES DURING THE FINANCIAL CRISIS

CAUSES AND CONSEQUENCES

BANKING AND BANKING DEVELOPMENTS

Additional books in this series can be found on Nova's website under the Series tab.

Additional E-books in this series can be found on Nova's website under the E-book tab.

ECONOMIC ISSUES, PROBLEMS AND PERSPECTIVES

Additional books in this series can be found on Nova's website under the Series tab.

Additional E-books in this series can be found on Nova's website under the E-book tab.

BANKING AND BANKING DEVELOPMENTS

BANK FAILURES DURING THE FINANCIAL CRISIS

CAUSES AND CONSEQUENCES

LAWRENCE C. ARMSTRONG
EDITOR

nova publishers

New York

For permission to use material from this book please contact us:
Telephone 631-231-7269; Fax 631-231-8175
Web Site: http://www.novapublishers.com

Library of Congress Cataloging-in-Publication Data

ISBN: 978-1-62618-615-6

Published by Nova Science Publishers, Inc. † New York

CONTENTS

PREFACE

Between January 2008 and December 2011, a period of economic downturn in the United States, 414 insured U.S. banks failed. Of these, 85 percent or 353 had less than $1 billion in assets. These small banks often specialize in small business lending and are associated with local community development and philanthropy. These small bank failures have raised questions about the contributing factors in the states with the most failures, including the possible role of local market conditions and the application of fair value accounting under U.S accounting standards. This book discusses the factors that contributed to the bank failures in states with the most failed institutions between 2008 and 2011 and what role, if any, fair value accounting played in these failures; the use of shared loss agreements in resolving troubled banks; and the effect of recent bank failures on local communities.

Chapter 1 - Between January 2008 and December 2011—a period of economic downturn in the United States—414 insured U.S. banks failed. Of these, 85 percent or 353 had less than $1 billion in assets. These small banks often specialize in small business lending and are associated with local community development and philanthropy. These small bank failures have raised questions about the contributing factors in the states with the most failures, including the possible role of local market conditions and the application of fair value accounting under U.S. accounting standards. As required by Pub. L. No. 112-88, this report discusses (1) the factors that contributed to the bank failures in states with the most failed institutions between 2008 and 2011 and what role, if any, fair value accounting played in these failures, (2) the use of shared loss agreements in resolving troubled banks, and (3) the effect of recent bank failures on local communities. GAO analyzed call report data, reviewed inspectors general reports on individual bank failures, conducted econometric modeling, and interviewed officials from federal and state banking regulators, banking associations, and banks, and market experts. GAO also coordinated with the FDIC Inspector General on its study.

GAO is not making any recommendations at this time. GAO plans to continue to monitor the progress of the ongoing activities of the accounting standard setters to address concerns with the loan loss provisioning model. The Board of Governors of the Federal Reserve System, the FDIC, and the Office of the Comptroller of the Currency provided technical comments that GAO incorporated as appropriate.

Chapter 2 - Public Law 112-88, signed into law on January 3, 2012, requires the Federal Deposit Insurance Corporation Office of Inspector General (FDIC OIG) to conduct a study on the impact of the failure of insured depository institutions. The study is quite broad and required the authors' office to address matters pertaining to shared-loss agreements (SLA), the significance of losses at institutions that failed, examiner implementation of appraisal guidelines, examiner assessment of capital adequacy and private capital investment in failing institutions, examiner implementation of loan workout guidance, the application and impact of formal enforcement orders, the impact of FDIC policies on investments in institutions, and the FDIC's handling of private equity company investments in institutions. The legislation included a number of topics under these broad matters, and these topics are addressed in detail in the author's report. The legislation required the author's office to conduct work at the FDIC, the Office of the Comptroller of the Currency (OCC), and the Board of Governors of the Federal Reserve System (FRB). The legislation also required the U.S. Government Accountability Office to study matters related to the causes of institution failures, fair value accounting, asset write-downs, the community impact of failures, and the feasibility and impact of SLAs.

Consistent with the legislation, the author's overall objective was to conduct a comprehensive study on the impact of the failure of insured depository institutions. The author's review timeframes were generally 2008 through 2011. In some cases, the author's data analysis preceded 2008, and in other cases the authors gathered information through September 30, 2012, updating data to the extent possible. As required, the author's scope included open and failed state member, state nonmember, and national banks regulated by the FRB, FDIC, and OCC, respectively. The author's evaluation scope did not include institutions formerly regulated by the Office of Thrift Supervision. In conducting their work, the authors interviewed agency officials, reviewed relevant policies and guidance, reviewed examination reports and working papers, analyzed institution financial data and agency enforcement action statistics, interviewed officials at open institutions, interviewed investment professionals, and surveyed borrowers of failed institutions. KPMG LLP assisted us with several areas of review. The authors conducted their evaluation from January 2012 through October 2012.

In: Bank Failures during the Financial Crisis
Editor: Lawrence C. Armstrong

ISBN: 978-1-62618-615-6

Chapter 1

FINANCIAL INSTITUTIONS: CAUSES AND CONSEQUENCES OF RECENT BANK FAILURES*

United States Government Accountability Office

WHY GAO DID THIS STUDY

Between January 2008 and December 2011—a period of economic downturn in the United States—414 insured U.S. banks failed. Of these, 85 percent or 353 had less than $1 billion in assets. These small banks often specialize in small business lending and are associated with local community development and philanthropy. These small bank failures have raised questions about the contributing factors in the states with the most failures, including the possible role of local market conditions and the application of fair value accounting under U.S. accounting standards. As required by Pub. L. No. 112-88, this report discusses (1) the factors that contributed to the bank failures in states with the most failed institutions between 2008 and 2011 and what role, if any, fair value accounting played in these failures, (2) the use of shared loss agreements in resolving troubled banks, and (3) the effect of recent bank failures on local communities.

GAO analyzed call report data, reviewed inspectors general reports on individual bank failures, conducted econometric modeling, and interviewed officials from federal and state banking regulators, banking associations, and banks, and market experts. GAO also coordinated with the FDIC Inspector General on its study.

GAO is not making any recommendations at this time. GAO plans to continue to monitor the progress of the ongoing activities of the accounting standard setters to address concerns with the loan loss provisioning model.

The Board of Governors of the Federal Reserve System, the FDIC, and the Office of the Comptroller of the Currency provided technical comments that GAO incorporated as appropriate.

* This is an edited, reformatted and augmented version of the Highlights of GAO-13-71, a report to congressional committees, dated January 2013.

WHAT GAO FOUND

Ten states concentrated in the western, midwestern, and southeastern United States—all areas where the housing market had experienced strong growth in the prior decade—experienced 10 or more commercial bank or thrift (bank) failures between 2008 and 2011 (see below). The failures of the smaller banks (those with less than $1 billion in assets) in these states were largely driven by credit losses on commercial real estate (CRE) loans. The failed banks also had often pursued aggressive growth strategies using nontraditional, riskier funding sources and exhibited weak underwriting and credit administration practices. The rapid growth of CRE portfolios led to high concentrations that increased the banks' exposure to the sustained real estate and economic downturn that began in 2007. GAO's econometric model revealed that CRE concentrations and the use of brokered deposits, a funding source carrying higher risk than core deposits, were associated with an increased likelihood of failure for banks across all states during the period. Several state regulatory and community banking association officials told GAO that in some cases, the losses failed banks incurred on their CRE loans were caused by declines in the value of the underlying collateral of impaired, collateral-dependent loans. However, data are not publicly available that indicate the extent to which loan losses were driven by such declines in collateral values. Fair value accounting also has been cited as a potential contributor to bank failures, but between 2007 and 2011 fair value accounting losses in general did not appear to be a major contributor, as over two-thirds of small failed banks' assets were not subject to fair value accounting. The Department of the Treasury and the Financial Stability Forum's Working Group on Loss Provisioning have observed that the current accounting model for estimating credit losses is based on historical loss rates, which were low in the prefinancial crisis years. They said that earlier recognition of loan losses could have potentially lessened the impact of the crisis, when banks had to recognize the losses through a sudden series of provisions to the loan loss allowance, thus reducing earnings and regulatory capital. The Financial Accounting Standards Board has issued a proposal for public comment for a loan loss provisioning model that is more forward-looking and focuses on expected losses, which would result in banks establishing earlier recognition of loan losses for the loans they underwrite and could incentivize prudent risk management practices. Moreover, it should help address the cycle of losses and failures that emerged in the recent crisis as banks were forced to increase loan loss allowances and raise capital when they were least able to do so.

The Federal Deposit Insurance Corporation (FDIC) used shared loss agreements to help resolve failed banks at the least cost during the recent financial crisis. Under a shared loss agreement, FDIC absorbs a portion of the loss on specified assets of a failed bank that are purchased by an acquiring bank. FDIC officials, state bank regulators, community banking associations, and acquiring banks of failed institutions GAO interviewed said that shared loss agreements helped to attract potential bidders for failed banks during the financial crisis. Bank officials that acquired failed banks confirmed that they would not have purchased them without FDIC's shared loss agreements because of uncertainty of the market and valuation of assets. FDIC said the benefits of shared loss agreements included reductions in its immediate cash needs, less disruption to failed bank customers, and the movement of assets quickly into the private sector. During 2008-2011, FDIC resolved 281 of 414 failures using shared loss agreements on assets purchased by the acquiring bank. As of December 31, 2011, Deposit

Insurance Fund (DIF) receiverships made shared loss payments totaling $16.2 billion. In addition, DIF receiverships are estimated to pay an additional $26.6 billion over the duration of the shared loss agreements, resulting in total estimated lifetime losses of $42.8 billion (see figure). By comparing the estimated cost of the shared loss agreements to the estimated cost of directly liquidating the failed banks' assets, FDIC estimates that the use of shared loss agreements saved the DIF over $40 billion. While total estimated lifetime losses of the shared loss agreements may not change, the timing of the losses may change and payments from shared loss agreements may increase as the terms of the agreements mature. FDIC officials stated that the acquiring banks are monitored for compliance with the terms and conditions of the shared loss agreements. FDIC is issuing guidance to the acquiring banks reminding them of these terms to prevent increased shared loss payments as these agreements approach maturity.

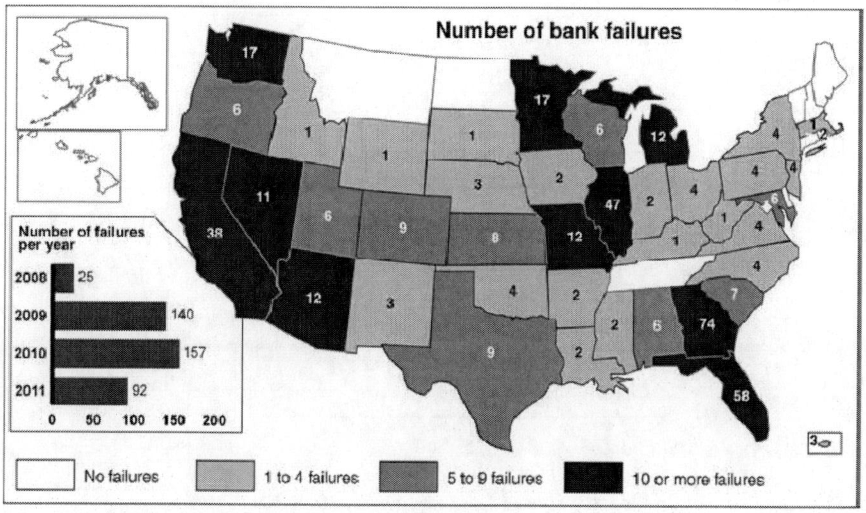

Source: GAO analysis of FDIC data: Map Resources (map).

Number of Bank Failures by State, 2008-2011.

The acquisitions of failed banks by healthy banks appears to have mitigated the potentially negative effects of bank failures on communities, although the focus of local lending and philanthropy may have shifted. First, while bank failures and failed bank acquisitions can have an impact on market concentration—an indicator of the extent to which banks in the market can exercise market power, such as raising prices or reducing availability of some products and services—GAO found only a limited number of metropolitan areas and rural counties were likely to have become significantly more concentrated. The lack of increases in concentration was because in many instances, the failed banks were acquired by out-of-market institutions. Second, GAO's econometric analysis of call report data from 2006 through 2011 found that failing small banks extended progressively less net credit as they approached failure, and that acquiring banks generally increased net credit after the acquisition. However, acquiring bank and existing peer bank officials GAO interviewed noted that in the wake of the bank failures, underwriting standards had tightened and thus credit was generally more available for small business owners who had good credit histories and strong financials than those that did not. Third, officials from regulators, banking associations, and banks GAO spoke with said that involvement in local philanthropy declined as small banks approached failure but generally increased after acquisition. Yet, these acquiring banks may not focus on the same philanthropic activities as did the failed banks. Finally, GAO econometrically analyzed the relationships among bank failures, income, unemployment, and real estate prices for all states and the District of Columbia (states) for the 1994 through 2011 period and found that bank failures in a state were more likely to affect its real estate sector than its labor market or broader economy.

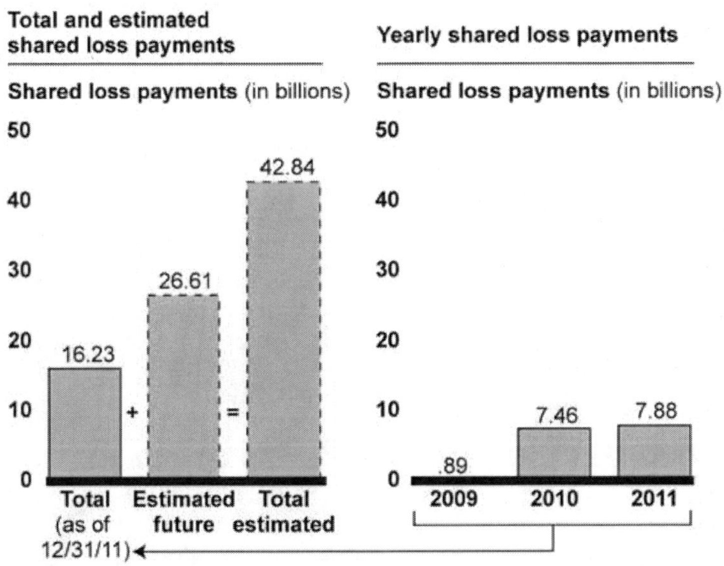

Source: GAO analysis of FDIC data.

Estimated Lifetime Losses and Yearly Shared Loss Payments, 2008-2011.

January 3, 2013

The Honorable Tim Johnson
Chairman
The Honorable Richard C. Shelby
Ranking Member
Committee on Banking, Housing, and Urban Affairs
United States Senate

The Honorable Spencer Bachus
Chairman
The Honorable Barney Frank
Ranking Member
Committee on Financial Services
House of Representatives

Between January 2008 and December 2011, 414 insured U.S. commercial banks and thrifts (banks) failed.[1] Of these, 85 percent (353), were small banks with less than $1 billion in assets. These small banks tend to be community banks that are depository institutions, with a relatively limited geographic scope of operations and often specialize in, among other things, providing credit to local small businesses. Community banks are also associated with local community development, leadership, and philanthropy.

These bank failures, which were concentrated in certain parts of the United States and occurred against the backdrop of the worst financial crisis since the Great Depression, raised a number of concerns. First, the number and proportion of failed banks varied across states, prompting questions about the role local market conditions and related economic factors played, particularly in those areas with the largest numbers of failures. Further, in an era of declining asset values and rising mortgage delinquencies, concerns have also been raised that the failures may have been due to losses recognized from the application of fair value accounting under U.S. generally accepted accounting principles (GAAP).[2] According to its critics, fair value accounting may have contributed to some bank failures by requiring the reduction of the book value of assets (write-downs) such as investments in mortgage-backed securities to abnormally low market prices, lowering earnings and depleting the banks' regulatory capital.[3] These critics thought that the write-downs were based on values in inactive or illiquid markets and did not specifically reflect the underlying value of the assets.[4] Moreover, they maintain that the write- downs created a procyclical effect in that they caused banks to sell assets in an attempt to boost regulatory capital, putting further downward pressure on market prices and triggering further write downs and depletion of capital. The large number of small bank failures has also raised concerns about the potential effect on the communities where the banks were located, particularly in terms of credit availability, income and employment, and philanthropic activity.

The Federal Deposit Insurance Corporation (FDIC) is required to resolve a bank failure in a manner that results in the least cost to the Deposit Insurance Fund (DIF).[5] The DIF is funded by assessments levied on insured banks and savings associations and is used to cover all deposit accounts at insured institutions, such as checking and savings accounts, up to the insurance limit. FDIC resolved most bank failures during 2008 through 2011 by facilitating their acquisitions by other banks and often by including a shared loss agreement, under which FDIC absorbed a portion of the loss on specified assets purchased by the acquiring bank.

In light of the questions raised about the recent failures, particularly those of small banks, and the potential costs to the DIF, Congress has required us to conduct a study of recent bank failures in states with 10 or more failures.[6] Accordingly, the objectives of our report are to discuss

(1) the factors that contributed to the failure of banks in states with 10 or more failures between 2008 and 2011, including the extent to which losses related to fair value accounting treatment affected the regulatory capital positions of failed banks;
(2) market factors that affected FDIC's choice of resolution method, or the amount of FDIC coverage offered on the shared loss agreements, and the costs that the DIF incurred as a result of these shared loss agreements; and
(3) the effect of recent small bank failures on local communities.

To address the factors that contributed to the recent bank failures, we analyzed data from FDIC's Historical Statistics on Banking–Failures and Assistance Transactions database, and Statistics on Depository Institutions as well as call report and thrift financial report data. In doing so, we reviewed information from FDIC on the policies and procedures it used to ensure that the data were complete and accurate and determined them to be reliable for our purposes. We reviewed material loss reviews (MLRs), failed bank reviews (FBR), and in-depth reviews (IDR) issued by the inspectors general (IG) of the federal banking regulators and estimated an econometric model to investigate bank characteristics that may have contributed to failure.[7] In addition, we analyzed call reports and thrift financial report data for failed and open commercial banks and thrifts to identify and compare trends in the use of fair value accounting. We also interviewed officials from federal banking regulators, state banking regulators, national and state banking organizations, and market experts and had two accounting experts, a former comptroller general and a professor of accountancy, review a draft of the report. To identify the costs the DIF has incurred to date under shared loss agreements, we obtained and analyzed FDIC loss payment information and the estimate of lifetime losses that FDIC develops for each failed institution. We determined that these estimates were sufficiently reliable. Also, we interviewed FDIC officials and reviewed and summarized FDIC policies and procedures for determining that shared loss agreements were the least costly method for resolving bank failures compared to other available resolution methods during this time period. We interviewed federal and state banking regulators, national and state banking associations, and market experts. We also conducted a cluster sampling of 10 failed small banks in three states and interviewed officials from acquiring and peer banks of these failed banks.

To address the effect of small bank failures on local communities, we estimated the change in market concentration from bank failures and acquisitions of failed banks using data from 2007 through 2012.[8] We measured market concentration using the Herfindahl-Hirschman Index (HHI), which is equal to the sum of the squared market shares of banks in a market.[9] We analyzed the impact of bank failures on the availability of credit using 2006 through 2011 call report data to estimate changes in the size of a bank's loan portfolio in the quarters leading up to failure for failed banks and in the quarters following acquisition of a failed bank (for acquiring banks).[10] We conducted an econometric modeling exercise designed to assess the relationship between bank failures and overall economic conditions in a state. Specifically we analyzed the relationship between bank failures, income, unemployment, and real estate prices for U.S. states and the District of Columbia, using data from1994 through 2011.[11] We interviewed federal and state banking regulators, national and state community banking organizations, market experts and officials from acquiring banks and peer banks of the failed banks that were part of our cluster sample. Appendix I provides a more detailed description of our scope and methodology.

We conducted this performance audit from February 2012 to December 2012 in accordance with generally accepted government auditing standards. Those standards require that we plan and perform the audit to obtain sufficient, appropriate evidence to provide a reasonable basis for our findings and conclusions based on our audit objectives.

BACKGROUND

A bank failure is the closing of a bank by a federal or state banking regulatory agency. One indicator of a bank's health is its relative level of regulatory capital, which cushions banks against losses from nonpayment of loans and other losses on assets. Regulators require banks to maintain certain minimum capital requirements to help ensure the safety and soundness of the banking system and generally expect banks to hold capital above these minimums at levels commensurate with their risks. Federal law generally requires federal banking regulators to close a bank that has become critically undercapitalized within a 90-day period.[12]

As figure 1 shows, 10 states experienced 10 or more bank failures between 2008 through 2011: Arizona, California, Florida, Georgia, Illinois, Michigan, Minnesota, Missouri, Nevada, and Washington, with the most failures occurring in California, Florida, Georgia, and Illinois. Together, failures in these 10 states comprised 298 of the 414 bank failures (72 percent) across all states during this time period.

Within these 10 states, 86 percent (257) of the failed banks were small institutions with assets of less than $1 billion at the time of failure, and 52 percent (155), had assets of less than $250 million (see table 1).

Twelve percent (36) were of medium-size banks with more than $1 billion but less than $10 billion in assets, and 2 percent (5) were large banks with assets of more than $10 billion at the time of failure.

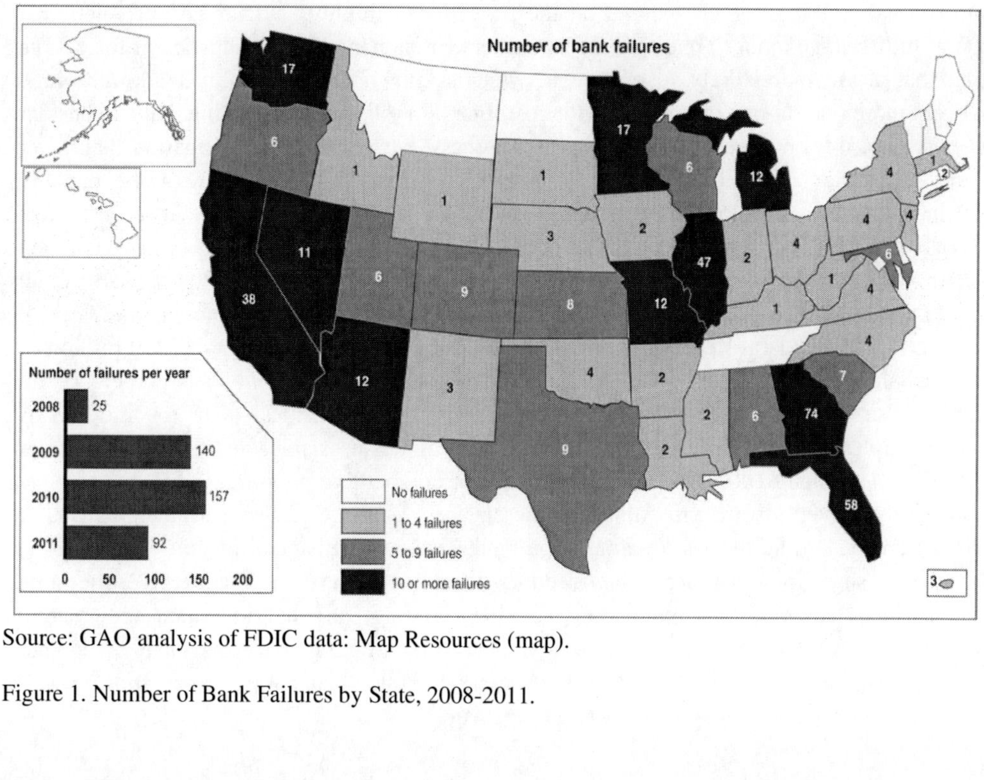

Source: GAO analysis of FDIC data: Map Resources (map).

Figure 1. Number of Bank Failures by State, 2008-2011.

Table 1. Bank Failures in States with 10 or More Failures by Asset Size, 2008-2011

State	Small banks (less than $1 billion)	Medium-size banks (more than $1billion but less than $10 billion)	Large banks (more than $10 billion)	Total
Arizona	12	0	0	**12**
California	21	14	3	**38**
Florida	53	4	1	**58**
Georgia	69	5	0	**74**
Illinois	40	7	0	**47**
Michigan	11	1	0	**12**
Minnesota	17	0	0	**17**
Missouri	12	0	0	**12**
Nevada	7	3	1	**11**
Washington	15	2	0	**17**
Total	257	36	5	**298**

Source: GAO analysis of FDIC data.

Small Banks and Community Lending

Small banks—those with less than $1 billion in assets—tend to differ from larger banks in their relationships with customers. Large banks are more likely to engage in what is called transactional banking, which focuses on the provision of highly standardized products that require little human input to manage and are underwritten using "hard" statistical information. Small banks are more likely to engage in what is known as relationship banking, which involves more one-on-one interaction with customers. In relationship banking, banks consider not only hard information in the underwriting process, but also "soft" information that is not readily available or quantifiable and is acquired primarily by working with the banking customer. Using this banking model, small banks may be able to extend credit to customers such as small business owners who might not be considered for a loan from a larger bank.[13]

As we have previously reported, small banks tend to have a larger portion of small business loans in their portfolios than larger banks.[14] The Board of Governors of the Federal Reserve System (Federal Reserve) reported that in 2011, banks with assets of $250 million or less accounted for 66.8 percent of all banking organizations but only 4.0 percent of all banking assets. Moreover, they held 13.7 percent of all small business loans (business loans equal to or less than $1 million) and 13.9 percent of business microloans (business loans equal to or less than $100,000).[15] In part because of competitive pressures, small banks have increasingly moved toward providing commercial real estate (CRE) loans rather than other types of credit. During the last decade, large banks and other financial institutions increased their market share for consumer loans, credit cards, and residential mortgages. Over the same period, small banks shifted their focus to CRE lending, an area in which they had a competitive advantage, according to market observers. Market observers have noted that small banks generally know their local CRE markets better than larger banks and are well positioned to gather specific information on properties.

Regulators define CRE loans to include acquisition, development, and construction (ADC) loans that are secured by real estate to finance land development and construction, including new construction, upgrades, and rehabilitation. CRE loans also include unsecured loans to finance commercial real estate, loans secured by multifamily properties, and loans secured by nonfarm nonresidential property. ADC loans generally are considered to be the riskiest class of CRE loans due to their long development times and because they can include properties (such as housing developments or retail space in a shopping mall) that are built before having firm commitments from buyers or lessees. In addition, by the time the construction phase is completed, market demand may have fallen, putting downward pressure on sales prices or rents, making this type of loan more volatile.

Financial Crisis (2007-2011)

The dramatic decline in the U.S. housing market that began in 2006 precipitated a decline in the price of mortgage-related assets, particularly mortgage assets based on nonprime loans in 2007. Some financial institutions found themselves so exposed that they were threatened with failure, and some failed because they were unable to raise capital or obtain liquidity as the value of their portfolios declined. Other institutions, ranging from government-sponsored enterprises such as Fannie Mae and Freddie Mac to large securities firms, were left holding "toxic" mortgages or mortgage-related assets that became increasingly difficult to value, were illiquid, and potentially had little worth. Moreover, investors not only stopped buying private-label securities backed by mortgages but also became reluctant to buy securities backed by other types of assets. Because of uncertainty about the liquidity and solvency of financial entities, the prices banks charged each other for funds rose dramatically, and interbank lending conditions deteriorated sharply. The resulting liquidity and credit crunch made the financing on which businesses and individuals depend increasingly difficult to obtain. By late summer of 2008, the ramifications of the financial crisis ranged from the continued failure of financial institutions to increased losses of individual wealth and reduced corporate investments and further tightening of credit that would exacerbate the emerging global economic slowdown.

Bank Regulators

Federal banking regulators—FDIC, Federal Reserve, and the Office of the Comptroller of the Currency (OCC)—are responsible for supervising the activities of banks. They are also responsible for taking corrective action when the banks' activities and overall performance present supervisory concerns or could result in financial losses to the DIF or violations of law or regulation.[16] The Federal Reserve is the primary regulator for state-chartered member banks (banks authorized to do business under charters issued by states) that are members of the Federal Reserve System and for bank and thrift holding companies. OCC is the primary regulator of national banks and federal thrifts, and FDIC is the primary regulator for state-chartered nonmember banks (i.e., state-chartered banks that are not members of the Federal Reserve System) and state-chartered thrifts.[17] In addition, FDIC insures the deposits of all federally insured banks, generally up to $250,000 per depositor, per insured bank. Prior to

July 21, 2011, the Office of Thrift Supervision (OTS) was the primary regulator of federally and state-chartered thrifts and thrift holding companies.[18] State-chartered banks are also subject to the supervision of their respective state banking regulators.

Table 2 shows the number of banks under federal supervision as of December 31, 2007, prior to the wave of bank failures, and their related level of assets. The vast majority of the 8,544 banks under supervision at that time were small banks (7,870 or 92 percent) whose assets comprised 11 percent of the total $13 trillion in assets under supervision. Of the 7,870 small banks under supervision as of December 31, 2007, 62 percent were supervised by FDIC, 18 percent by OCC, 10 percent by the Federal Reserve, and 9 percent by OTS. During this time period, about 3.6 percent of small banks in the 10 states that were supervised by FDIC failed, followed by 3.2 percent that were supervised by the Federal Reserve, and 2.5 percent supervised by OCC and OTS.

FDIC acts as the receiver of failed banks and is charged with evaluating various resolution strategies in order to facilitate the sale of assets belonging to failed depository institutions. The 1991 Federal Deposit Insurance Corporation Improvement Act (FDICIA) requires FDIC to resolve failed institutions using the least costly method to the DIF, or the least-cost transaction.[19]

Congress enacted FDICIA in response to the savings and loan crisis, and the law contained a number of reforms, including some designed to address criticisms that federal regulators had not taken prompt and forceful actions to minimize or prevent losses to the deposit insurance funds caused by bank failures.

FDIC Resolution Methods for Failed Institutions

FDIC is required to resolve failed institutions using the least costly method to the DIF, and FDIC evaluates various resolution strategies to identify the least costly method. FDIC primarily uses two methods to resolve failing banks and thrifts: purchase and assumption (P&A) transactions (the direct sale of a failed bank to another, healthier bank) and deposit payoffs.

A P&A transaction is a resolution in which an acquiring institution purchases some or all of the assets of a failed bank or thrift and assumes some or all of the liabilities, including all insured deposits. Some P&As include a shared loss agreement in which FDIC absorbs a portion of the loss on a specified pool of assets (such as loans), which helps maximize asset recoveries and minimize FDIC losses.

FDIC executes a deposit payoff only if it does not receive a bid for a P&A transaction that meets the least cost test—the process by which FDIC selects the least costly option to the DIF. There are three types of deposit payoffs. The first is a straight deposit payoff, in which FDIC pays deposited amounts due up to the insured limits. The second type is an insured deposit transfer, which allows FDIC to transfer the insured deposits to a healthy institution to limit service interruptions for insured depositors. The third type is the creation of a new depository institution in the same community of the failed bank in order to conduct an orderly liquidation of the insured deposits, also referred to as a deposit insurance national bank (DINB).[20]

Table 2. Numbers, Asset Size, and Percentage of Banks and Failed Banks in the 10 States by Size, as of 2007Q4 and 2008-2011

		Federal Reserve		FDIC		OCC		OTS		Total	
Number of supervised banks as of 2007Q4 (assets in billions)	All banks	878	$1,518.20	5,205	$2,195.13	1,635	$7,785.23	826	$1,551.97	**8,544**	**$13,050.54**
	Small banks	789	$171.92	4,909	$871.89	1,455	$293.47	717	$155.37	**7,870**	**$1,492.65**
Number of supervised banks that failed between 2008-2011 in the 10 states (assets in billions)	All banks	29	$18.57	196	$87.54	46	$49.16	27	$384.74	**298**	**$540.01**
	Small banks	25	$9.68	178	$47.18	36	$8.11	18	$4.13	**257**	**$69.10**
Percent of supervised banks in 2007Q4 that failed between 2008-2010 in the 10 states (assets in billions)	All banks	3.3%	1.2%	3.8%	4.0%	2.8%	0.6%	3.3%	24.8%	**3.5%**	**4.1%**
	Small banks	3.2%	5.6%	3.6%	5.4%	2.5%	2.8%	2.5%	2.7%	**3.3%**	**4.6%**

Source: GAO analysis of FDIC data.

Note: Small banks are defined as banks with asset under $1 billion.

Fair Value, Historical Cost, and Impairment Accounting

GAAP establishes the basis on which items reported on a bank's balance sheet should be measured. Currently, assets and liabilities are reflected in the balance sheet at fair value, historical cost, or another basis, such as lower-of-cost or fair value.

- Fair value. Fair value is the price that would be received to sell an asset or paid to transfer a liability in an orderly transaction between market participants at the measurement date. Fair value accounting standards under GAAP establish a standardized framework for measuring the fair value of an asset or liability.[21] According to the Securities and Exchange Commission, fair value is most prevalently used to measure "financial" assets and liabilities, such as investment securities and derivative instruments. Fair value measurements that are required on a quarterly basis (or each reporting period) are often referred to as "recurring." For some assets and liabilities that are measured at fair value on a recurring basis, such as securities designated for trading, unrealized gains or losses flow through the bank's earnings in the income statement and affect regulatory capital. For certain other assets and liabilities that are measured at fair value on a recurring basis, such as securities designated as available for sale, unrealized fair value gains and losses generally do not impact earnings, and thus, generally are not included in regulatory capital calculations. Instead, these gains or losses are recorded through other comprehensive income (OCI), unless the institution determines that a decline in fair value below amortized cost constitutes an other- than-temporary impairment (OTTI) in which case the instrument is written down to its fair value, with credit losses reflected in earnings.[22]
- Historical cost. Measurement using historical cost can be done in several ways, but the general concept is to record items on the balance sheet using the original amount paid or received, with adjustments when appropriate in subsequent periods for depreciation, amortization, principal pay downs, or impairment. Generally, loans that a bank holds for investment (HFI), for example, are recorded at amortized cost, net of an impairment allowance for estimated credit losses.[23] Such loans typically comprise the bulk of assets held by FDIC-insured banks.
- Loan impairment accounting: GAAP requires financial institutions to maintain an allowance for loan losses (loan loss allowance) at a level that is appropriate to cover estimated credit losses incurred as of the balance sheet date for their entire portfolio of HFI loans. Under GAAP, institutions must recognize impairment on HFI loans when credit losses are determined to be probable and reasonably estimable, that is, when, based on current information and events, it is probable that an institution will be unable to collect all amounts due (i.e., both principal and interest) according to the contractual terms of the original loan agreement. An increase in the loan loss allowance results in a charge to expenses, termed a provision for loan losses (loan loss provision), except in the case where there are recoveries of amounts previously charged off. Loan loss provisions reduce the net interest income earned as part of a bank's earnings, and regulatory capital declines.[24] Impairment accounting standards under GAAP set forth the measurement methods for estimating the amount of impairment attributable to individually impaired loans. Regulators generally require

institutions to establish policies and procedures for determining the loan loss allowance based on GAAP requirements.[25] Under GAAP, credit losses for an individually impaired loan are measured based on the present value of expected future cash flows discounted at the loan's effective interest rate (the contractual interest rate adjusted for any net deferred loan fees or costs, premium, or discount existing at the origination or acquisition of the loan), except that as a practical expedient, impairment may be measured based on the loan's observable market price, or, if the loan is a collateral- dependent loan, the fair value of the collateral.[26] GAAP requires the impairment measurement to be based on the fair value of collateral when foreclosure is probable.

Loan Classifications

In examinations, federal banking examiners review a sample of loans and banks' internal ratings of loans to determine the adequacy of credit risk administration and identify loans that have a higher degree of risk of nonpayment. As part of this review, examiners determine which loans are considered "pass," due to their having a lower risk of nonpayment, as well as those that are adversely "classified" because they have a higher risk of nonpayment. There are three adverse classification categories used by the federal banking regulators: "substandard", "doubtful", and "loss".

Loans subject to adverse classifications plus the internal ratings that banks apply to their loan portfolios are incorporated into how each bank calculates its loan loss allowance. Therefore, an increase in the amount of loans adversely classified substandard or doubtful typically results in a bank's updating its loan loss allowance estimates to reflect the increased risk in those loans. Loans or portions of loans that are classified loss are removed from the bank's balance sheet because they are considered uncollectible and their continuance as bankable assets is not warranted. This loss amount is charged against the loan loss allowance, which reduces the allowance.

Charge offs also cause regulatory capital to decline to the extent that additional provision expenses are needed if the loss has not been previously recognized through the loan loss allowance.

Bank Failures Were Largely Related to Nonperforming Real Estate Loans but Also Highlight Impact of Impairment Accounting and Loan Loss Provisioning

In the 10 states with 10 or more failures between 2008 and 2011, failures of small and medium-size banks were largely associated with high concentrations of CRE loans, and in particular, ADC loans, and inadequate management of the risks associated with these loans. The rapid growth of their CRE portfolios resulted in concentrations that exceeded regulatory thresholds for heightened scrutiny and increased the banks' exposure to the sustained real estate and economic downturn that began in 2007.

In addition, these failed banks had often pursued aggressive growth strategies using nontraditional, riskier funding sources and exhibited weak underwriting and credit administration practices. Large bank failures in the 10 states were associated with some of the same factors—high-risk growth strategies that relied on nontraditional residential mortgage products, weak underwriting and risk controls, and excessive concentrations that increased these banks' exposure to the real estate market downturn.

We found that losses related to bank assets and liabilities subject to fair value accounting contributed little to bank failures overall, largely because most banks' assets and liabilities were not recorded at fair value.

Several state regulators and community banking association officials told us that at some small failed banks, declining collateral values of impaired collateral-dependent loans—particularly CRE and ADC loans—drove both credit losses and charge offs and resulted in reductions to regulatory capital.

However, data are not publicly available that indicate the extent to which credit losses or charge offs at the failed banks were driven by declines in the fair value of the collateral. The Department of the Treasury (Treasury) and the Financial Stability Forum's Working Group on Loss Provisioning (Working Group) observed that the current accounting model for estimating credit losses is based on historical loss rates, which were low in the years before the financial crisis.[27]

They noted that earlier recognition of loan losses could have potentially reduced the procyclicality in the recent crisis. To address this issue, the Financial Accounting Standards Board (FASB) has issued a proposal for public comment for a loan loss provisioning model that is more forward-looking and focuses on expected losses, which would result in banks establishing earlier recognition of loan losses for loans they underwrite and could incentivize prudent risk management practices.

Failures of Small and Medium-Size Banks in Our 10 States Were Largely Associated with High Concentrations of Risky CRE Loans

Failures of almost all small and medium-size banks in our 10 states were associated with high concentrations of CRE lending, particularly the higher risk ADC lending segment, and inadequate management of the risks associated with these high concentrations.[28]

Eighty-eight percent of the 251 IG reviews that we obtained for small and medium failed banks cited high concentrations of CRE and ADC loans as a primary contributing factor to the failures. Figure 2 shows that the quarterly average loan balances of CRE lending and the subset of ADC lending as a percentage of the total loan balances at the 258 small banks that failed between 2008 and 2011 increased significantly in the years prior to the housing market downturn.

Small banks that did not fail exhibited markedly slower growth rates of these types of loans as well as substantially lower levels of these loans. The trends for the 35 medium-size banks were similar over this time period.

The rapid growth in CRE and the subset of ADC lending led to concentrations—measured through the ratio of total CRE loans to total risk-based capital—that exceeded regulatory thresholds for heightened scrutiny and increased the banks' exposure to the risks associated with a sustained downturn in the real estate market and economy.

Guidelines issued by federal banking regulators in 2006 provided that banks with ADC concentrations greater than 100 percent or CRE concentrations greater than 300 percent when the outstanding balance of the institution's CRE portfolio has increased by 50 percent or more during the prior 36 months would be subject to greater regulatory scrutiny.[29] CRE concentrations at small failed banks grew from 333 percent in December 2001 to 535 percent in June 2008, while ADC concentrations grew from 104 percent to 259 percent. Small banks that did not fail exhibited significantly lower concentrations. Overall, CRE concentrations grew from 210 percent to 276 percent over the same time period, while ADC concentrations grew from 46 to 71 percent. We found similar trends for medium-size banks.

With the downturn in the housing market and onset of the financial crisis, the level of nonperforming loans began to rise, as did the level of subsequent charge offs.[30] The rising level of nonperforming loans, particularly ADC loans, appears to be the key factor driving the decline in regulatory capital and resulting failures of small and medium banks in the 10 states between 2008 and 2011.

In December 2001, only 2 percent of ADC loans at the small failed banks were classified as nonperforming. With the onset of the financial crisis, the level of nonperforming ADC loans increased quickly to 11 percent by June 2008 and 46 percent by June 2011. As banks began to deem nonperforming loans or portions of these loans uncollectible, the level of net charge offs also began to rise.[31] In December 2001, net charge offs of ADC loans at small failed banks were less than 1 percent. By June 2008, net charge offs were 2 percent, and by June 2011, 12 percent.

FDIC staff told us that small banks first began incurring credit-related losses in their consumer loan and credit card portfolios and later in their construction-related portfolios. Particularly in the southeastern and southwestern United States, ADC projects began to stall because developers could not find buyers or tenants for their completed or ongoing projects. Further, many banks had made loans to developers for the purpose of constructing primary residences, and demand for these residences fell sharply. FDIC staff also noted that ADC loans, in particular, were usually based entirely on collateral values, and that repaying the loans depended on selling the developed properties. They added that rapidly declining real estate values meant that collateral values dropped beneath the outstanding balance of the loans, making it difficult for developers to refinance their loans if they could not pay down the principal amount to a level acceptable to the lender.

CRE, and especially ADC, concentrations in failed banks often were correlated to poor risk management and risky funding sources. The IG reviews noted that in the majority of the failures, management exercised poor oversight of the risks associated with high CRE and ADC concentrations and engaged in weak underwriting and credit administration practices. In many cases, the IG reviews noted that the failed banks did not maintain an adequate loan loss allowance. In other instances, failed banks had engaged in out-of-territory lending, that is, participating in CRE and ADC loans outside of their normal geographical trade areas where they did not have experience.

Further, 28 percent (84) of the 298 failed banks in the 10 states were young banks that had been chartered for less than 10 years at the time of failure. Both FDIC and OCC staff said a number of these banks that later failed were formed to take advantage of the CRE and ADC market as it was picking up and did not have the experience necessary to manage the risks associated with high concentrations in these loans. FDIC staff noted that in many cases, young failed banks departed sharply from the approved business plan originally filed with FDIC upon receiving their charter by aggressively pursuing growth in higher risk ADC loans.

The IG reviews noted that in general failed small and medium banks had often pursued aggressive growth strategies using riskier funding sources, such as brokered deposits.[32] We found that for small failed banks, the average percent of total deposits that were brokered deposits increased from 3 percent in December 2001 to 20 percent in December 2008, and for medium-size failed banks, from 3 percent to 28 percent. For small and medium-size banks that did not fail, the level of brokered deposits was considerably lower, increasing from 2 percent to 6 percent and from 4 to 13 percent, respectively, over the same time period. According to a 2011 FDIC study, high rate deposits, which can include brokered deposits, appear more likely to lead a bank to take greater risk because, all else being equal, to net the same amount a bank must earn more on its assets for a high rate deposit than for a low rate deposit.[33] Moreover, once a bank is not well capitalized, federal law prohibits banks from renewing or accepting brokered deposits, which makes it difficult to replace these funds when they mature.[34]

Several state banking regulators and one federal banking regulator noted that other small and medium banks also exhibited high levels of CRE and ADC concentrations prior to the onset of the financial crisis, but did not fail. They attributed the nonfailure of these institutions to better risk management practices. For example, they noted that these banks tended to engage in more sound underwriting and maintained higher capital levels than the banks that failed.

Similarly, an FDIC IG study issued in October 2012 found that some banks with high ADC concentrations were able to weather the recent financial crisis without experiencing a corresponding decline in their overall financial condition. The factors that the IG identified that contributed to their success included a well-informed and active board, strong management, sound credit administration and underwriting practices, and adequate capital. In addition, the IG found that the banks in their sample did not rely on brokered deposits to fund growth and had significantly diversified their loan portfolio by shifting their loan mix away from ADC loans and to shrink the volume of ADC loans in response to the economic decline.[35]

The IG reviews also identified the decline in the fair value of real-estate related investment securities as a contributing factor to the failure of some small and medium-size banks. The IG reviews noted that about 10 percent of failed small and medium-size banks had made investments in instruments such as private label residential mortgage-backed securities (MBS) and preferred stock of the housing-related government-sponsored enterprises (GSE), Fannie Mae and Freddie Mac, which subsequently declined in value. When the real-estate market began to deteriorate in 2007, residential MBS securities began experiencing significant price declines as a result of credit rating downgrades that reflected the decline in the quality of the underlying mortgages.

On September 7, 2008, Treasury and the Federal Housing Finance Agency announced that the GSEs had been placed into conservatorship. GSEs' equity prices dropped considerably in response, and, as a result, those banks that held sizable amounts of the GSEs' preferred stock suffered substantial losses.

Econometric Analysis Suggests That Riskier Lending and Funding Sources Were Associated with an Increased Likelihood of Bank Failure Nationwide

Our econometric analysis suggests that across the country, banks with high concentrations of ADC loans and a greater use of brokered deposits were more likely to fail from 2008 to 2011, while banks with greater capital adequacy and better asset quality were less likely to fail.

To investigate factors associated with bank failures across the United States, we analyzed data on FDIC-insured commercial banks and state-chartered savings banks from 2006-2011.[36] We collected data on characteristics that described a bank's capital adequacy; asset quality; earnings; liquidity; ADC lending; multifamily real estate lending; non-farm, non-residential real estate lending; commercial real estate lending not secured by real estate; brokered deposits funding; and size. We then used an econometric model to estimate the likelihood of failure as a function of these characteristics, controlling for factors that affect the likelihood of failure of all banks, such as the market for the banks' products and services and overall economic conditions.[37]

We found that greater amounts of ADC lending and greater reliance on brokered deposits were associated with an increased likelihood of failure, while higher asset quality and better capital adequacy were associated with a reduced likelihood of failure, all else being equal. Banks were more likely to fail if they had higher concentrations of ADC loans three to eight quarters in the past. Banks were also more likely to fail if they relied more heavily on brokered deposits six to eight quarters in the past. However, banks were less likely to fail if they had better capital adequacy in the past six quarters or if they had better asset quality in the past eight quarters.

Separate analyses of banks by size yielded results that were generally consistent with our aggregate results. To allow for the possibility that different factors were associated with the failure of banks of different sizes, we repeated the analysis separately for small banks and medium- size banks.[38]

We found that ADC lending was associated with an increase in the likelihood of failure for both types of banks. We also found that capital adequacy was associated with a decreased likelihood of failure for both small and medium-size banks and that asset quality was associated with a decreased likelihood of failure for small banks.

Our results likely reflect both factors that are generally associated with the likelihood that a bank fails and the specific characteristics of the time period we analyzed, and therefore our results may not be generalizeable to other time periods. Furthermore, our results reflect average relationships between bank characteristics and the likelihood of failure for all of the observations we used.

As such, they may not reflect the specific circumstances of any one bank. Finally, the list of characteristics we analyzed highlights important characteristics of banks that are related to the likelihood of failure, but because many other characteristics play a role in whether or not a bank fails, our list of characteristics is likely not exhaustive. Specifically, we did not completely control for a number of factors thought to drive the failures such as risk management practices or excessive growth.

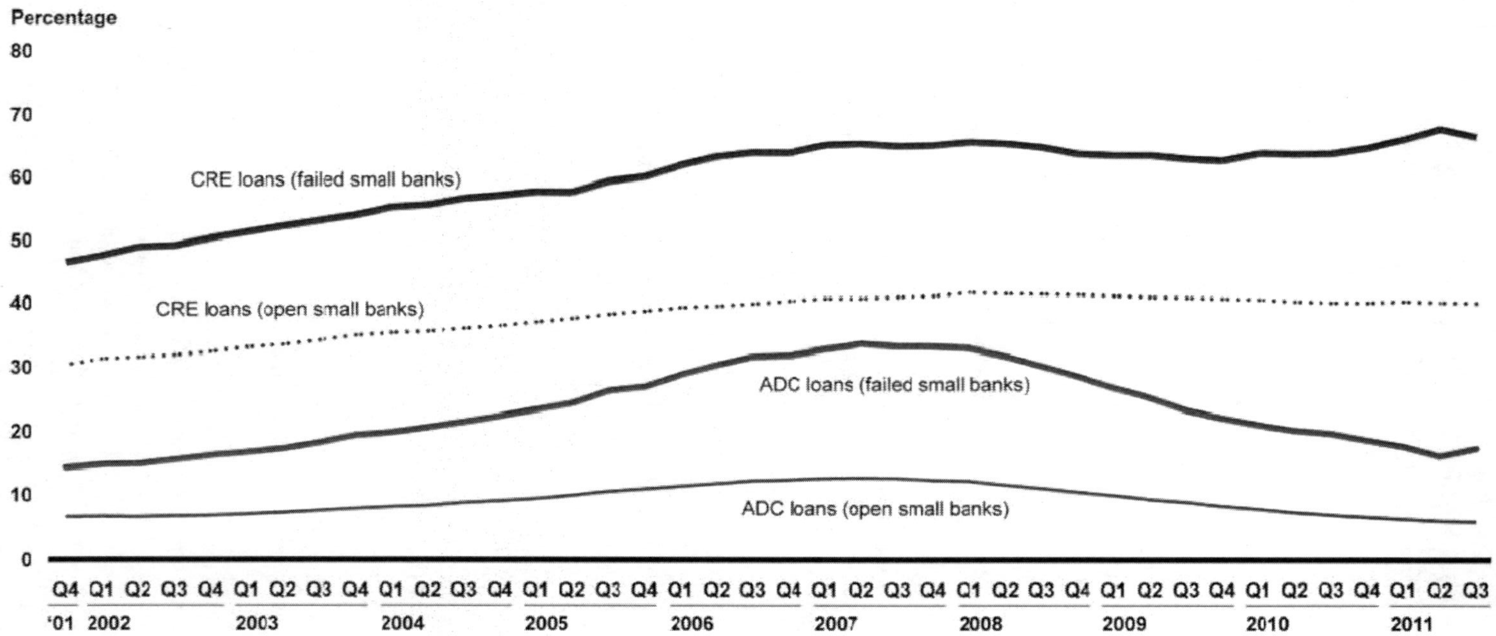

Source: GAO analysis of FDIC call report data.

Figure 2. Quarterly Average CRE and ADC Loan Balances as a Percentage of Total Loan Balances at Failed and Open Small Banks in the 10 States, 2001-2011.

Most Large Bank Failures in the 10 States Were Primarily Associated with Losses from Subprime and Nontraditional Residential Mortgage Loans

The four largest failures in our 10 states—Washington Mutual Bank (WaMu); IndyMac Bank (IndyMac), FSB; Bank United, FSB; and Downey Savings and Loan, FA— were caused primarily by management's pursuit of a high-risk growth strategy that relied on high-risk residential mortgages. According to the IGs' review, these banks had developed excessive concentrations in risky nontraditional loan products, such as payment option ARMs, Alt-A loans, and nonprime loans, and had inadequate underwriting and risk controls.[39] For example, according to the Treasury IG, as its primary business, IndyMac originated high-risk residential mortgage loans or bought loans from others, including mortgage origination brokers, and packaged them together in securities that it sold on the secondary market to other banks, thrifts, or investment banks. IndyMac maintained mortgage servicing rights for the loans it sold. The IG noted that IndyMac held the loans in its "available for sale" portfolio from the time they were packaged until they were sold to investors. The IG's review noted that Indy Mac had engaged in an aggressive growth strategy focusing on Alt-A and other nontraditional loan products—often making loans without verification of the borrower's income—insufficient underwriting, credit concentrations in residential real estate in the California and Florida markets, and heavy reliance on noncore funding such as brokered deposits. When home prices declined in the second half of 2007 and the secondary mortgage market collapsed, IndyMac was left with $10.7 billion in loans it could not sell. Its reduced liquidity was further exacerbated in late June 2008 when account holders withdrew $1.55 billion during the month. OTS closed IndyMac on July 11, 2008, and named FDIC as receiver. FDIC re-opened the bank on July 14, 2008, as IndyMac Federal Bank, F.S.B. and later sold it to OneWest Bank, F.S.B. in March 2009.

As another example, the joint FDIC and Treasury IGs' review noted that payment-option ARMs at WaMu grew to represent as much as half of all loan originations and approximately $59 billion(47 percent), of the home loans on WaMu's balance sheet at the end of 2007. In addition to payment option ARMs, WaMu's business strategy included underwriting subprime loans, home equity loans, and home equity lines of credit to high-risk borrowers. In line with that strategy, WaMu purchased and originated subprime loans, which represented approximately $16 billion (13 percent), of WaMu's 2007 home loan portfolio. The joint IG review noted that home equity products totaled $63.5 billion (27 percent), of WaMu's loans secured by residential real estate in 2007—a 130 percent increase from 2003. After the mortgage market meltdown in mid-2007, WaMu began experiencing severe losses due to loan charge offs and provisions for loan losses—$1 billion between fourth quarter 2007 and first quarter 2008 and another $3 billion by second quarter 2008—and its stock price decreased by 55 percent. The joint IG review also noted that with the failure of IndyMac in July 2008, WaMu's liquidity was stressed as it encountered significant deposit withdrawals. The Federal Home Loan Bank of San Francisco also began to limit WaMu's borrowing capacity. As a result, WaMu began offering deposit rates in excess of competitors in order to bring in deposits to improve liquidity. Shortly thereafter, Lehman Brothers collapsed on September 15, 2008, and within the following 8 days, WaMu incurred net deposit outflow of $16.7 billion, creating a second liquidity crisis. WaMu's ability to raise funds to improve its liquidity position was hindered by, among other things, its borrowing capacity limits, share price decline, and portfolio losses, according to the IG review. On September 25, 2008, OTS closed WaMu and appointed FDIC as receiver; FDIC sold WaMu to JP Morgan Chase & Co.

In contrast, one of the five largest bank failures in our 10 states during the period resulted, in part from CRE and ADC loans. Specifically, the FDIC IG identified contributing factors to the failure of the fifth largest bank, United Commercial Bank (UCB), as high concentrations in CRE and ADC loans and heavy reliance on nontraditional funding sources to support its expansion efforts, all of which increased the bank's risk profile. For example, between 2005 and 2009, ADC concentrations grew from 72 percent to 211 percent of total capital. According to the IG, UCB's board and management failed to control the risks associated with the institution's rapid expansion. As the commercial real estate market declined, losses and provisions associated with ADC and CRE concentrations eroded the bank's earnings and capital and led to inadequate liquidity.[40] The California Department of Financial Institutions closed UCB and appointed FDIC receiver on November 6, 2009.

Credit Losses and Charge-offs from Nonperforming Loans Contributed Significantly to Bank Failures Nationwide, but Losses due to Fair Value Accounting Did Not

Concerns have been raised that recent bank failures may have been driven, in part, by unrealized losses resulting from changes in the fair value of certain assets and liabilities and that such losses had a procyclical impact on banks' balance sheets. Based on our analysis, fair value losses related to investments in certain types of mortgage-related investment securities were a contributing factor in some bank failures; but, fair value related losses in general contributed little to the decline in net interest income and regulatory capital that failed banks experienced overall once the financial crisis began.

We analyzed the assets and liabilities on the balance sheets of failed banks nationwide that were subject to fair value accounting between 2007 and 2011. We found that generally over two-thirds of the assets of all failed commercial banks (small, medium-size, and large) were classified as held-for-investment (HFI) loans, and, as discussed earlier, were not subject to fair value accounting.[41] For example, small failed commercial banks held an average of 77 percent of their assets as HFI loans in 2008 compared to small open commercial banks, which held an average of 69 percent in such loans. Small failed thrifts, as well as failed and open medium-size and large commercial banks and thrifts, exhibited similar percentages.

Investment securities classified as available for sale (AFS) represented the second-largest percentage of assets for all failed and open banks over our 5-year time period.[42] For example, in 2008, small failed commercial banks held an average of 10 percent of their assets as AFS securities, while small open banks averaged 16 percent. Generally, AFS securities are recorded at fair value on a recurring basis with changes in fair value recorded in OCI; however, these fair value changes do not impact earnings or regulatory capital, unless the institution determines that those fair value changes constituted an other-than- temporary impairment with credit losses reflected in the income statement through earnings, thereby reducing regulatory capital.[43]

Several other asset and liability categories are recorded at fair value on a recurring basis through income or at the lower of cost or fair value under certain circumstances. However, together these categories did not account for a significant percentage of total assets at either failed or open commercial banks or thrifts. For example, in 2008, assets and liabilities recorded at fair value on a recurring basis through income at small failed banks ranged from 0.00 percent to 0.03 percent. As a consequence, fair value changes of these assets and liabilities, generally, were not a key driver in institutions' financial performance.[44]

Declines in regulatory capital at failed banks in the 10 states and the rest of the United States were driven by rising levels of credit losses related to nonperforming loans held by the banks and subsequent charge offs of these loans. For failed commercial banks and thrifts of all sizes nationwide, we found that the credit losses, which resulted from nonperforming HFI loans, were the largest contributors to the institutions' overall losses when compared to any other asset class. These losses had a greater negative impact on institutions' net interest income and regulatory capital levels than those recorded at fair value. For example, from 2008 to 2011, credit losses at small failed commercial banks accounted for on average of over 140 percent of net interest income (see figure 3), compared with 24 percent for small open commercial banks. Net losses from other income categories did not represent a significant percent of net interest income for either small failed or open commercial banks.[45]

Declining Collateral Values Contributed to Credit Losses and Charge Offs at Small Failed Banks

While fair value accounting did not play a significant role in bank failures, several state regulators and community banking association officials told us that at some failed community banks, declining collateral values of impaired collateral-dependent loans—particularly CRE and ADC loans—drove both credit losses and charge-offs and resulted in reductions to regulatory capital.

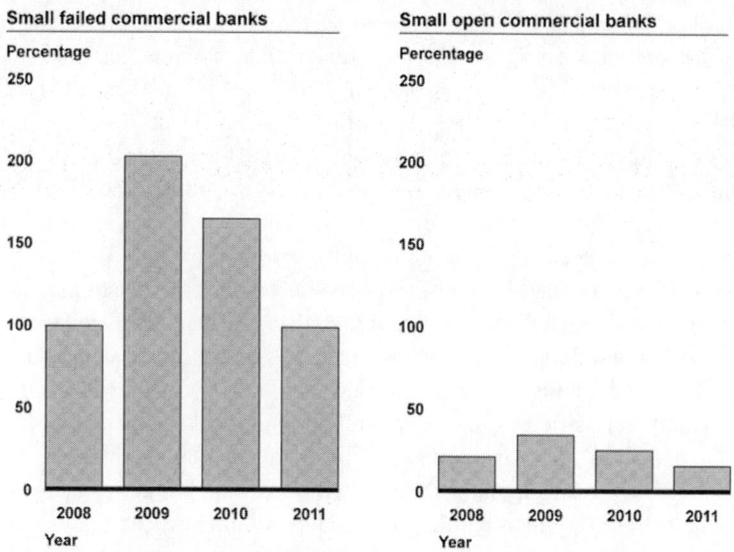

Source: GAO analysis of call report and thrift financial report data.

Figure 3. Credit Losses as a Percentage of Net Interest Income for Small Failed Commercial Banks and Small Open Commercial Banks in All States, 2008-2011.

Under GAAP, when a creditor such as a bank has determined that a loan is impaired it must establish the amount of the impairment on the basis of the present value of expected future cash flows, discounted at the loan's effective interest rate (the contractual interest rate adjusted for any net deferred loan fees or costs, premium, or discount existing at the origination or acquisition of the loan). However, as a practical expedient to measuring the discounted expected cash flows, impairment may also be measured in one of two other ways: either using the loan's observable market price, or if the loan is collateral-dependent, the "fair value" of the collateral. A loan is considered "collateral dependent" when the repayment of the debt will be provided solely by the sale or operation of the underlying collateral and there are no other available and reliable sources of repayment.

Federal banking regulators have issued guidance allowing banks to choose one of these three methods on a loan-by-loan basis for measuring impairment on an individually impaired loan, except for an impaired collateral-dependent loan. In that case, the regulators require that banks determine the amount of the loan impairment and the required increase to the loan loss allowance using the fair value of the collateral (the fair value of collateral method).[46] The guidance directs banks to consider the appraised value of the collateral as the starting point for determining its fair value.[47] In addition, the guidance provides that any portion of the loan balance on an impaired collateral dependent loan that exceeds the fair value of the collateral (less costs to sell in certain circumstances) and can be identified as uncollectible should generally be classified as a loss and charged off against the loan loss allowance. This principle applies when the repayment of the debt will be provided solely by the sale of the underlying real estate collateral (as opposed to the operation of the collateral) and there are no other available and reliable sources of repayment.

As discussed earlier, many failed banks' had high concentrations in ADC loans, which are considered the riskiest class of CRE loans because they can include properties that are built before having firm purchase or lease commitments from buyers or lessees. For many of these loans, market demand had fallen by the time the construction phase was completed, putting downward pressure on sales prices or rents. Data are not publicly available that indicate the extent to which credit losses or charge-offs at the failed banks were driven by declines in the collateral values of impaired collateral-dependent CRE or ADC loans.[48] However, several state regulators and state banking associations from the 10 states that we spoke with said that such declines in the collateral underlying impaired CRE and ADC loans were significant drivers in the levels of credit losses and charge-offs, and thus declines in regulatory capital, experienced by failed community banks, especially in those areas where real estate assets prices declined severely. Some state banking associations said that these effects were exacerbated by federal bank examiners' classification of collateral-dependent loans and their evaluation of appraisals used by banks to support impairment analysis of these loans. First, two state banking associations said that during examinations federal bank examiners adversely classified some performing collateral- dependent loans. These associations stated that in these instances, borrowers were making interest and principal payments as agreed; however, regulators questioned borrowers' future capacity to repay the loan. As such, the banks were then required to conduct an impairment analysis based on the appraised value of the collateral, which resulted in significant credit losses and charge-offs. Second, another association expressed concerns about the appraisals used to determine the fair value of the collateral and examiners' judgments concerning these appraisals. This association said that after the financial crisis began, examiners questioned some of the appraisals banks had obtained and made adjustments to them, driving larger valuation allowances, and when required, larger write-downs, than may have been warranted.

FDIC, Federal Reserve, and OCC staff agreed that the underlying collateral value of collateral-dependent loans that many failed banks had held had declined noticeably. However, they noted that regulatory guidance issued in October 2009 directed examiners not to require banks to write down loans to an amount less than the loan balance solely because the value of the underlying collateral had declined.[49] The guidance stated that for many CRE projects, the value of the collateral and the repayment of the loan both depended on the cash flows that the underlying project was expected to generate. Because of this linkage, collateral values are considered an important indicator of project viability and could signal changes that would adversely affect the cash flow available to service or repay the loan. The guidance stated that in making decisions to write down loans, bank examiners are to first focus on the adequacy of cash flows to service the debt, including cash flows from the operation of the collateral, and support from financially responsible guarantors or other bona fide repayment sources. However, the guidance noted that if these sources did not exist, and the only likely repayment source was the sale of the collateral, then examiners would direct the bank to write down the loan balances to the fair value of the collateral, less estimated costs to sell in certain circumstances. For example, one Federal Reserve staff told us that at some failed banks, ADC loans were being extended on an interest-only basis with no evidence that the borrower would be able to repay the principal and with underlying collateral whose value had declined by a very significant amount. In those cases, examiners questioned whether the banks would ever be repaid the principal owed. Absent any evidence the borrowers could pay through other means, the examiners would require a write-down under such circumstances. The guidance also addressed the appraisals banks obtained to support their impairment analyses. The guidance stated that examiners were generally not expected to challenge the appraisals obtained by banks unless they found that any underlying facts or assumptions about the appraisal were inappropriate or could support alternative assumptions.[50]

One banking association we spoke with noted that the required use of the fair value of collateral method to measure impairment resulted in larger increases to the loan loss allowance and loan loss provisions and resulting reductions in capital than would have occurred if the regulators had allowed the banks to use the present value of expected future cash flows method. This could occur particularly in those instances where repayment of the loan depended on the operation, as opposed to the sale, of the underlying collateral (e.g. rent collected from an apartment building). In such instances, as one of the valuation techniques used to determine appraised value, which is the starting point for applying the fair value of collateral method, expected cash flows from the income source are to be discounted using the market interest rate. The banking association also noted that the impairment amounts associated with the fair value of collateral method were greater because the market interest rate used in the appraisal process to discount the expected future cash flows was higher than the effective interest rate used under the present value of expected cash flows method.

FDIC and Federal Reserve staff told us that the federal banking regulators required banks to use the fair value of collateral method when determining the appropriate impairment amount of a collateral-dependent loan for consistency and comparability as well as for safety and soundness reasons. The effective interest rate used under the present value of expected cash flows method is the contractual interest rate on the loan and essentially a historical rate. Federal Reserve staff said that because different loans have different effective interest rates, values obtained using the present value of expected cash flows method are not comparable across loans or banks. Federal Reserve staff said that the fair value of collateral method facilitated comparability because it required the use of the same interest rate—the market interest rate—to value collateral.

Federal Reserve staff also said that the fair value of collateral method promotes safety and soundness by ensuring that a loan that is impaired is not carried on the books at a higher value than what can be obtained if the collateral were liquidated. FDIC staff agreed that the fair value of collateral method generally results in larger increases to the loan loss allowance for individually impaired loans and thus higher loan loss provisions than the present value of expected future cash flows method. From a safety and soundness perspective, they said that federal bank examiners require that the loan loss allowance be adequate within the confines of GAAP to absorb the potential losses on loans. Further, they said that the decision to require the use of the fair value of collateral method to determine the appropriate increase to the loan loss allowance, and, if required, the write-down and charge-off of an impaired collateral-dependent loan reflected long-standing examination practices.

Current Accounting Practices for Loss Provisioning May Have Delayed Reporting of Credit Losses during the Recent Crisis

Treasury and the Working Group have observed that the current accounting model for determining credit losses is based on historical loss rates, which were low in the years before the financial crisis. Under GAAP, the accounting model for estimating credit losses is commonly referred to as an "incurred loss model" because the timing and measurement of losses are based on estimating losses that have been incurred as of the balance sheet date, indicating a probable loss. In a 2009 speech, the Comptroller of the Currency, who was a co-chair of the Working Group, noted that in a long period of benign economic conditions, such as the years prior to the recent downturn, historical loan loss rates would typically be low. As a result, justifying significant loan loss provisioning to increase loan loss allowance can be difficult under the incurred loss model.[51] Treasury and the Working Group said that earlier recognition of loan losses could have potentially reduced the procyclicality of provisioning in the recent crisis—when banks had to recognize increases in their incurred credit losses through a sudden series of loan loss provisions, reducing earnings and regulatory capital—while still providing the necessary transparency to users of financial reports on changes in credit trends.[52]

In a 2010 speech, the chief national bank examiner for the OCC noted that the existing accounting rules made it difficult for examiners to require banks to make provisions to increase their loan loss allowances when it became clear that credit troubles were on the horizon. He said the result was that when subsequent charge-offs on impaired loans occurred, the allowances were not there to support them, and the higher provision levels that were then needed reduced capital, accelerating the spiral into insolvency for many banks.[53] FDIC and Federal Reserve staff also said that the existing accounting rules restricted examiners' ability to require banks to increase their loan loss allowances to recognize credit losses that were expected to occur in the future even as the examiners saw banks developing high concentrations of CRE and ADC loans and loosening underwriting standards. They also noted that the incurred loss model in effect creates "hurdles" for the examiners, outside auditors, and bank management who see credit trends and have the experience to know that problems are brewing but cannot incorporate this knowledge of growing risk into provisioning adequately for expected loan losses.

FDIC staff said that examiners can require banks to increase regulatory capital (i.e. by increasing shareholder equity) if they believe the level of the bank's capital or loan loss allowance does not adequately address the credit risk in the loan portfolio.[54] However, FDIC staff said that it is important for the loan loss allowance methodology to reflect best practices in credit risk management, so that bank management is forced to think about the potential amount of losses they might expect from the loans they are making. Similarly, Federal Reserve staff said that if management at the failed banks had been required to recognize loan losses earlier for the types of loans they were underwriting, it might have provided an incentive for them to not concentrate so heavily in the loans that later resulted in significant losses.

To address this issue, Treasury and the Working Group called for accounting standards setters to reevaluate the incurred loss model underlying current loan loss provisioning requirements and to reevaluate the existing accounting standards to develop forward-looking loan loss provisioning practices that incorporated a broader range of available credit information. In January 2011 FASB published a Supplementary Document, pursuant to a joint project with the International Accounting Standards Board (IASB) which proposed a model based on expected losses.[55] For the purpose of determining impairment allowance, financial assets that were managed on an open portfolio would be split into two groups: the "good book" and the "bad book," with an allowance computed for both books separately.[56] The division of the good book and bad book portfolios is based on an evaluation of the degree of uncertainty about collectability. The bad book requires the entire amount of expected credit losses over the remaining life of the portfolio to be recognized immediately. The good book requires the higher of (1) the time proportional expected credit losses or (2) the credit losses expected to occur within the foreseeable future. The time proportional expected credit losses represents a portion of expected lifetime losses based on the age of the financial assets relative to their expected life.

Some comment letters received in response to the proposal expressed concerns about potential complexities in the application of the proposed model, including uncertainty as to how institutions would actually estimate expected losses over the life of a portfolio. For example, the proposed approach for the good book required dual computations and introduced the need to estimate the expected remaining life of each portfolio in order to apply a "time proportional" approach. Concerns were also expressed about how companies would divide the portfolio into the good book and bad book and how transfers between the two books would occur. Based on the comments received, FASB and IASB began developing a revised credit impairment approach that would divide portfolios into three buckets of assets that determined the timing and amount of credit losses.[57] However, as a result of comments received regarding the understandability, operability, and auditability of this proposal, FASB announced on August 1, 2012, that it would instead explore a revised approach. In its Summary Board Decisions of August 22, 2012, FASB stated it was considering an alternative approach to impairment measurement called the "Current Expected Credit Loss Model". Under this model, the credit deterioration (or improvement) reflected in the income statement would include changes in the estimate of expected credit losses resulting from, but not limited to (1) changes in the credit risk of assets held by the entity, (2) changes in historical loss experience for assets like those held at the reporting date, (3) changes in conditions since the previous reporting date, and (4) changes in reasonable and supportable forecasts about the future. Such a model would recognize losses, if any, earlier than the current incurred loss model. On December 20, 2012, FASB issued a proposal for public comment regarding this model.[58]

In their comment letters to FASB on its proposals, federal banking regulators stated that they support the development of improved impairment standards and in particular an impairment standard that is more forward looking and recognizes credit losses earlier than the current incurred loss model.[59] FDIC staff said that given the unprecedented nature of the financial crisis, it was not clear to what extent recent bank failures would have been prevented had an expected loss model been in effect instead of the incurred loss model. However, they said that loan loss allowances under an expected loss model would certainly have been higher than they were at the beginning of the financial crisis, which would have provided banks' earnings and capital more protection against the rising credit losses.

We agree that loan loss allowances were not adequate to absorb the wave of credit losses that occurred when the financial crisis began, in part because current accounting standards for loan loss provisioning require banks to estimate losses using an incurred loss model and that earlier recognition of loan losses could have potentially reduced the procyclicality in the recent crisis. FASB is in the process of taking important steps to address this issue by proposing a model for loan loss provisioning that is more forward-looking and focuses on expected losses instead of incurred losses. Although examiners have the flexibility to require banks to increase regulatory capital if they determine that capital or loan loss allowances do not adequately address the credit risk in the loan portfolio, we agree with federal banking regulators that it is important for the loan loss reserving methodology to reflect best practices in credit risk management. Doing so would not only result in bank managements' establishing loan loss allowances for the loans they underwrite that reflect expected losses, but also could incentivize prudent risk management practices. Moreover, it should help address the cycle of losses and failures that emerged in the recent crisis as banks were forced to write down impaired loans and increase loan loss allowance and raise capital when they were least likely to be able to do so.

FDIC Used Shared Loss Agreements to Attract Bidders at Least Cost to the Deposit Insurance Fund

During the recent financial crisis, FDIC used shared loss agreements to help resolve failed financial institutions at the least cost to the DIF.[60] FDIC officials, state bank regulators, community banking associations, and acquiring banks of failed institutions we interviewed told us that shared loss agreements helped to attract potential bidders interested in purchasing the failed banks. According to FDIC officials, at the height of the financial crisis in 2008, FDIC sought bids for whole bank purchase and assumption agreements with little success. Banks that we spoke to said that, because of uncertainties about the market and the value of the assets, they would not have purchased the failed banks without FDIC's shared loss agreements. According to acquiring banks and peer banks we interviewed, while total estimated lifetime losses of the shared loss agreements may not change, the timing of the losses may change and payments from shared loss agreements may increase as the terms of the shared loss agreements mature. FDIC officials stated that the acquiring institutions were being monitored for compliance with the terms and conditions of the shared loss agreements. FDIC is issuing guidance to the acquiring institutions reminding them of the terms to prevent increased shared loss payments as these agreements mature and expire.

FDIC Used Shared Loss Agreements to Attract Bidders for Failed Banks

For most of FDIC's history, purchase and assumption transactions (the direct sale of a failed bank to another, healthier bank) have been the preferred resolution method for failed banks. FDIC has said that such sales are generally less costly than directly paying off depositors of the failed bank and keep customers with insured deposits from suffering any loss of service.[61] FDIC strives to effect a whole bank purchase and assumption agreement, in which essentially all of the failed bank's deposits, assets, and certain liabilities are sold and transferred to the acquiring institution.[62] From January 2008 through December 31, 2011, FDIC was appointed as receiver for the 414 failed banks, with $662 billion in book value of failed bank assets. FDIC used purchase and assumption agreements to resolve 394 failed institutions amounting to approximately $652 billion in failed institution assets, which represents 98 percent of the total assets of failed banks and thrifts since 2008 (see figure 4).

However, FDIC was only able to resolve so many of these banks with purchase and assumption agreements because it offered to share in the losses incurred by the acquiring institution. According to FDIC officials, at the height of the financial crisis in 2008, FDIC sought bids for whole bank purchase and assumption agreements with little success. Potential acquiring banks we interviewed told us that they did not have sufficient capital to take on the additional risks that the failed institutions' assets represented. Because shared loss agreements had worked well during the savings and loan crisis of the 1980s and early 1990s, FDIC decided to use this method to solicit bids to provide potential buyers some protection on the purchase of failed bank assets, reduce immediate cash needs, keep assets in the private sector, and minimize disruptions to banking customers.[63] Under the agreements, FDIC generally agrees to pay 80 percent for covered losses with the acquiring bank covering the remaining 20 percent.[64]

Resolution type	Number of failed banks	Total assets (dollars in billions)
Purchase and assumption	394	$652
Direct payout and insured deposit transfers	20	10
	Total 414	**Total $662**

Source: GAO analysis of FDIC data.

Figure 4. FDIC's Resolution Methods, 2008-2011.

From 2008 to the end of 2011, FDIC resolved 281 of the 414 failures (68 percent) by providing a shared loss agreement (see figure 5).[65] Banks that we spoke to said that, because of uncertainties in the market and the value of the assets, they would not have purchased the failed banks without FDIC's shared loss agreements. By comparing the estimated cost of the shared loss agreements versus the estimated cost of directly liquidating the failed bank, FDIC claims that the use of shared loss agreements saved the DIF over $40 billion.

In 2012, FDIC has been able to resolve more failed institutions without having to offer to share in the losses. For example, year to date as of September 30, 2012, there had been 43 bank failures, and FDIC has only had to agree to share losses on 18 of those failures (42 percent). Additionally, some potential bidders were willing to accept shared loss agreements with lower than 80-percent coverage.

FDIC Monitors Acquiring Institutions' Adherence to Agreements' Terms and Conditions

FDIC officials stated that the acquiring institutions were being monitored for compliance with the terms and conditions of the shared loss agreements. As shown in figure 6, FDIC estimated the DIF receiverships would have to pay $42.8 billion over the life of the agreements.[66] As of the end of 2011, FDIC had paid out about $16.2 billion under the agreements, and FDIC estimated it would have to pay an additional $26.6 billion over the life of the agreements. Shared loss payment claims may be submitted unevenly over the life of the agreements.

FDIC estimates that most of those losses will be experienced at the beginning of the agreement and will increase somewhat in the final year of the agreement. For financial reporting purposes for year-end 2012, for example, FDIC assumes in its commercial shared loss agreement that 40 percent of the lifetime losses occur in the first year and approximately 18 percent occur in the 5th and final year of the agreement. FDIC officials stated that they monitor the agreements to ensure the acquirer is adhering to the terms and conditions for proper loss recognition.

Additionally, FDIC is issuing guidance reminding them of the terms of the agreements to prevent an increase in shared loss payments as the agreements mature and expire due to inappropriate loss claims. The uneven claims do not change the total estimated lifetime losses, but affect the year in which the losses are incurred. FDIC revises its estimate of lifetime losses for financial reporting (and management purposes) each year based on current market conditions.

Year	Number of shared loss agreements	Estimated lifetime losses (dollars in billions)
2008	3	$3.29
2009	90	19.92
2010	130	15.98
2011	58	3.65
	Total **281**	**Total** **$42.84**

Source: GAO analysis of FDIC data.

Figure 5. Shared Loss Agreements Entered into by Year, 2008-2011.

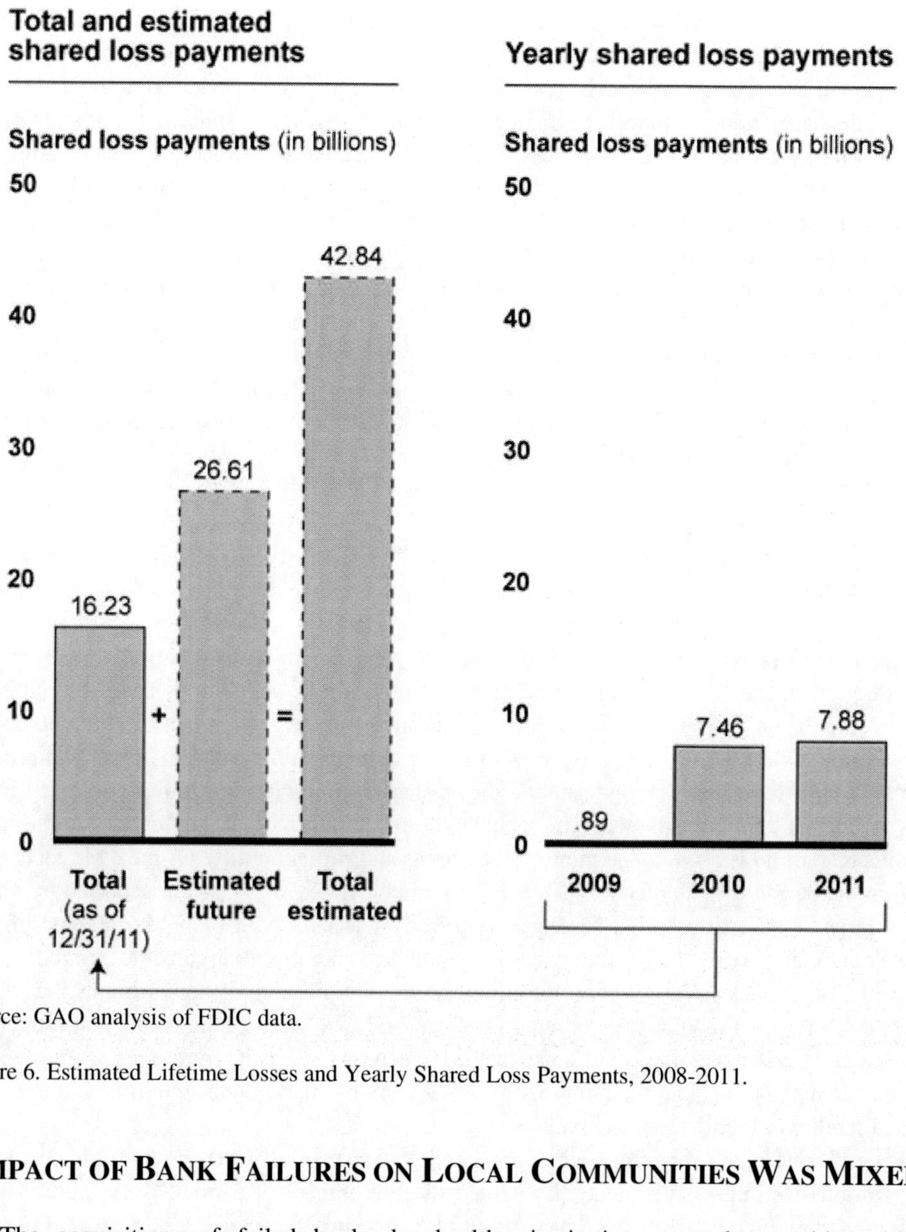

Source: GAO analysis of FDIC data.

Figure 6. Estimated Lifetime Losses and Yearly Shared Loss Payments, 2008-2011.

IMPACT OF BANK FAILURES ON LOCAL COMMUNITIES WAS MIXED

The acquisitions of failed banks by healthy institutions may have mitigated the potentially negative effects of bank failures on communities, although the focus of local lending and philanthropy may have shifted. First, while bank failures and failed bank acquisitions can increase market concentration— thereby potentially impacting banks' ability to exercise market power, such as raising prices or reducing availability of some products and services,—our analysis suggests that a limited number of metropolitan areas and rural counties were likely to have become significantly more concentrated. This is because in many instances the failed banks were acquired by out-of-market institutions. Second, our analysis of call report data from 2007 to 2011 found that failing small banks extended progressively less net credit as they approached failure, but that acquiring banks generally increased net credit as measured by changes in loan balances. However, officials of acquiring banks and surviving peer banks of failed banks in Georgia, Nevada, and Michigan we interviewed noted that in the wake of the bank failures, underwriting standards had tightened and thus credit was generally more readily available for small business owners who had better credit histories and stronger financials than for those who did not. Further, several bank officials said that new lending in certain kinds of loans was restricted in certain areas, such as collateral dependent loans in areas where asset values declined severely. Third, regulators, banking associations, and banks we spoke with said that involvement in local philanthropy declined as small banks approached failure but generally increased after acquisition. However, these acquiring banks may not focus on the same philanthropic activities as the failed bank did. Finally, our analysis of personal income, unemployment, house prices, and bank failures in states from 1994 to 2011 suggests that bank failures are more likely to affect the real estate sector in a state than the labor market or overall economy in a state.

With Exceptions, Bank Failures Have Not Resulted in Significant Increases in Local Market Concentration

Bank failures and failed bank acquisitions had a significant impact on market concentration in a limited number of metropolitan areas and rural counties. Market concentration is an indicator of the extent to which firms in the market can have the potential to exercise market power—that is, raise prices, reduce output, diminish innovation, or otherwise harm customers as a result of diminished competitive constraints or incentives. Bank failures and failed bank acquisitions have the potential to affect market concentration—and thus market power—in some metropolitan areas and rural counties. Of the 414 banks that failed in the period from January 1, 2008, to December 31, 2011, 393 were acquired by other banks. In some cases, the failed bank was acquired by a bank with branches in some of the same geographic areas as the failed bank's branches, thereby changing the numbers and relative sizes of banks doing business in those areas. The failures of the 21 banks that were not acquired also led to changes in the numbers and relative sizes of the banks that remained in the areas where the failed banks had been located. As a result, these bank failures and failed bank acquisitions had the potential to affect banking market concentration and the cost and availability of credit and other banking services.

Federal and state banking regulators and national and state community banking organizations we interviewed generally agreed that the impact of a small bank failure in an urban area would likely differ from the impact of failure in a rural area. Urban areas typically have a number of financial institutions, including other small banks, which can meet the community's needs if one community bank fails. But several interviewees stated that the severity of the effect of a bank failure on a rural county with just one bank whose branches were located entirely within the county would likely depend on whether the bank was acquired or the bank's assets were liquidated through a direct payout. If a bank was resolved through a direct payout, the community might find it had less access to credit and other banking services than it would have if the failed bank were purchased by a healthy bank.

However, our analysis showed that market concentration likely increased after a bank failure and acquisition in a small percentage of both urban and rural communities.[67] We analyzed the impact of bank failures and failed bank acquisitions on local credit markets using data for the period from June 2007 to June 2012 to calculate the Herfindahl-Hirschman Index (HHI), a key statistical measure used to assess market concentration and the potential for firms to exercise their ability to influence market prices.[68] The HHI reflects the number of firms in the industry and each firm's market share. It is calculated by summing the squares of the market shares of each firm competing in the market. The HHI also reflects the distribution of market shares of the top firms and the composition of the market outside the top firms. The HHI is measured on a scale of 0 to 10,000, with larger values indicating more concentration. According to the Department of Justice (DOJ) and the Federal Trade Commission (FTC), markets in which the value of the HHI is between 1,500 and 2,500 points are considered to be moderately concentrated, and those in which the value of the HHI is in excess of 2,500 points are considered to be highly concentrated, although other factors also play a role.

We estimated the difference between pre- and postfailure HHIs for each local market as of June 30 of each year from 2007 to 2011 using deposits to measure banks' market shares.[69] We defined local markets as metropolitan statistical areas and micropolitan statistical areas (collectively, metropolitan areas) and rural counties (counties that are not components of metropolitan areas) as identified by the Census Bureau as of December 2009.[70] Table 3 summarizes the number of markets where at least one deposit-taking branch of a failed bank was doing business as of June 30 of each year from 2007 to 2011 and the number of markets in which the difference between pre- and postfailure HHI was at least 100 and the postfailure HHI was 1,500 or more, the benchmark for raising significant competitive concerns. Our results suggest that a small number of the markets affected by bank failures and failed bank acquisitions were likely to have become significantly more concentrated. For example, 8 of the 188 metropolitan areas affected by bank failures and failed bank acquisitions between June 30, 2009, and June 29, 2010, met the criteria for raising significant competitive concerns. Similarly, 5 of the 68 rural counties affected by bank failures during the same time period met the same criteria. Our analysis also showed that in most markets, bank failures and failed bank acquisitions were likely to have no impact on market concentration. For example, 120 of the 188 metropolitan areas affected by bank failures between June 30, 2009, and June 29, 2010, likely experienced no change in market concentration as a result of those failures and acquisitions. Similarly, 62 of the 68 rural counties affected by bank failures and failed bank acquisitions during the same period likely experienced no change in concentration as a result. The failed banks in these markets were acquired by banks that had not previously been operating in the markets, so the failures and acquisitions had no impact on market concentration in the area. In general, a small number of markets were likely to become significantly more concentrated as a result of the bank failures and bank acquisitions because, in most instances, the acquiring bank was a bank that had not previously been operating in the community.

Although the number of markets with potentially significant competitive effects is small, households and businesses in those markets may face higher prices or reduced availability of at least some banking products and services. These competitive effects are more likely to impact banking products and services that are more local in scope, such as checking account services or lines of credit. However, customers may be able to obtain some products and services from banks outside their local market, and the extent to which the market for any particular banking product or service is local as opposed to regional, national, or even international, is likely to vary.

Table 3. Impact of Bank Failures and Failed Bank Acquisitions on Market Concentration, 2007-2012

	June 30, 2007–June 29, 2008	June 30, 2008–June 29, 2009	June 30, 2009–June 29, 2010	June 30, 2010–June 29, 2011	June 30, 2011–June 29, 2012
Metropolitan areas	**942**	**942**	**942**	**942**	**942**
Number with bank failures	4	150	188	124	102
Number with changes in market concentration that are consistent with potentially significant competitive effects from bank failures and failed bank acquisitions	0	6	8	3	8
Number with changes in concentration that are not consistent with potentially competitive effects from bank failures and failed bank acquisitions	0	45	60	31	28
Number with no change in concentration from bank failures and failed bank acquisitions	4	99	120	90	66
Rural counties	**1331**	**1331**	**1331**	**1331**	**1331**
Number with bank failures	2	31[a]	68	32	45
Number with changes in concentration that are consistent with potentially significant competitive effects from bank failures and failed bank acquisitions	0	7	5	5	5
Number with changes in concentration that are not consistent with potentially competitive effects from bank failures and failed bank acquisitions	0	3	1	0	3
Number with no change in concentration and failed bank acquisitions	2	21	62	27	37

Source: GAO analysis of Census Bureau, FDIC, and OCC data.

Note: A market had a failed bank if one or more banks with deposits in that market as of June 30 failed over the next 12 months. The change in concentration is the difference between the pre- and post-failure HHI. The prefailure HHI for each year is the HHI calculated using banks' market shares as of June 30 of each year. The postfailure HHI is the HHI calculated as of June 30 of each year assuming that all the bank failures and failed bank acquisitions that occurred over the next 12 months occurred at the beginning of the period. Markets with changes in concentration that are consistent with potentially significant competitive effects of bank failures and failed bank acquisitions are those in which the postfailure HHI is at least 1,500 and the difference between the pre- and postfailure HHI is at least 100. Markets with no change in concentration are those in which difference between and pre- and postfailure HHI is zero. Markets with changes in concentration that are not consistent with potentially significant competitive effects of bank failures and failed bank acquisitions are those in which the difference between the pre- and postfailure HHI is greater than zero but either the postfailure HHI is less than 1,500 or the difference between the pre- and post-failure HHI is less than 100. We used a bank's share of total deposits in a market to measure its market share in that market. However, a bank's share of total deposits in a market may be measured with error, depending upon how banks allocate deposits to their branches when reporting branch level deposits. Furthermore, a bank's share of total deposits in a market may not reflect its share of the market for other banking products and services. In addition, this table focuses on the impact of bank failures and failed bank acquisitions on market concentration, but many other factors contribute to the actual amount of concentration in a market. Finally, the HHI can only indicate the potential for firms to exercise market power and it does not imply that firms will actually choose to exercise market power if they have it.

[a] Number includes Glascock, GA, because the one bank doing business in that county on June 30, 2008, failed and was not acquired by another bank in the next 12 months.

Our analysis of market concentration has limitations and thus should be interpreted with caution. In particular, a bank's share of total deposits in a market may be measured with some error, depending upon how banks allocate deposits to their branches when reporting branch-level deposits to FDIC. Furthermore, a bank's share of total deposits in a market may not reflect its share of the market for other banking products and services. In addition, our analysis focuses on the impact of bank failures and failed bank acquisitions on market concentration. However, many other factors contribute to the actual amount of concentration in a market, including changes in banks' business models over time, fluctuations in consumer demand, and entry into and exit from the market by non-bank financial institutions. Finally, the HHI can only indicate the potential for firms to exercise market power and does not imply that firms will actually choose to exercise market power if they have it.

Acquiring Banks Mitigated the Decline in Credit Extension due to Failing Institutions

The amount of credit extended by failing banks fell as the banks approached failure and their balance sheets deteriorated, but the amount of credit extended by acquiring banks remained positive even after the acquisition of a failed bank. We used FDIC and Federal Financial Institutions Examination Council (FFIEC) data from 2006 through 2011 to estimate the net credit that all failing banks extended in the quarters before they failed and by acquiring banks in the quarters following their acquisition of a failed bank.[71] Estimates from our modeling procedure suggest that, on average, net credit extended by banks that failed in the period from 2008 to 2011 decreased continuously over the eight quarters prior to failure and became negative about five quarters prior to failure, indicating that failing banks were contracting and reducing the overall amount of credit they provided (see figure 7). Our estimates also suggest that net credit extended by banks that acquired failed banks during the same period generally decreased immediately after the acquisition and then partially recovered, but always remained positive. It follows that, on average, acquiring banks continued to expand the amount of credit they made available, albeit more slowly than they did prior to the acquisition of the failed bank.

To examine the robustness of our results, we repeated our analysis for small and medium-sized banks as separate groups. Our estimates for small and medium-size banks suggest that net credit extended by failed banks in these categories followed a pattern similar to that shown in figure 7, declining continuously in the quarters preceding failure and becoming negative four to five quarters before failure. Net credit extended by small acquiring banks declined on average immediately following the acquisition of a failed bank and then partially recovered, but remained positive except in the first quarter following the acquisition. For medium- sized acquiring banks, net credit appears to have declined more slowly following the acquisition of a failed bank, remaining positive for several quarters but actually becoming negative around a year after acquiring the failed bank. Overall, however, our estimates suggest that failing banks extend less and less credit as they fail and that acquiring banks continue to extend additional credit after they acquire a failed bank.

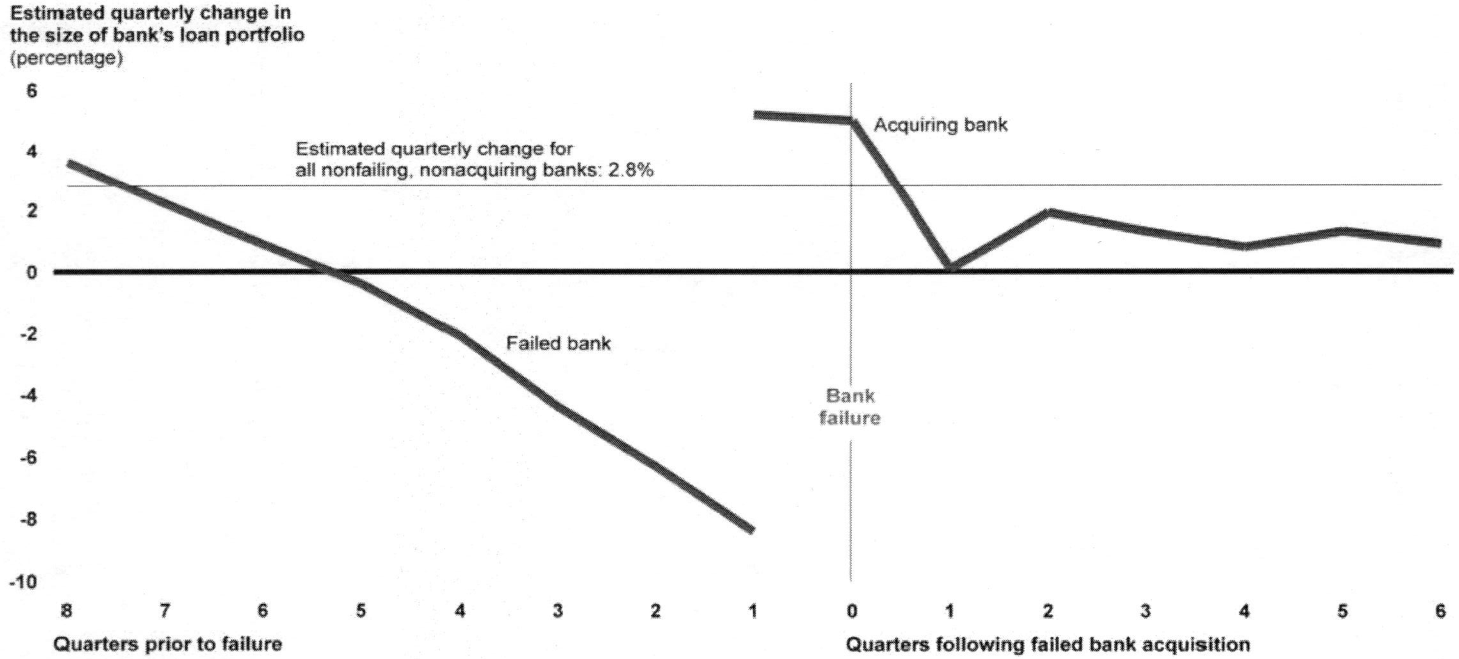

Source: GAO analysis of FDIC and FFIEC data.

Note: Net credit extended by a bank in a quarter is calculated as the percent change in the size of the bank's loan portfolio over the quarter and thus reflects the overall effect of actions that increase the size of a bank's loan portfolio, such as originating new loans or purchasing loans, and actions that decrease the size of a bank's loan portfolio, such as charging off delinquent loans or selling loans. Estimates reflect average relationships between bank characteristics and net credit extended by banks for all of the observations we used and thus may not reflect trends in net credit extended by any one bank.

Figure 7. Estimated Net Credit Extended by Failing, Acquiring, and Nonfailing, Nonacquiring Banks, 2008-2011.

Our results likely reflect both factors that are generally associated with net credit extended by banks and factors that are specific to the particular time period we analyzed. Thus, the extent to which our results can be generalized to other time periods is limited. Furthermore, our results reflect average relationships between bank characteristics and net credit extended by banks for all of the observations we used. As such, they may not reflect the particular circumstances of any one bank. In addition, we note that the list of characteristics we analyzed is meant to highlight important characteristics of banks that are related to the provision of credit, but many other factors—including demand for credit by borrowers—play a role in the net amount of credit a bank extends and our list of characteristics is not exhaustive. Finally, we used the change in the size of a bank's loan portfolio over a quarter to measure the net amount of credit it extended over that quarter. However, several factors affect the size of a bank's loan portfolio outside of making new loans, including charging off delinquent loans.[72] Thus, the change in the size of a bank's loan portfolio is a measure of the net effect of increases in the amount of credit a bank is extending, but it is an imperfect proxy for new loan originations.

According to Interviews with Banks, Acquisitions Generally Mitigated Other Potential Impacts of Small Bank Failures on Communities

We interviewed officials of selected acquiring banks of small failed banks and open peers of these banks that were their competitors (peers) in Georgia, Nevada, and Michigan to learn about the effects of the failures on local communities in those states. According to banks in urban and rural areas in the three states that we interviewed, acquisitions of failed small banks mitigated some potential negative effects on the cost and availability of credit and on philanthropic contributions in these communities. For example, officials from acquiring banks in the three states we interviewed told us that, since taking over the failed banks, they had increased lending and noted that the failed banks had generally ceased making new loans in the community prior to their failures. Several acquiring and peer banks in the three states said that credit was more readily available for small business owners who had good credit histories and strong financials. Several acquiring and peer banks in the three states we interviewed noted that in the wake of the bank failures, underwriting standards had tightened, making it harder for some borrowers who may have been able to obtain loans prior to the bank failures than to obtain them afterward.[73] For example, several bankers said that they would not consider making new loans to small business owners with weak credit histories. Several banks we interviewed also said that finding new high-quality borrowers was difficult.

However, the bankers we interviewed also said that new lending for certain types of loans could be restricted in certain areas. Bankers in all three states said that the CRE market, and in particular the ADC market, had contracted, and new lending in this area had declined significantly. For example, one acquiring banker in the Atlanta area said that upon acquiring the failed bank it made all of its lending products available, thus considerably expanding the types of credit available to the community. However, this banker said that the bank no longer made new CRE loans and that much of the growth in new lending had been in small business and commercial and industrial lending. This banker also noted that ADC lending had largely ceased in the Atlanta area and that CRE loans were now focused on owner-occupied properties, which are considered less risky than other types of CRE loans.

Several acquiring and peer banks in the three states stated that weak demand due to economic uncertainty, particularly among high quality borrowers, was inhibiting growth in new loans.[74] A few banks in the three states noted that competition, particularly for customers with good credit has pushed interest rates to lower levels. However, one bank in Michigan noted that even with the lack of demand for credit, larger acquiring banks tended to bring more products and services to the community.

One peer bank in Georgia indicated that failed banks acquired via shared loss agreements had negatively impacted competition because the acquired banks received significant loss coverage on potential credit losses that peer banks did not. This bank said that it might have to absorb larger credit losses than acquiring banks for comparable loans. For example, this bank said that the acquiring banks had driven down real estate values in the local market by selling off assets such as collateralized loans covered by shared loss agreements at depressed prices. As a result of these sales, existing collateralized assets might have to be reappraised at the lower values, possibly leading to further credit losses. However, officials of several acquiring banks told us that the shared loss agreements gave them more time to work out problem loans held by existing customers and allowed them to hold onto the assets.[75]

Federal and state banking regulators, national and state banking associations, and acquiring and existing bank officials we interviewed in Georgia, Nevada, and Michigan told us that involvement in local philanthropy declines as community banks approach failure but generally increases after they have been acquired. State banking regulators and national and state community banking associations we interviewed told us that failed community banks were highly involved in local philanthropic activities before the recession—for example, by designating portions of their earnings for community development or other charitable activities. Many community bank board members and managers were leaders in the community who supported local charities and civic groups. Acquiring bank officials we interviewed told us that they had generally increased philanthropic activities compared to the failed community banks during the economic downturn and in the months before failure. However, acquiring banks may or may not focus on the same philanthropic activities as the failed banks. For example, one large acquiring bank official told us that it made major charitable contributions to large national or statewide philanthropic organizations and causes and focused less on the local community charities to which the failed bank had contributed. However, another acquirer told us that by retaining the failed bank's employees, it had been able to continue contributing to the charities the employees had previously selected.

Bank Failures in a State Are More Likely to Affect the Real Estate Sector than the Labor Market or Broader Economy

To assess the relationship between bank failures and overall economic conditions in a state, we used an econometric model to analyze the relationships among four variables—bank failures, income, unemployment, and real estate prices—for U.S. states and the District of Columbia (states) using data for the period from 1994 through 2011.[76] Our results are limited by several factors and thus should be interpreted with caution. First the econometric procedure we used is a useful diagnostic tool but it is based largely on timing patterns in the variables as opposed to actual causality. Second, as with the results of our other analyses, they may not generalize to other time periods or, in this case, to the national, city, or county level.

Third, the model reflects average relationships among the variables and thus may not apply to the specific circumstances of any one state.

Finally, the specific group of variables we analyzed was chosen to highlight particular relationships and may not contain all of the variables that contribute to explaining personal income, unemployment, house prices, or failed bank deposits in states.

Our analysis suggests that bank failures in a state were more likely to affect its real estate sector than its labor market or broader economy. The results suggest that failed banks' share of deposits in a state—our measure for bank failures—do not impact personal income in a state in the sense that past values of failed banks' share of deposits do not help explain the current level of personal income in a state (table 4).[77]

Similarly, past values of personal income in a state do not appear to help explain the current value of failed banks' share of deposits in a state. In particular, this analysis did not suggest that bank failures in a state were associated with a decline in personal income in that state.

To the extent that there is a relationship between the unemployment rate and failed banks' share of deposits in a state, it appears that the unemployment rate has more bearing on failed banks' share of deposits than vice versa. Past values of the unemployment rate appear to partially explain the current value of failed banks' share of deposits. However, we did not find evidence that past values of failed banks' share of deposits in a state help explain the current value of the unemployment rate.

Failed banks' share of deposits and the house price index in a state appear to be significantly related to each other. Past values of failed banks' share of deposits appear to help explain the current value of the house price index in a state, and vice versa. Altogether, these results suggest that the impact of bank failures on a state's economy is most likely to appear in the real estate sector and are less likely to appear in the overall labor market or in the broader economy.

Table 4. Summary of Relationships among Bank Failures, Personal Income, Unemployment, and Real Estate Prices in U.S. States, 1994-2011

Variable	Variable may be explained in part by past values of			
	Personal income	**Unemployment**	**house prices**	**Failed bank deposits**
Personal income	—	Yes	In some specifications	No
Unemployment	Yes	—	In some specifications	No
House prices	In some specifications	Yes	—	Yes
Failed bank deposits	No	Yes	Yes	—

Source: GAO analysis of data from the Bureau of Economic Analysis, Bureau of Labor Statistics, Federal Deposit Insurance Corporation, and the Federal Housing Finance Agency.

Note: The extent to which our results can be generalized to other time periods or other geographic units–either larger units, such as nations, or smaller units, such as cities or counties—is limited.

AGENCY COMMENTS

We provided a draft of this report to the Federal Reserve, FDIC, and OCC for review and comment. The agencies did not provide formal written comments, but provided written technical comments, which we incorporated as appropriate.

Gene L. Dodaro
Comptroller General of the United States

APPENDIX I. OBJECTIVES, SCOPE AND METHODOLOGY

The objectives of our report were to review (1) the factors that contributed to the failure of banks in states with 10 or more failures between 2008 and 2011, including the extent to which losses related to fair value accounting treatment affected the regulatory capital positions of failed banks; (2) market factors that affected the Federal Deposit Insurance Corporation's (FDIC) choice of resolution method, or the amount of FDIC coverage offered on the shared loss agreements, and the costs that the DIF incurred as a result of these shared loss agreements; and (3) the effect of recent small bank failures on local communities.

To address the factors that contributed to the failures of banks in states with 10 or more failures between 2008 and 2011, including the extent to which losses related to fair value accounting treatment affected the regulatory capital positions of failed banks, we used data from FDIC's Historical Statistics on Banking–Failures and Assistance Transactions (HSOB) database to identify states that met the criterion. We identified 10 states that experienced 10 or more failures (the 10 states) over the relevant time period. We then used data from the HSOB database to develop characteristics that described the failed banks in these 10 states, such as asset size, charter type, bank type, length of operations and failed bank assets as a percentage of total assets. We reviewed material loss reviews (MLR), failed bank reviews (FBR), and in-depth reviews (IDR) issued by the inspectors general (IG) of the federal banking regulators for these same institutions and summarized the factors they identified as contributing to the failures. [78] We then used data from FDIC's Statistics on Depository Institutions (SDI) database to develop trend statistics for the period 2001 through 2011 that described bank characteristics in the years leading up to the failures for these institutions. In conducting our analyses, we carried out a data reliability assessment of the HSOB and SDI databases. To do so, we reviewed information on the processes and procedures FDIC uses to help ensure that data entered into these databases are accurate and complete. We also reviewed the data for missing values, and, where we observed instances of such, determined the reason. On the basis of this information, we determined that these data were reliable for our purposes. We also interviewed officials from FDIC, the Board of Governors of the Federal Reserve System, and the Office of the Comptroller of the Currency (federal banking regulators), state banking regulators from the 10 states, national banking organizations, state community banking organizations from 7 of the 10 states, and market experts to obtain their views on the causes of bank failures in the 10 states.[79]

We also estimated, as a function of the bank characteristics discussed above, the likelihood that a bank might fail. More specifically, we analyzed nationwide data from FDIC and Federal Financial Institutions Examination Council (call report data) on FDIC-insured commercial banks and state- chartered savings banks for the period from 2006 through 2011.[80] We examined characteristics that describe a bank's capital adequacy, asset quality, earnings, liquidity, CRE lending, brokered deposits funding, and size. We used econometric models to estimate the relationships between these characteristics and the likelihood that a bank fails.[81] We included indicators for each quarter to control for factors affecting the likelihood of failure that are common to all banks at the same time, such as changes in the regulatory environment, the market for bank products and services, and the overall economy. In conducting our analyses, we carried out a data reliability assessment of the FDIC and FFIEC call report data. To do so, we reviewed information on the processes and procedures used to help ensure that these data were complete and accurate. We also reviewed the data for missing values, and, where we observed instances of such, determined the reason. On the basis of this information, we determined that these data were reliable for our purposes.

To address the extent to which losses related to fair value accounting treatment affected the regulatory capital positions of failed banks, we identified and reviewed those accounting standards under U.S. generally accepted accounting principles (GAAP) that pertain to fair value, historical cost, and impairment accounting and identified those assets and liabilities on banks' balance sheets that are subject to each. We also reviewed guidance issued by the federal banking regulators as to the application of these standards. We then analyzed bank call report and thrift financial data from 2007 through 2011 for failed and open commercial banks and thrifts nationwide to identify and compare trends in (1) the use of historical cost accounting and fair value accounting and (2) the extent to which losses were credit related. In conducting our analysis, we followed the methodology used by the Securities and Exchange Commission in their 2008 report on mark-to-market accounting, which examined the linkages that occurred between fair value accounting and bank failures that occurred in 2008.[82] We also reviewed reports issued by the Department of the Treasury and the Financial Stability Forum's Working Group on Loss Provisioning to obtain views on the adequacy of current accounting models for loan loss provisioning and reviewed proposals issued by accounting standard setters to revise the current accounting model and comment letters received in response to these proposals. We provided a copy of the draft report to two accounting experts, a former comptroller general and a professor of accountancy for their review.

To address the market factors that affected FDIC's choice of resolution method, or the amount of FDIC coverage offered on shared loss agreements, and the costs the Deposit Insurance Fund (DIF) incurred as a result of the shared loss agreements, we first obtained and analyzed FDIC loss payment information from its New Financial Environment accounting system. To identify the future costs to the DIF that will result from shared loss agreements, we obtained and analyzed the estimate of lifetime losses that FDIC develops for each failed institution. We determined that these estimates were reliable for purposes of financial reporting. Also, we interviewed FDIC officials and reviewed and summarized FDIC policies and procedures in order to assess how FDIC determined that shared loss agreements were the least costly method for resolving bank failures during this time period. In order to describe factors in the market environment from 2008 through 2011 that may have affected the choice of resolution method or the structure of FDIC shared loss agreements, we interviewed officials from federal banking regulators, state banking regulators from the 10 states, national banking organizations, state community banking organizations from 7 of the 10 states, and market experts.

To assess the effect of recent small bank failures on local communities, we first assessed the impact of nationwide bank failures and failed bank acquisitions on concentration in local credit markets using data for the period from June 2007 through June 2012 by calculating the Herfindahl- Hirschman Index (HHI)—a commonly used measure to assess the competitive environment and enforce U.S. antitrust laws. Market concentration is an indicator of the extent to which firms in the market can exercise market power, that is, to raise prices, reduce output, diminish innovation, or otherwise harm customers as a result of diminished competitive constraints or incentives. The HHI is equal to the sum of the squares of the market shares of each firm in the market and thus reflects both the number of firms in the market and each firm's relative size.[83] The HHI ranges from 10,000 (if there is a single firm in the market) to a number approaching zero (in the case of a perfectly competitive market). Department of Justice (DOJ) and Federal Trade Commission (FTC) guidelines suggest that markets with an HHI of less than 1,500 are unconcentrated, those with HHIs between 1,500 and 2,500 are moderately concentrated, and those with HHIs greater than 2,500 are concentrated. They also suggest that a change in a market's HHI of 100 or more that results in an HHI of more than 1,500 may raise significant competitive concerns, while a change in a market's HHI of 200 or more that results in an HHI of 2,500 is presumed to be likely to enhance market power.

We compared the pre- and postfailure HHIs for each local market across the country as of June 30 of each year from 2007 through 2011. We defined local markets as metropolitan statistical areas and micropolitan statistical areas (collectively, metropolitan areas) and rural counties (counties that are not components of metropolitan areas) as identified by the Census Bureau as of December 2009. We used data on FDIC- insured institutions, including commercial banks, savings banks, savings associations, and insured branches of foreign banks from FDIC's Survey on Deposits database. We defined a banking organization as the collection of all banks that are subsidiaries of the same bank or thrift holding company, or the consolidated bank for those banks that are not subsidiaries of a holding company. We identified a banking organization as doing business in a market if at least one of the banks in that banking organization had at least one deposit-taking branch in that market.[84] We used deposits to measure a banking organization's market share. We calculated the prefailure HHI for each local market as of June 30 of each year by summing the squared market shares of each banking organization doing business in that market as of that date. We calculated the postfailure HHIs for each local market by treating the bank failures and acquisitions that occurred during the period from June 30 of one year to June 29 of the next year as if they occurred at the beginning of the period. We assigned deposits in failed banks that were acquired to the acquiring bank, and we assigned deposits in failed banks that were not acquired to other banks in the market proportionally. Although we included failed banks of all sizes in this analysis, over 90 percent of the bank failures were of small banks, and thus the analysis largely reflects the impact of their failures on market concentration. In conducting our analyses, we carried out a data reliability assessment of the Survey on Deposits database. To do so, we reviewed information on the processes and procedures FDIC uses to help ensure that data entered into this database are accurate and complete. We also reviewed the data for missing values, and, where we observed instances of such, determined the reason. On the basis of this information, we determined that these data were reliable for our purposes.

Our analysis of market concentration has limitations and thus should be interpreted with caution. In particular, a bank's share of total deposits in a market may be measured with some error, depending upon how banks allocate deposits to their branches when reporting branch-level deposits to FDIC. Furthermore, a bank's share of total deposits in a market may not reflect its share of the market for other banking products and services. In addition, our analysis focuses on the impact of bank failures and failed bank acquisitions on market concentration. However, many other factors contribute to the actual amount of concentration in a market, including changes in banks' business models over time, fluctuations in consumer demand, and entry into and exit from the market by non-bank financial institutions. Finally, the HHI can only indicate the potential for firms to exercise market power and does not imply that firms will actually choose to exercise market power in ways that are detrimental to consumers.

We also assessed the impact of bank failures on the availability of credit by using 2006-2011 call report data to estimate changes in the size of a bank's loan portfolio in the quarters leading up to failure for failed banks and in the quarters following acquisition of a failed bank (for acquiring banks). We used the change in the size of a bank's loan portfolio over a quarter as a proxy for the net amount of credit it extended over that quarter. The change in the size of a bank's loan portfolio over a quarter reflects the net effects of new loan originations, loan purchases, charge- offs, loan sales and securitizations, and other factors. As a result, it reflects net credit extended by a bank rather than the extension of new credit only. We first estimated the relationship between the characteristics of banks that were associated with the likelihood of failure and changes in the size of banks' loan portfolios. We then used our estimates to predict the average change in the size of a bank's loan portfolio in the quarters leading up to failure for failed banks and in the quarters following acquisition of a failed bank (for acquiring banks).[85] We conducted this analysis for all banks, and then for small banks and medium-size banks. We did not conduct a separate analysis for large banks because there were insufficient observations.

We assessed the relationship between bank failures and overall economic conditions in a state by analyzing the relationship between bank failures, income, unemployment, and real estate prices for U.S. states, including the District of Columbia, using data for the period from 1994 through 2011. We measured bank failures in a state as the fraction of deposits in a state that were in banks that failed during the past year using data from FDIC. Although we included failed banks of all sizes in this analysis, over 90 percent of the bank failures were of small banks, and thus the analysis largely reflects the impact of their failures. We measured income in a state using state personal income, adjusted for inflation, from the Bureau of Economic Analysis. We measured unemployment in a state using the unemployment rate from the Bureau of Labor Statistics. We measured real estate prices using house price indices for single-family detached properties with conventional conforming mortgages from FHFA. We assessed the reliability of data from each of these sources and found it to be sufficiently reliable for our purposes. For each variable, we estimated the relationship between the variable, its past values, and past values of the other three variables. We used a technique that controls for time-invariant characteristics of states, that controls for features of the national economy that affect all states at the same time, and that allows for the possibility that all four variables are jointly determined and affected by each other.[86] We then estimated the likelihood that the past values of each variable help explain current values of the other variables.

We interviewed officials from federal banking regulators, state banking regulators from the 10 states, a national banking and community banking organizations, and state community banking organizations from 7 of the 10 states and market experts. We also conducted a cluster sampling of 10 failed small banks in three states and interviewed officials from 18 acquiring and existing peer banks of these failed banks to obtain their views of the effects of the failures on their communities. [87]The three states we chose to focus on were Georgia, Nevada, and Michigan. The three states reflect the three major areas where the bank failures were concentrated—the southeast, southwest, and Midwest. They reflect states with either highest numbers of bank failures or highest failure rates. They also reflect the economic conditions that contributed to the bank failures—high unemployment rates, and for two states, high declines in house prices.

For each of the states selected, we selected several failed small banks within a targeted metropolitan area and nonmetropolitan area within the state. Reviewing several failed banks within the same state allowed us to more carefully evaluate the impact of other contributing factors associated with the failures, for example, size of the failed institution, purchase agreement terms, number of surrounding banks, characteristics of the acquiring bank, and feedback from nearby existing small banks without the complexities created by differences in economic climates that can occur across states.

In determining which failed banks to review, we obtained and reviewed data on the failed banks in these three states, as well as the acquiring banks (if the failed banks were not liquidated), and the peer banks that currently operate in the same geographic area as the failed banks. We focused on failed banks that were small banks, typically defined as banks with less than $1 billion in assets. For each state, we chose at least three failed banks to target—two that failed within a metropolitan statistical area and one that failed in a nonmetropolitan statistical area. Within each state, to the extent possible we chose failed banks that represented different types of resolutions (whole bank purchase, whole bank purchase with a shared loss agreement, and liquidation) and different types of acquiring banks (other state chartered community banks, out of state regional banks, and national banks). Once we chose the failed banks to target, we then examined the population of existing peer banks within the same county or zip code; that is, other small banks. Our first priority was to choose peer banks that were headquartered in the same county, but if none existed, we looked for small banks from nearby counties or zip codes that had branches in the same community as the target failed bank.

We conducted this performance audit from February 2012 to December 2012 in accordance with generally accepted government auditing standards. Those standards require that we plan and perform the audit to obtain sufficient, appropriate evidence to provide a reasonable basis for our findings and conclusions based on our audit objectives. We believe that the evidence obtained provides a reasonable basis for our findings and conclusions based on our audit objectives.

APPENDIX II. FDIC RESOLUTION METHODS FOR FAILED INSTITUTIONS AND THE LEAST COST TEST PROCESS

The Federal Deposit Insurance Corporation (FDIC) has two primary types of closing transactions, with multiple variations of both, to resolve failing institutions:

- Purchase and Assumption. A resolution transaction in which a healthy institution purchases some or all of the assets of the failed financial institution and assumes some or all of the liabilities, including all insured deposits.
  - Basic Purchase and Assumption. Assets transferring to the acquiring institution (AI) are limited to cash and cash-equivalents.
  - Modified Purchase and Assumption. Cash and a portion of the loan portfolio (loan pools) transfer to the acquiring institution.
  - Whole Bank Purchase and Assumption. The acquiring institution assumes essentially all assets and liabilities.
  - Whole Bank Purchase and Assumption with Shared loss Agreements (SLA). Specific assets assumed by the assuming institution are covered (FDIC reimburses the acquiring institution or shares in loan losses).
  - Bridge Bank Resolution Transaction. A type of purchase and assumption transaction for which FDIC itself acts temporarily as the assuming institution.
- Deposit Payoff Transaction. A resolution strategy that occurs when there is no assuming institution, and FDIC directly pays the insured amounts to the depositor and becomes the subrogated holder of the claim.
  - Straight Deposit Payoff. This is only executed if FDIC does not receive a bid for the purchase and assumption transaction, thus no liabilities are assumed and no assets are purchased by an acquiring institution.
  - Insured Deposit Transfer. The deposits and secured liabilities of a failed institution are transferred to a healthy institution. This means no assets are purchased.
  - Deposit Insurance National Bank (DINB) – Insured deposits are transferred to a newly charted federal financial institution, which is operated for a limited period of time by the FDIC to permit depositors to make an orderly withdrawal of funds.
  - Open Bank Assistance. FDIC determines it is least costly to the DIF to provide assistance rather than close the failing bank.[88]

Least Cost Test Process

FDIC is required to resolve failed institutions using the least costly method to the DIF. FDIC contacts qualified insured depository institutions to bid on deposits and the failing bank's assets. After all bids are received, FDIC selects the least costly option to the DIF, which may include a purchase and assumption transaction with accompanying shared loss agreements. Figure 8 provides an overview of the least cost test process.

The authority to approve any resolution transaction, including any shared loss provisions, rests with the FDIC Board of Directors (BOD). The FDIC Division of Resolutions and Receiverships (DRR) Franchise and Asset Marketing Branch (FAMB) must obtain approval from the BOD before executing a resolution transaction. Because the FAMB must obtain approval before executing a resolution transaction, FAMB, Risk Management Supervision and Legal begin preparing a Failing Bank Board Case (FBC) immediately following notification from the bank's primary regulator that it has been identified as a potential failing institution.

FBC provides a history of the failing institution, an economic overview, comparable market and demographic data, and FDIC's estimated cost to liquidate the institution. This cost assumes a payout of insured deposits and a liquidation of all assets by FDIC. The FBC is prepared prior to the receipt of any bids and therefore, any premium paid by the successful bidder for the assets or deposits is not considered in this analysis and subsequently reduces FDIC's liquidation costs. In addition to information related to the failing institution, the FBC also includes a broad set of delegations allowing FDIC staff to approve and implement a resolution strategy. Once approved by the BOD, the BOD delegates authority to the Director of DRR to approve the transaction that resolves the financial institution at the least cost to the DIF.

The FAMB presents resolution strategies including a whole bank purchase and assumption transaction with and without shared loss agreements for approval from the BOD. The whole bank purchase and assumption transaction is the preferred method of resolution strategy. Under the whole bank purchase and assumption transaction, essentially all assets and liabilities are transferred to a healthy institution. This type of transfer includes transferring performing and nonperforming assets based on competitive bids. If no acceptable bids are received, a new depository institution in the same community as the failing bank may be organized to assume the insured deposits in order to payout those deposits, and to temporarily perform certain functions to wind up the affairs of the bank in an orderly fashion.

The FAMB marketing specialist starts marketing the bank to qualified institutions when the bank is issued a Prompt Corrective Action notice by its primary regulator. The FAMB marketing process involves getting asset and liability information from the failing institution and allowing the potential acquiring institutions to review this information. FAMB generates a bid list of qualified depository institutions that are approved by the primary regulators and is used to solicit bids. FDIC targets banks that are usually double the size of the failing bank and are financially stable. The bidders sign confidentiality agreements in order to review the failing banks' information. FDIC performs a LCT analysis on all bids that are received.

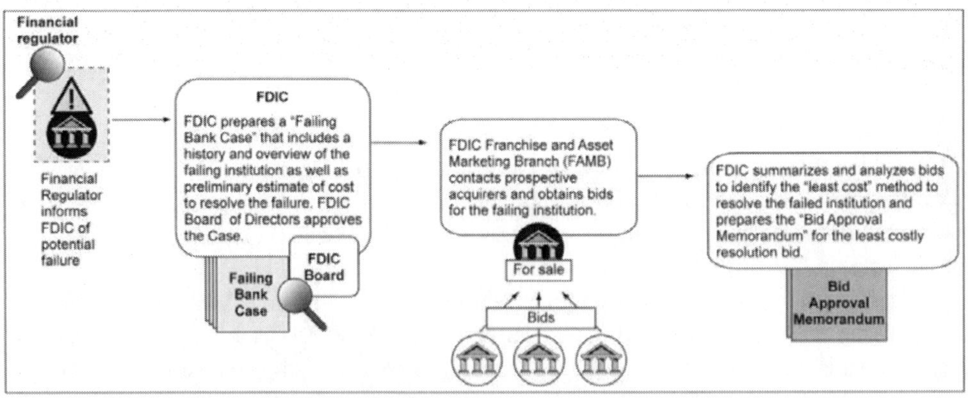

Source: GAO (analysis); Art Explosion (images).

Figure 8. FDIC's Least Cost Test Process.

The bids are submitted to FAMB for evaluation. These bids may contain several elements related to the bidder's valuation of the bank. Once all the bids have been received, FAMB compiles the bids and creates the Bid Summary Report. The Bid Summary Report indicates if a bid is conforming or nonconforming, as well as identifies other key information, including the proposed terms of the bid. A conforming bid follows the standard terms of the transaction and bid instructions, while a nonconforming bid is submitted with contingencies or conditions that deviate from the standard terms of the transaction and bid instructions. Conforming bids are always considered and evaluated when determining the least costly resolution. Nonconforming bids are considered as well, if they can be analyzed.

FAMB completes the LCT Analysis that is contained in the LCT Excel Workbooks including the bank's balance sheet, asset loss and recovery information, uninsured deposit estimate, bids and the Shared loss Worksheet (LSW), if applicable. The LSW is used to estimate the cost of a shared loss transaction. This cost may include an estimate of the initial cash outlay by FDIC or the acquirer, shared loss payments, payments to creditors left behind in the receivership, monitoring costs for those shared loss covered assets, FDIC receivership costs, and future estimated recoveries on assets retained by the receivership. Losses and recoveries are estimated by the financial advisors hired by the FDIC to perform the asset valuations.

After completing the LCT Analysis, the Bid Approval Memorandum addressed to the Director of DRR is prepared. The Bid Approval includes a description of all bids received, and a summary of the estimated cost to liquidate the institution, as well as the least costly transaction. The Director of DRR has the delegation of authority from the FDIC BOD to approve the least costly bid. The Director of DRR signs the memorandum to indicate approval of the winning bid.

APPENDIX III. GAO ANALYSIS OF BANK CHARACTERISTICS AND THE LIKELIHOOD OF FAILURE

We conducted an econometric analysis to estimate the relationship between bank characteristics and the likelihood of bank failure, using data on FDIC-insured commercial banks and state-chartered savings banks (banks) for the period from 2006 through 2011 along with data on banks that failed during the period from 2008 through 2011 and their acquiring banks. We used a discrete-time hazard model to estimate the likelihood that a bank fails in a quarter as a function of its balance sheet characteristics in the previous quarter, including capital adequacy; asset quality; earnings; liquidity; brokered deposits use; ADC lending; nonfarm, nonresidential real estate lending; multifamily real estate lending; commercial real estate, construction, and land development lending not secured by real estate; and size.

- Capital adequacy. Capital adequacy measures the net worth or solvency of the bank. Bank capital performs several important functions, such as absorbing losses, promoting public confidence, restricting excessive asset growth, and providing protection to depositors and the FDIC insurance fund. We calculated capital adequacy as bank equity capital as a percent of total assets.

- Asset quality. Asset quality measures the quality of the bank's assets, which may include losses not yet reflected in capital. The primary factor affecting overall asset quality is the quality of the loan portfolio and the credit administration program. We calculated asset quality as performing assets as a percent of total assets, where performing assets are total assets less assets 90 days or more past due but still accruing interest, assets in nonaccrual status, and other real estate owned.
- Earnings. Earnings measure profitability. Earnings absorb losses and augment capital, provide the initial safeguard against the risks of engaging in the banking business, and represent the first line of defense against capital depletion resulting from reduced asset values. We calculated earnings as bank net income as a percent of total assets.
- Liquidity. Liquidity represents the ability to fund assets and meet obligations as they become due, and it is essential in all banks to compensate for expected and unexpected balance sheet fluctuations and to provide funds for growth. One component of liquidity is the extent to which a bank relies on stable funding sources. We calculated liquidity as stable liabilities as a percent of total liabilities, where stable liabilities are total liabilities less federal funds purchased and securities sold under agreements to repurchase, demand notes issued to the U.S. Treasury and other borrowed money, time deposits over the limit for insured deposits held in domestic offices, deposits held in foreign offices, and trading liabilities net of revaluation losses on derivatives.
- Brokered deposits. Brokered deposits measure reliance on high-cost and potentially volatile funding sources. We calculated brokered deposits—deposits accepted through a deposit broker—as a percent of total liabilities.
- ADC loans. ADC loans measure concentration in one type of risky lending. We calculated ADC loans as a percent of total assets.
- Nonfarm, nonresidential real estate loans. Non-farm, non-residential real estate loans measure concentration in one type of risky lending. We calculated non-farm, non-residential real estate loans as a percent of total assets.
- Multifamily real estate loans. Multifamily real estate loans measure concentration in one type of risky lending. We calculated multifamily real estate loans as a percent of total assets.
- Commercial real estate, construction, and land development loans not secured by real estate. Commercial real estate, construction, and land development loans not secured by real estate measure concentration in one type of risky lending. We calculated these loans as a percent of total assets.
- Size. Size accounts for other factors that are correlated with the likelihood of failure, such as product mix or business model, that may vary by bank size. We calculated size as the natural logarithm of total assets.

We included indicators for each quarter to control for factors affecting the likelihood of failure that are common to all banks at the same time, such as the regulatory environment, the state of the market for bank products and services, and the condition of the overall economy. We adjusted the standard errors of our estimates to reflect the lack of independence between observations on the same bank in different quarters. Specifically, we clustered our standard errors by bank to allow for arbitrary correlation between observations on the same bank in different quarters and we multiplied our standard errors by the square root of the average number of observations per bank to reflect the fact that the series of observations on a single bank constitutes a single observation in our model. We used a similar model to estimate the likelihood that a bank fails in a quarter based on the characteristics of its balance sheet two quarters in the past, three quarters in the past, and so on up to eight quarters in the past.

To allow for the possibility that different factors were associated with the failure of banks of different sizes, we repeated the analysis separately for small and medium-sized banks. Small banks are banks with average assets of less than $1 billion and medium-sized banks are banks with average assets of at least $1 billion and less than $10 billion. The number of failures of large banks—banks with average assets of $10 billion or more—was too small to permit us to separately analyze this group of banks.

Table 5. Bank Characteristics Associated with the Likelihood of Failure, 2008-2011

Bank size	Lagged factors that increase the likelihood of failure in the current quarter	Lagged factors that decrease the likelihood of failure in the current quarter	Number of lags (quarters)
All banks			
	Brokered deposits[c], ADC loans[a]	Asset quality[b]	8
	Brokered deposits[c], ADC loans[a]	Asset quality[b]	7
	Brokered deposits[c], ADC loans[a]	Asset quality[a], capital adequacy[b]	6
	ADC loans[a]	Asset quality[a], capital adequacy[b]	5
	ADC loans[b]	Asset quality[a], capital adequacy[a]	4
	ADC loans[c]	Asset quality[a], capital adequacy[a]	3
		Asset quality[b], capital adequacy[a]	2
		Asset quality[c], capital adequacy[a]	1
Small banks (average assets less than $1 billion)			
	ADC loans[a]	Asset quality[b]	8
	ADC loans[a]	Asset quality[b]	7
	ADC loans[a]	Asset quality[a], capital adequacy[c]	6
	ADC loans[a]	Asset quality[a], capital adequacy[a]	5
	ADC loans[b]	Asset quality[a], capital adequacy[a]	4
		Asset quality[a], capital adequacy[a]	3
		Asset quality[b], capital adequacy[a]	2
		Capital adequacy[a]	1
Medium-sized banks (average assets $1-10 billion)			
	ADC loans[b]		8
	ADC loans[c]		7
			6
			5
			4
		Capital adequacy[b]	3
		Capital adequacy[b]	2
		Capital adequacy[b]	1

Source: GAO analysis of data from FDIC and the Federal Financial Institutions Examinations Council.

[a] Significant at the 1 percent level.

[b] Significant at the 5 percent level.

[c] Significant at the 10 percent level.

We found that ADC lending and brokered deposits were associated with an increased likelihood of failure, while asset quality and capital adequacy were associated with a reduced likelihood of failure, all else being equal (see table 5). A bank was more likely to fail in a quarter if it had high concentrations of ADC loans on its balance sheet in the past, specifically, three, four, five, six, seven, or eight quarters in the past. A bank was also more likely to fail in a quarter if it relied heavily on brokered deposits six, seven, or eight quarters in the past. On the other hand, a bank was less likely to fail in a quarter if it had more adequate capital in the previous six quarters and if it had better asset quality in the previous eight quarters.

Our analyses of small and medium-sized banks generated results that were broadly consistent with our analysis of all banks. A small bank was more likely to fail in a quarter if it had high concentrations of ADC loans on its balance sheet four, five, six, seven, or eight quarters in the past, while a medium-sized bank was more likely to fail in a quarter if it had high concentrations of ADC loans seven or eight quarters in the past. However, a small bank was less likely to fail in a quarter if it had better capital adequacy in the previous six quarters and a medium-sized bank was less likely to fail in a quarter if it had better capital adequacy in the previous three quarters. Finally, a small bank was less likely to fail in a quarter if its asset quality was better in the period from two quarters in the past to eight quarters in the past.

Our results likely reflect both factors that are generally correlated with the likelihood of failure and factors that are specific to the particular time period we analyzed. Thus, the extent to which our results can be generalized to other time periods is limited. Furthermore, our results reflect average relationships between bank characteristics and the likelihood of failure for all of the observations we used. As such, they may not reflect the particular circumstances of any one bank. Finally, we note that the list of characteristics we analyzed is meant to highlight important characteristics of banks that are related to the likelihood of failure, but many other factors play a role in whether or not a bank fails and our list of characteristics is not exhaustive.

APPENDIX IV. ANALYSIS OF THE IMPACT OF FAIR VALUE ACCOUNTING ON RECENT COMMERCIAL BANK FAILURES

We analyzed bank call reports from 2007 through 2011 for failed and open commercial banks to identify and compare trends in (1) the use of historical cost accounting and fair value accounting and (2) the extent to which losses were credit-related for small, medium-size, and large institutions. We define small failed banks as those that had $1 billion or less in assets at the time of failure, medium-size failed banks as those that had between $1 billion and $10 billion at the time of failure, and large failed banks as those that had over $10 billion in assets at the time of failure. Overall our analysis showed that fair value-related losses contributed very little to the decline in net interest income and regulatory capital experienced by failed commercial banks of all sizes (small, medium-size, and large) once the financial crisis began in 2007. Similarly, fair value losses at open commercial banks of all sizes were also limited. Instead, this analysis showed that the commercial bank failures were driven by rising levels of credit losses related to nonperforming loans held by the banks. Further, these losses had a greater negative impact on institutions' net interest income and regulatory capital levels than those recorded at fair value. We analyzed failed thrifts separately. (See app. V.)

Fair Value, Historical Cost, and Impairment Accounting

U.S. generally accepted accounting principles (GAAP) establish the basis on which items reported on a bank's balance sheet should be measured. Currently, assets and liabilities are reflected in the balance sheet at fair value, historical cost, or another basis, such as lower-of-cost or fair value.

- Fair Value: Fair value is the price that would be received to sell a asset or paid to transfer a liability in an orderly transaction between market participants at the measurement date. Fair value accounting standards under GAAP establish a standardized framework for measuring the fair value of an asset or liability.[89] According to the Securities and Exchange Commission, fair value is most prevalently used to measure "financial" assets and liabilities, such as investment securities and derivative instruments. Fair value measurements that are required on a quarterly basis (or each reporting period) are often referred to as "recurring." Fair value measurements that are not required on a regular basis are often referred to as "nonrecurring." For some assets and liabilities that are measured at fair value on a recurring basis, such as securities designated for trading, unrealized gains or losses flow through the bank's earnings in the income statement and affect regulatory capital. For other assets and liabilities that are measured at fair value on a recurring basis, such as securities designated as available for sale, unrealized fair value gains and losses generally do not impact earnings, and thus, generally are not included in regulatory capital calculations. Instead, these gains or losses are recorded through other comprehensive income (OCI), unless the institution determines that a decline in fair value below amortized cost constitutes an other than temporary impairment (OTTI) in which case the instrument is written down to its fair value, with credit losses reflected in earnings.[90] The OTTI decision for a given asset is a judgmental decision of the bank, considering various factors related to the severity and duration of the decrease in the value of the asset. Unrealized changes in fair value and OTTI-related write-downs that are recognized in earnings in the income statement directly impact regulatory capital levels.
- Historical Cost: Measurement using historical cost can be done in several ways, but the general concept is to record items on the balance sheet using the original amount paid or received, with adjustments when appropriate in subsequent periods for depreciation, amortization, principal pay downs, or impairment. Generally, loans that a bank holds for investment (HFI), for example, are recorded at amortized cost, net of an impairment allowance for estimated credit losses.[91] Such loans typically comprise the bulk of assets held by FDIC-insured banks.
- Loan Impairment Accounting: GAAP requires financial institutions to maintain an allowance for loan losses (loan loss allowance) at a level that is appropriate to cover estimated credit losses incurred as of the balance sheet date for their entire portfolio of HFI loans. Under GAAP, institutions must recognize impairment on HFI loans

when credit losses are determined to be probable and reasonably estimable, that is, when, based on current information and events, it is probable that an institution will be unable to collect all amounts due (i.e., both principal and interest) according to the contractual terms of the original loan agreement. An increase in the loan loss allowance results in a charge to expenses, termed a provision for loan losses. Impairment accounting standards under GAAP set forth the measurement methods for estimating the credit losses attributable to individually impaired loans. Regulators generally require institutions to establish policies and procedures for determining the loan loss allowance based on GAAP requirements.[92]

Most Assets and Liabilities at Failed and Open Commercial Banks Were Not Measured at Fair Value between 2007 and 2011

Assets Measured at Amortized Cost

During the period of our study, loans HFI represented on average over two-thirds of most commercial banks' total assets (table 1). HFI loans are not measured at fair value, but instead are measured on an amortized- cost basis, net of an impairment allowance for estimated credit losses.

Table 6 indicates that small and medium-size commercial banks generally had slightly higher percentages of loans classified as HFI loans than large commercial banks. Also, compared to open commercial banks, failed commercial banks held a higher percentage of HFI loans.

Assets and Liabilities Measured at Fair Value through Earnings on a Recurring Basis

Assets measured at fair value through earnings on a recurring basis comprised mainly trading assets, nontrading derivative assets, and nonfinancial assets such as servicing rights for mortgages for which the fair value option has been elected.[93]

Trading Assets

Trading assets generally include both debt and marketable equity securities bought and held primarily to be sold in the near term. Trading activities typically involve active and frequent buying and selling to generate profits on short-term movements in market prices. Trading assets also include derivative contracts held for trading purposes in gain positions. Table 7 shows that trading assets did not represent a significant percentage of failed commercial banks' assets from 2007 through 2011.

Table 7 also indicates that failed commercial banks held fewer trading assets than open commercial banks. Large open commercial banks in particular tended to have larger percentages of trading assets than failed commercial banks of similar size.

Table 6. HFI Loans as a Percentage of Total Assets for Failed and Open Commercial Banks, 2007-2011

Asset size	Description	2007	2008	2009	2010	2011
Failed banks						
< $1 billion	HFI loans	78.30%	77.48%	74.25%	70.73%	68.38%
>$1 billion, <$10 billion	HFI loans	72.46%	73.01%	69.90%	69.20%	77.39%
>$10 billion	HFI loans	60.80%	56.25%	58.85%	77.20%	—[a]
Open banks						
< $1 billion	HFI loans	—[b]	69.47%	67.68%	65.11%	62.47%
>$1 billion, <$10 billion	HFI loans	—[b]	68.62%	66.89%	63.64%	61.95%
>$10 billion	HFI loans	—[b]	52.72%	50.99%	51.30%	49.63%

Source: GAO analysis of FDIC call report data.

[a] No large commercial banks failed in 2011.

[b] Pub. L. No.112-88 requires us to analyze bank failures that occurred since 2008. As such, we analyzed trends for both failed banks and open banks from 2008 through 2011. For failed banks, we also obtained 2007 data to determine any additional trends prior to the failures.

Table 7. Trading Assets as a Percentage of Total Assets for Failed and Open Commercial Banks, 2007-2011

Asset size	Description	2007	2008	2009	2010	2011
Failed banks						
< $1 billion	Trading assets	0.05%	0.03%	0.00%	0.02	0.00%
>$1 billion, <$10 billion	Trading assets	0.17%	0.14%	0.03%	0.01%	0.00%
>$10 billion	Trading assets	0.04%	0.04%	0.05%	0.11	—[a]
Open banks						
< $1 billion	Trading assets	—[b]	0.06%	0.04%	0.02%	0.02%
>$1 billion, <$10 billion	Trading assets	—[b]	0.27%	0.16%	0.28%	0.19%
>$10 billion	Trading assets	—[b]	9.76%	7.82%	7.22%	7.03%

Source: GAO analysis of FDIC call report data.

[a] No large commercial banks failed in 2011.

[b] Pub. L. No.112-88 requires us to analyze bank failures that occurred since 2008. As such, we analyzed trends for both failed banks and open banks from 2008 through 2011. For failed banks, we also obtained 2007 data to determine any additional trends prior to the failures.

Nontrading Assets

Nontrading assets measured at fair value on a recurring basis include, among other things, nontrading derivative contracts in gain positions. Most commercial banks did not have any significant holdings of such nontrading assets (table 8). Even for open commercial banks that have relatively more of such nontrading assets than failed institutions, the level of these assets is less than 0.15 percent of their total assets.

Nonfinancial Assets

Nonfinancial assets measured at fair value through earnings on a recurring basis consist of mortgage servicing rights (MSR) for which a fair value option has been elected. Failed commercial banks did not have significant amounts of such nonfinancial assets (table 9). Failed commercial banks also had fewer such nonfinancial assets than open commercial banks, particularly large open commercial banks.

Liabilities

Liabilities measured at fair value through earnings on a recurring basis include trading liabilities such as securities an institution sold but did not own and therefore is obligated to purchase at a future date (short positions), derivative contracts held for trading purposes in loss positions, nontrading derivative contracts in loss positions, and those liabilities for which a bank elects to measure at fair value on a recurring basis under the fair value option. Failed commercial banks did not have a significant amount of such liabilities (table 10). Failed commercial banks also had fewer such liabilities than open commercial banks, particularly large open banks.

Table 8. Nontrading Assets Measured at Fair Value through Earnings on a Recurring Basis as a Percentage of Total Assets for Failed and Open Commercial Banks, 2007-2011

Asset size	Description	2007	2008	2009	2010	2011
Failed banks						
< $1 billion	Nontrading assets	0.00%	0.00%	0.00%	0.00%	0.00%
>$1 billion, <$10 billion	Nontrading assets	0.00%	0.00%	0.00%	0.00%	0.00%
>$10 billion	Nontrading assets	0.00%	0.00%	0.00%	0.00%	—[a]
Open banks						
< $1 billion	Nontrading assets	—[b]	0.03%	0.01%	0.00%	0.00%
>$1 billion, <$10 billion	Nontrading assets	—[b]	0.03%	0.04%	0.05%	0.06%
>$10 billion	Nontrading assets	—[b]	0.13%	0.02%	0.02%	0.01%

Source: GAO analysis of FDIC call report data.

[a] No large commercial banks failed in 2011.

[b] Pub. L. No. 112-88 requires us to analyze bank failures that occurred since 2008. As such, we analyzed trends for both failed banks and open banks from 2008 through 2011. For failed banks, we also obtained 2007 data to determine any additional trends prior to the failures.

Table 9. Nonfinancial Assets Measured at Fair Value through Earnings on a Recurring Basis as a Percentage of Total Assets for Failed and Open Commercial Banks, 2007-2011

Asset size	Description	2007	2008	2009	2010	2011
Failed banks						
< $1 billion	Nonfinancial assets	0.00%	0.00%	0.00%	0.00%	0.00%
>$1 billion, <$10 billion	Nonfinancial assets	0.00%	0.00%	0.00%	0.00%	0.00%
>$10 billion	Nonfinancial assets	0.00%	0.00%	0.00%	0.00%	__[a]
Open banks						
< $1 billion	Nonfinancial assets	__[b]	0.05%	0.09%	0.08%	0.07%
>$1 billion, <$10 billion	Nonfinancial assets	__[b]	0.24%	0.34%	0.27%	0.23%
>$10 billion	Nonfinancial assets	__[b]	1.08%	1.31%	1.19%	1.08%

Source: GAO analysis of FDIC call report data.

[a] No large commercial banks failed in 2011.

[b] Pub. L. No. 112-88 requires us to analyze bank failures that occurred since 2008. As such, we analyzed trends for both failed banks and open banks from 2008 through 2011. For failed banks, we also obtained 2007 data to determine any additional trends prior to the failures.

Table 10. Trading Liabilities Measured at Fair Value through Earnings on a Recurring Basis as a Percentage of Total Assets for Failed and Open Commercial Banks, 2007-2011

Asset size	Description	2007	2008	2009	2010	2011
Failed banks						
< $1 billion	Liabilities	0.00%	0.00%	0.00%	0.00%	0.00%
>$1 billion, <$10 billion	Liabilities	0.01%	0.00%	0.00%	0.00%	0.00%
>$10 billion	Liabilities	0.01%	0.02%	0.03%	0.06%	—[a]
Open banks						
< $1 billion	Liabilities	—[b]	0.00%	0.00%	0.00%	0.00%
>$1 billion, <$10 billion	Liabilities	—[b]	0.06%	0.05%	0.04%	0.06%
>$10 Billion	Liabilities	—[b]	4.61%	3.43%	3.33%	3.37%

Source: GAO analysis of FDIC call report data.

[a] No large commercial banks failed in 2011.

[b] Pub. L. No. 112-88 requires us to analyze bank failures that occurred since 2008. As such, we analyzed trends for both failed banks and open banks from 2008 through 2011. For failed banks, we also obtained 2007 data to determine any additional trends prior to the failures.

Assets Measured at Fair Value on a Nonrecurring Basis through Income

Securities Held to Maturity

Investments in debt securities classified as held-to-maturity (HTM) are measured at amortized cost, but if any decline in fair value below amortized cost is other than temporary, credit losses are recognized in earnings. The HTM category includes only debt securities that management has both the positive intent and ability to hold until maturity. As illustrated in table 11, investment securities accounted for as HTM represented less than 2 percent of assets held for failed banks with less than $10 billion in assets. For failed banks with more than $10 billion in assets, HTM ranged between 3 percent and 14 percent, particularly because of one large bank with a high percentage of HTM securities. On average, open banks held about 3 percent of HTM securities.

Securities Available for Sale

Investments in debt securities that are not classified as trading securities or as HTM securities are classified as available-for-sale (AFS) securities. AFS securities also include equity securities that have readily determinable fair values and are not classified as trading securities. If the fair value of an AFS security declines below its amortized cost, and the decline is other than temporary, credit losses are recognized in earnings.

As illustrated in table 12, AFS securities represented the largest percentage of assets held after HFI loans. For failed banks, AFS assets ranged between 9 percent and 18 percent of total assets compared to 12 percent and 20 percent for open banks. On average, open banks with less than $10 billion in total assets held the highest percentages of AFS securities.

As a result of an April 2009 change to the relevant GAAP standard, an OTTI loss of either an AFS or HTM debt security, in certain circumstances, is separated into (1) the credit loss amount, which is recognized in earnings and (2) the loss amount related to all other factors (noncredit loss), which is recognized in OCI, net of applicable taxes. We discuss the impact of this change later on in this appendix.

Table 11. HTM Securities as a Percentage of Total Assets for Failed and Open Commercial Banks, 2007-2011

Asset size	Description	2007	2008	2009	2010	2011
Failed banks						
< $1 billion	HTM securities	1.17%	1.14%	0.63%	0.32%	0.43%
>$1 billion, <$10 billion	HTM securities	0.82%	1.38%	1.09%	0.14%	0.00%
>$10 billion[a]	HTM securities	13.60%	5.04%	2.80%	4.88%	—[b]
Open banks						
< $1 billion	HTM securities	—[c]	2.51%	2.37%	2.22%	2.17%
>$1 billion, <$10 billion	HTM securities	—[c]	2.63%	2.56%	2.97%	3.10%
>$1 0 billion	HTM securities	—[c]	0.69%	1.12%	0.84%	1.02%

Source: GAO analysis of FDIC call report data.

[a] One large bank with a high percentage of HTM securities accounted for most of the HTM securities. Excluding this bank, the percentages ranged from x to x.

[b] No large commercial banks failed in 2011.

[c] Pub. L. No.112-88 requires us to analyze bank failures that occurred since 2008. As such, we analyzed trends for both failed banks and open banks from 2008 through 2011. For failed banks, we also obtained 2007 data to determine any additional trends prior to the failures.

Table 12. AFS Securities as a Percentage of Total Assets for Failed and Open Commercial Banks, 2007-2011

Asset size	Description	2007	2008	2009	2010	2011
Failed banks						
< $1 billion	AFS securities	10.51%	10.15%	9.61%	9.47%	9.50%
>$1 billion, <$10 billion	AFS securities	15.56%	11.97%	10.92%	13.22%	10.01%
>$1 billion	AFS securities	9.94%	16.47%	18.31%	12.52%	—[a]
Open banks						
< $1 billion	AFS securities	—[b]	16.16%	16.47%	17.68%	19.79%
>$1 billion, <$10 billion	AFS securities	—[b]	15.59%	16.19%	17.06%	18.83%
>$10 billion	AFS securities	—[b]	12.68%	15.91%	17.94%	18.28%

Source: GAO analysis of FDIC call report data.

[a] No large commercial banks failed in 2011.

[b] Pub. L. No. 112-88 requires us to analyze bank failures that occurred since 2008. As such, we analyzed trends for both failed banks and open banks from 2008 through 2011. For failed banks, we also obtained 2007 data to determine any additional trends prior to the failures.

Assets Measured at the Lower of Cost or Fair Value

Loans Held for Sale

Under GAAP, loans originated with the intent to sell in the secondary market to government-sponsored entities and other investors (including other FDIC-insured institutions) are carried at the lower of cost or fair value, unless the institution has elected to account for the loans at fair value under the fair value option. Institutions can transfer loans into or out of the HFS classification as a result of changes in intentions regarding whether the loans will be sold or held for investment. Transfers between the HFS and HFI categories, however, are recorded at the lower of cost or fair value.[94]

As indicated in table 13, HFS loans did not represent a significant percent of assets held by commercial banks. On average, failed banks with less than $10 billion in assets held less than 2 percent of HFS loans with small banks accounting for less than one-half of 1 percent of such assets. Large failed banks have a higher percent of HFS loans than open large banks. In 2007 and 2008, a few large banks started transferring HFS loans into their HFI portfolios as a result of the 2007 contraction in the secondary mortgage market. Appendix VI provides further analysis of these transfers.

Table 13. HFS Loans as a Percentage of Total Assets for Failed and Open Commercial Banks, 2007-2011

Asset size	Description	2007	2008	2009	2010	2011
Failed banks						
< $1 billion	HFS loans	0.42%	0.22%	0.26%	0.29%	0.26%
>$1 billion, <$10 billion	HFS loans	1.17%	1.36%	1.35%	0.73%	0.05%
>$10 billion	HFS loans	3.08%	4.19%	3.01%	0.65%	—[a]
Open banks						
< $10 billion	HFS loans	—[b]	0.32%	0.47%	0.54%	0.53%
>$1billion, <$10 billion	HFS loans	—[b]	1.34%	0.83%	0.93%	0.96%
>$10 Billion	HFS loans	—[b]	1.52%	1.58%	1.45%	1.21%

Source: GAO analysis of FDIC call report data.

[a] No large commercial banks failed in 2011.

[b] Pub. L. No. 112-88 requires us to analyze bank failures that occurred since 2008. As such, we analyzed trends for both failed banks and open banks from 2008 through 2011. For failed banks, we also obtained 2007 data to determine any additional trends prior to the failures.

Table 14. OREO Assets as a Percentage of Total Assets for Failed and Open Commercial Banks, 2007-2011

Asset size	Description	2007	2008	2009	2010	2011
Failed banks						
< $1 billion	OREO	0.36%	1.35%	2.88%	5.13%	7.78%
>$1 billion, <$10 billion	OREO	0.26%	0.83%	2.10%	2.61%	2.30%
>$10 billion	OREO	0.04%	0.39%	0.63%	0.78%	—[a]
Open banks						
< $1 billion	OREO	—[b]	0.37%	0.71%	0.98%	1.05%
>$1 billion, <$10 billion	OREO	—[b]	0.26%	0.55%	0.78%	0.80%
>$10 billion	OREO	—[b]	0.10%	0.15%	0.24%	0.22%

Source: GAO analysis of FDIC call report data.

[a] No large commercial banks failed in 2011.

[b] Pub. L. No. 112-88 requires us to analyze bank failures that occurred since 2008. As such, we analyzed trends for both failed banks and open banks from 2008 through 2011. For failed banks, we also obtained 2007 data to determine any additional trends prior to the failures.

Other Real Estate Owned

Other Real Estate Owned (OREO) usually includes assets repossessed through a foreclosure process for defaulted loans. Generally, assets acquired through, or in lieu of, loan foreclosure are held for sale and are initially recorded at the estimated fair value of the collateral less costs to sell at the date of foreclosure, establishing a new cost basis. Subsequent to foreclosure, periodic valuations are performed and the assets are carried at the lower of their cost basis or estimated fair value less cost to sell.[95]

Table 14 shows that early in 2007 and 2008, commercial banks had little exposure to foreclosed assets. However, as the crisis deepened and the real estate downturn became more severe, delinquencies increased rapidly and banks foreclosed more properties, particularly smaller institutions. Compared to open banks, failed banks had a larger share of OREO assets.

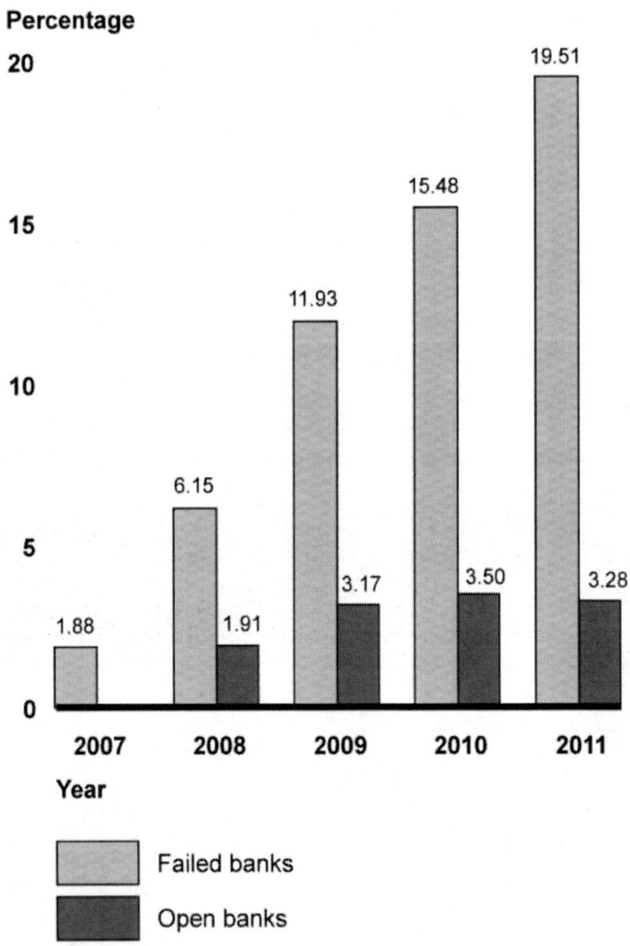

Source: GAO analysis of FDIC call report data.

Figure 9. Nonperforming Loans as a Percentage of Total Loans for Small Failed and Open Commercial Banks, 2007-2011.

Declines in Regulatory Capital at Failed Commercial Banks due to Rising Levels of Nonperforming Loans and Resulting Increased Credit Losses

Small Commercial Banks

The reduction in capital for small failed commercial banks was driven by increases in their provisions for loan losses. As the financial crisis that began in 2007 progressed, the levels of nonperforming loans rose from an average of less than 2 percent of total loans in 2007 to over 6 percent in 2008, and to nearly 20 percent in 2011 (see figure 9).

The rising levels of nonperforming loans appear to be the key factor driving the increases in provisions for loan losses and the resulting reduction in net interest income and regulatory capital. For small failed banks, credit losses were by far the largest contributor to these institutions' losses relative to any other asset class. For example, from 2008 through 2011, credit losses accounted for on average over 140 percent of net interest income while net losses from the sale of OREO averaged about 15 percent of net interest income (see figure 10). During that same period, net losses from the sale of AFS and HTM securities averaged less than 4 percent. Net losses from recurring fair value measurements were less than one-tenth of 1 percent.

The level of nonperforming loans experienced by small failed banks far exceeds the levels of nonperforming loans experienced by open banks of similar size (see figures 10 and 11). Also, the magnitude of the credit losses experienced by open banks is significantly less than what the failed banks have experienced.

Medium-Size Commercial Banks

The high levels of nonperforming loans experienced in 2009 and 2010 drove the extent of credit losses during those years for medium-size failed banks. The levels of nonperforming loans for these banks went from less than 2 percent in 2007 to over 6 percent in 2008 and to over 14 percent in 2010 (see figure 12). During that same time frame, nonperforming loan levels for open banks of similar size were about one-third.

The large credit losses generally drove the failed commercial banks' decrease in earnings and regulatory capital. For example, from 2007 to 2011, credit losses averaged over 181 percent of net interest income while net losses from the sale of OREO averaged close to10 percent of net interest income (see figure 13). During that same period, net losses from the sale of AFS and HTM securities, as well as losses from trading (recurring fair value) averaged about 9 percent and 0.09 percent of net interest income, respectively. Sales of HFS loans, on the other hand, had a positive impact on net interest income.

In contrast, medium-size open banks experienced far fewer credit losses during the 2008-2011 time period (see figure 14).

Large Failed Commercial Banks

Nonperforming loans for the three large commercial banks that failed between 2008 and 2011—United Commercial Bank (UCB), Colonial Bank (Colonial), and Westernbank Puerto Rico (Westernbank) also far exceeded the levels of nonperforming loans experienced generally for open banks of similar size (figure15).

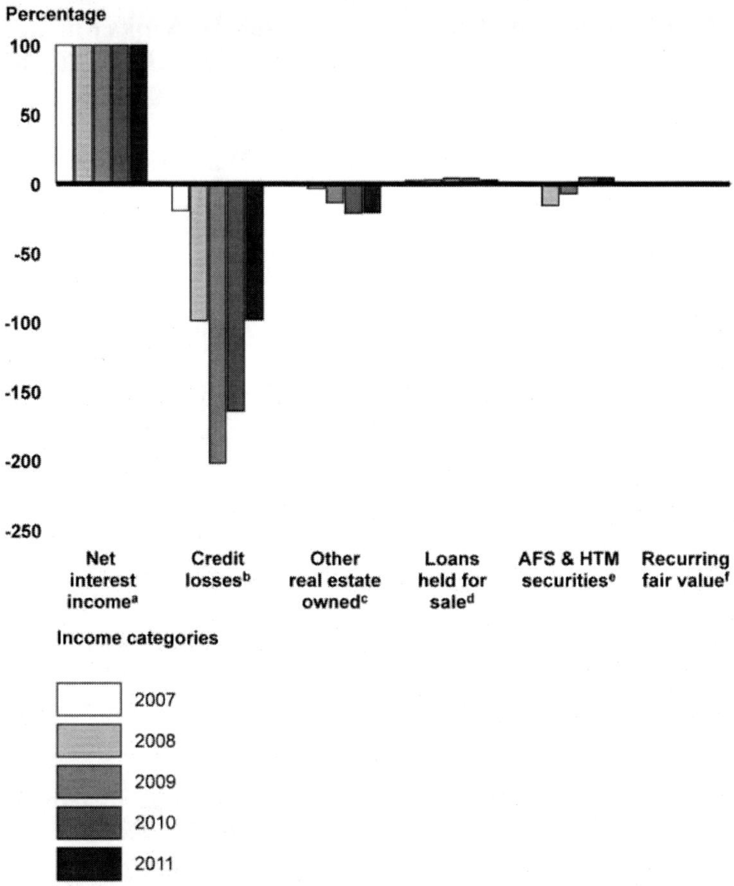

Source: GAO analysis of FDIC call report data.

[a] Net interest income is reported in the call report, schedule report of income. We show net interest income as 100 percent and for each income category calculate its percentage of net interest income.

[b] Credit losses are based on provisions for loan and lease losses as reported in the call report, schedule report of income.

[c] The impact on income of other real estate owned is based on net gains (losses) on sales of OREO as reported in the call report, schedule report of income , which includes gains and losses recognized upon sale of foreclosed property and fair value losses recognized prior to sale.

[d] The impact on income of HFS loans is based on net gains (losses) on sales of loans and leases as reported in the call report, schedule report of income, which includes gains and losses recognized upon sale and fair value losses recognized prior to sale.

[e] The impact on income of AFS and HTM securities is based on realized gains (losses) on AFS and HTM securities as reported in the call report, schedule report of income, which includes impairment losses recognized.

[f] The impact on income of recurring fair value measurements is based on trading revenues and net gains (losses) on assets and liabilities accounted for under the fair value option as reported in the call report, schedule report of income.

Figure 10. Income Categories as a Percentage of Net Interest Income for Small Failed Commercial Banks, 2007-2011.

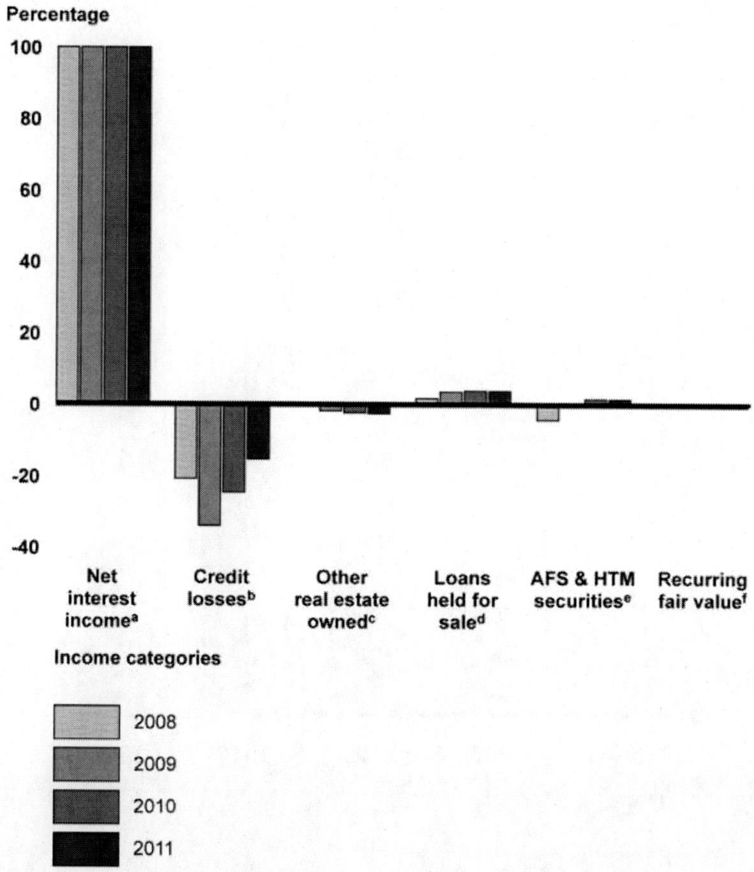

Source: GAO analysis of FDIC call report data.

[a] Net interest income is reported in the call report, schedule report of income. We show net interest income as 100 percent and for each income category calculate its percentage of net interest income.

[b] Credit losses are based on provisions for loan and lease losses as reported in the call report, schedule report of income.

[c] The impact on income of other real estate owned is based on net gains (losses) on sales of OREO as reported in the call report, schedule report of income, which includes gains and losses recognized upon sale of foreclosed property and fair value losses recognized prior to sale.

[d] The impact on income of HFS loans is based on net gains (losses) on sales of loans and leases as reported in the call report, schedule report of income, which includes gains and losses recognized upon sale and fair value losses recognized prior to sale.

[e] The impact on income of AFS and HTM securities is based on realized gains (losses) on AFS and HTM securities as reported in the call report, schedule report of income, which includes impairment losses recognized.

[f] The impact on income of recurring fair value measurements is based on trading revenues and net gains (losses) on assets and liabilities accounted for under the fair value option as reported in the call report, schedule report of income.

Figure 11. Income Categories as Percentage of Net Interest Income for Small Open Commercial Banks, 2008-2011.

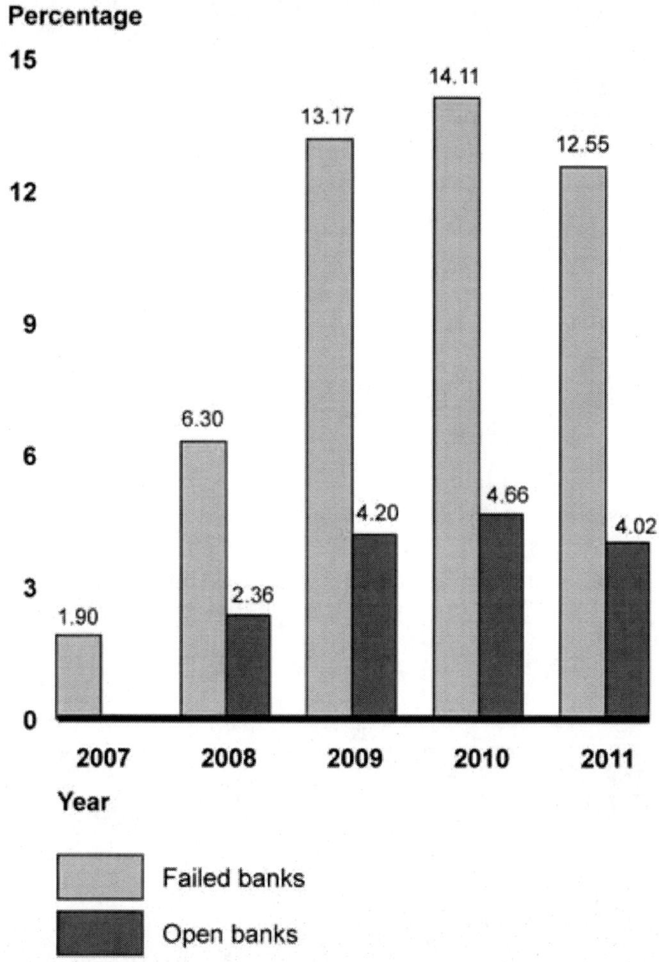

Source: GAO analysis of FDIC call report data.

Figure 12. Nonperforming Loans as a Percentage of Total Loans for Medium-Size Commercial Banks, 2007-2011.

UCB

In 2007, UCB had less than 1 percent of nonperforming loans. However, in 2008, the levels of nonperforming loans rose rapidly to almost 4 percent, and nearly tripled in 2009 (see figure 15). In its 2008 Form 10-K, UCB disclosed that it recorded a net loss of $68 million in 2008 compared with a net income of $102 million in 2007. The decline was primarily the result of an increase in the provision for loan losses of about $263 million for 2008, compared to $20 million for 2007. The increased provision for loan losses was the result of increases in classified residential construction loans and specific allowances on individually impaired residential construction loans located in distressed areas of California and Nevada.

UCB's credit losses were by far the largest contributor to the bank's overall losses relative to any other asset class (figure16). For example, from 2007 through 2009, credit losses accounted for on average over 123 percent of net interest income.

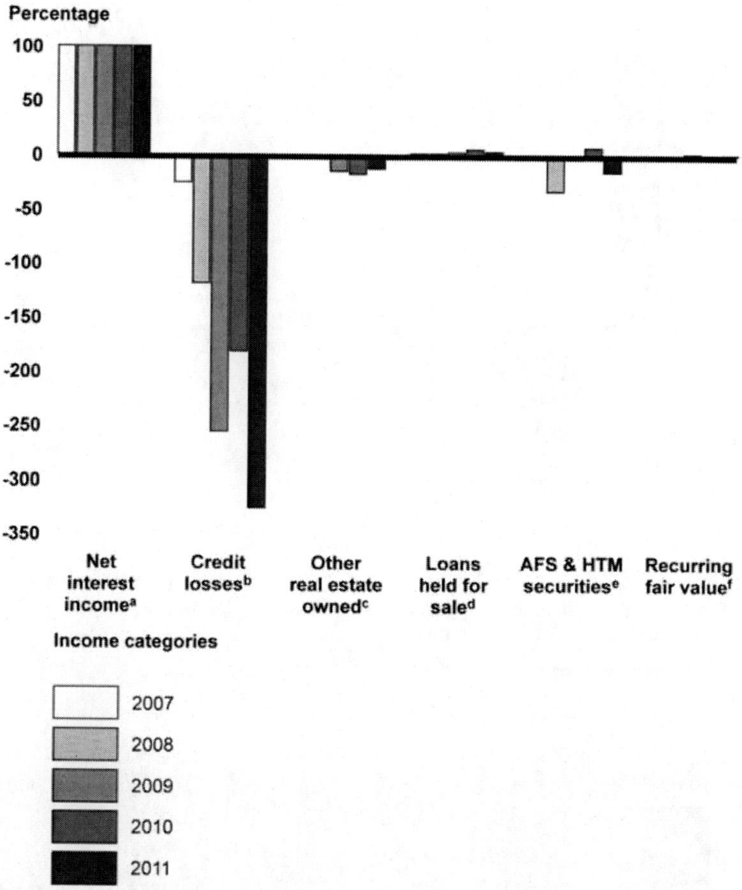

Source: GAO analysis of FDIC call report data.

[a] Net interest income is reported in the call report, schedule report of income. We show net interest income as 100 percent and for each income category calculate its percentage of net interest income.

[b] Credit losses are based on provisions for loan and lease losses as reported in the call report, schedule report of income.

[c] The impact on income of other real estate owned is based on net gains (losses) on sales of OREO as reported in the call report, schedule report of income, which includes gains and losses recognized upon sale of foreclosed property and fair value losses recognized prior to sale.

[d] The impact on income of HFS loans is based on net gains (losses) on sales of loans and leases as reported in the call report, schedule report of income, which includes gains and losses recognized upon sale and fair value losses recognized prior to sale.

[e] The impact on income of AFS and HTM securities is based on realized gains (losses) on AFS and HTM securities as reported in the call report, schedule report of income, which includes impairment losses recognized.

[f] The impact on income of recurring fair value measurements is based on trading revenues and net gains (losses) on assets and liabilities accounted for under the fair value option as reported in the call report, schedule report of income.

Figure 13. Income Categories as a Percentage of Net Interest Income for Medium- size Failed Commercial Banks, 2007-2011.

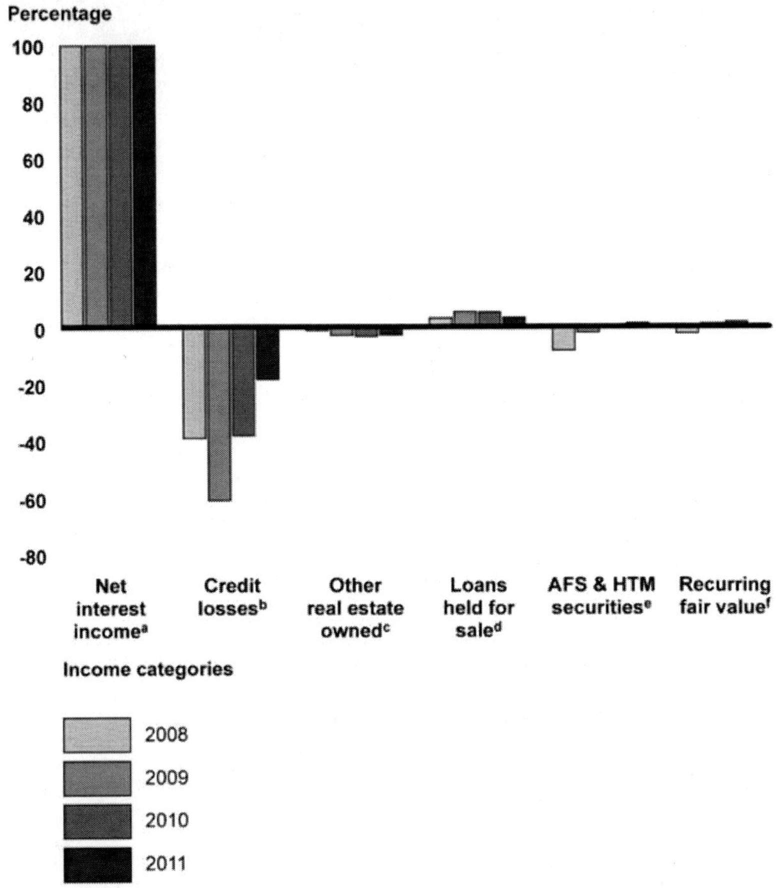

Source: GAO analysis of FDIC call report data.

[a] Net interest income is reported in the call report, schedule report of income. We show net interest income as 100 percent and for each income category calculate its percentage of net interest income.

[b] Credit losses are based on provisions for loan and lease losses as reported in the call report, schedule report of income.

[c] The impact on income of other real estate owned is based on net gains (losses) on sales of OREO as reported in the call report, schedule report of income, which includes gains and losses recognized upon sale of foreclosed property and fair value losses recognized prior to sale.

[d] The impact on income of HFS loans is based on net gains (losses) on sales of loans and leases as reported in the call report, schedule report of income, which includes gains and losses recognized upon sale and fair value losses recognized prior to sale.

[e] The impact on income of AFS and HTM securities is based on realized gains (losses) on AFS and HTM securities as reported in the call report, schedule report of income, which includes impairment losses recognized.

[f] The impact on income of recurring fair value measurements is based on trading revenues and net gains (losses) on assets and liabilities accounted for under the fair value option as reported in the call report, schedule report of income.

Figure 14. Income Categories as a Percentage of Net Interest Income for Open Medium-size Banks, 2008-2011.

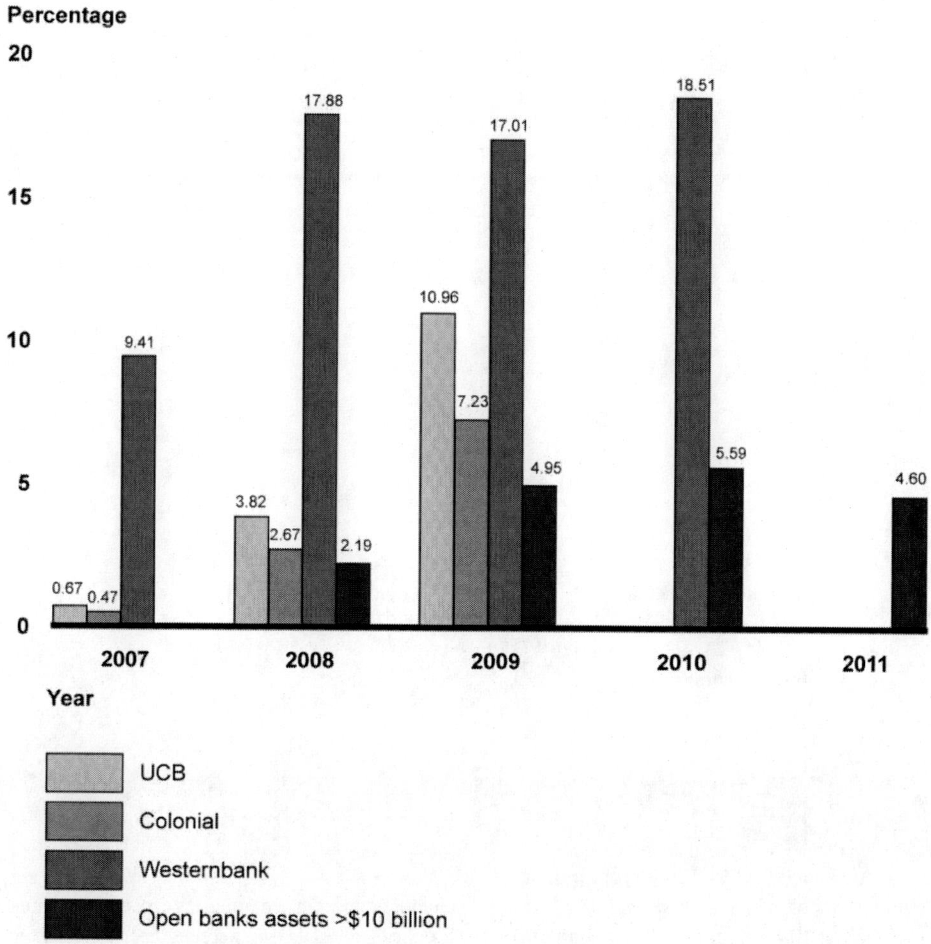

Source: GAO analysis of FDIC call report data.

Note: For each large failed commercial bank, we provided data for 2007 and for the following years until the bank failed. UCB and Colonial failed in 2009 and Westernbank failed in 2010.

Figure 15. Nonperforming Loans as a Percentage of Total Loans for Large Failed Commercial Banks, 2007-2011.

Colonial

In 2008 Colonial had less than one-half of 1 percent of nonperforming loans (figure 15). However, in 2008, nonperforming loans had jumped to nearly 3 percent of total loans, reflecting rapid deteriorations in the quality of its loan portfolio. By 2009, the level of nonperforming loans had more than doubled again to 7.23 percent. In its material loss review, the Treasury IG found that from 2006 through 2009, Colonial charged off $998 million of loans, of which $752 million (75 percent) were losses within the acquisition, development, and construction (ADC) loan portfolio. In addition, loan delinquencies significantly increased and, as of June 2009, 25 percent of the ADC loan portfolio was 90 days past due or in nonaccrual status. During that same quarter, Colonial also had $377 million in unrealized securities losses in its other mortgage-backed securities portfolio.

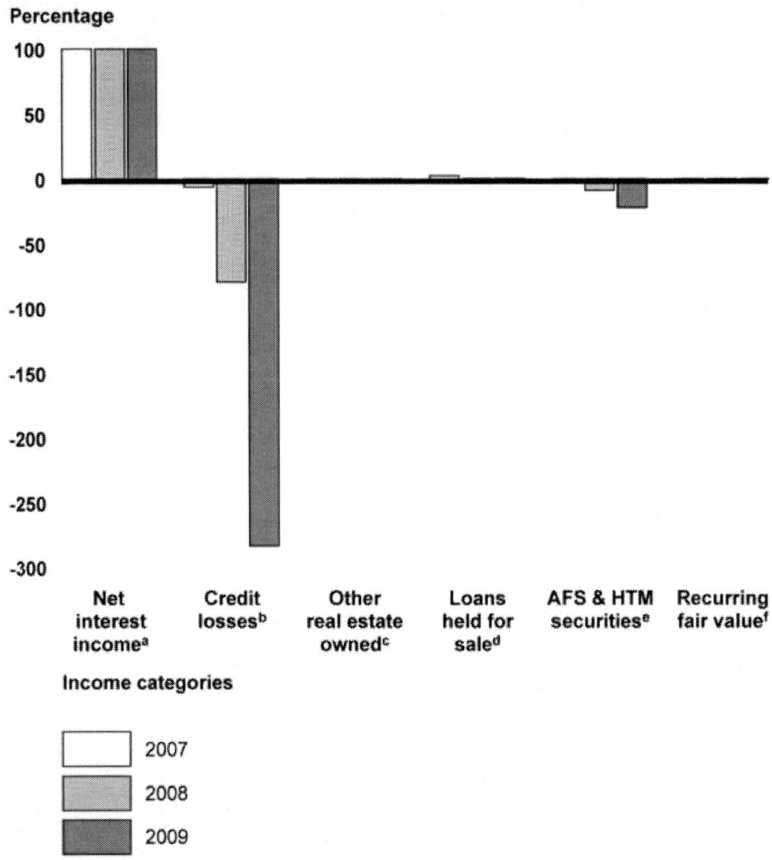

Source: GAO analysis of FDIC call report data.

[a] Net interest income is reported in the call report, schedule report of income. We show net interest income as 100 percent and for each income category calculate its percentage of net interest income.

[b] Credit losses are based on provisions for loan and lease losses as reported in the call report, schedule report of income.

[c] The impact on income of other real estate owned is based on net gains (losses) on sales of OREO as reported in the call report, schedule report of income, which includes gains and losses recognized upon sale of foreclosed property and fair value losses recognized prior to sale.

[d] The impact on income of HFS loans is based on net gains (losses) on sales of loans and leases as reported in the call report, schedule report of income, which includes gains and losses recognized upon sale and fair value losses recognized prior to sale.

[e] The impact on income of AFS and HTM securities is based on realized gains (losses) on AFS and HTM securities as reported in the call report, schedule report of income, which includes impairment losses recognized.

[f] The impact on income of recurring fair value measurements is based on trading revenues and net gains (losses) on assets and liabilities accounted for under the fair value option as reported in the call report, schedule report of income. UCB did not report any losses in this category during this period.

Figure 16. Income Categories as a Percentage of Net Interest Income for United Commercial Bank, 2007-2009.

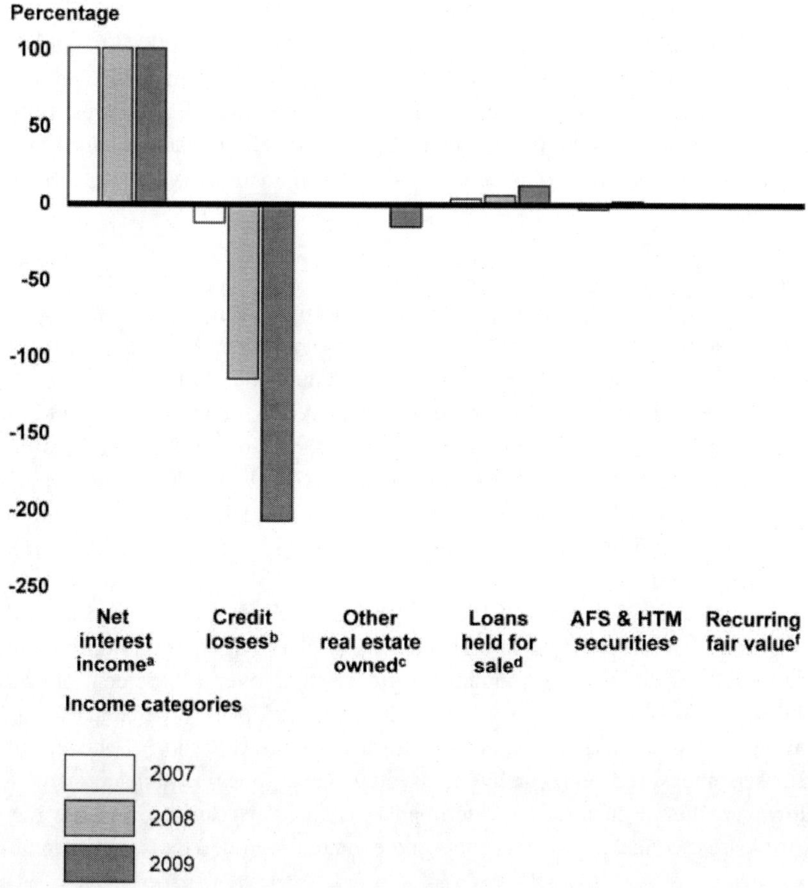

Source: GAO analysis of FDIC call report data.

[a] Net interest income is reported in the call report, schedule report of income. We show net interest income as 100 percent and for each income category calculate its percentage of net interest income.

[b] Credit losses are based on provisions for loan and lease losses as reported in the call report, schedule report of income.

[c] The impact on income of other real estate owned is based on net gains (losses) on sales of OREO as reported in the call report, schedule report of income, which includes gains and losses recognized upon sale of foreclosed property and fair value losses recognized prior to sale.

[d] The impact on income of HFS loans is based on net gains (losses) on sales of loans and leases as reported in the call report, schedule report of income, which includes gains and losses recognized upon sale and fair value losses recognized prior to sale.

[e] The impact on income of AFS and HTM securities is based on realized gains (losses) on AFS and HTM securities as reported in the call report, schedule report of income, which includes impairment losses recognized.

[f] The impact on income of recurring fair value measurements is based on trading revenues and net gains (losses) on assets and liabilities accounted for under the fair value option as reported in the call report, schedule report of income.

Figure 17. Income Categories as a Percentage of Net Interest Income for Colonial National Bank, 2007-2009.

By and large, Colonial's credit losses were the primary drivers of the decline in net interest income (see figure 17). For example, from 2007 through 2009, Colonial's credit losses accounted for on average over 110 percent of net interest income, while net losses from the sale of OREO averaged about 6 percent. During that same period, net losses from the sale of AFS and HTM securities averaged less than 2 percent of net interest income and the bank's fair value losses were less than 1 percent of net interest income, whereas HFS loan sales generated income.

Westernbank

In 2007, Westernbank was already experiencing significant levels of nonperforming loans, which approached 10 percent of its total loans (figure 15). According to the Treasury IG's material loss review, Westernbank's board and management's lending strategy focused on growth in CRE, ADC, and asset-based lending (ABL) portfolios without mitigating controls in place to keep pace with the changing loan portfolio. The IG noted that as Puerto Rico's economy sank into recession, ABL, CRE and ADC loans that were originated and renewed based on weak loan underwriting practices and deficient credit administration practices caused the precipitous deterioration of asset quality and increasingly high levels of adversely classified assets.

During the period 2007 through 2010, Westernbank's credit losses contributed the most to the bank's overall losses relative to any other asset class (figure 18). For example, from 2007 through 2010, credit losses accounted for, on average, over 125 percent of net interest income while net losses from the sale of OREO averaged over 7 percent of net interest income. During that same period, revenues from the sale of AFS and HTM securities, HFS loans, and assets measured at recurring fair value had a positive impact on net interest income. However, the credit losses Westernbank sustained necessitated a large increase in provisions for losses, which stressed earnings and eventually eroded the bank's capital.

OTTI Losses on HTM and AFS Debt Securities as a Percentage of Net Interest Income

In April 2009, the Financial Accounting Standards Board (FASB) amended the GAAP standard on OTTI to modify when charges stemming from declines in the fair value of debt securities classified as AFS and HTM below amortized cost are recorded in earnings.[96] Under the previous standard, an entity was required to consider relevant factors in determining whether an impairment of a debt security was other than temporary, in which case the entire loss was recognized in earnings.[97] However, some critics of this standard believed that during the recent financial crisis banks were recording significant OTTI losses to their earnings, and thus regulatory capital, to account for impaired assets, such as mortgage-backed securities that they had no immediate intention of selling and on which they expected the fair value would recover in the future when the financial markets improved. Under the new standard, if (a) the entity does not intend to sell a debt security and (b) it is not more likely than not that the entity will be required to sell the debt security before recovery of its amortized cost basis less any current-period credit loss, the amount of the OTTI representing the credit loss is recognized in earnings and the amount related to all other factors is recognized in OCI. In contrast, the amount of OTTI recorded in earnings for a debt security is the entire difference between the security's amortized cost basis and its fair value if the entity intends to sell the security or it is more likely than not that the entity will be required to sell the debt security prior to recovery of its amortized cost basis.

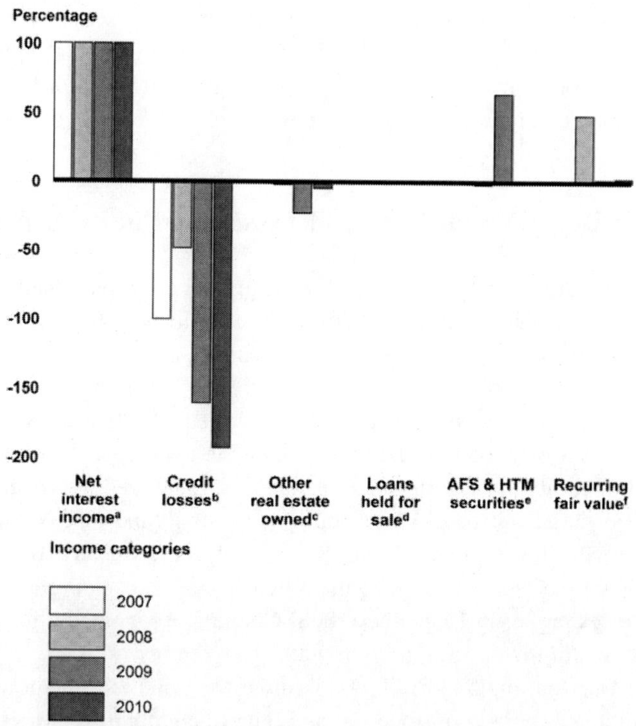

Source: GAO analysis of FDIC call report data.

[a] Net interest income is reported in the call report, schedule report of income. We show net interest income as 100 percent and for each income category calculate its percentage of net interest income.

[b] Credit losses are based on provisions for loan and lease losses as reported in the call report, schedule report of income.

[c] The impact on income of other real estate owned is based on net gains (losses) on sales of OREO as reported in the call report, schedule report of income, which includes gains and losses recognized upon sale of foreclosed property and fair value losses recognized prior to sale.

[d] The impact on income of HFS loans is based on net gains (losses) on sales of loans and leases as reported in the call report, schedule report of income, which includes gains and losses recognized upon sale and fair value losses recognized prior to sale.

[e] The impact on income of AFS and HTM securities is based on realized gains (losses) on AFS and HTM securities as reported in the call report, schedule report of income, which includes impairment losses recognized.

[f] The impact on income of recurring fair value measurements is based on trading revenues and net gains (losses) on assets and liabilities accounted for under the fair value option as reported in the call report, schedule report of income.

Figure 18. Income Categories as a Percentage of Net Interest Income for Westernbank, 2007-2010.

Figure 19 shows total OTTI losses and the breakdown of the noncredit- related portion recognized in OCI and the credit-related portion recognized in earnings. Although the changes were adopted in April of 2009, the changes were not captured in bank call reports until the first quarter of 2010, as a result, no data on OTTI are available prior to first quarter of 2010. Also, because most of the large banks that failed did so prior to the first quarter of 2010, there were no OTTI data recorded for the large banks past that date. Nevertheless, based on the limited reported data on OTTI, the results of the analysis show that generally OTTI losses recognized in earnings accounted for less than 2 percent of net interest income in 2010 and 2011 at failed and open banks of all sizes.

Impact of Goodwill and Other Intangible Assets on Equity Capital

Goodwill refers to the excess of the cost of an acquired entity over the net of the amounts assigned to assets acquired and liabilities assumed. Goodwill is tested for impairment on an annual basis with any impairment charge recognized in net income and therefore decreasing equity capital. Generally, one trigger for assessing goodwill and other intangibles for impairment is if the fair value of the business unit acquired falls below its carrying amount. As figures 20 and 21 show, goodwill and other intangible expenses, on average, represented less than 2 percent of equity capital for failed institutions, compared to less than 1 percent for open institutions. For large failed banks, the ratio of goodwill and other intangible expenses to capital showed higher levels in 2008 and 2009 mainly because of two institutions, UCB and Colonial Bank. These two banks recognized higher than expected goodwill expenses in 2008 and 2009. For example, in December 2008, Colonial recognized a goodwill and other intangible expense totaling over $579 million, and in September of 2009, UCB recognized a similar noncash charge totaling $433 million. Without the goodwill impairment transactions of these two institutions, the ratio of goodwill and other intangible expenses to capital would have been 0.13 percent and 0.88 percent in 2008 and 2009, respectively.

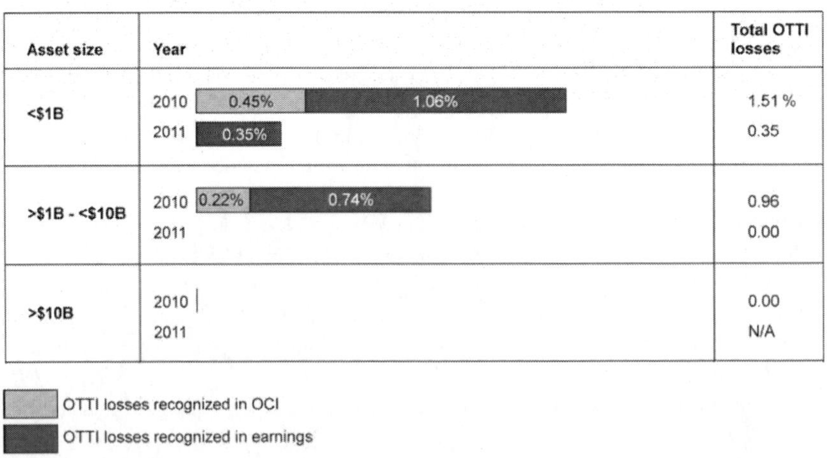

Source: GAO analysis of FDIC call report data.

Figure 19. OTTI Losses on HTM and AFS Debt Securities as a Percentage of Net Interest Income for Failed Banks.

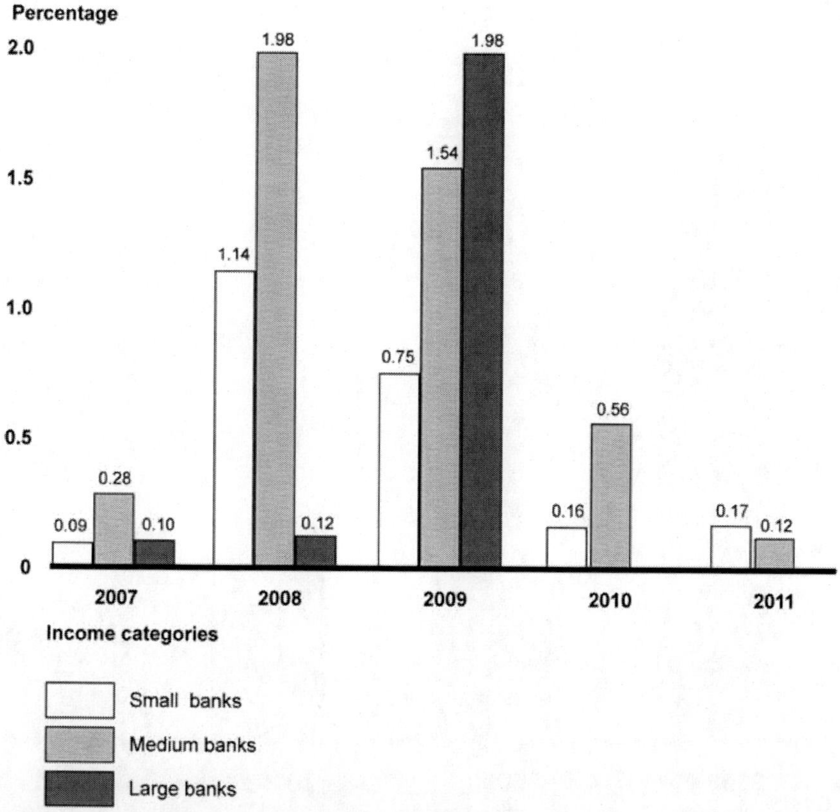

Source: GAO analysis of FDIC call report data.

Note: The ratio of goodwill and other intangible expenses to capital showed higher levels in 2008 and 2009 mainly because of two institutions, UCB and Colonial Bank. These two banks recognized higher than expected goodwill expenses in 2008 and 2009 because of 2007 bank mergers and acquisitions in Florida and Nevada that later became impaired primarily due to declining bank market valuations and increased credit costs. For example, in December 2008, Colonial recognized a goodwill and other intangible expense totaling over $579 million, and in September of 2009, UCB recognized a similar noncash charge totaling $433 million. Without the goodwill impairment transactions of these two institutions, the ratio of goodwill and other intangible expenses to capital would have been 0.13 percent and 0.88 percent in 2008 and 2009, respectively.

Figure 20. Goodwill and Other Intangible Expenses as a Percentage of Equity Capital (Failed Banks), 2007-2011.

Impact of Other Comprehensive Income on Equity Capital

As discussed earlier, the accumulated OCI includes the unrealized fair value gains and losses on AFS securities (including fair value losses unrelated to credit factors). In addition, when a debt security is transferred from AFS to HTM, the unrealized holding gains or losses continues to be reported in this account, and it is amortized over the remaining life of the security as an adjustment of yield. We determined the extent to which negative changes in OCI impacted institutions' equity capital.

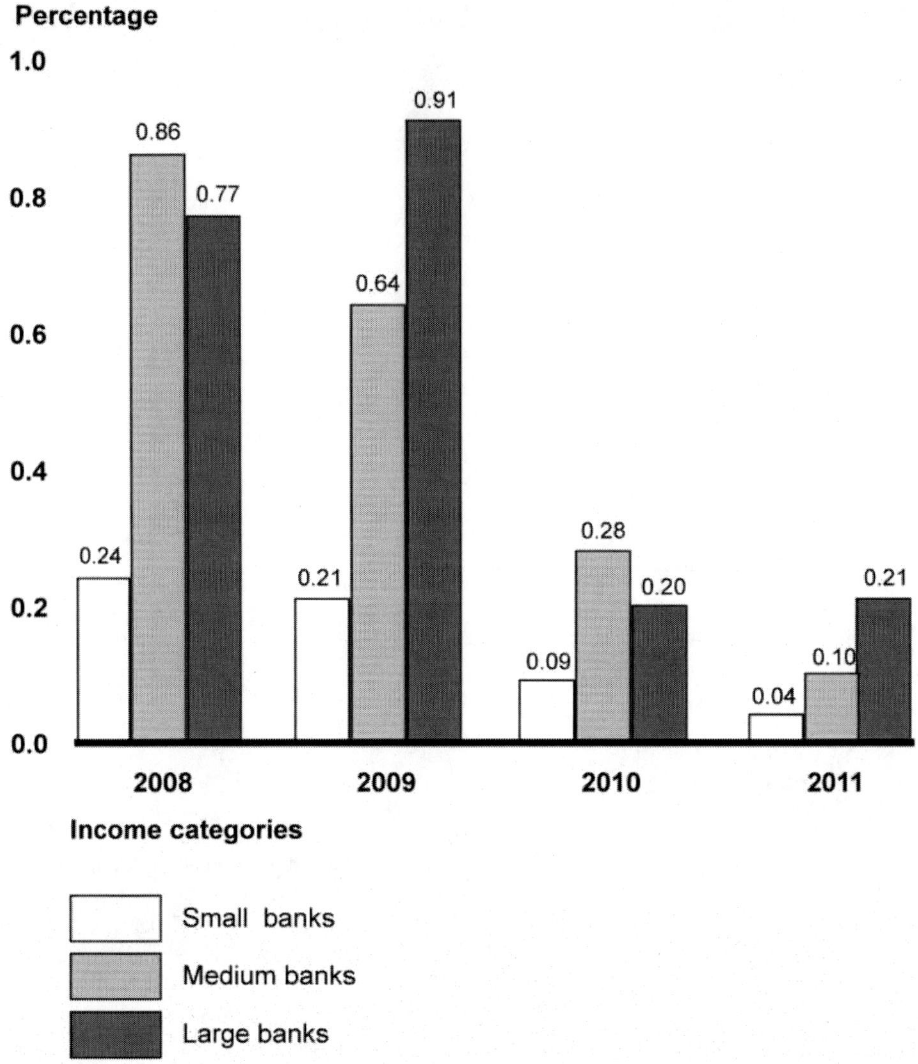

Source: GAO analysis of FDIC call report data.

Figure 21. Goodwill and Other Intangible Expenses as a Percentage of Equity Capital (Open Banks), 2008-2011.

As table 15 shows, for small failed and open banks, the year-to-date (YTD) and accumulated OCI decreases were smaller than for medium- size and large failed and open banks. Generally, larger banks had larger decreases in 2008 and 2009, principally due to two large banks, Colonial and Westernbank. Colonial had a YTD OCI of over $(318) million during the fourth quarter of 2008, and $ (200) million during the first quarter of 2009, while Westernbank had a YTD OCI of over $ (100) million during the second and third quarters of 2008. These unrealized fair value losses had a slightly larger impact on larger banks with more than $10 billion in assets. Larger failed banks had larger negative changes in OCI, hence larger negative impact on equity than open institutions of similar size.

Table 15. YTD and Accumulated OCI as a Percentage of Equity Capital

Asset size	Description	2007	2008	2009	2010	2011
Failed banks						
< $1 billion	YTD OCI	-0.05%	-1.92%	-0.21%	0.53%	15.17%
>$1 billion, <$10 billion	YTD OCI	0.10%	-1.81%	-0.06%	2.58%	1.83%
>$10 billion	YTD OCI	0.48%	-5.77%	5.57%	4.25%	—[a]
< $1 billion	AOCI	-0.57%	-2.15%	-2.70%	-0.06%	11.17%
>$1 billion, <$10 billion	AOCI	-0.93%	-2.50%	-6.56%	-1.61%	-2.25%
>$10 billion	AOCI	-1.00%	-6.32%	-3.69%	0.18%	N/A[a]
Open banks						
< $1 billion	YTD OCI	—[b]	-0.70%	0.54%	0.59%	1.90%
>$1 billion, <$10 billion	YTD OCI	—[b]	-1.12%	0.66%	0.65%	1.09%
>$10 billion	YTD OCI	—[b]	-2.96%	2.54%	1.51%	0.71%
< $1 billion	AOCI	—[b]	-0.39%	0.46%	1.43%	1.99%
>$1 billion, <$10 billion	AOCI	—[b]	-1.42%	-0.94%	0.48%	0.91%
>$10 billion	AOCI	—[b]	-4.64%	-3.41%	-0.67%	-0.15%

Source: GAO analysis of FDIC call report data.

[a] No large commercial banks failed in 2011.

[b] Pub. L. No. 112-88 requires us to analyze bank failures that occurred since 2008. As such, we analyzed trends for both failed banks and open banks from 2008 through 2011. For failed banks, we also obtained 2007 data to determine any additional trends prior to the failures.

APPENDIX V. ANALYSIS OF THE IMPACT OF FAIR VALUE ACCOUNTING ON RECENT THRIFT INSTITUTION FAILURES

We analyzed thrifts financial reports from 2007 through 2011 for failed and open thrift institutions to identify and compare trends in (1) the use of historical cost accounting and fair value accounting and (2) the extent to which losses were credit-related for small, medium-size, and large institutions. We define small failed thrifts as those that had $1 billion or less in assets at the time of failure, medium-size failed thrifts as those that had between $1 billion and $10 billion at the time of failure, and large failed thrifts as those that had over $10 billion in assets at the time of failure. Overall we found that fair value-related losses contributed very little to the decline in net interest income and regulatory capital experienced by failed thrifts of all sizes (small, medium-size, and large) once the financial crisis began. Similarly, fair value losses at open thrifts of all sizes were also limited. Instead, we found that the thrift failures were driven by rising levels of credit losses related to nonperforming loans held by the thrifts. Further, these losses had a greater negative impact on thrift institutions' net interest income and regulatory capital levels than those recorded at fair value. We analyzed failed banks separately. (See app. IV.)

Fair Value, Historical Cost, and Impairment Accounting

U. S. generally accepted accounting principles (GAAP) establish the basis on which items reported on a financial institution's balance sheet should be measured, including a thrift. Currently, assets and liabilities are reflected in the balance sheet at fair value, historical cost, or another basis, such as lower-of-cost or fair value.

- Fair Value: Fair value is the price that would be received to sell an asset or paid to transfer a liability in an orderly transaction between market participants at the measurement date.. Fair value accounting standards under GAAP establish a standardized framework for measuring the fair value of an asset or liability.[98] According to the Securities and Exchange Commission, fair value is most prevalently used to measure "financial" assets and liabilities, such as investment securities and derivative instruments. Fair value measurements that are required on a quarterly basis (or each reporting period) are often referred to as "recurring." Fair value measurements that are not required on a regular basis are often referred to as "nonrecurring."For some assets and liabilities that are measured at fair value on a recurring basis, such as securities designated for trading, unrealized gains or losses flow through the thrift's earnings in the income statement and affect regulatory capital. For other assets and liabilities measured at fair value on a recurring basis, such as securities designated as available for sale, unrealized fair value gains and losses generally do not impact earnings, and thus, generally are not included in regulatory capital calculations. Instead, these gains or losses are recorded through other comprehensive income (OCI), unless the institution determines that a decline in fair value below amortized cost constitutes an other than temporary impairment (OTTI), in which case the instrument is written down to its fair value, with credit losses reflected in earnings.[99] The OTTI decision for a given asset is a judgmental decision of the thrift, considering various factors related to the severity and duration of the decrease in the value of the asset. Unrealized changes in fair value and OTTI-related write-downs that are recognized in earnings in the income statement directly impact regulatory capital levels.
- Historical Cost: Measurement using historical cost can be done in several ways, but the general concept is to record items on the balance sheet using the original amount paid or received, with adjustments when appropriate in subsequent periods for depreciation, amortization, principal pay downs, or impairment. Generally, loans that a thrift designates as held-for-investment (HFI), for example, are recorded at amortized cost, net of an impairment allowance for estimated credit losses.[100] Such loans typically comprise the bulk of assets held by thrifts.
- Loan Impairment Accounting: GAAP requires financial institutions to maintain an allowance for loan losses (loan loss allowance) at a level that is appropriate to cover estimated credit losses incurred as of the balance sheet date for their entire portfolio of HFI loans. Under GAAP, institutions must recognize impairment on HFI loans when credit losses are determined to be probable and reasonably estimable, that is, when, based on current information and events, it is probable that an institution will be unable to collect all amounts due (i.e., both principal and interest) according to the contractual terms of the original loan agreement. An increase in the loan loss allowance results in a charge to expenses, termed a provision for loan losses. Impairment accounting standards under GAAP set forth the measurement methods for estimating the credit losses attributable to individually impaired loans. Regulators

generally require institutions to establish policies and procedures for determining the loan loss allowance based on GAAP requirements.

Most Failed Small and Medium-Size Thrifts Did Not Measure a Significant Percentage of Assets at Fair Value over the 2007-2011 Period

Assets Measured at Amortized Cost

During the period of our study, HFI loans represented on average over two thirds of most thrift institutions total assets (table 1). HFI loans are not recorded at fair value, but instead are measured on an amortized-cost basis, net of an impairment allowance for estimated credit losses. Table 16 indicates that small and medium-size thrifts generally had slightly higher percentages of loans classified as HFI loans than large thrifts. Also, compared to open thrifts, failed thrifts held a higher percentage of HFI loans.

Table 16. HFI Loans as a Percentage of Total Assets for Failed and Open Thrifts, 2007-2011

Asset size	Description	2007	2008	2009	2010	2011
Failed thrifts						
< $1 billion	HFI loans	77.67%	77.62%	73.65%	66.80%	70.20%
>$1 billion, <$10 billion	HFI loans	81.24%	83.02%	78.27%	65.43%	69.56%
Open thrifts						
>$10 billion	HFI loans	68.91%	75.42%	72.19%	—[a]	—[a]
< $1 billion	HFI loans	70.69%	71.65%	69.91%	67.20%	64.87%
>$1 billion, <$10 billion	HFI loans	71.12%	68.61%	63.41%	59.82%	61.01%
>$10 billion	HFI Loans	65.25%	67.03%	60.85%	58.47%	55.51%

Source: GAO analysis of FDIC thrift financial report data.

[a] No large thrifts failed in 2010 or 2011.

Table 17. Trading Assets as a Percentage of Total Assets for Failed and Open Thrifts, 2007-2011

Asset size	Description	2007	2008	2009	2010	2011
Failed thrifts						
< $1 billion	Trading assets	0.00%	0.00%	0.00%	0.01	0.00%
>$1 billion, <$10 billion	Trading assets	0.00%	0.13%	0.20%	0.05%	0.00%
>$10 billion	Trading assets	1.28%	0.35%	0.00%	—[a]	—[a]
Open thrifts						
< $1 billion	Trading assets	0.19%	0.12%	0.04%	0.01%	0.01%
>$1 billion, <$10 billion	Trading assets	0.56%	1.53%	1.68%	0.89%	0.03%
>$10 billion	Trading assets	0.52%	0.37%	0.43%	0.11%	0.17%

Source: GAO analysis of FDIC thrift financial report data.

[a] No large thrifts failed in 2010 or 2011.

Assets and Liabilities Measured at Fair Value through Earnings on a Recurring Basis through Income

Assets measured at fair value through earnings on a recurring basis comprised mainly trading assets, nontrading derivative assets, and nonfinancial assets such as servicing rights for mortgages for which the fair value option has been elected.[101]

Trading Assets

Trading assets generally include both debt and marketable equity securities bought and held primarily to be sold in the near term. Trading activities typically involve active and frequent buying and selling to generate profits on short-term movements in market prices. Trading assets also include derivative contracts held for trading purposes in gain positions. Table 17 shows that trading assets did not represent a significant percentage of failed thrifts' assets from 2007-2011.

Nontrading Assets

Nontrading assets measured at fair value on a recurring basis include, among other things, nontrading derivative contracts in gain positions. Most thrifts did not have any significant holdings of such nontrading assets (table 18). Even for open thrifts that have relatively more of such nontrading assets than failed thrifts, the level of these assets is less than 2.75 percent of their total assets.

Nonfinancial Assets

Nonfinancial assets measured at fair value through earnings on a recurring basis consist of mortgage servicing rights (MSRs) for which a fair value option has been elected. Failed thrifts did not have significant amounts of such nonfinancial assets (table 19). Failed thrifts also generally had fewer such nonfinancial assets than open thrifts. However, large failed thrifts generally had larger levels of such nonfinancial assets than most of the open thrifts because Washington Mutual, the largest thrift institution that failed, had a sizable level of mortgage servicing rights on its books.

Table 18. Nontrading Assets Measured at Fair Value through Earnings on a Recurring Basis as a Percentage of Total Assets for Failed and Open Thrifts, 2007-2011

Asset size	Description	2007	2008	2009	2010	2011
Failed thrifts						
< $1 billion	Nontrading assets	0.33%	0.26%	0.28%	2.94%	14.68%
>$1 billion, <$10 Billion	Nontrading assets	0.02%	0.30%	0.50%	0.03%	0.01%
>$10 billion	Nontrading assets	0.87%	1.24%	1.15%	—[a]	—[a]
Open thrifts						
< $1 billion	Nontrading assets	0.80%	0.76%	0.41%	0.29%	0.48%
>$1 billion, <$10 billion	Nontrading assets	0.34%	1.32%	1.68%	1.40%	1.03%
>$10 billion	Nontrading assets	1.76%	1.71%	2.10%	2.71%	2.34%

Source: GAO analysis of FDIC thrift financial report data.

[a] No large thrifts failed in 2010 or 2011.

Table 19. Nonfinancial Assets Measured at Fair Value through Earnings on a Recurring Basis as a Percentage of Total Assets for Failed and Open Thrifts, 2007-2011

Asset size	Description	2007	2008	2009	2010	2011
Failed thrifts						
< $1 billion	Nonfinancial assets	0.04%	0.04%	0.08%	0.14%	0.37%
>$1 billion, <$10 billion	Nonfinancial assets	0.25%	0.27%	0.34%	0.21%	0.19%
>$10 billion	Nonfinancial assets	2.21%	1.18%	1.28%	—[a]	—[a]
Open thrifts						
< $1 billion	Nonfinancial Assets	0.19%	0.19%	0.18%	0.20%	0.26%
>$1 billion, <$10 Billion	Nonfinancial Assets	0.29%	0.28%	0.42%	0.33%	0.42%
>$10 billion	Nonfinancial Assets	0.86%	0.84%	0.39%	0.31%	0.29%

Source: GAO analysis of FDIC thrift financial report data.
[a] No large thrifts failed in 2010 or 2011.

Liabilities

Liabilities measured at fair value through earnings on a recurring basis include trading liabilities such as securities an institution sold but did not own and therefore is obligated to purchase at a future date (short positions), derivative contracts held for trading purposes in loss positions, nontrading derivative contracts in loss positions, and those liabilities for which a bank elects to measure at fair value on a recurring basis under the fair value option. Failed thrifts did not have a significant amount of such trading liabilities (table 20). Failed thrifts also had fewer such trading liabilities than open thrifts, particularly large open thrifts.

Assets Measured at Fair Value on a Non-Recurring Basis through Income

Securities Held to Maturity

Investments in debt securities classified as held to maturity (HTM) are measured at amortized cost but if any decline in fair value is other than temporary, credit losses are recognized in earnings. The held-to-maturity category includes only debt securities that management has both the positive intent and ability to hold until maturity.

Table 20. Liabilities Measured at Fair Value through Earnings on a Recurring Basis as a Percentage of Total Assets for Failed and Open Thrifts, 2007-2011

Asset size	Description	2007	2008	2009	2010	2011
Failed thrifts						
< $1 billion	Liabilities	0.01%	0.01%	0.00%	0.01%	0.02%
>$1 billion, <$10 billion	Liabilities	0.00%	0.05%	0.04%	0.12%	0.30%
>$1 billion	Liabilities	0.04%	0.15%	0.13%	—[a]	—[a]
Open thrifts						
< $1 billion	Liabilities	0.26%	0.19%	0.00%	0.00%	0.00%
>$1 billion, <$10 billion	Liabilities	0.30%	1.87%	2.41%	1.69%	1.53%
>$1 billion	Liabilities	1.06%	0.48%	0.15%	0.76%	0.76%

Source: GAO analysis of FDIC thrift financial report data.
[a] No large thrifts failed in 2010 or 2011.

As illustrated in table 21, investment securities classified as HTM represented less than 4 percent of assets held for failed thrifts with less than $10 billion in assets. For failed thrifts with more than $10 billion in assets, HTM securities ranged between 2 percent and 5 percent. HTM securities for open thrifts were not available.

Securities Available for Sale

Investments in debt securities that are not classified as trading securities or as HTM securities are classified as available-for-sale (AFS) securities. AFS securities also include equity securities that have readily determinable fair values and are not classified as trading securities. If the fair value of an AFS security declines below its amortized cost, and the decline is other than temporary, credit losses are recognized in earnings.

As illustrated in table 22, AFS securities represented the largest percentage of assets held after loans HFI. For failed thrifts, AFS securities ranged between 6 percent and 10 percent of total assets compared to 12 percent and 20 percent for open thrifts. On average, large open thrifts held the highest percentages of AFS securities.

As a result of an April 2009 change to the relevant GAAP standard, an OTTI loss of either an AFS or HTM debt security, in certain circumstances, is separated into (1) the credit loss amount, which is recognized in earnings and (2) the loss amount related to all other factors (noncredit loss), which is recognized in other comprehensive income, net of applicable taxes.

Table 21. HTM Securities as a Percentage of Total Assets for Failed Thrifts, 2007-2011 Failed thrifts

Asset size	Description	2007	2008	2009	2010	2011
< $1 billion	HTM securities	2.08%	1.16%	1.32%	1.71%	0.33%
>$1 billion, <$10 billion	HTM securities	2.8%	3.1%	2.7%	3.5%	0.2%
>$10 billion	HTM securities	1.79%	4.94%	3.01%	—[a]	—[a]

Source: GAO analysis of FDIC thrift financial report data.

[a] No large thrifts failed in 2010 or 2011.

Table 22. AFS Securities as a Percentage of Total Assets for Failed and Open Thrifts, 2007-2011

Asset size	Description	2007	2008	2009	2010	2011
Failed thrifts						
< $1 billion	AFS securities	8.36%	7.63%	7.88%	9.65%	7.87%
>$1 billion, <$10 billion	AFS securities	5.60%	5.28%	4.99%	8.52%	8.47%
>$10 billion	AFS securities	8.44%	6.29%	7.88%	—[a]	—[a]
Open thrifts						
< $1 billion	AFS securities	11.50%	10.96%	11.05%	11.66%	12.74%
>$1 billion, <$10 billion	AFS securities	12.11%	12.48%	15.50%	19.05%	19.62%
>$10 billion	AFS securities	14.56%	13.92%	14.85%	19.32%	20.20%

Source: GAO analysis of FDIC thrift financial report data.

[a] No large thrifts failed in 2010 or 2011.

Assets Measured at the Lower- of-Cost-or-Fair-Value

Loans Held for Sale

Under GAAP, HFS loans originated with the intent to sell in the secondary market to government-sponsored entities and other investors (including other FDIC-insured institutions) are carried at the lower of cost or fair value, unless the institution has elected to account for the loans at fair value under the fair value option. Institutions can transfer loans into or out of the HFS classification as a result of changes in intentions regarding whether the loans will be sold or HFI. Transfers between categories, however, are recorded at the lower of cost or fair value.[102]

HFS loans did not represent a significant percentage of assets held by thrifts. On average, failed thrifts with less than $10 billion in assets held about 5 percent of their assets in HFS loans (table 23). With the exception of 2007, the percentage of HFS assets are generally lower for failed thrifts with over $10 billion in assets compared to open thrifts of similar size. In 2007 and 2008, a few large thrifts started transferring a significant amount of HFS loans into their HFI portfolio as a result of the tightening in the secondary market for nonagency mortgage loans. Appendix VI provides further analysis of these transfers.

Other Real Estate Owned

Other Real Estate Owned (OREO) usually includes assets repossessed through a foreclosure process for defaulted loans. Generally, assets acquired through, or in lieu of, loan foreclosure are held for sale and are initially recorded at the estimated fair value of the collateral less costs to sell at the date of foreclosure, establishing a new cost basis. Subsequent to foreclosure, periodic valuations are performed and the assets are carried at the lower of their cost basis or estimated fair value less cost to sell.[103]

In early 2007 and 2008, thrift institutions had little exposure to foreclosed assets (table 24). However, as the financial crisis deepened and the real estate downturn became more severe, delinquencies increased rapidly and thrifts foreclosed more properties, particularly smaller thrifts. Compared to open thrifts, failed thrifts had a larger share of OREO assets.

Table 23. HFS Loans as a Percentage of Total Assets for Failed and Open Thrifts, 2007-2011

Asset size	Description	2007	2008	2009	2010	2011
Failed thrifts						
< $1 billion	HFS loans	2.82%	2.55%	1.95%	2.18%	0.18%
>$1 billion, <$10 billion	HFS loans	3.45%	1.60%	2.36%	5.13%	1.12%
>$10 billion	HFS loans	6.81%	1.26%	1.05%	—[a]	—[a]
Open thrifts						
< $1 billion	HFS loans	1.07%	1.13%	1.20%	1.28%	1.02%
>$1 billion, <$10 billion	HFS loans	2.07%	2.13%	2.61%	2.19%	1.38%
>$10 billion	HFS loans	5.30%	2.29%	1.47%	0.96%	2.41%

Source: GAO analysis of FDIC thrift financial report data.

[a] No large thrifts failed in 2010 or 2011.

Table 24. OREO Assets as a Percentage of Total Assets for Failed and Open Thrifts, 2007-2011

Asset size	Description	2007	2008	2009	2010	2011
Failed thrifts						
< $1 billion	OREO	0.33%	1.16%	2.34%	4.16%	6.07%
>$1 billion, <$10 billion	OREO	0.18%	0.84%	1.73%	1.81%	2.47%
>$10 billion	OREO	0.26%	0.96%	4.19%	—[a]	—[a]
Open thrifts						
< $1 billion	OREO	0.17%	0.34%	0.69%	0.91%	0.95%
>$1 billion, <$10 billion	OREO	0.11%	0.32%	0.54%	0.47%	0.42%
>$10 billion	OREO	0.14%	0.30%	0.33%	0.41%	0.35%

Source: GAO analysis of FDIC thrift financial report data.

[a] No large thrifts failed in 2010 or 2011.

Declines in Regulatory Capital at Failed Thrifts Due to Rising Levels of Nonperforming Loans and Resulting Increased Credit Losses

Small Failed Thrifts

For small failed thrifts, as the financial crisis that began in 2007 progressed, the levels of nonperforming loans rose from an average of less than 2 percent of total loans in 2007 to over 13 percent in 2011 (figure 22).

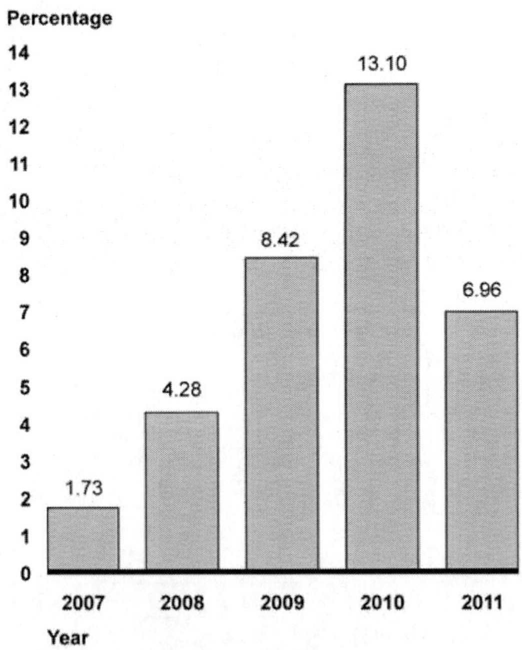

Source: GAO analysis of FDIC thrift financial report data.

Figure 22. Nonperforming Loans as a Percentage of Total Loans for Small Failed Thrifts, 2007-2011.

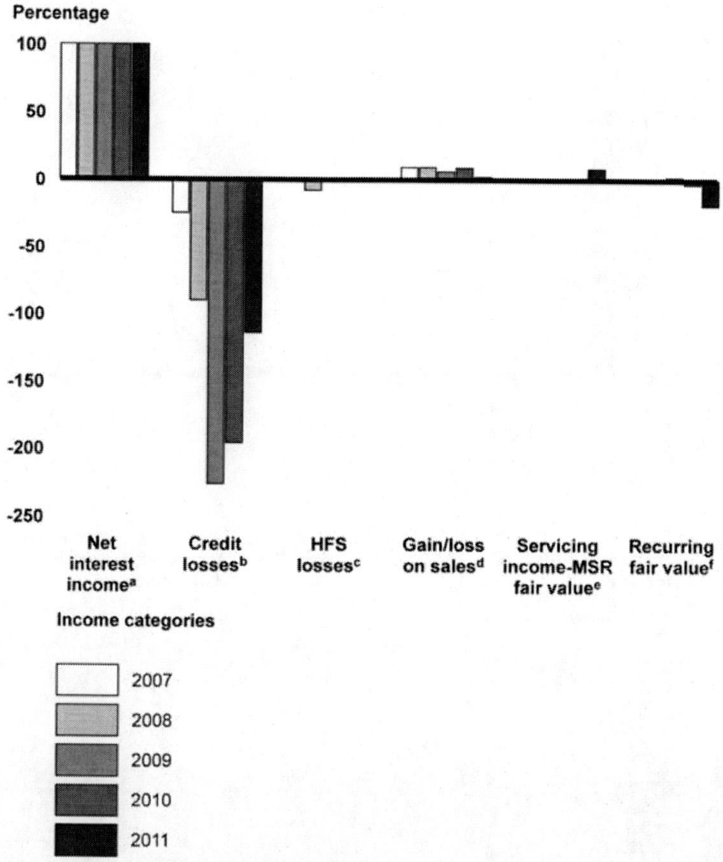

Source: GAO analysis of FDIC thrift financial report data.

[a] Net interest income reported in the thrift financial report, schedule statement of operations. We show net interest income as 100 percent and for each income category calculate its percentage of net interest income.

[b] Credit losses are based on provisions for losses on interest bearing assets as reported in the thrift financial report schedule statement of operations, which includes fair value losses recognized on foreclosed property and impairment losses recognized on debt and equity securities.

[c] The impact on income of losses on HFS loans is based on the lower-of-cost-or-fair-value adjustments made to HFS assets as reported in the thrift financial report schedule statement of operations of the thrift financial report, which does not include gains or losses recognized upon sale.

[d] The impact on income of gain/loss on sales is based on the sale of HFS assets and AFS securities as reported in the thrift financial report schedule statement of operations, which does not include impairment losses.

[e] The impact on income of servicing income is based on mortgage loan servicing fees and servicing amortization and valuation adjustments as reported in the thrift financial report schedule statement of operations.

[f] The impact on income of recurring fair value measurements is based on gains and losses on financial assets and liabilities carried at fair value as reported in the thrift financial report schedule statement of operations.

Figure 23. Income Categories as a Percentage of Net Interest Income for Small Failed Thrifts, 2007-2011.

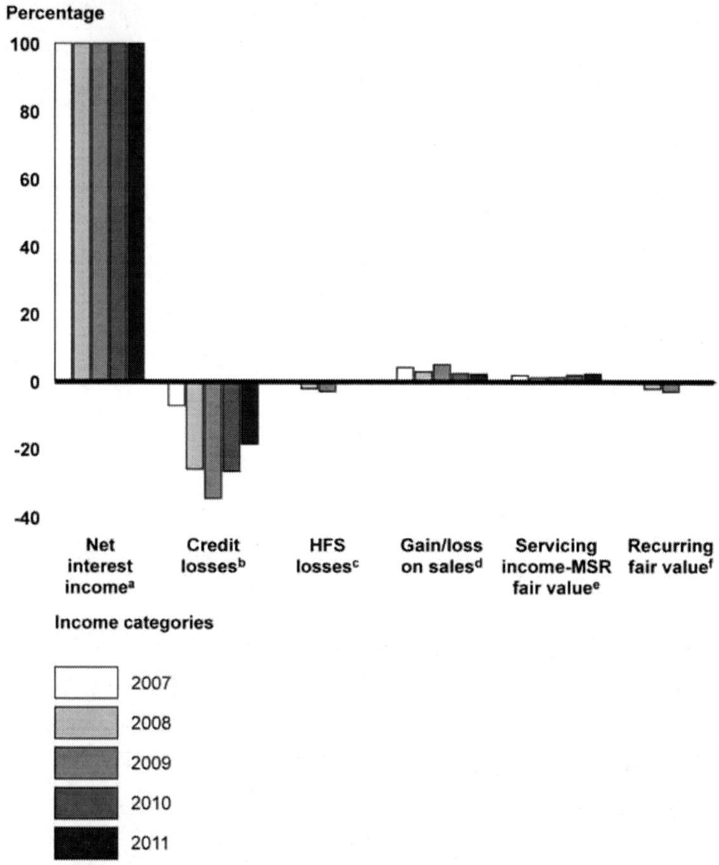

Source: GAO analysis of FDIC thrift financial report data.

[a] Net interest income reported in the thrift financial report, schedule statement of operations. We show net interest income as 100 percent and for each income category calculate its percentage of net interest income.

[b] Credit losses are based on provisions for losses on interest bearing assets as reported in the thrift financial report schedule statement of operations, which includes fair value losses recognized on foreclosed property and impairment losses recognized on debt and equity securities.

[c] The impact on income of losses on HFS loans is based on the lower-of-cost-or-fair-value adjustments made to HFS assets as reported in the thrift financial report schedule statement of operations of the thrift financial report, which does not include gains or losses recognized upon sale.

[d] The impact on income of gain/loss on sales is based on the sale of HFS assets and AFS securities as reported in the thrift financial report schedule statement of operations, which does not include impairment losses.

[e] The impact on income of servicing income is based on mortgage loan servicing fees and servicing amortization and valuation adjustments as reported in the thrift financial report schedule statement of operations.

[f] The impact on income of recurring fair value measurements is based on gains and losses on financial assets and liabilities carried at fair value as reported in the thrift financial report schedule statement of operations.

Figure 24. Income Categories as a Percentage of Net Interest Income for Small Open Thrifts, 2007-2011.

The rising levels on nonperforming loans appear to be the key factor driving the increases in provisions for credit losses and the resulting reduction in net interest income and regulatory capital. For failed small thrifts, credit losses were by far the largest contributor to these institutions' losses relative to any other asset class. For example, from 2007 to 2011, credit losses accounted for on average over 130 percent of net interest income while net losses from the sale of HFS assets averaged about 2 percent of net interest income (figure 23). During that same period, net losses from recurring fair value measurements were less than 4 percent.

In contrast, the magnitude of credit losses experienced by small open thrifts from 2007 through 2011 was significantly less than what the failed thrifts experienced (figure 24).

Medium-Size Thrifts

The level of nonperforming loans for medium-size failed thrifts grew from less than 2 percent in 2007 to over 9 percent in 2009 (figure 25). As with the small failed thrifts, the rising levels of nonperforming loans appear to be the key factor driving the increases in credit losses for medium-size failed thrifts.

The large credit losses largely drove the failed thrifts' decrease in earnings and regulatory capital. For example, from 2007 through 2009, credit losses accounted for on average over 133 percent of net interest income of medium-size failed thrifts while net losses from HFS assets averaged less than one half of 1 percent of net interest income (figure 26).

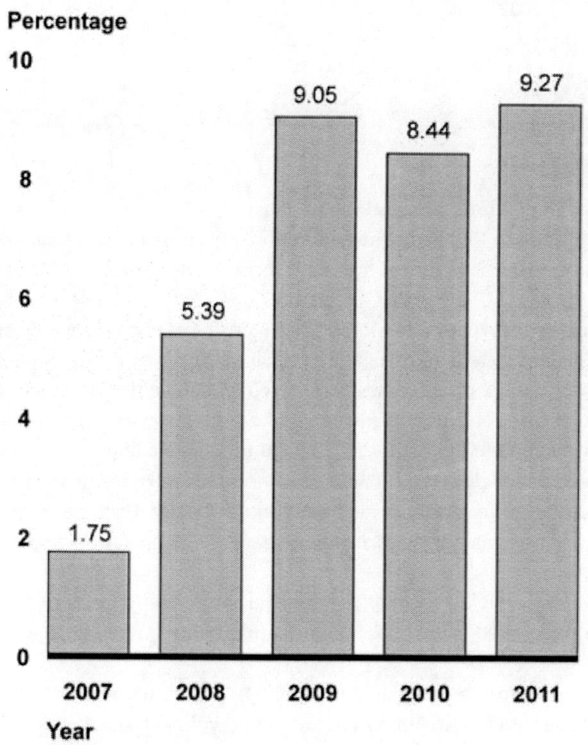

Source: GAO analysis of FDIC thrift financial report data.

Figure 25. Nonperforming Loans as a Percent of Total Loans for Medium-Size Failed Thrifts, 2007-2011.

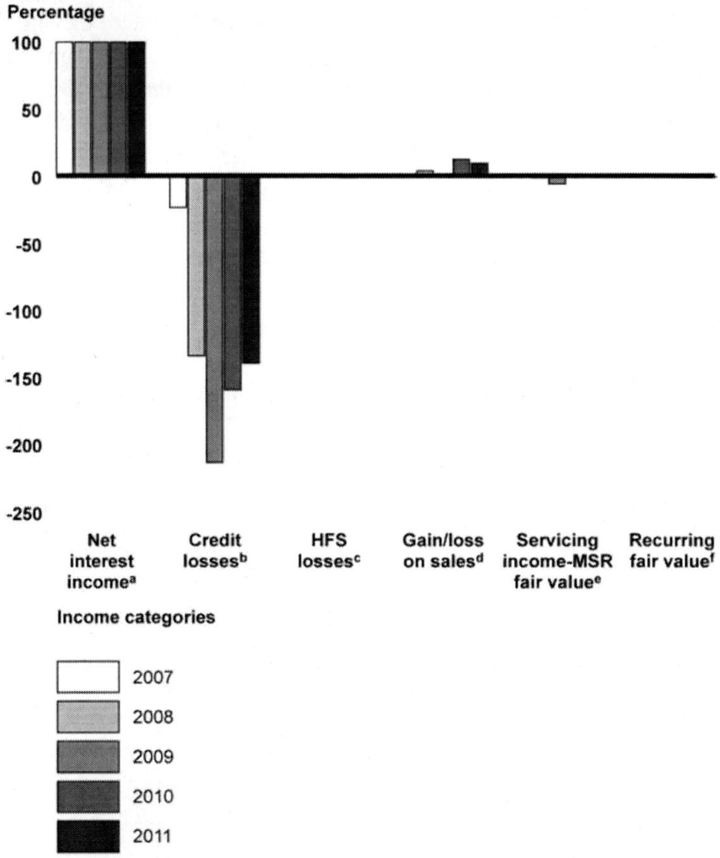

Source: GAO analysis of FDIC thrift financial report data.

[a] Net interest income reported in the thrift financial report, schedule statement of operations. We show net interest income as 100 percent and for each income category calculate its percentage of net interest income.

[b] Credit losses are based on provisions for losses on interest bearing assets as reported in the thrift financial report schedule statement of operations, which includes fair value losses recognized on foreclosed property and impairment losses recognized on debt and equity securities.

[c] The impact on income of losses on HFS loans is based on the lower-of-cost-or-fair-value adjustments made to HFS assets as reported in the thrift financial report schedule statement of operations of the thrift financial report, which does not include gains or losses recognized upon sale.

[d] The impact on income of gain/loss on sales is based on the sale of HFS assets and AFS securities as reported in the thrift financial report schedule statement of operations, which does not include impairment losses.

[e] The impact on income of servicing income is based on mortgage loan servicing fees and servicing amortization and valuation adjustments as reported in the thrift financial report schedule statement of operations.

[f] The impact on income of recurring fair value measurements is based on gains and losses on financial assets and liabilities carried at fair value as reported in the thrift financial report schedule statement of operations.

Figure 26. Income Categories as a Percentage of Net Interest Income for Medium- size Failed Thrifts, 2007-2011.

During that same time frame, the magnitude of the credit losses experienced by open medium-size thrifts was significantly less (figure 27).

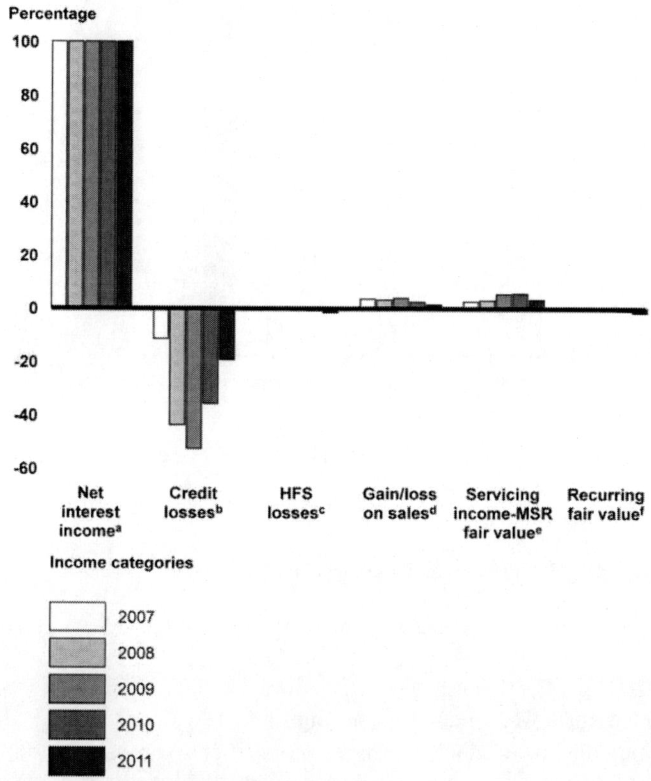

Source: GAO analysis of FDIC thrift financial report data.

[a] Net interest income reported in the thrift financial report, schedule statement of operations. We show net interest income as 100 percent and for each income category calculate its percentage of net interest income.

[b] Credit losses are based on provisions for losses on interest bearing assets as reported in the thrift financial report schedule statement of operations, which includes fair value losses recognized on foreclosed property and impairment losses recognized on debt and equity securities.

[c] The impact on income of losses on HFS loans is based on the lower-of-cost-or-fair-value adjustments made to HFS assets as reported in the thrift financial report schedule statement of operations of the thrift financial report, which does not include gains or losses recognized upon sale.

[d] The impact on income of gain/loss on sales is based on the sale of HFS assets and AFS securities as reported in the thrift financial report schedule statement of operations, which does not include impairment losses.

[e] The impact on income of servicing income is based on mortgage loan servicing fees and servicing amortization and valuation adjustments as reported in the thrift financial report schedule statement of operations.

[f] The impact on income of recurring fair value measurements is based on gains and losses on financial assets and liabilities carried at fair value as reported in the thrift financial report schedule statement of operations.

Figure 27. Income Categories as a Percentage of Net Interest Income for Medium- Size Open Thrifts, 2007-2011.

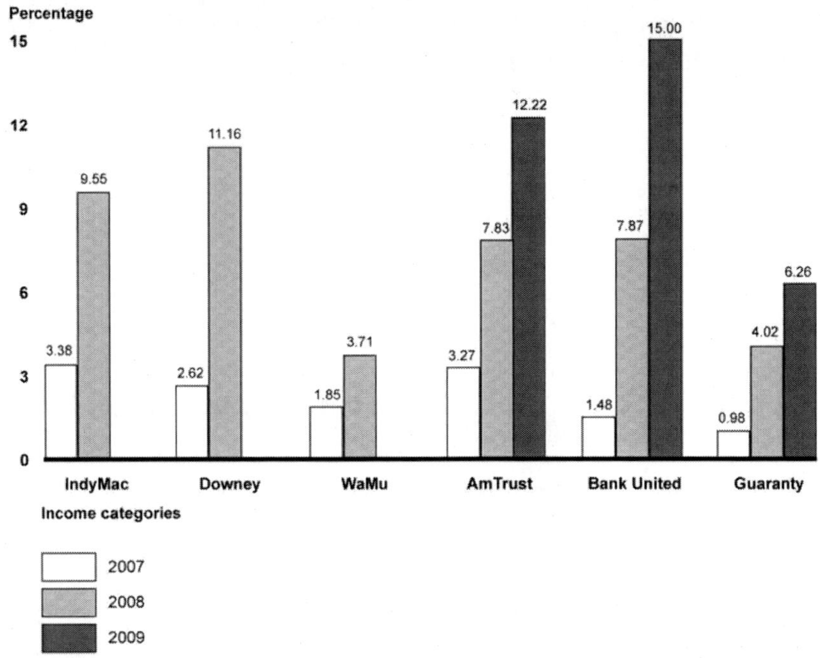

Source: GAO analysis of FDIC thrift financial report data.

Figure 28. Nonperforming Loans as a Percent age of Total Loans for Large Failed Thrifts, 2007-2009.

Large Failed Thrifts

The large failed thrifts' decrease in earnings and regulatory capital also was mostly driven by the rising levels of nonperforming loans. For example, in 2007 large thrifts' nonperforming loans averaged about 2 percent of their total assets compared with 7.36 percent in 2008, when WaMu, IndyMac, and Downey failed (figure 28). However, from 2008 through 2009, nonperforming loans for AmTrust, BankUnited, and Guaranty, the large thrifts that failed in 2009, grew from an average of almost 7.36 percent to over 10 percent.

The large credit losses largely drove the failed thrifts' decrease in earnings and regulatory capital. For example, from 2007 to 2009, credit losses accounted for on average close to 300 percent of net interest income while net losses from HFS assets and recurring fair averaged about 2 percent and 4.5 percent, respectively. During that same time period, the magnitude of credit losses at open thrifts of similar size averaged only about 33 percent (figures 29 and 30).

IndyMac

The recognition of incurred credit losses and losses recognized for the decrease in fair value of its portfolio of HFS loans, investment securities, and derivatives contributed to the decline in regulatory capital at IndyMac (figure 31). According to its 2007 Form 10-K, IndyMac was severely impacted by worsening credit conditions as home prices and home sales declined. As a result, it experienced a significant increase in delinquencies in many products, and thus recorded significant charges, related to credit risk in its HFI portfolio and other construction portfolios. In addition, IndyMac recorded significant fair value losses in its loans held for sale, investment- and noninvestment-grade securities and residual securities. Offsetting these decreases in fair value was an increase in fair value of the bank's MSRs.

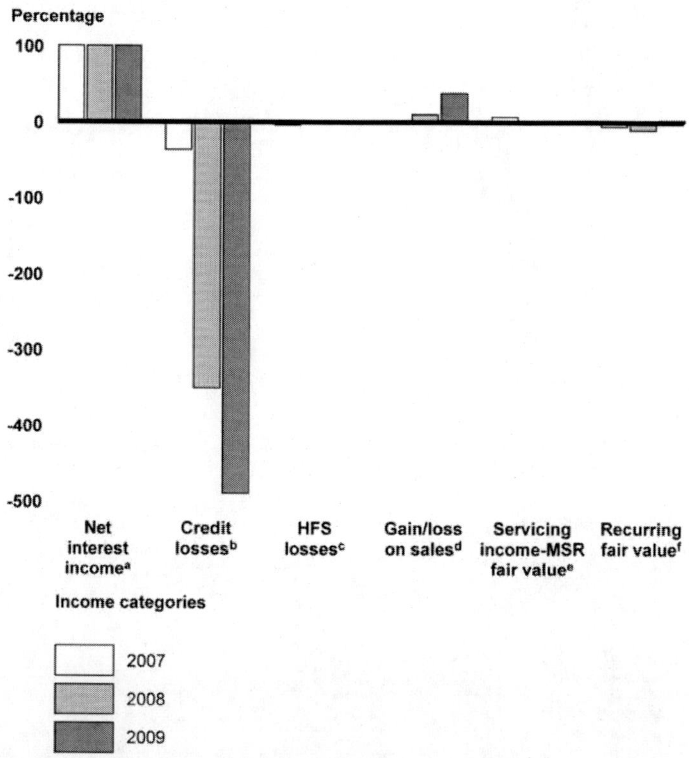

Source: GAO analysis of FDIC thrift financial report data.

[a] Net interest income reported in the thrift financial report, schedule statement of operations. We show net interest income as 100 percent and for each income category calculate its percentage of net interest income.

[b] Credit losses are based on provisions for losses on interest bearing assets as reported in the thrift financial report schedule statement of operations, which includes fair value losses recognized on foreclosed property and impairment losses recognized on debt and equity securities.

[c] The impact on income of losses on HFS loans is based on the lower-of-cost-or-fair-value adjustments made to HFS assets as reported in the thrift financial report schedule statement of operations of the thrift financial report, which does not include gains or losses recognized upon sale.

[d] The impact on income of gain/loss on sales is based on the sale of HFS assets and AFS securities as reported in the thrift financial report schedule statement of operations, which does not include impairment losses.

[e] The impact on income of servicing income is based on mortgage loan servicing fees and servicing amortization and valuation adjustments as reported in the thrift financial report schedule statement of operations.

[f] The impact on income of recurring fair value measurements is based on gains and losses on financial assets and liabilities carried at fair value as reported in the thrift financial report schedule statement of operations.

Figure 29. Income Categories as a Percentage of Net Interest Income for Large Failed Thrifts, 2007-2009.

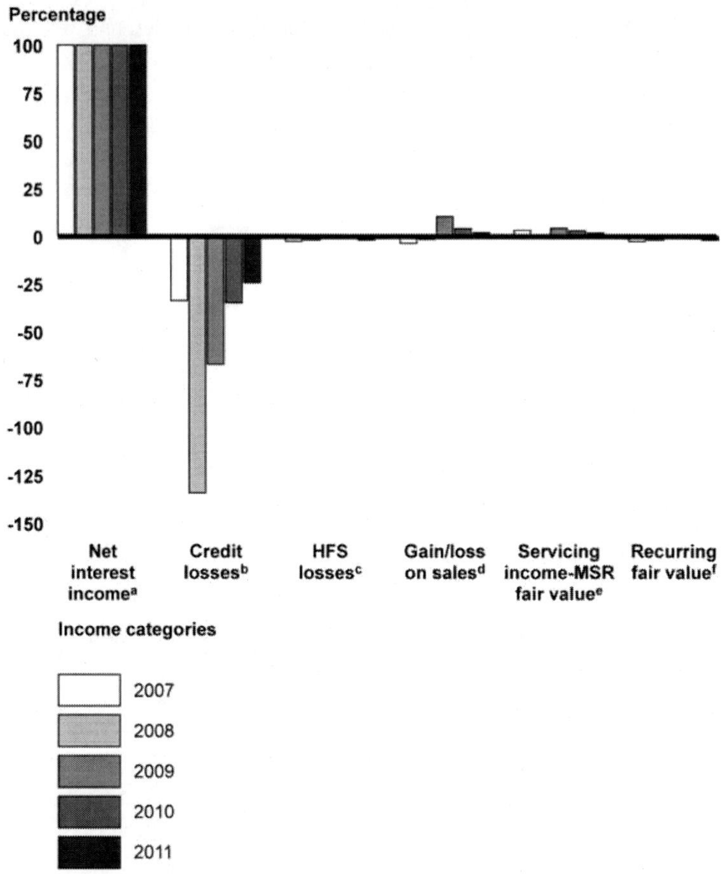

Source: GAO analysis of FDIC thrift financial report data.

[a] Net interest income reported in the thrift financial report, schedule statement of operations. We show net interest income as 100 percent and for each income category calculate its percentage of net interest income.

[b] Credit losses are based on provisions for losses on interest bearing assets as reported in the thrift financial report schedule statement of operations, which includes fair value losses recognized on foreclosed property and impairment losses recognized on debt and equity securities.

[c] The impact on income of losses on HFS loans is based on the lower-of-cost-or-fair-value adjustments made to HFS assets as reported in the thrift financial report schedule statement of operations of the thrift financial report, which does not include gains or losses recognized upon sale.

[d] The impact on income of gain/loss on sales is based on the sale of HFS assets and AFS securities as reported in the thrift financial report schedule statement of operations, which does not include impairment losses.

[e] The impact on income of servicing income is based on mortgage loan servicing fees and servicing amortization and valuation adjustments as reported in the thrift financial report schedule statement of operations.

[f] The impact on income of recurring fair value measurements is based on gains and losses on financial assets and liabilities carried at fair value as reported in the thrift financial report schedule statement of operations.

Figure 30. Income Categories as a Percentage of Net Interest Income for Large Open Thrifts, 2007-2011.

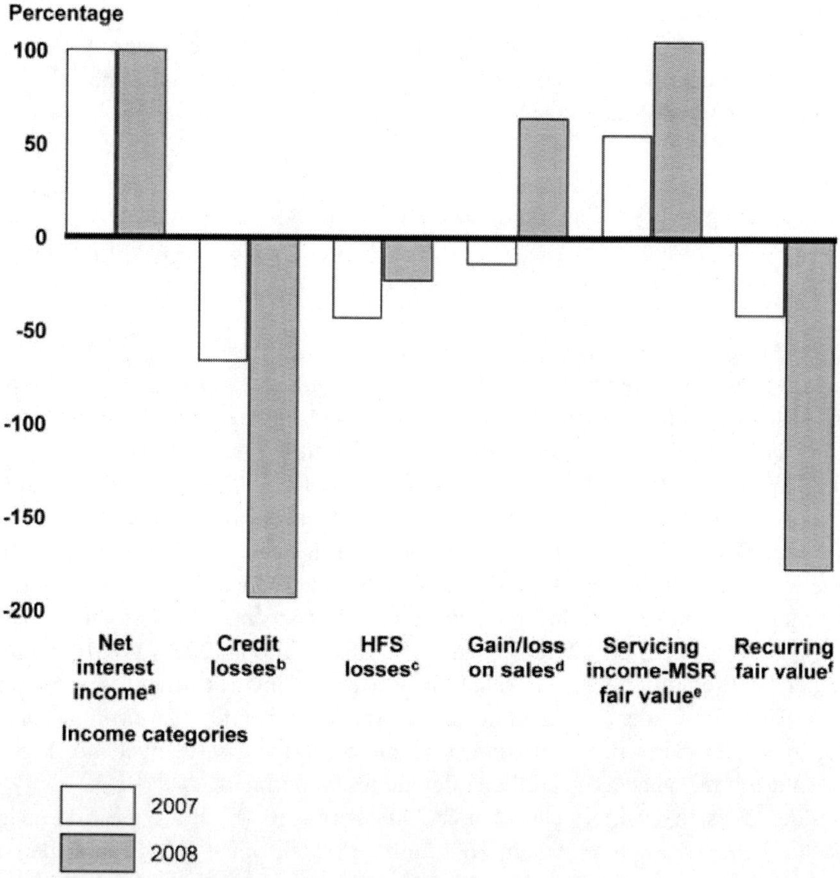

Source: GAO analysis of FDIC thrift financial report data.

[a] Net interest income reported in the thrift financial report, schedule statement of operations. We show net interest income as 100 percent and for each income category calculate its percentage of net interest income.

[b] Credit losses are based on provisions for losses on interest bearing assets as reported in the thrift financial report schedule statement of operations, which includes fair value losses recognized on foreclosed property and impairment losses recognized on debt and equity securities.

[c] The impact on income of losses on HFS loans is based on the lower-of-cost-or-fair-value adjustments made to HFS assets as reported in the thrift financial report schedule statement of operations of the thrift financial report, which does not include gains or losses recognized upon sale.

[d] The impact on income of gain/loss on sales is based on the sale of HFS assets and AFS securities as reported in the thrift financial report schedule statement of operations, which does not include impairment losses.

[e] The impact on income of servicing income is based on mortgage loan servicing fees and servicing amortization and valuation adjustments as reported in the thrift financial report schedule statement of operations.

[f] The impact on income of recurring fair value measurements is based on gains and losses on financial assets and liabilities carried at fair value as reported in the thrift financial report schedule statement of operations.

Figure 31. IndyMac Income Categories as a Percentage of Net Interest Income, 2007-2008.

IndyMac also recognized its largest write-downs for its noninvestment grade securities in 2007 and attributed a significant portion of these write- downs to incurred credit losses embedded in these securities. During 2008, IndyMac recognized additional charges for credit losses and related write-downs.

Downey

According to regulatory filings, credit losses were the most significant cause of decline in income at Downey, and there were no losses recognized for recurring fair value measurements (figure 32).

Washington Mutual

Figure 33 shows that credit losses were the most significant cause of declines in income at WaMu. Although WaMu recognized fair value losses during the review period, these losses were significantly less than the credit losses recognized during the same periods. In its 2007 Form 10-K, WaMu disclosed that it recorded a net loss for 2007 of $67 million compared with net income of $3.56 billion in 2006. It noted the decline was primarily the result of significant credit deterioration in its single- family residential mortgage loan portfolio and significant disruptions in the capital markets, including the sudden and severe contraction in secondary mortgage market liquidity for nonconforming residential loan products. Based on disclosures made it its 2007 annual regulatory filing, during 2007 WaMu recognized approximately $500 million of fair value losses for trading securities, which primarily consisted of below investment grade retained interests in credit card securitizations, and $200 million of losses for fair value write-downs of nonconforming residential mortgage loans HFS. In contrast, it recognized $3.1 billion of credit losses during that year.

According to its first and second quarter 2008 Forms 10-Q, during the first quarter of 2008, WaMu recognized approximately $600 million of fair value gains due to derivatives that economically hedged the fair value of MSRs, which were partially offset by fair value declines in the related MSRs. During the second quarter of 2008, WaMu recognized losses on the derivatives it used to economically hedge the fair value of MSRs, which again were partially offset by gains in the fair value of its MSRs. In addition to the fair value effects of hedging activities, WaMu recognized approximately $500 million of fair value losses for credit card retained interests and securities backed by Alt-A loans that were accounted for as trading securities during the first 6 months of 2008, which was significantly less than the $9.4 billion of credit losses recognized during the same period.

AmTrust

Credit losses resulting from increased nonperforming loan levels were the main driver for the decline in income at AmTrust (figure 34). In 2007, AmTrust's nonperforming loans were already over 3 percent of its total loans and had more than doubled in 2008. In 2009, AmTrust's nonperforming loans climbed to over 12 percent. The Treasury IG's material loss review for AmTrust identified significant losses in AmTrust's loan portfolio associated with its high concentrations of ADC loans and high-risk residential mortgage loans, including interest-only, reduced documentation, and subprime loans. As the levels on nonperforming loans increased rapidly in 2008 and 2009, AmTrust's net losses exceeded $513 million and $308 million, respectively. From 2007 to 2009, AmTrust's credit losses averaged close to 250 percent of net interest income. The substantial credit losses associated with AmTrust's growing nonperforming loans eroded the bank's earnings and capital. On November 4, 2009, OTS notified AmTrust that it had become significantly undercapitalized and required AmTrust to file a capital restoration plan by November 30, 2009. On December 1, 2009, AmTrust informed OTS that its efforts to raise capital were unsuccessful, and that there were no known near-term investors or acquirers.

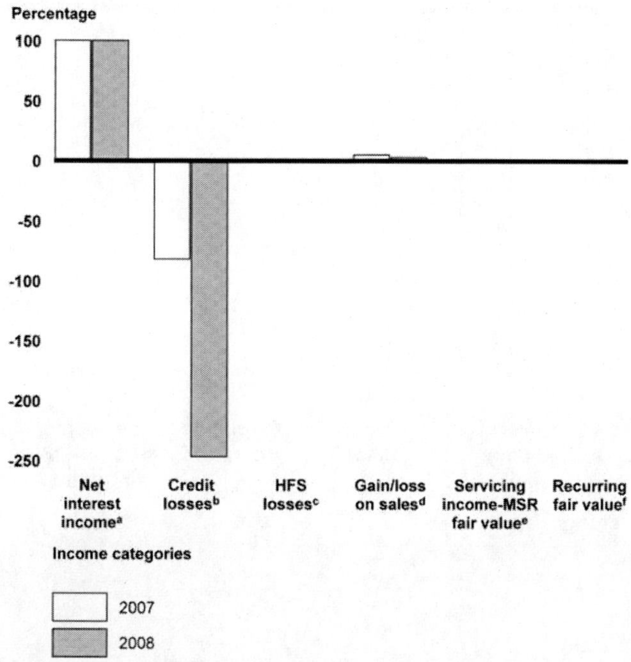

Source: GAO analysis of FDIC thrift financial report data.

[a] Net interest income reported in the thrift financial report, schedule statement of operations. We show net interest income as 100 percent and for each income category calculate its percentage of net interest income.

[b] Credit losses are based on provisions for losses on interest bearing assets as reported in the thrift financial report schedule statement of operations, which includes fair value losses recognized on foreclosed property and impairment losses recognized on debt and equity securities.

[c] The impact on income of losses on HFS loans is based on the lower-of-cost-or-fair-value adjustments made to HFS assets as reported in the thrift financial report schedule statement of operations of the thrift financial report, which does not include gains or losses recognized upon sale.

[d] The impact on income of gain/loss on sales is based on the sale of HFS assets and AFS securities as reported in the thrift financial report schedule statement of operations, which does not include impairment losses.

[e] The impact on income of servicing income is based on mortgage loan servicing fees and servicing amortization and valuation adjustments as reported in the thrift financial report schedule statement of operations.

[f] The impact on income of recurring fair value measurements is based on gains and losses on financial assets and liabilities carried at fair value as reported in the thrift financial report schedule statement of operations.

Figure 32. Downey Income Categories as a Percent of Net Interest Income, 2007-2008.

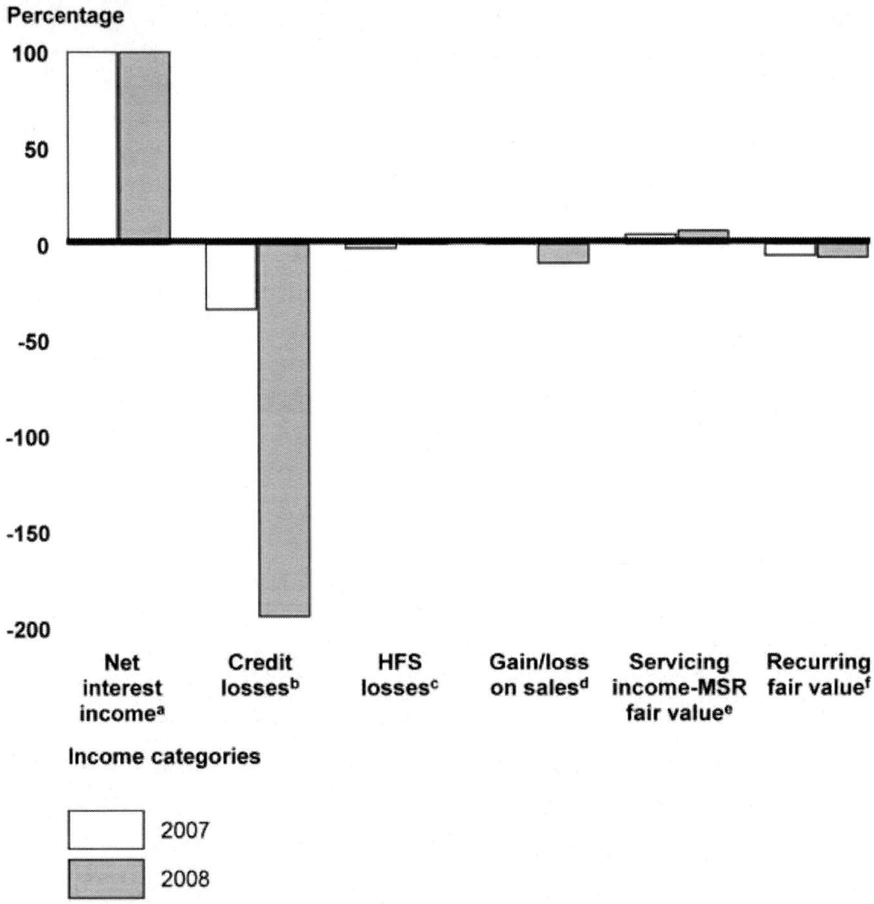

Source: GAO analysis of FDIC thrift financial report data.

[a] Net interest income reported in the thrift financial report, schedule statement of operations. We show net interest income as 100 percent and for each income category calculate its percentage of net interest income.

[b] Credit losses are based on provisions for losses on interest bearing assets as reported in the thrift financial report schedule statement of operations, which includes fair value losses recognized on foreclosed property and impairment losses recognized on debt and equity securities.

[c] The impact on income of losses on HFS loans is based on the lower-of-cost-or-fair-value adjustments made to HFS assets as reported in the thrift financial report schedule statement of operations of the thrift financial report, which does not include gains or losses recognized upon sale.

[d] The impact on income of gain/loss on sales is based on the sale of HFS assets and AFS securities as reported in the thrift financial report schedule statement of operations, which does not include impairment losses.

[e] The impact on income of servicing income is based on mortgage loan servicing fees and servicing amortization and valuation adjustments as reported in the thrift financial report schedule statement of operations.

[f] The impact on income of recurring fair value measurements is based on gains and losses on financial assets and liabilities carried at fair value as reported in the thrift financial report schedule statement of operations.

Figure 33. Washington Mutual Income Categories as a Percentage of Net Interest Income, 2007-2008.

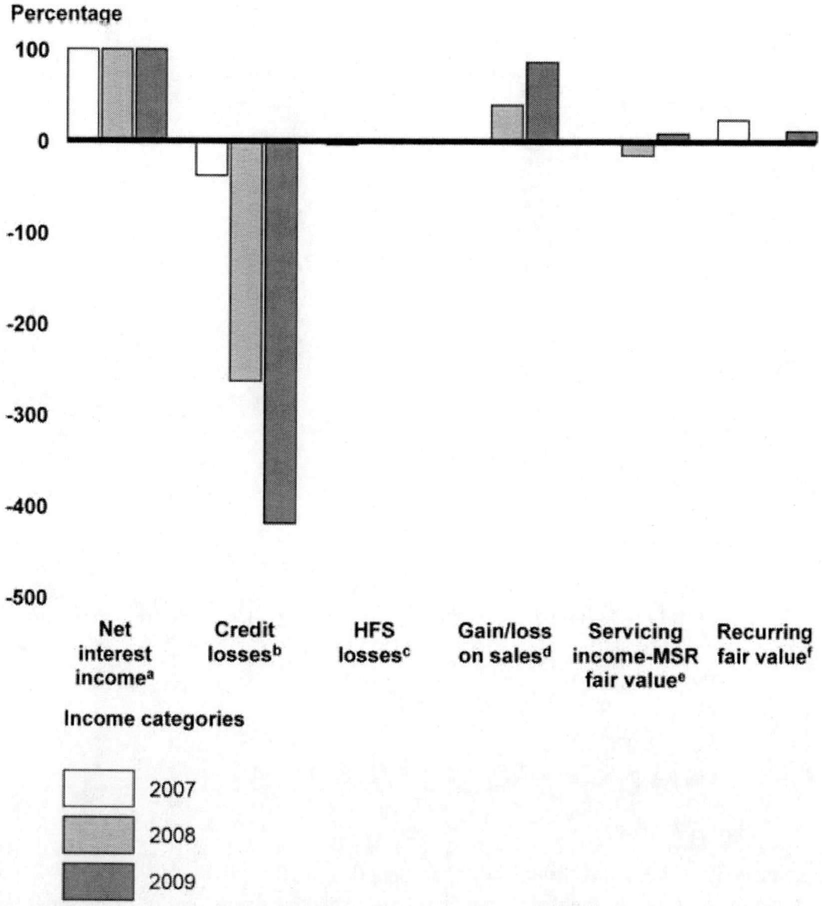

Source: GAO analysis of FDIC thrift financial report data.

[a] Net interest income reported in the thrift financial report, schedule statement of operations. We show net interest income as 100 percent and for each income category calculate its percentage of net interest income.

[b] Credit losses are based on provisions for losses on interest bearing assets as reported in the thrift financial report schedule statement of operations, which includes fair value losses recognized on foreclosed property and impairment losses recognized on debt and equity securities.

[c] The impact on income of losses on HFS loans is based on the lower-of-cost-or-fair-value adjustments made to HFS assets as reported in the thrift financial report schedule statement of operations of the thrift financial report, which does not include gains or losses recognized upon sale. dThe impact on income of gain/loss on sales is based on the sale of HFS assets and AFS securities as reported in the thrift financial report schedule statement of operations, which does not include impairment losses.

[e] The impact on income of servicing income is based on mortgage loan servicing fees and servicing amortization and valuation adjustments as reported in the thrift financial report schedule statement of operations.

[f] The impact on income of recurring fair value measurements is based on gains and losses on financial assets and liabilities carried at fair value as reported in the thrift financial report schedule statement of operations.

Figure 34. AmTrust Income Categories as a Percentage of Net Interest Income, 2007-2009.

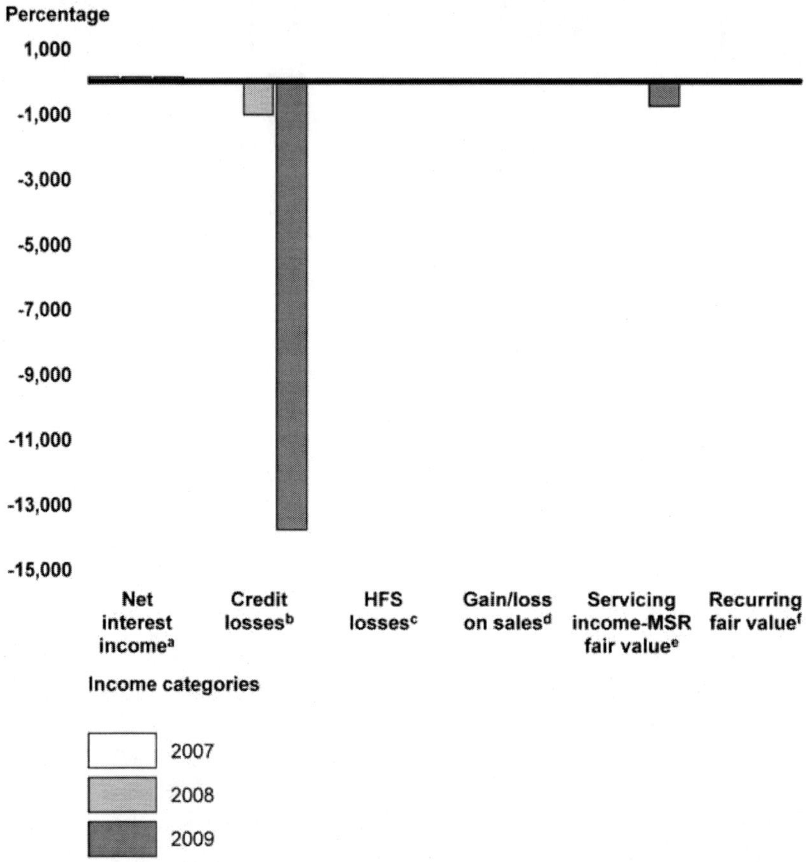

Source: GAO analysis of FDIC thrift financial report data.

[a] Net interest income reported in the thrift financial report, schedule statement of operations. We show net interest income as 100 percent and for each income category calculate its percentage of net interest income.

[b] Credit losses are based on provisions for losses on interest bearing assets as reported in the thrift financial report schedule statement of operations, which includes fair value losses recognized on foreclosed property and impairment losses recognized on debt and equity securities.

[c] The impact on income of losses on HFS loans is based on the lower-of-cost-or-fair-value adjustments made to HFS assets as reported in the thrift financial report schedule statement of operations of the thrift financial report, which does not include gains or losses recognized upon sale.

[d] The impact on income of gain/loss on sales is based on the sale of HFS assets and AFS securities as reported in the thrift financial report schedule statement of operations, which does not include impairment losses.

[e] The impact on income of servicing income is based on mortgage loan servicing fees and servicing amortization and valuation adjustments as reported in the thrift financial report schedule statement of operations.

[f] The impact on income of recurring fair value measurements is based on gains and losses on financial assets and liabilities carried at fair value as reported in the thrift financial report schedule statement of operations.

Figure 35. BankUnited Income Categories as a Percentage of Net Interest Income, 2007-2009.

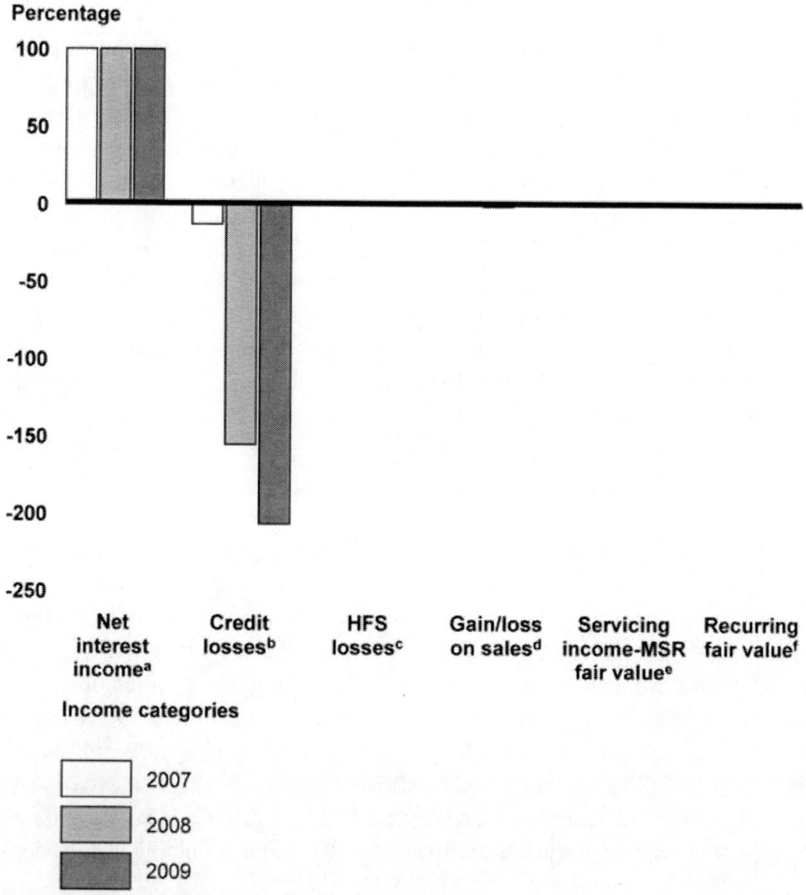

Source: GAO analysis of FDIC thrift financial report data.

[a] Net interest income reported in the thrift financial report, schedule statement of operations. We show net interest income as 100 percent and for each income category calculate its percentage of net interest income.

[b] Credit losses are based on provisions for losses on interest bearing assets as reported in the thrift financial report schedule statement of operations, which includes fair value losses recognized on foreclosed property and impairment losses recognized on debt and equity securities.

[c] The impact on income of losses on HFS loans is based on the lower-of-cost-or-fair-value adjustments made to HFS assets as reported in the thrift financial report schedule statement of operations of the thrift financial report, which does not include gains or losses recognized upon sale.

[d] The impact on income of gain/loss on sales is based on the sale of HFS assets and AFS securities as reported in the thrift financial report schedule statement of operations, which does not include impairment losses.

[e] The impact on income of servicing income is based on mortgage loan servicing fees and servicing amortization and valuation adjustments as reported in the thrift financial report schedule statement of operations.

[f] The impact on income of recurring fair value measurements is based on gains and losses on financial assets and liabilities carried at fair value as reported in the thrift financial report schedule statement of operations.

Figure 36. Guaranty Income Categories as a Percentage of Net Interest Income, 2007-2009.

BankUnited

Credit losses resulting from increased nonperforming loan levels were the main driver for the decline in income at BankUnited. In 2007, BankUnited nonperforming loans were just below 2 percent of its total loans. However, by December 2007, BankUnited's payment option adjustable rate mortgages increased to $7.5 billion, comprising 52 percent of its total assets. The rapid decline in real estate market resulted in the deterioration of the thrift's asset quality and a rise in nonperforming loans, which led to significant credit losses that diminished earnings. For example, in 2007, BankUnited's credit losses averaged about 27 percent of net interest income, but in 2008, BankUnited's credit losses substantially increased to an average of 1,000 percent of net interest income (figure 35). BankUnited's losses during the first quarter of 2009 almost reached 14,000 percent of net interest income. The increase in BankUnited's nonperforming real estate loans in all categories, totaling $1.8 billion as of March 31, 2009, resulted in increases in its loan loss allowance and large losses that significantly diminished the thrift's earnings and capital.

Guaranty

Large credit losses resulting from increased nonperforming loan levels coupled with significant losses in nonagency mortgage-backed securities were the main drivers for the decline in income and resulting failure at Guaranty. Guaranty held a substantial level of nontraditional mortgage loans with option ARM features concentrated in volatile real estate markets such as California, Florida, and Arizona. In its regulatory filing for third quarter 2008, Guaranty disclosed that credit losses for nonperforming loans increased from $33 million in December 2007 to $58 million in March of 2008, and to $99 million in June of 2008. From 2008 to 2009, Guaranty's credit losses averaged 181 percent of net interest income (figure 36). In 2008, Guaranty also sustained a $1.2 billion loss in the value of its $3.5 billion nonagency mortgage backed securities portfolio. The mounting losses depleted its capital.

APPENDIX VI. ANALYSIS OF HFI LOANS COMPARED TO HFS LOANS OF LARGE BANKS

Loans held for investment (HFI) recorded at amortized cost represent for most banks the largest proportion of their assets between 2007 and 2011. Conversely, loans held for sale (HFS) represented a much smaller share of assets for most of the larger banks and thrifts. However, as a result of severe contraction in the secondary market for mortgage-backed securities in 2007, several of the large banks and thrifts that failed between 2008 and 2011 determined that a significant amount of real estate loans that had been designated as HFS prior to the market disruption were no longer held for sale and transferred the loans to HFI. HFI loans are those loans that the bank has the intent and ability to hold for the foreseeable future or until maturity or payoff.[104] Failed institutions' primary reason for reclassifying HFS loans to HFI was to better reflect their prevailing intentions in light of the severity and duration of unfavorable secondary market conditions that existed during the crisis, especially if they did not anticipate liquidity to return in the foreseeable future. In addition, HFS loans are more susceptible to earnings volatility particularly when real estate values are falling because the accounting standards require that these loans be carried on the balance sheet at the lower of cost or fair value, with any declines reflected in current earnings.[105] Loans held for investment, by contrast, are reported on the balance sheet at amortized cost, net of an impairment allowance for estimated credit losses (loan loss allowance). Impairment on HFI loans must be recognized when credit losses are determined to probable and estimable. An increase to the loan loss allowance results in a charge to expenses, termed a provision for loan losses, which reduces current earnings. We discuss five large commercial banks and thrifts that failed between 2008 and 2011 that reclassified significant amounts of HFS loans to HFI during the financial crisis: AmTrust Bank (AmTrust); IndyMac Bank (IndyMac); Washington Mutual Bank (Wamu); Downey Savings and Loan, FB (Downey); and United Commercial Bank (UCB).

AmTrust

From the first quarter of 2007 to the first quarter of 2008, AmTrust's HFS loans ranged between about 12 percent to 21 percent of its total assets (figure 37). In July 2008, AmTrust began curtailing the volume of its HFS loans, which included a large volume of acquisition, development, and construction loans.

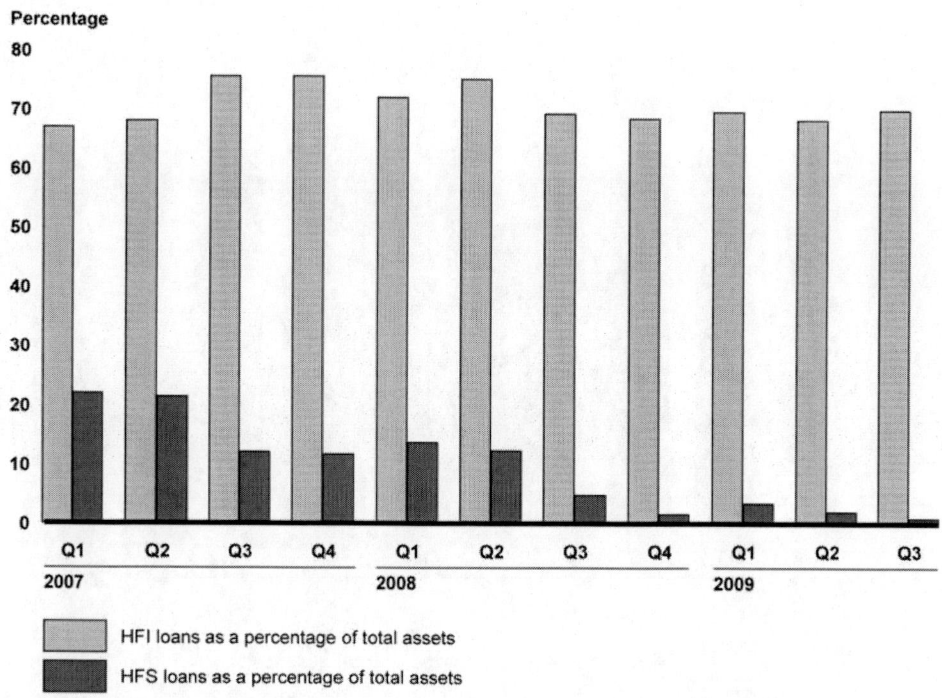

Source: GAO analysis of FDIC thrift financial report data.

Figure 37. Amtrust Volume of HFI Loans Compared to HFS Loans as a Percentage of Total Assets.

IndyMac

IndyMac was the failed bank with the largest share of HFS loans as a percent of its total assets. From the first quarter of 2007 to the third quarter of 2007, IndyMac's HFS loans ranged between about 36 percent to 42 percent of its total assets (figure 38). However, as of the fourth quarter of 2007, it started curtailing the volume of its HFS loans, which included significant amounts of payment option adjustable rate mortgage loans. In its regulatory filing with the Securities Exchange Commission (SEC), IndyMac reported that in the fourth quarter of 2007, it transferred HFS loans with an original cost basis of $10.9 billion to HFI loans as it no longer intended to sell these loans given the extreme disruption in the secondary mortgage market.

WaMu

From the first quarter of 2007 to the fourth quarter of 2007, WaMu's HFS loans declined from 8.5 percent to 1.7 percent of its total assets (figure 39). The company reported in its regulatory filings with the SEC that it transferred $17 billion of real estate loans designated as HFS loans to its HFI loan portfolio, which represented substantially all of its loans designated as HFS prior to the market disruption.

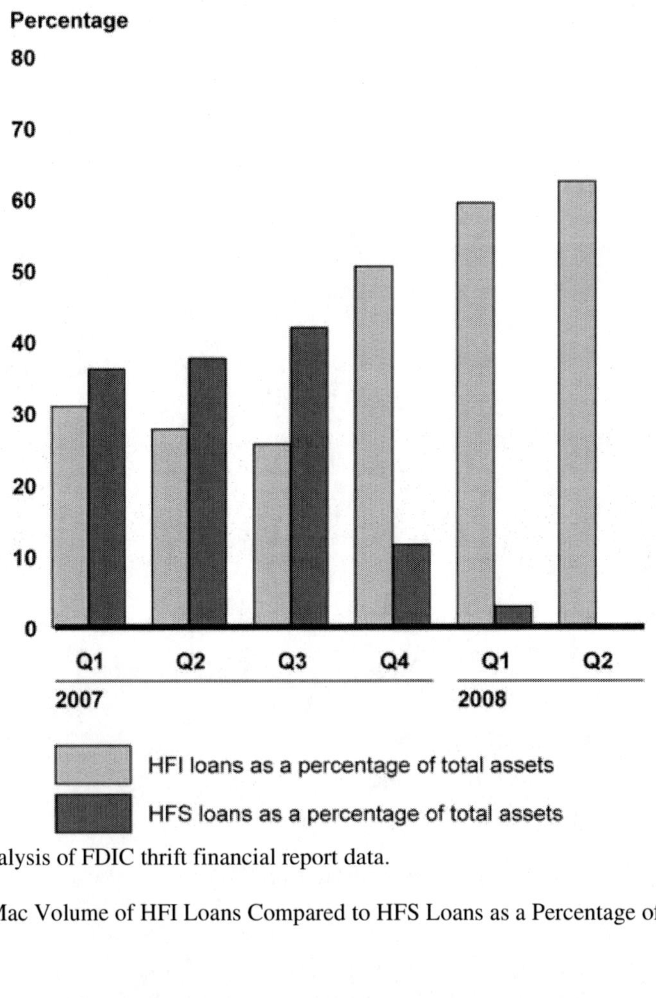

Source: GAO analysis of FDIC thrift financial report data.

Figure 38. IndyMac Volume of HFI Loans Compared to HFS Loans as a Percentage of Total Assets.

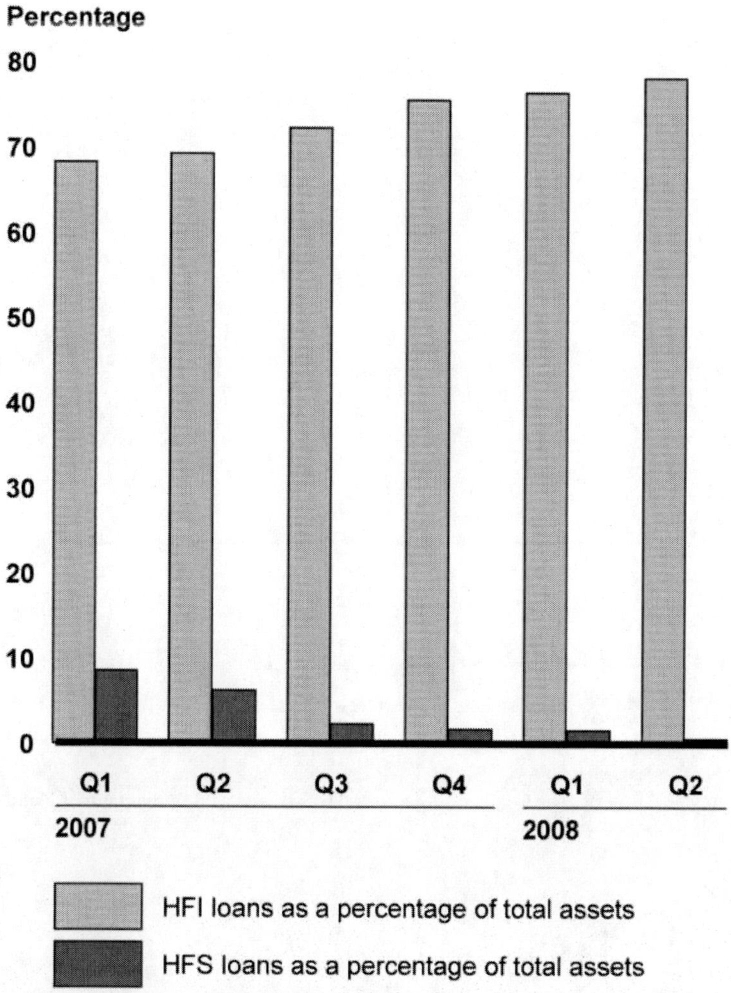

Source: GAO analysis of FDIC thrift financial report data.

Figure 39. WaMu Volume of HFI Loans Compared to HFS Loans as a Percent age of Total Assets.

Downey

From first quarter of 2007 to third quarter of the same year, Downey's volume of HFS loans declined from 1.8 percent to 0.6 percent (figure 40). Downey disclosed in a regulatory filing dated August 2007 that total loans and mortgage-backed securities, including those designated HFS, declined $818 million during the second quarter of 2007to a total of $12.4 billion. The company also disclosed in regulatory filings that during the third quarter of 2008, loans HFI increased $119 million while loans HFS declined $78 million.

UCB

From first quarter 2007 to first quarter of 2008, UCB's HFS loans ranged between 0.9 percent and 1.7 percent of total assets (figure 41). In the second quarter of 2008 it began curtailing its HFS portfolio.

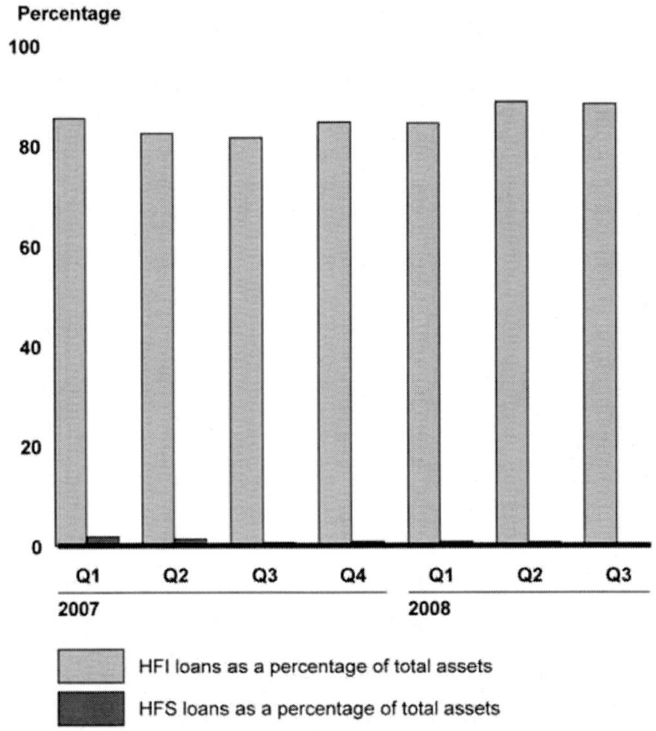

Source: GAO analysis of FDIC thrift financial report data.

Figure 40. Downey Volume of HFI Loans compared to HFS Loans as a Percentage of Total Assets.

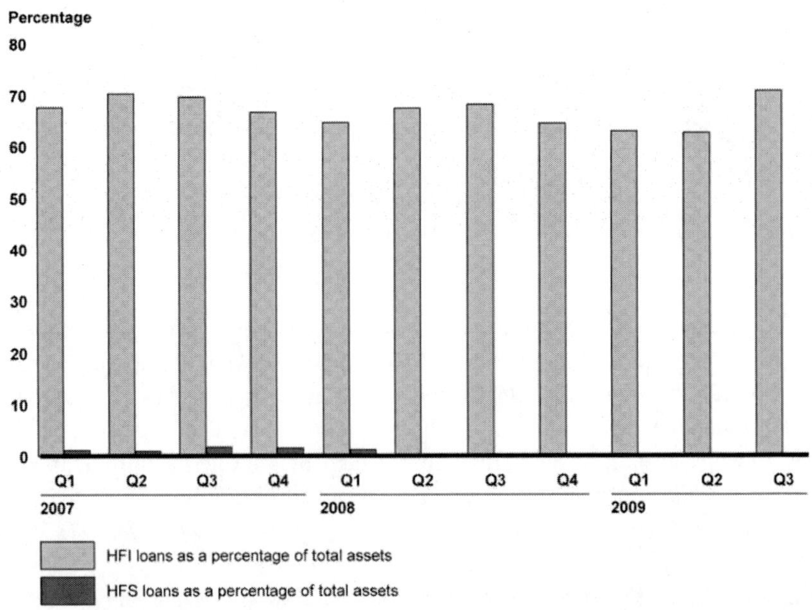

Source: GAO analysis of FDIC call report data.

Figure 41. UCB Volume of HFI Loans Compared to HFS Loans as a Percentage of Total Assets.

APPENDIX VII. GAO ANALYSIS OF NET CREDIT EXTENDED BY FAILING BANKS AND ACQUIRING BANKS

To analyze the impact of bank failures on credit availability, we estimated net credit extended by failing banks in the quarters leading up to failure and by acquiring banks in the quarters following acquisition of a failed bank. We used the change in the size of a bank's loan portfolio over a quarter to measure the net amount of credit it extended over that quarter. Several factors affect the size of a bank's loan portfolio. It grows when the bank makes new loans or purchases existing loans. It shrinks when the bank charges off a delinquent loan; when the bank forecloses on a delinquent real estate loan, charges off the difference between the market and face values of the loan, and reclassifies the collateral as "other real estate owned;" and when a the bank sells or securitizes a loan. It also changes when loans are paid down, extended, or repurchased. Thus, the change in the size of a bank's loan portfolio is a measure of the net effect of increases in the amount of credit a bank is extending (e.g., from making new loans or purchasing loans) and reductions in the amount of credit a bank is extending (e.g., from charging-off delinquent loans or selling loans).

We used FDIC and Federal Financial Institutions Examination Council (FFIEC data on FDIC-insured commercial banks and savings banks (banks) over the period from 2006 through 2011. We first used an econometric model to estimate the relationship between net credit extended by banks and the characteristics of banks associated with the likelihood of failure—capital adequacy; asset quality; earnings; liquidity; ADC lending; nonfarm, nonresidential real estate lending; commercial real estate lending not secured by real estate; multifamily real estate lending; brokered deposits funding; and size. We included indicators for each quarter to control for factors affecting net credit extension that are common to all banks at the same time, such as the regulatory environment, the state of the market for bank products and services, and the condition of the overall economy. We have observations on each bank over one or more quarters (a panel) so we also included indicators for each bank to control for unobserved characteristics of banks that do not change over time. We estimated the parameters of the model using observations on all banks. We then used the estimated parameters along with observations on failed banks and acquiring banks to predict net credit extended by failing banks over the 2 years preceding failure and to predict net credit extended by acquiring banks over the period from one quarter preceding acquisition of a failed bank to six quarters following the acquisition of a failed bank. To examine the robustness of our results, we repeated our analysis separately for small and medium-sized banks. The number of large failed banks was not large enough for us to separately analyze large banks. We used this approach because it allowed us to connect net credit extended by failed and acquiring banks to the characteristics of the balance sheets, rather than just their status as failed or acquiring banks, as these categories may not fully reflect the factors associated with net credit extension. In addition, our approach allowed us to improve our estimates by incorporating banks that neither failed nor acquired a failed bank as a control group since they may have had balance sheet characteristics that were similar to the characteristics of failed or acquiring banks for a period of time.

As shown in table 25, our econometric model suggests that many of the characteristics that help explain the likelihood of failure also help explain net credit extended by banks. Our estimates suggest that capital adequacy and asset quality were associated with more net credit, while ADC lending was associated with less net credit, all else being equal. In addition, higher earnings, nonfarm, nonresidential real estate lending, multifamily real estate lending, and size were also associated with less net credit, all else being equal.

Our analysis of small banks produced estimates that are generally similar to the results of our baseline analysis of all banks. For medium-sized banks, our estimates suggest that net credit was positively associated with asset quality and negatively associated with size, but it was not significantly associated with any other characteristics.

Table 25. Estimated Effect of Bank Characteristics on Net Credit, 2006-2011

Characteristic	All banks	Small banks	Medium-sized banks
Capital adequacy	2.005[a]	2.119[a]	0.221
	(0.0720)	(0.0729)	(0.289)
Asset quality	0.76[a]	0.738[a]	0.617[a]
	(0.0493)	(0.0503)	(0.176)
Earnings	-4.168[a]	-4.407[a]	0.376
	(0.314)	(0.336)	(0.644)
Liquidity	0.0133	0.0215	-0.0706
	(0.0199)	(0.0213)	(0.0565)
ADC lending	-0.467[a]	-0.489[a]	-0.0203
	(0.0358)	(0.0378)	(0.0878)
Non-farm, non-residential real estate lending	-0.555[a]	-0.549[a]	-0.170
	(0.0339)	(0.0342)	(0.153)
Multifamily real estate lending	-0.818[a]	-0.854[a]	-0.339
	(0.133)	(0.141)	(0.425)
Commercial real estate, construction, and land development loans not secured by real estate	-0.327 [a]	-0.315[a]	-0.228
	(0.0844)	(0.0817)	(0.619)
Brokered deposits	0.0208	0.00301	0.111
	(0.0301)	(0.0254)	(0.0707)
Size	-6.046[a]	-3.926[a]	-13.70[a]
	(0.941)	(0.979)	(2.302)
Observations	168,225	155,664	10,520
R-squared	10,520	0.406	0.060
Number of banks	8,307	7,644	548

Source: GAO analysis of data from FDIC and the Federal Financial Institutions Examinations Council.

Notes: This table shows the estimated parameters and standard errors for a regression of net credit extended by banks on capital adequacy, asset quality, earnings, liquidity, ADC lending, nonfarm, nonresidential real estate lending, multifamily real estate lending, commercial real estate lending not secured by real estate, brokered deposits, size, indicators for each quarter, and indicators for each bank. Parameters were estimated separately using observations on all banks, on small banks only, and on medium-sized banks only. Parameters for quarter and bank indicators are not reported. We used t-tests to determine statistical significance.

[a] Significant at the 1 percent level.

We used the estimates from our econometric model to predict net credit extended by failing banks in the eight quarters preceding failure and by acquiring banks from the quarter preceding failure to six quarters following the acquisition of a failed bank (table 26). To do so, we first calculated the predicted value of net credit for every bank in every quarter using the actual values of the independent variables for each observation and the parameters we estimated with our baseline econometric model for all banks. Next, we calculated the average of the predicted values for observations on failed banks in the last quarter prior to failure to produce the average net credit extended by failing banks in the last quarter prior to failure. Similarly, we calculated the average of the predicted values for observations on failed banks two quarters prior to failure, the average of the predicted values of the observations on failed banks three quarters prior to failure, and so on up to eight quarters prior to failure. We also calculated the average of the predicted values for observations on acquiring banks one quarter prior to acquisition of a failed bank, the average of the predicted values for observations on acquiring banks the quarter they acquired a failed bank, the average of the predicted values for observations on acquiring banks the quarter after they acquired a failed bank, and so on up to six quarters after acquiring a failed bank.

Finally, we calculated the average of the predicted values for observations on open, nonacquiring banks to produce average predicted net credit for these banks for all quarters. We repeated these steps using only observations on small banks along with the estimated parameters for small banks and also using only observations on medium-sized banks along with the estimated parameters for medium-sized banks.

Our estimates suggest that, on average, net credit extended by banks that failed in the period from 2008 through 2011 decreased continuously over the eight quarters prior to failure and actually became negative about five quarters prior to failure, indicating that failing banks were contracting the sizes of their loan portfolios and reducing the overall amount of credit they were providing. Our estimates also suggest that net credit extended by banks that acquired failed banks during the same period generally decreased immediately after the acquisition and then partially recovered, but remained positive. Acquiring banks continued to expand the amount of credit they were making available, albeit more slowly than they did prior to the acquisition of the failed bank.

The results of our separate analysis of small and medium-size banks are broadly similar to the results of our baseline analysis of all banks, with the exception of medium-size acquiring banks. On average, net credit extended by both small and medium-size failing banks declined continuously in the quarters preceding failure and became negative 4-5 quarters prior to failure. On average, net credit extended by small acquiring banks declined immediately following the acquisition of a failed bank and then partially recovered, but remained positive except in the first quarter following the acquisition. For medium-size acquiring banks, on average, net credit appears to have declined more slowing following the acquisition of a failed bank, remaining positive for several quarters but actually becoming negative around a year after acquiring the failed bank. Overall, however, our estimates suggest that failing banks extended less and less credit as they failed and that that acquiring banks continued to extend additional credit after they acquired failed banks.

The results of this analysis are subject to several limitations and should be interpreted with caution. As discussed above, we used the change in the size of a bank's loan portfolio over a quarter to measure the net amount of credit it extended over the quarter. This measure reflects the net effects of new loan originations, loan purchases, charge-offs, loan sales and securitizations, and other factors, and does not reflect only the extension of new credit. Our results likely reflect both factors that are generally associated with net credit extended by banks and factors that are specific to the particular time period we analyzed. Thus, the extent to which our results can be generalized to other time periods is limited. Furthermore, our results reflect average relationships between bank characteristics and net credit extended by banks for all of the observations we used. As such, they may not reflect the particular circumstances of any one bank or local community. Finally, we note that the list of characteristics we analyzed is meant to highlight important characteristics of banks that are related to the provision of credit, but many other factors—including demand for credit by borrowers— play a role in the amount of credit a bank extends and our list of characteristics is not exhaustive.

Table 26. Estimated Net Credit Extended by Failing, Acquiring, and Nonfailing, Nonacquiring Banks, 2008-2011

	Failing banks, quarters prior to failure (percent)								Average net credit extended by non-failing, non-acquiring banks (percent)
	8	**7**	**6**	**5**	**4**	**3**	**2**	**1**	—
All banks	3.6	2.2	0.9	-0.4	-2.1	-4.4	-6.3	-8.4	2.8
Small banks	3.6	2.2	0.8	-0.5	-2.2	-4.6	-6.8	-8.8	2.8
Medium-sized banks	3.9	3	1.9	1.1	-0.3	-1.2	-3.5	-4.2	2.5
	Acquiring banks, quarters following failed bank acquisition (percent)								
	-1	**0**	**1**	**2**	**3**	**4**	**5**	**6**	—
All banks	5.2	5.0	0.1	1.9	1.3	0.8	1.3	0.9	2.8
Small banks	7.0	6.4	-1.4	1.5	1.5	1.4	1.6	1.2	2.8
Medium-sized banks	3.3	3.6	2.2	1.4	0.0	-1.4	-0.8	-1.7	2.5

Source: GAO analysis of data from FDIC and the Federal Financial Institutions Examinations Council.

Note: Table cells contain average predicted net credit extended by failing banks in quarters prior to failure and by acquiring banks in quarters following acquisition of a failed bank. We used an econometric model to estimate the relationship between net credit extended by banks and the characteristics of banks associated with the likelihood of failure—capital adequacy, asset quality, earnings, liquidity, ADC lending, nonfarm, nonresidential real estate lending, commercial real estate lending not secured by real estate, multifamily real estate lending, brokered deposits funding, and size. We included indicators for each quarter to control for factors affecting the likelihood of failure that are common to all banks at the same time and we included indicators for each bank to control for unobserved characteristics of banks that do not change over time. We estimated the parameters of the model using observations on all banks. We used the estimated parameters along with observations on failed banks and acquiring banks to predict average net credit extended by failing banks over the two years preceding failure and to predict net credit extended by acquiring banks over the period from one quarter preceding to six quarters following the acquisition of a failed bank. We used the estimated parameters along with observations on open, non-acquiring banks to predict average net credit extended by these banks in all quarters. We repeated this procedure using only observations on small banks and using only observations on medium-sized banks.

APPENDIX VIII. GAO ANALYSIS OF THE EFFECT OF BANK FAILURES ON STATE ECONOMIC CONDITIONS

To assess the relationship between bank failures and overall economic conditions in a state, we used an econometric model to analyze the relationship between bank failures, income, unemployment, and real estate prices for U.S. states and the District of Columbia (states) using data for the period from 1994 through 2011. That is, we estimated four sets of relationships: (1) the relationship between personal income and past values of personal income, past values of the unemployment rate, past values of the house price index, and past values of failed banks' share of deposits; (2) the relationship between the unemployment rate and past values of the unemployment rate, past values of personal income, past values of the house price index, and past values of failed banks' share of deposits; (3) the relationship between the house price index and past values of the house price index, past values of personal income, past values of the unemployment rate, and past values of failed banks' share of deposits; and (4) the relationship between failed banks' share of deposits and past values of failed banks' share of deposits, past values of personal income, past values of the unemployment rate, and past values of the house price index.

Limitations

The results of our analysis are limited by several factors and thus should be interpreted with caution. First, we used the concept of Granger causality to determine the extent to which variables are associated with each other. However, Granger causality only measures whether the current value of one variable is correlated with past values of another variable and it does not imply that one variable is the result of or the effect of another variable. In addition, our results likely reflect factors specific to the time period we analyzed and may not apply to other time periods. Second, our results likely reflect relationships among the variables at the state level and may not generalize to other geographic units—either larger units, such as a nation, or smaller units, such as cities or counties. Furthermore, our results reflect average relationships among the variables and thus may not apply to the specific circumstances of any one state. Finally, the specific group of variables we analyzed was chosen to highlight particular relationships and may not contain all of the variables that contribute to explaining personal income, unemployment, house prices, or failed bank deposits in states.

Analysis

We measured bank failures in a state as the fraction of deposits in a state that were in banks that failed during the past year. We measured income in a state using state personal income, adjusted for inflation. We measured unemployment in a state using the unemployment rate. We measured real estate prices using house price indices for single-family detached properties with conventional conforming mortgages. For each variable, we estimated the relationship between the variable, its past values, and past values of the other three variables. We used a technique that controls for time-invariant characteristics of states, that controls for features of the national economy that affect all states at the same time, and that allows for the possibility that all four variables are jointly determined and affected by each other. We then estimated the likelihood that the past values of each variable help explain current values of the other variables.

We used data on the price level, state gross domestic product, and state personal income from the Bureau of Economic Analysis; on state unemployment rates from the Bureau of Labor Statistics; on deposits and failures of commercial banks, savings banks, savings associations, and insured branches of foreign banks (banks) from the Federal Deposit Insurance Corporation (FDIC); and on house prices in states from the Federal Housing Finance Administration (FHFA) for the period from 1994 to 2011 for U.S. states and the District of Columbia (states).

We used linear dynamic panel models to estimate relationships among bank failures, income, unemployment, and house prices in states. Linear dynamic panel models are appropriate for analysis of panels with a large number of cross-section units and a small number of time periods, dynamic dependent variables that depend on past values of themselves, potentially endogenous explanatory variables, fixed cross-section effects, and heteroskedasticity and autocorrelation within cross-section units but not across them. We separately estimated the parameters of four equations—one each for failed bank deposits, personal income, unemployment, and house prices—in which the dependent variable is a linear function of past values of itself, as well as past values of the other three variables, indicators for each state, and indicators for each year. For example, for the personal income equation, personal income was the dependent variable and was a linear function of past values of personal income, past values of unemployment, failed bank deposits, and house prices, indicators for each state, and indicators for each year. Then, we used Granger causality tests to assess the extent to which the dependent variable is "Granger caused" by the other three variables in the sense that past values of the other three variables help explain the current value of the dependent variable. For example, for the personal income equation, we used Granger causality tests to assess whether past values of unemployment, failed bank deposits, and house prices help explain the current value of personal income. We chose the number of past values by starting with six past values and then using F-tests to determine if fewer past values were appropriate. We also examined our models for the presence of first-order autocorrelation. Linear dynamic panel models use lagged values of variables as instruments. However, instrument proliferation can overfit endogenous variables and fail to expunge their endogenous components. To address this limitation, we examined specifications with the default number of instruments and with a severely reduced number of instruments.

In general, our results suggest that bank failures in a state were more likely to affect its real estate sector than its labor market or overall economy (table 27). We did not find evidence of a significant relationship between personal income in a state and failed banks' share of deposits in a state. Our results suggest that failed banks' share of deposits in a state did not "cause" personal income in a state in the sense that past values of failed banks' share of deposits do not help explain the current level of personal income. Similarly, past values of personal income do not help explain the current value of failed banks' share of deposits.

To the extent that there was a relationship between the unemployment rate and failed banks' share of deposits in a state, it appears that the unemployment rate had more bearing on failed banks' share of deposits than vice versa. Past values of unemployment appear to partially explain the current value of failed banks' share of deposits, but failed banks' share of deposits did not help explain the current value of unemployment.

Finally, failed banks' share of deposits and the house price index in a state appear to be significantly related to each other. Past values of failed banks' share of deposits appeared to help explain the current value of the house price index in a state, and vice versa. Altogether, these results suggest that the effects of bank failures on a state's economy were more likely to appear in the real estate sector and less likely to appear in the labor market or in the broader economy.

Table 27. Granger Causality Tests for Personal Income, Unemployment, House Price, and Failed Bank Deposit Equations, 1994-2011

Equation	Granger causality test: Personal income	Unemployment	House prices	Failed bank deposits
Panel A. Default number of instruments				
Personal income (4 lags, 323 instruments)	—	33.44 (0.00)	32.33 (0.00)	0.90 (0.93)
Unemployment (4 lags, 323 instruments)	12.63 (0.01)	—	36.93 (0.00)	7.07 (0.13)
House prices (6 lags, 250 instruments)	15.85 (0.02)	15.17 (0.02)	—	31.71 (0.00)
Failed bank deposits (6 lags, 241 instruments)	8.90 (0.18)	15.28 (0.02)	27.46 (0.00)	—
Panel B. Restricted instrument count				
Personal income (3 lags, 60 instruments)	—	9.45 (0.02)	4.70 (0.20)	4.11 (0.25)
Unemployment (4 lags, 56 instruments)	12.69 (0.01)	—	3.14 (0.54)	1.54 (0.82)
House prices (4 lags, 56 instruments)	7.10 (0.13)	15.00 (0.01)	—	12.86 (0.01)
Failed bank deposits (2 lags, 65 instruments)	2.27 (0.32)	6.55 (0.04)		—

Source: GAO analysis of data from the Bureau of Economic Analysis, the Bureau of Labor Statistics, FDIC, and FHFA.

Notes: Cells contain the chi-squared statistics and p-values (in parentheses) of F-tests of the null hypothesis that the lagged values of the variable in the column header are jointly equal to zero in the regression of the variable in the row header on lagged values of itself and the other three variables. The lag length for each equation is determined by starting with a model with 6 lags and then using F- tests to identify the highest order lags that are not jointly significant at the 10 percent level.

End Notes

[1] In this report, we refer to both these types of financial institutions as banks unless otherwise indicated. Commercial banks accept depositsmake business loansand offer related servicesThey serve individuals but focus primarily on servicing and making loans to businesses. Thrifts accept deposits and make loans, particularly for home mortgages. No banks failed in 2005 or 2006, and only three failed in 2007.

[2] Fair value accounting is a financial reporting approach that requires or permits financial institutions to measure and report on an ongoing basis certain financial assets and liabilities at the price that would be received to sell an asset or paid to transfer a liability in an orderly transaction between market participants at the measurement date.

[3] Regulatory capital can be measured as total capital or tier 1 capital. Total capital consists of the sum of tier 1 and tier 2 capital. Tier 1 capital consists primarily of equity capital and retained earnings (the profits a bank has earned but has not paid out to shareholders in the form of dividends). Tier 2 capital includes subordinated debt, a portion of loan loss allowances, and certain other instruments.

[4] An inactive or illiquid market is one in which observable inputs such as quoted prices are not available due to infrequent transactions.

[5] 12 U.S.C. § 1823(c)(4).

[6] Pub. L. No. 112-88, § 3, 125 Stat. 1899, 1902 (2012). As part of this act, the FDIC Inspector General (IG) must also conduct a separate study on the impact of bank failures.

[7] Section 38(k) of the Federal Deposit Insurance Act (FDI Act) requires that the inspector general of the appropriate federal banking agency complete an MLR of the agency's supervision of a failed institution when the projected loss to the DIF is material to, among other things, ascertain why the institution's problems resulted in a material loss to the DIF. 12 U.S.C. § 1831o(k). Prior to the enactment of the Dodd-Frank Wall Street and Consumer Protection Act (Dodd-Frank Act) on July 21, 2010, the FDI Act defined a material loss to the DIF as the greater of $25 million or 2 percent of the institution's total assets. The Dodd-Frank Act amended the FDI Act to define a material loss to the DIF for the period January 1, 2010, to December 31, 2011, as an estimated loss in excess of $200 million; for the period January 1, 2012, to December 31, 2013, as an estimated loss in excess of $150 million; and on or after January 1, 2014, as an estimated loss in excess of $50 million. Pub. L. No. 111-203, § 987. The Dodd-Frank Act also created new reporting requirements—the failed bank review, or FBR—for failures that resulted in losses below the "material loss" threshold. The Inspector General, every six months, shall conduct FBRs to determine the grounds identified by the federal banking agency or state bank supervisor for appointing FDIC as receiver, and whether any "unusual circumstances" exist that might warrant an IDR of the loss. If an in-depth review is warranted, the Inspector General must prepare the IDR consistent with the requirements of an MLR.

[8] Market concentration is an indicator of the extent to which firms in a market can exercise power by raising prices, reducing output, diminishing innovation, or otherwise harming customers as a result of reduced competitiveness. A key variable used in this analysis, deposits in bank branches, is available annually as of June 30 of each year, so we used observations for 12-month periods starting on June 30 of each year from 2007 through 2011 to cover the period from 2008 to 2011. Data on bank failures for the first half of 2012 are used to create observations on the 12month period beginning on June 30, 2011.

[9] The HHI is one of the measures of market concentration that government agencies, including Department of Justice (DOJ) and Federal Trade Commission (FTC), use to enforce U.S. antitrust laws. DOJ and FTC often calculate the HHI as the first step in providing insight into potentially anticompetitive conditions in an industry. However, the HHI is a function of firms' market shares, and market shares may not fully reflect the competitive significance of firms in the market. Thus, DOJ and FTC use the HHI in combination with other evidence of competitive effects when evaluating market concentration.

[10] We used data for 2006 through 2011 to analyze data on banks that failed in 2008 through 2011 up to 8 quarters prior to their failures.

[11] We used data for the longest time period for which data on personal income, unemployment, real estate prices, and deposits in failed banks for U.S. states and the District of Columbia are all available.

[12] Section 38 of the FDI Act requires federal banking regulators to classify banks into one of five capital categories and take increasingly severe actions, known as prompt corrective action, as a bank's capital level deteriorates. 12 U.S.C. § 1831o. A bank is declared critically undercapitalized if its tangible equity is equal to or less than 2 percent of its total assets. Tangible equity is equal to the amount of Tier 1 capital plus outstanding cumulative perpetual preferred stock minus all intangible assets not previously deducted, except certain purchased mortgage-servicing rights.

[13] Although no commonly accepted definition of a community bank exists, the term often is associated with smaller banks (e.g., under $1 billion in assets) that provide relationship banking services to the local community. For the purposes of this report, we use the term "small" banks and "community" banks interchangeably.

[14] See GAO, *Troubled Asset Relief Program: Status of Programs and Implementation of GAO recommendations*, GAO-11-74 (Washington, D.C.: Jan.12, 2011).

[15] Board of Governors of the Federal Reserve System, *Report to Congress on the Availability of Credit to Small Businesses*, (Sept. 2012). In addition, our analysis indicates that between 2007 and 2011, banks with assets of about $1 billion or more made an average of 85-90 percent of their small business loans in markets where they had branches, and at least 95 percent of banks with assets of $1 billion or more made at least half of their small business loans in markets where they had branches.

[16] Until 1989, thrift deposits were federally insured by the Federal Savings and Loan Insurance Corporation (FSLIC), which was created by the National Housing Act, 48 Stat. 1246 (1934). After experiencing solvency

problems in connection with the savings and loan crisis of the 1980s, FSLIC was abolished and its insurance function was transferred to FDIC by the Financial Institutions Reform, Recovery, and Enforcement Act of 1989, Pub. L. No. 101-73, § 401, 103 Stat. 183 (1989).

17 The responsibilities of the Federal Reserve include supervising and regulating banks and other important financial institutions to ensure the safety and soundness of the nation's banking and financial system and to protect the credit rights of consumers.

18 The Dodd-Frank Act eliminated OTS. Supervisory authority previously vested in OTS was transferred to the OCC for federal savings associations, to FDIC for state savings associations, and to the Federal Reserve for thrift holding companies and their subsidiaries, other than depository institutions. The transfer of these powers was completed on July 21, 2011, and OTS was officially dissolved 90 days later (Oct. 19, 2011).

19 Pub. L. No. 102-242, § 141, 105 Stat. 2236, 2273 (1991), codified at 12 U.S.C. § 1823(c)(4).

20 See appendix II for more information on FDIC's resolution methods for failed institutions and its least cost test process.

21 In 2006, the Financial Accounting Standards Board issued Statement of Financial Accounting Standards (SFAS) No. 157, *Fair Value Measurements*, which defined fair value, established a framework for measuring fair value under GAAP, and required expanded disclosures about fair value measurements. SFAS No. 157 became effective for an entity's first fiscal year beginning after November 15, 2007. Prior to its issuance, fair value measurement principles were not consistently defined and codified in a single accounting standard, which led to the potential for disparate fair value measurement practices under different accounting standards. SFAS No. 157 was intended to provide a single set of measurement principles to be uniformly applied for fair value measurement when GAAP requires or permits reporting entities to measure or disclose the fair value of an asset or liability. However, SFAS No. 157 did not change which assets and liabilities are subject to fair value accounting or when fair value should be applied, as other previously existing accounting standards provide the requirement or permission to measure assets and liabilities at fair value. SFAS 157 was subsequently codified as Accounting Standards Council (ASC) 820 and amended, and additional staff guidance was issued on the application of fair value accounting.

22 OCI refers to revenues, expenses, gains, and losses that are included in comprehensive income but excluded from net income. Comprehensive income is the total non-owner change in equity for a reporting period. An other-than-temporarily impaired instrument is one whose fair value has fallen below its amortized cost and its value is not expected to recover to its amortized cost through the holding period. As a result of an April 2009 change to the relevant GAAP standard, an OTTI of either a debt security classified as available-for-sale or held-to-maturity in certain circumstances in separated into the (1) credit loss amount recognized in earnings and (2) the amount related to all other factors (non-credit loss) recognized in OCI, net of applicable taxes.

23 Essentially, amortized cost is outstanding principal adjusted for any charge offs, deferred fees or costs, and unamortized discount or premium.

24 Net interest income is the difference between the interest income recognized on earning assets and the interest expense on deposits and other borrowed funds. Increases in the loan loss allowance for credit losses on nonperforming loans are charged to the bank's expenses on the income statement, thus reducing its net interest income. Reductions in a bank's income are reflected in its earnings, which are included in retained earnings, a component of regulatory capital.

25 Section 121 of FDICIA requires that the accounting principles used for regulatory reporting should be no less stringent than GAAP in order to facilitate prompt corrective action to resolve failed banks at the least cost to the DIF.

26 GAAP defines a loan to be a collateral-dependent loan when the repayment of the debt will be provided solely by the sale or operation of the underlying collateral, and there are no other available and reliable sources of repayment.

27 See Financial Stability Forum, *Report of the FSF Working Group on Provisioning* (March 2009) and Department of the Treasury, *A New Foundation: Rebuilding Financial Supervision and* Regulation (June 2009). The Financial Stability Forum (FSF) was a group consisting of major national financial authorities such as finance ministries, central bankers, and international financial bodies. Its Working Group on Provisioning was co-chaired by the Securities and Exchange (SEC) Commissioner and the Chair of the Technical Committee of the International Organization of Securities Commissions, and the Comptroller of the Currency and Chair of the Joint Forum. In April 2009, the FSF was re- launched as the Financial Stability Board and its membership expanded and mandate broadened to promote financial stability.

28 We reported similar findings in GAO, *Banking Regulation: Enhanced Guidance on Commercial Real Estate Risks Needed*, GAO-11-489 (Washington, D.C.: May19, 2011).

29 On December 12, 2006, federal banking regulators issued *Concentrations in Commercial Real Estate Lending, Sound Risk Management Practices* to reinforce existing regulations and guidelines for real estate lending and safety and soundness. The Joint Guidance stated that the federal banking regulators had observed an increasing trend in the number of banks with concentrations in CRE loans and noted that such concentration may make institutions more vulnerable to cyclical CRE markets. 71 Fed. Reg. 74,580 (Dec. 12, 2006).

[30] Nonperforming loansare defined as loans that are 90 days or more past due and loans on which the bank is no longer accruing interest. Institutions must estimate the credit losses on nonperforming loans and increase the loan loss allowance accordingly.

[31] Net charge offs are the total amount of loans that are charged off (removed from the balance sheet because of uncollectibility), less amounts recovered on loans previously charged off.

[32] A "brokered deposit" is defined as a deposit obtained, directly or indirectly, from or through the mediation or assistance of a deposit broker. The term "deposit broker" is defined by statute as "(A) any person engaged in the business of placing deposits, or facilitating the placement of deposits, of third parties with insured depository institutions or the business of placing deposits with insured depository institutions for the purpose of selling interests in those deposits to third parties; and (B) an agent or trustee who establishes a deposit account to facilitate a business arrangement with an insured depository institution to use the proceeds of the account to fund a prearranged loan," subject to certain exclusions. 12 U.S.C. § 1831f(g). The broker pools large-denomination deposits from many small investors and markets the pooled deposits to financial institutions, usually in blocks nearing $100,000, and negotiates a higher rate for the pooled certificates of deposit. In contrast, core deposits are largely derived from a bank's regular customer base, and are typically the most stable and least costly source of funding with the lowest interest rates.

[33] FDIC, *Study on Core Deposits and Brokered Deposits*, (Washington D.C.: July 2011).

[34] 12 U.S.C. § 1831f; 12 C.F.R. § 337.6(b). FDIC may, on a case-by-case basis, waive the prohibition on renewing and accepting brokered deposits for banks that are adequately capitalized (but not well capitalized) if it finds that the acceptance of such deposits does not constitute an unsafe or unsound practice.

[35] FDIC Office of the Inspector General, Acquisition, office of Audits and *Evaluations, Acquisition Development, and Construction Loan Concentration Study*, no. EVAL-13-001 October 2012. The IG had identified 436 institutions that had an ADC concentration of 100 percent or greater as of December 2007 and were in satisfactory condition as of April 2011. From those, the IG chose a sample of 18 institutions that had ADC concentrations of 300 percent or more. The IG noted that it did not identify a significant number of banks with high concentrations in 2007 that were in satisfactory condition in 2011, which it stated was reflective of how difficult it was for institutions with exceedingly high ADC concentrations to mitigate the concentration risk during an economic downturn.

[36] We excluded savings associations and insured branches of foreign banks from our analysis because these institutions did not report data on key variables for the time period we analyzed.

[37] We used a discrete-time hazard model to estimate how various variables impacted the likelihood that a bank would fail in a future time period. See appendix III for more details on our econometric model.

[38] The number of failures of large banks (average assets of $10 billion or more) was too small to analyze separately.

[39] Payment option ARMs are a type of adjustable rate mortgage that allows borrowers to make minimum payments that do not cover principal or all accrued interest, but can result in increased loan balances over time (negative amortization). Typically after 5 years, or if the loan balance increases to a cap specified in the mortgage terms, payments recast to include an amount that will fully amortize the outstanding balance over the remaining years of the loan.

[40] The IG further noted that management controls were insufficient to prevent inaccuracies, omissions, and misrepresentations that affected key UCB financial statements, prompting the bank's audit committee to start an investigation in May 2009. UCB reported that its 2008 financial statements were materially inaccurate and required revision. The investigation and inaccurate financial statements made it harder for UCB to raise the capital the bank needed in 2009 to absorb substantial provisions and losses associated with its loan portfolio.

[41] We analyzed commercial banks and thrifts separately for this section because the call report and the thrift financial report categorize and group income statement items in different formats and because thrift financial report filers were not required to report the fair value of certain types of assets and liabilities.

[42] Investments in debt securities that are not classified as trading securities or as HTM securities are classified as available-for-sale (AFS) securities. AFS securities also include equity securities that have readily determinable fair values and are not classified as trading securities.

[43] As a result of an April 2009 change to the relevant GAAP standard, an OTTI loss on either a debt security classified as AFS or held-to-maturity in certain circumstances is separated into (1) the credit loss amount, which is recognized in earnings and (2) the amount related to all other factors (noncredit loss), which is recognized in OCI, net of applicable taxes. See appendix IV for further discussion of the impact of this change on the balance sheet of failed and open banks.

[44] Appendices IV and V provide more information on the various bank assets and liabilities subject to fair value accounting in open and failed small, medium-size, and large commercial banks and thrifts.

[45] See appendix IV and V.

[46] Interagency Policy Statement on the Allowance for Loan and Lease Losses (December 2006) and Policy Statement on Prudent Commercial Real Estate Loan Workouts (October 2009). GAAP requires the use of the fair value of the collateral method when foreclosure is probable on collateral-dependent loans.

[47] According to the guidance, an institution should consider the appraised value of the collateral as the starting point for determining its fair value but should also consider other factors and events in its environment that could

have affected the current fair value of the collateral since the appraisal was performed. For example, the timing of when the cash flows are expected to be received from the underlying collateral could affect the fair value of the collateral if the timing was not contemplated in the appraisal. This generally results in the appraised value of the collateral being greater than the institution's estimate of the collateral's fair value (less costs to sell).

48 Neither bank call reports nor thrift financial reports specify the nature of credit losses or charge offs reported by banks and thrifts.

49 Policy Statement on Prudent Commercial Real Estate Loan Workouts.

50 In GAOwe reported that interviews with officials from 43 banks in different parts of the country had identified multiple concerns with examiner treatment of CRE loans and related issues. As part of its mandated study under Pub. L. No. 112-88, the FDIC IG reviewed examiner classification of loans reported by the institution as current, as well as the policies and procedures examiners use for evaluating the appraised values of property securing real estate loans and the extent to which those policies and procedures were followed.

51 Remarks by John C. Dugan, Comptroller of the Currency before the Institute of International Bankers, *Loan Loss Provisioning and Pro-cyclicality*, (Mar. 2, 2009). He also noted that by building up a large loan loss allowance when times were good, banks could recognize and deal with credit problems early. Later, when the loan losses materialize, the loan loss allowance can absorb the losses without impairing capital, keeping the bank safe, sound, and able to continue extending credit. He also said that in theory, the loan loss allowance could have an important macroeconomic benefit as well. He said that allowing banks to recognize losses early should result in charges against earnings (and possibly capital) during the favorable part of an economic cycle, because banks anticipated higher future losses when the cycle turned negative. At the same time, charges would be reduced during downturns, since banks anticipated smaller losses when the cycle turns positive. In other words, the loan loss reserving process can have the important economic benefit of being counter cyclical.

52 Several empirical studies have found evidence linking lower levels of loan loss allowances to procyclicality in the banking system and, conversely, that higher levels of loan loss allowances reduce procyclicality. For example, a 2009 Federal Reserve Bank of Richmond study compared the incurred loss model as implemented in the United States and the dynamic provisioning model as implemented in Spain, which is intended to build loan loss allowances to protect banks against losses expected but not yet identified in the loan portfolio. The authors conducted an empirical simulation and concluded that a dynamic provisioning framework could have allowed for a build-up of allowances during the boom years in the United States and the need to provision for loan losses would have been significantly lower during the financial crisis of 2007–2009. See Eliana Balla and Andrew McKenna, "*Dynamic Provisioning: A Countercyclical Tool for Loan Loss Reserves*," Economic Quarterly 95(4), (fall 2009), 383-418. Similarly, a 2012 Bank for International Settlements study examined Asian banks provisioning practices in the aftermath of the Asian financial crisis of the late 1990s to determine whether these banks were provisioning in a manner that reduced procyclicality. Based on a sample of 240 banks in 12 Asian countries, the researchers found that loan loss allowances and provisioning levels were generally higher in the run-up to the recent financial crisis. The researchers reported that countercyclical loan loss provisioning—increasing provisioning in good times in response to rising levels of risk dominated in emerging Asian economies and ameliorated swings in bank earnings and the macroeconomy. See Frank Packer and Haibin Zhu, "*Loan Loss Provisioning Practices of Asian Banks*," Bank For International Settlements, Working Paper No. 375, (April 2012).

53 Remarks by Tim Long, Senior Deputy Comptroller for Bank Supervision Policy and Chief National Bank Examiner, AICPA National Conference on Banks and Savings Institutions (September 14, 2009).

54 Staff from the federal banking regulators told us that FDICIA precludes them from requiring banks to follow loan loss provisioning accounting methodologies that are not GAAP-compliant. Section 121(a) of FDICIA states that accounting principles applicable to reports or statements that federal banking regulators require insured depository institutions to file must, among other things, result in financial statements and reports of condition that accurately reflect the capital of such institutions and facilitate their effective supervision. 12 U.S.C. § 1831n(a)(1). Section 121(a) also requires such accounting principles to be uniform and consistent with GAAP. 12 U.S.C. § 1831n(a)(2)(A). If a federal banking regulator determines that the application of any generally accepted accounting principle to any insured depository institution is inconsistent with the objectives described in (1), it may prescribe an accounting principle which is applicable to such institutions which is no less stringent than GAAP.

55 Expected losses are those losses that result from specified past, present, and future events. Unexpected losses, on the other hand, are losses that are unanticipated due to various economic or other factors that cannot be controlled by bank management.

56 FASB, Supplementary Document: *Accounting for Financial Instruments and Revisions to the Accounting for Derivative Instruments and Hedging Activities: Impairment* (January 2011).

57 According to this concept, Bucket 1 assets would be evaluated collectively for impairment if they do not meet the definition of Bucket 2 or 3, including loans that have suffered changes in credit loss expectations as a result of macroeconomic events that are not specific to either a group of loans or a specific loan. Conversely, Bucket 2 assets would include those that have been affected by observable events that indicate a direct relationship to possible future defaults; however, the specific assets in danger of default are not known. Bucket 3 assets would

consist of loans for which information is available that specifically identifies credit losses that are expected to, or have, occurred on the individual assets.

[58] FASB Exposure Draft, "*Financial Instruments—Credit Losses (Subtopic 825-15)*", (December 20,2012).

[59] Federal Reserve staff said that it is important that the accounting standards setters are addressing expected losses via their development of an expected loss model for loan loss provisioning because other ongoing efforts to address procyclicality in the banking system are focused solely on unexpected credit losses. They noted that proposed standards under Basel III, which is intended to strengthen the global regulatory framework related to bank capital, address unexpected losses in their proposed capital measures but not expected loan losses. The Basel Committee on Banking Supervision, which drafted the proposed Basel III framework, stated it strongly supports the accounting standard setters' initiative to promote stronger loan loss provisioning practices by moving towards an expected loss model and that it sees its work and that of the accounting standards setters as complementary in addressing procyclicality. See Basel Committee on Banking Supervision, *Basel III: A Global Regulatory Framework For More Resilient Banks And Banking Systems* (December 2010).

[60] As part of FDIC's annual financial statement audit, GAO evaluates the controls over the least cost test process, total estimated lifetime losses, and shared loss payments. We found no material weaknesses in these controls. Most recent audit results can be found in GAO-12-416. Appendix II provides more information on FDIC's least cost test process.

[61] A bank we spoke with expressed concern that failed banks acquired via shared loss agreements had negatively impacted competition because the acquired banks received significant loss coverage on potential credit losses that peer banks did not. We discuss these views later in the report.

[62] In a whole bank purchase and assumption agreement, the acquiring institution typically assumes all of the deposits and essentially all of the assets of the failed institution.

[63] The majority of the commercial and residential loan assets are purchased under shared loss agreements, where FDIC agrees to share in future losses and recoveries experienced by the acquirer on those assets covered under the agreement.

[64] Losses on the covered assets are shared between the acquirer and FDIC in its receivership capacity of the failed institution when losses occur through the sale, foreclosure, loan modification, or charge-off of loans in accordance with terms of the shared loss agreements. The majority of the agreements are for 8 to 10 years.

[65] The agreements covered about $135 billion of total remaining covered assets purchased by the acquiring institutions as of December 31, 2011.

[66] Any shared loss payments are made from receivership funds from the specific failed institution or, if those are insufficient, from the DIF.

[67] Appendix I contains a complete description of our analysis.

[68] The HHI is one of the measures of market concentration that government agencies, including DOJ and FTC, use to enforce U.S. antitrust laws. DOJ and FTC often calculate the HHI as the first step in providing insight into potentially anticompetitive conditions in an industry. However, the HHI is a function of firms' market shares, and market shares may not fully reflect the competitive significance of firms in the market. Thus, DOJ and FTC use the HHI in combination with other evidence of competitive effects when evaluating market concentration.

[69] We calculated the prefailure HHI for June 30 of each year using banks' market shares as of June 30 of each year. We calculated the postfailure HHI for June 30 of each year assuming that the bank failures and failed bank acquisitions that occurred over the next 12 months occurred at the beginning of the period. Although we included failed banks of all sizes in this analysis, over 90 percent of the bank failures were of small banks.

[70] Metropolitan and micropolitan statistical areas are geographic entities defined by the Office of Management and Budget for use by federal statistical agencies in collecting, tabulating and publishing federal statistics. A metro area contains a core urban of 50,000 or more population, and a micro area contains an urban core of at least 10,000 (but less than 50,000) population. Each metro or micro area consists of one or more counties and includes the counties in the core urban area, as well as any adjacent counties that have a high degree of social and economic integration with the urban core.

[71] We used an econometric model to estimate net credit extended by banks during a quarter as a function of the capital adequacy; asset quality; earnings; liquidity; ADC lending; non-farm, non-residential real estate lending; multifamily real estate lending; commercial real estate lending not secured by real estate; brokered deposits; size; and other factors. We also included indicators for each quarter to control for factors affecting the likelihood of failure that are common to all banks at the same time, such as the regulatory environment, the state of the market for bank products and services, and the condition of the overall economy. We then used the results of our model to predict net credit extended by failing banks in the quarters leading up to their failure and by acquiring banks in the quarters following acquisition of a failed bank. See appendix VII for more information on our econometric model.

[72] For example, the loan portfolio grows when the bank makes new loans or purchases existing loans. It shrinks when the bank charges off a delinquent loan; when the bank forecloses on a delinquent real estate loan, charges off the difference between the market and face values of the loan, and reclassifies the collateral as

"other real estate owned;" and when a the bank sells or securitizes a loan. It also changes when loans are paid down, extended, or repurchased.

[73] Our results are not generalizable to all local communities that experienced small bank failures.

[74] We attempted to contact groups representing small businesses in the communities that were part of our sample to obtain their views on credit availability and loan demand, but did not receive any responses. However, a recent survey conducted by the National Federation of Independent Business noted that 90 percent of 740 small business owners surveyed reported that all their credit needs were met or that they were not interested in borrowing. National Federation of Independent Business, "*Small Business Economic Trends*" survey (July 2012).

[75] The FDIC IG is required under Pub. L. No. 112-88 to evaluate, among other things, the impact of shared loss agreements on existing banks and the borrowers of banks that fail, including FDIC's policies and procedures for monitoring LSAs, including those designed to ensure institutions are not imprudently selling assets as a depressed value and the extent to which LSAs provide incentives for loan modifications and other means of increasing the probability of commercial assets being considered performing.

[76] Although we included failed banks of all sizes in this analysis, over 90 percent of the bank failures were of small banks.

[77] Our measure of bank failures captures both the size of the failing banks and their share of the deposits (a proxy for their weight in a state), whereas the absolute number of failures or the simple failure rate does not. We used the concept of Granger causality to determine the extent to which variables are associated with each other. Granger causality measures whether the current value of one variable is correlated with past values of another variable, but it does not imply that one variable is the result of or the effect of another variable. See appendix VIII.

[78] Section 38(k) of the Federal Deposit Insurance Act (FDI Act) requires that the inspector general of the appropriate federal banking agency complete an MLR of the agency's supervision of a failed institution when the projected loss to the DIF is material to, among other things, ascertain why the institution's problems resulted in a material loss to the DIF. 12 U.S.C. § 1831o(k). Prior to the enactment of the Dodd-Frank Wall Street and Consumer Protection Act (Dodd-Frank Act) on July 21, 2010, the FDI Act defined a material loss to the DIF as the greater of $25 million or 2 percent of the institution's total assets. The Dodd-Frank Act amended the FDI Act to define a material loss to the DIF for the period January 1, 2010, to December 31, 2011, as an estimated loss in excess of $200 million; for the period January 1, 2012, to December 31, 2013, as an estimated loss in excess of $150 million; and on or after January 1, 2014, as an estimated loss in excess of $50 million. Pub. L. No. 111-203, § 987. The Dodd-Frank Act also created new reporting requirements—the failed bank report, or FBR—for failures that resulted in losses below the "material loss" threshold. The inspector general, every six months, shall conduct FBRs to determine the grounds identified by the federal banking agency or state bank supervisor for appointing FDIC as receiver, and whether any "unusual circumstances" exist that might warrant an IDR of the loss. If an IDR is warranted, the inspector general must prepare the IDR consistent with the requirements of an MLR.

[79] Three state banking associations declined our request for an interview.

[80] We excluded savings associations and insured branches of foreign banks from our analysis because these institutions did not report data on key variables for the time period we analyzed.

[81] We employed discrete-time hazard models. For more information on these econometric models, see appendix III.

[82] Securities and Exchange Commission, "*Report and Recommendations Pursuant to Section 133 of the Emergency Economic Stabilization Act of 2008: Study on Mark-to- Market Accounting*," (December 2008).

[83] For example, a market with four firms with market shares of 30 percent, 30 percent, 20 percent, and 20 percent would have an HHI of 2,600 (900 + 900 + 400 + 400).

[84] A branch is any location, or facility, of a financial institution, including its main office, where deposit accounts are opened, deposits are accepted, checks paid, and loans are granted. Branches include, but are not limited to, brick and mortar locations, detached drive-in facilities, seasonal offices, offices on military bases or government installations, paying/receiving stations or units, and Internet and Phone Banking locations where a customer can open accounts, make deposits and borrow money. A branch does not include automated teller machines (ATMs), consumer credit offices, contractual offices, customer bank communication terminals (CBCT), electronic fund transfer units (EFTU), or loan production offices (FDIC, Summary of Deposits Reporting Instructions, June 30, 2011).

[85] For more information on these econometric models, see appendix VII.

[86] For more information on the linear dynamic panel approach, see appendix VIII.

[87] We attempted to interview local organizations representing the perspective of small businesses that relied for credit on the failed banks in our sample, but the organizations did not respond to our interview requests.

[88] Prior to 2010, a systemic risk determination would have permitted open bank assistance to an individual insured depository institution (IDI). However, since the passage of the Dodd-Frank Act on July 21, 2010, the systemic risk determination authority under section 13 of the FDI Act is limited to IDIs put in an FDIC receivership. Accordingly, open bank assistance is no longer an option. In an open bank assistance agreement, the FDIC provided financial assistance to an operating insured bank or thrift determined to be in danger of closing.

[89] In 2006, the Financial Accounting Standards Board issued Statement of Financial Accounting Standards (SFAS) No. 157, *Fair Value Measurements*, which defined fair value, established a framework for measuring fair value under GAAP, and required expanded disclosures about fair value measurements. SFAS No. 157 became effective in 2008. Prior to its issuance, fair value measurement principles were not consistently defined and codified in a single accounting standard, which led to the potential for disparate fair value measurement practices under different accounting standards. SFAS No. 157 was intended to provide a single set of measurement principles to be uniformly applied for fair value measurement when GAAP requires or permits reporting entities to measure or disclose the fair value of an asset or liability. However, SFAS No. 157 did not change which asset and liabilities are subject to fair value accounting or when fair value should be applied, as other previously existing accounting standards provide the requirement or permission to measure assets and liabilities at fair value. SFAS 157 was subsequently codified as ASC 820 and amended, and additional staff guidance was issued on the application of fair value accounting.

[90] OCI refers to revenues, expenses, gains, and losses that are included in comprehensive income but excluded from net income. Comprehensive income is the total non-owner change in equity for a reporting period. An other-than-temporarily impaired instrument is one whose fair value has fallen below its amortized cost and its value is not expected to recover to its amortized cost through the holding period. As a result of an April 2009 change to the relevant GAAP standard, an OTTI of either a debt security classified as available-for-sale or held-to-maturity in certain circumstances in separated into the (1) credit loss amount recognized in earnings and (2) the amount related to all other factors (non-credit loss) recognized in OCI, net of applicable taxes.

[91] Essentially, amortized cost is outstanding principal, adjusted for any charge-offs, deferred fees or costs, and unamortized discount or premium.

[92] Section 121 of the Federal Deposit Insurance Corporation Improvement Act requires that the accounting principles used for regulatory reporting should be no less stringent than GAAP in order to facilitate prompt corrective action to resolve failed banks at the least cost to the DIF.

[93] ASC 825 (formerly FAS 159), "*The Fair Value Option for Financial Assets and Financial Liabilities*," (February 2007) allows a one-time election to report certain financial instruments at fair value. At initial recognition for certain financial assets and liabilities, an entity may irrevocably elect fair value as the initial and subsequent measurement attribute, with changes in fair value included in current earnings.

[94] The OCC Bank Accounting Advisory Series states that a bank should transfer loans from the HFI category to the HFS category when it no longer has the intent and ability to hold the loans for the foreseeable future or until maturity or payoff. However, such changes in intent followed by subsequent sales of the loan in the near term would likely cause increased skepticism and scrutiny by the auditor and examiner, especially if the sale or transfer occurs during the period the bank originally considered its foreseeable future.

[95] See, for example, FDIC Financial Institution Letter 62-2008 Guidance on Other Real Estate.

[96] Financial Accounting Standards Board Staff Position No. FAS 115-2: "Recognition and Presentation of Other-Than-Temporary Impairments," (April 9, 2009).

[97] ASC 320 (formerly FAS 115): "*Accounting for Certain Investments in Debt and Equity Securities*," May 1993.

[98] In 2006, the Financial Accounting Standards Board issued Statement of Financial Accounting Standards (SFAS) No. 157, *Fair Value Measurements*, which defined fair value, established a framework for measuring fair value under GAAP, and required expanded disclosures about fair value measurements. SFAS No. 157 became effective in 2008. Prior to its issuance, fair value measurement principles were not consistently defined and codified in a single accounting standard, which led to the potential for disparate fair value measurement practices under different accounting standards. SFAS No. 157 was intended to provide a single set of measurement principles to be uniformly applied for fair value measurement when GAAP requires or permits reporting entities to measure or disclose the fair value of an asset or liability. However, SFAS No. 157 did not change which asset and liabilities are subject to fair value accounting or when fair value should be applied, as other previously existing accounting standards provide the requirement or permission to measure assets and liabilities at fair value. SFAS 157 was subsequently codified as Accounting Standards Council (ASC) 820 and amended, and additional staff guidance was issued on the application of fair value accounting.

[99] OCI refers to revenues, expenses, gains, and losses that are included in comprehensive income but excluded from net income. Comprehensive income is the total non-owner change in equity for a reporting period. An other-than-temporarily impaired instrument is one whose fair value has fallen below its amortized cost and its value is not expected to recover through the holding period. As a result of an April 2009 change to the relevant GAAP standard, an OTTI of either a debt security classified as available-for-sale or held- to-maturity in certain circumstances in separated into the (1) credit loss amount recognized in earnings and (2) the amount related to all other factors (non-credit loss) recognized in OCI, net of applicable taxes.

[100] Essentially, amortized cost is outstanding principal, adjusted for any charge offs, deferred fees or costs, and unamortized discount or premium.

[101] ASC 825 (formerly FAS 159), "*The Fair Value Option for Financial Assets and Financial Liabilities*," (February 2007) allows a one-time election to report certain financial instruments at fair value. At initial recognition for certain financial assets and liabilities, an entity may irrevocably elect fair value as the initial and subsequent measurement attribute, with changes in fair value included in current earnings.

[102] The OCC Bank Accounting Advisory Series states that a bank should transfer loans from the held-for-investment category to the HFS category when it no longer has the intent and ability to hold the loans for the foreseeable future or until maturity or payoff. However, such changes in intent followed by subsequent sales of the loan in the near term, would likely cause increased skepticism and scrutiny by the auditor and examiner, especially if the sale or transfer occurs during the period the bank originally considered its foreseeable future.

[103] See, for example, FDIC Financial Institution Letter 62-2008: Guidance on Other Real Estate.

[104] Call report instructions, schedule report of income RI-C.

[105] FASB Statement No. 65, *Accounting for Certain Mortgage Banking Activities* (SFAS 65), Paragraph 6, states that a mortgage loan transferred to a long-term investment classification shall be transferred at the lower of cost or fair value on the transfer date. Any difference between the carrying amount of the loan and its outstanding principal balance shall be recognized as an adjustment to yield by the interest method.

In: Bank Failures during the Financial Crisis
Editor: Lawrence C. Armstrong

ISBN: 978-1-62618-615-6

Chapter 2

COMPREHENSIVE STUDY ON THE IMPACT OF THE FAILURE OF INSURED DEPOSITORY INSTITUTIONS*

Federal Deposit Insurance Corporation

EXECUTIVE SUMMARY

Why We Did the Study

Public Law 112-88, signed into law on January 3, 2012, requires the Federal Deposit Insurance Corporation Office of Inspector General (FDIC OIG) to conduct a study on the impact of the failure of insured depository institutions. The study is quite broad and required our office to address matters pertaining to shared-loss agreements (SLA), the significance of losses at institutions that failed, examiner implementation of appraisal guidelines, examiner assessment of capital adequacy and private capital investment in failing institutions, examiner implementation of loan workout guidance, the application and impact of formal enforcement orders, the impact of FDIC policies on investments in institutions, and the FDIC's handling of private equity company investments in institutions. The legislation included a number of topics under these broad matters, and these topics are addressed in detail in our report. The legislation required our office to conduct work at the FDIC, the Office of the Comptroller of the Currency (OCC), and the Board of Governors of the Federal Reserve System (FRB). The legislation also required the U.S. Government Accountability Office to study matters related to the causes of institution failures, fair value accounting, asset write-downs, the community impact of failures, and the feasibility and impact of SLAs.

Consistent with the legislation, our overall objective was to conduct a comprehensive study on the impact of the failure of insured depository institutions. Our review timeframes were generally 2008 through 2011. In some cases, our data analysis preceded 2008, and in other cases we gathered information through September 30, 2012, updating data to the extent possible. As required, our scope included open and failed state member, state nonmember,

---

* This is an edited, reformatted and augmented version of the Office of Inspector General, Report No. EVAL-13-002, dated January 2013.

and national banks regulated by the FRB, FDIC, and OCC, respectively. Our evaluation scope did not include institutions formerly regulated by the Office of Thrift Supervision. In conducting our work, we interviewed agency officials, reviewed relevant policies and guidance, reviewed examination reports and working papers, analyzed institution financial data and agency enforcement action statistics, interviewed officials at open institutions, interviewed investment professionals, and surveyed borrowers of failed institutions. KPMG LLP assisted us with several areas of review. We conducted our evaluation from January 2012 through October 2012.

Background

Regulator Responsibilities for Overseeing Insured Depository Institutions and Resolving Them When They Fail

Examining Institutions. The FDIC, OCC, and FRB oversee the nation's insured depository institutions to ensure they operate in a safe and sound manner. The regulators assess the condition of institutions through off-site monitoring and on-site examinations. The regulators have longstanding policies for examiners to review an institution's lending and loan review functions, assess capital adequacy, and recommend improvements, if needed. Every financial institution must maintain an Allowance for Loan and Lease Losses (ALLL), basically a reserve that covers estimated credit losses on individually evaluated loans determined to be impaired as well as estimated credit losses inherent in the remainder of the loan and lease portfolio. If examiners disagree with an institution's risk rankings or determine that additional loans should be classified, the institution must update its ALLL estimates to be consistent with generally accepted accounting principles (GAAP). If loans are classified as loss, they are charged off the institution's balance sheet. The ALLL directly impacts the institution's capital level.

Another part of reviewing an institution's lending and loan review function is considering the collateral values of loans. The December 2010 *Interagency Appraisal and Evaluation Guidelines* require examiners to consider the size and the nature of an institution's real estate-related activities when assessing the appropriateness of its appraisal program, and assess whether the methods, assumptions, and value conclusions are reasonable when reviewing an appraisal or evaluation for individual transactions.

When regulators determine that an institution's condition is less than satisfactory, they may take a variety of supervisory actions, including informal and formal enforcement actions, to address identified deficiencies. Each regulator has somewhat different approaches to enforcement actions.

Resolving Failed Institutions. Chartering agencies are generally required by law to promptly close *Critically Undercapitalized* institutions that cannot be recapitalized. The FDIC is also required by law to resolve failing institutions in the least costly manner. The FDIC frequently enters into SLAs with acquiring institutions (AIs) of failed bank assets, and these agreements guarantee that the FDIC will share in a portion of future asset losses and recoveries for a specific time period. In return, the AI agrees to manage the failed bank assets consistently with its legacy assets, pursue residential loan modifications on qualified loans, and work to minimize losses on those assets.

The FDIC was aware of the need for additional capital in the banking system, and, in August 2009, the FDIC Board of Directors issued FDIC's *Final Statement of Policy on Qualifications for Failed Institution Acquisitions* (PCI SOP), which provided guidance to private capital investors (PCI) interested in acquiring or investing in failed institutions. The guidance was aimed at encouraging such investment while ensuring that such PCIs had adequate capital and management expertise and protections against insider transactions.

Study Results

The financial crisis had devastating impacts on the banking industry, businesses, communities, and consumers. Over 400 institutions have failed and several of the country's largest institutions have required government intervention to remain solvent. Commercial real estate (CRE) collateral values have fallen by more than 42 percent. Construction starts remain partially complete and continue to detract from the quality of neighborhoods and home values. Trillions of dollars of household wealth have vanished, and almost 18 million loans have faced foreclosure since 2007. Unemployment peaked at 10 percent in October 2009 and remains stubbornly high.

Events leading to the financial crisis and subsequent efforts to resolve it involved the dynamic interplay of laws passed by the Congress, regulatory rules, agency-specific policies and practices, and the real estate and financial markets in ways that are continuing to play out. In that regard, our study indicated:

- The markets drove behaviors that were not always prudent. Banks expanded lending to keep pace with rapid growth in construction and real estate development, rising mortgage demands, and increased competition. Many of the banks that failed did so because management relaxed underwriting standards and did not implement adequate oversight and controls. For their part, many borrowers who engaged in commercial or residential lending arrangements did not always have the capacity to repay loans and pursued many construction projects without properly considering the risks involved. Ultimately, these loans created significant losses for the institutions involved and often left the FDIC with the challenge of managing and disposing of troubled assets.
- In response to unprecedented circumstances, the regulators generally fulfilled their supervisory and resolution responsibilities as defined by statutes, regulations, accounting standards, and interagency guidance in place at the time. In addition, the regulators reacted to a rapidly changing economic and financial landscape by establishing and revising supervisory policies and procedures to address key risks facing the industry. While not a focus of this study, our report does acknowledge, however, material loss review findings that showed the FRB, OCC, and FDIC could have provided earlier and greater supervisory attention to troubled institutions that failed. For its part, among other initiatives associated with resolutions, the FDIC reinstituted the use of SLAs with AIs and took steps to promote private capital investments in failing institutions.

We also made the following specific observations related to P.L. 112-88's required matters of review.

- The FDIC's resolution methods—including the SLAs that we studied—were market-driven. Often, failing banks with little or no franchise value and poor asset quality did not attract sufficient interest from viable bidders to enable the FDIC to sell the banks without a loss-share guarantee. The FDIC used SLAs to keep failed bank assets in the banking sector, support failed bank asset values, and preserve the solvency of the Deposit Insurance Fund (DIF). The FDIC has established controls over its SLA monitoring program, which help protect the FDIC's interests, promote loan modifications, and require equal treatment of SLA and legacy loans. We did find, however, that the FDIC should place additional emphasis on monitoring commercial loan extension decisions to ensure that AIs do not inappropriately reject loan modification requests as SLAs approach termination. In addition, we concluded that the FDIC needs to formulate a better strategy for mitigating the impact of impending portfolio sales and SLA terminations on the DIF so that the FDIC will be prepared to address the potentially significant volume of asset sale requests.
- The majority of community banks failed as a result of aggressive growth, asset concentrations, poor underwriting, and deficient credit administration coupled with declining real estate values. These factors led to write-downs and charge-offs on delinquent and non-performing real estate loans as opposed to examiner-required write-downs or fair value accounting losses.
- The regulators have longstanding policies for classifying problem assets, monitoring appraisal programs, assessing capital adequacy, evaluating CRE loan workouts, and administering enforcement actions, when warranted. The regulators also have processes and controls, training programs, and job aids to help ensure examiner compliance and consistency. We found that examiners generally followed relevant policies and implemented them appropriately. For example, examiners usually did not classify as loss loans that the institution claimed were paying as agreed without justification, nor did they question or reduce the appraised values of assets securing such loans. However, examiners did not always document the procedures and steps that they performed to assess institutions' appraisal and workout programs. We also noted that the regulators had different approaches to enforcement actions, particularly related to non-problem banks.
- The FDIC has investment-related policies in place to protect the DIF and to ensure the character and fitness of potential investors. These policies are largely based in statute. By their nature, such policies are going to have an impact on investments in institutions. The FDIC approved most change-in-control and merger applications, although approval rates were lower for states such as California, Florida, and Nevada that were heavily impacted by the financial crisis. The FDIC has policies and procedures for certain aspects of the review of PCIs, and the FDIC generally followed those policies. PCI purchases of failed institutions accounted for 10 percent of total failed bank assets acquired. Finally, we identified instances where the FDIC did not accept proposed open bank investments and instead closed an institution. However, in each case, we found that the FDIC identified concerns with the proposed investment related to safety and soundness issues, proposed management,

or proposed business plans or determined that the proposed transaction would not present the least loss option to the DIF.

Recommendations and Regulator Comments

While the regulators generally implemented their policies appropriately, our study identified certain areas for improvement and issues warranting management attention. In the interest of strengthening the effectiveness of certain supervisory activities and helping ensure the success of the FDIC's ongoing resolution efforts, we made seven recommendations in the following areas:

- **SLA Program.** We made recommendations related to developing additional controls for monitoring AIs' commercial loan modification efforts and developing a more formal strategy for mitigating the impact of impending portfolio sales and SLA terminations on the DIF.
- **Appraisals and Workouts.** We made several recommendations related to clarifying how examiners should review institutions' appraisal programs and strengthening examiner documentation requirements to more clearly define examination methodologies and procedures performed to assess institutions' appraisal and workout programs. These recommendations should help to assure agency management that examiners are consistently applying relevant guidance.
- **Enforcement Orders.** We recommended that the regulators study differences between the types of enforcement actions that are used by the regulators and the timing of such actions to determine whether there are certain approaches that have proven to be more effective in mitigating risk and correcting deficiencies that should be implemented by all three regulators.

The FDIC, OCC, and FRB provided written responses to a draft of this report. The regulators concurred with our recommendations and proposed actions that adequately address the intent of our recommendations.

Beyond these specific recommendations, any changes to policies, practices, and approaches discussed in this report would involve the Congress and require continued discussion and deliberation among the regulators and industry representatives. Such dialogue will be critical to sustaining recovery efforts, ensuring stability and confidence in the financial system, and helping prevent future crises.

INTRODUCTION

This report presents the results of a study required by *Public Law 112-88* (P.L. 112-88). The law requires the Federal Deposit Insurance Corporation Office of Inspector General (FDIC OIG) to conduct a comprehensive study on the impact of the failure of insured depository institutions. The study is quite broad and addresses a number of matters pertaining to Shared-Loss Agreements (SLA), the significance of losses at institutions that failed, examiner implementation of appraisal guidelines, examiner assessment of capital adequacy and private capital investment in failing institutions, examiner implementation of loan workout guidance, the application and impact of formal enforcement orders, the impact of FDIC policies on investments in institutions, and the FDIC's handling of private equity company investments in institutions.

Consistent with the legislation, our overall objective was to conduct a comprehensive study of the impact of the failure of insured depository institutions. Our review timeframes were generally 2008 through 2011. In some cases, our data analysis preceded 2008, and in other cases we gathered information through September 30, 2012, updating data to the extent possible. As required, our scope included open and failed state member, state nonmember, and national banks regulated by the Board of Governors of the Federal Reserve System (FRB), the FDIC, and the Office of the Comptroller of the Currency (OCC), respectively. Our evaluation scope did not include institutions formerly regulated by the Office of Thrift Supervision (OTS).

In conducting our work, we interviewed agency officials, reviewed relevant policies and guidance, reviewed examination reports and working papers, analyzed institution financial data and agency enforcement action statistics, interviewed officials at open institutions, and surveyed borrowers of failed institutions. KPMG LLP assisted us with several areas of review. We conducted our evaluation from January 2012 through October 2012 in accordance with the Council of the Inspectors General on Integrity and Efficiency's *Quality Standards for Inspection and Evaluation.* Our study approach is referenced throughout this report and presented more fully in Appendix 1. Our methodology for sampling is discussed in Appendix 2. Appendix 10 provides a glossary of certain terms used in this report, and Appendix 11 provides a list of acronyms used in this report. Other appendices provide additional detail on the matters discussed in this report to facilitate readability.

BACKGROUND

To provide context for the matters addressed in this report, this section discusses the events leading up to, and the impact of, the financial crisis; the examination and resolution processes; and the study requirements of P.L. 112-88.

Events Leading up to, and the Impact of, the Financial Crisis

The financial crisis that began in 2007 had a profound and lasting impact on the banking industry and broader economy. In January 2011, the Financial Crisis Inquiry Commission reported[1] that while the vulnerabilities that created the potential for crisis were years in the making, it was the collapse of the housing bubble—fueled by low interest rates, easy and available credit, scant regulation, and toxic mortgages—that was the spark that ignited a string of events, which led to a full-blown crisis in the fall of 2008. Trillions of dollars in risky mortgages had become embedded throughout the financial system. When the bubble burst, hundreds of billions of dollars in losses in mortgages and mortgage-related securities shook markets as well as financial institutions that had significant exposures to those mortgages and had borrowed heavily against them.

In February 2010, the Congressional Oversight Panel reported that the bubble in residential property also did much to fuel the bubble in commercial property.[2] Companies involved in residential real estate, construction, and home furnishing grew rapidly as a result of the residential bubble and expanded the demand for office and industrial space. Many new retail properties were also built to serve new residential developments and the consumer credit-driven economy. *Commercial real estate (CRE) loans* accounted for more than one-third of community bank lending. Delinquencies for such loans more than doubled between 2008 and the date of the Panel's 2010 report.

Real estate-secured lending, both residential and commercial, grew at FDIC-insured financial institutions for more than a decade until shortly after the real estate bubble burst in the summer of 2007. From December 2000 to March 2008, real estate-secured loans grew 101 percent, from $2.4 trillion to $4.8 trillion. Figure 1 depicts growth in real estate-secured lending leading up to the financial crisis. Real estate lending includes *1-4 family residential loans*; *multi-family residential loans* such as apartments; other CRE loans such as office buildings; and *acquisition, development, and construction (ADC) loans*. ADC loans are considered to be the riskiest class of CRE loans because of long development times and because they can include properties that are built on speculation.

As the economy deteriorated beginning in 2006 and loan portfolio weaknesses emerged, institutions increased their loan loss reserves to recognize estimated incurred losses. Doing so put greater pressure on their earnings and ability to maintain adequate capital. From 2007 through 2011, FDIC-insured institutions provisioned almost $727 billion for loan and lease losses. Institutions that ultimately failed generally experienced higher rates of increases in reserves because their loan portfolios contained more distressed assets. Figure 2 shows the level and trend of average *Allowance for Loan and Lease Losses* (ALLL) to total loans and leases from December 2005 to June 2011.

As the downturn in the economy continued, loan growth became restricted and financial institutions began to actually experience losses. Exposures to residential mortgages were a primary cause of distress among the largest failed financial institutions, while losses in ADC and other types of CRE loans, often related to residential real estate lending, figured prominently in many smaller institution failures. From 2007 through 2011, FDIC-insured institutions charged off almost $632 billion in loans. As shown in Figure 3, average net charge-off rates peaked at the end of 2009 for all FDIC-insured institutions.

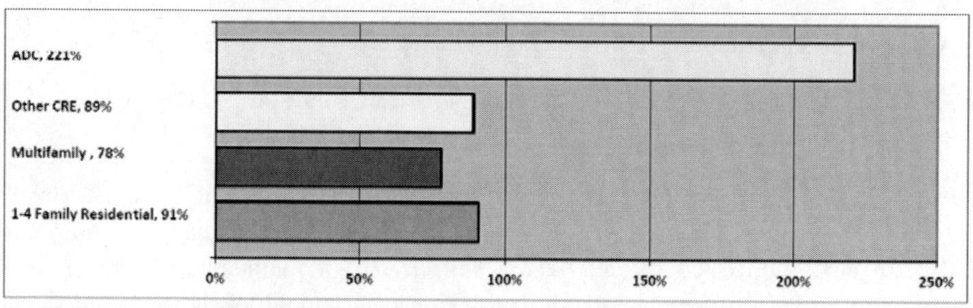

Source: OIG analysis of FDIC *Quarterly Banking Profile reports.*

Figure 1. Growth in Real Estate-Secured Lending—December 2000 through March 2008.

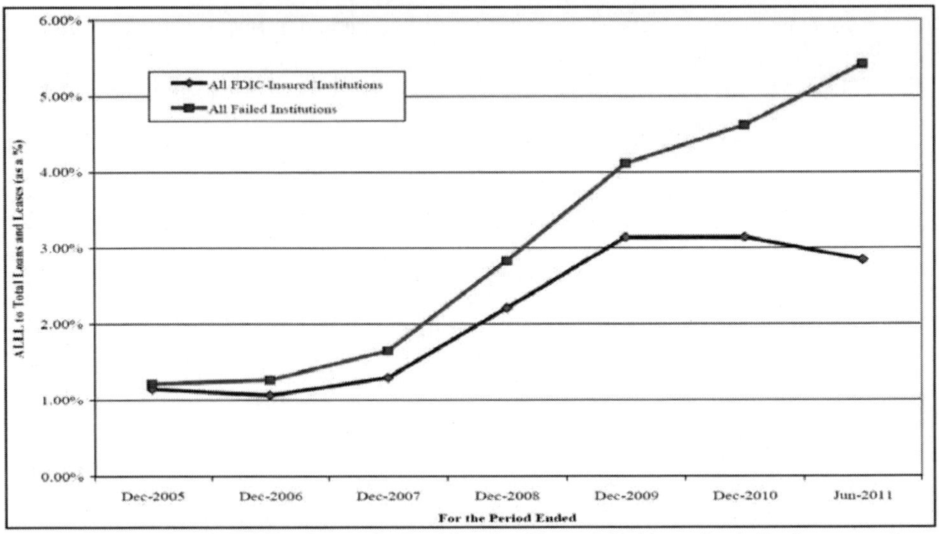

Source: OIG analysis of FDIC's Quarterly Banking Profile and *Uniform Bank Performance Reports* (UBPR) for failed financial institutions.

Figure 2. Allowance for Loan and Lease Losses to Total Loans and Leases.

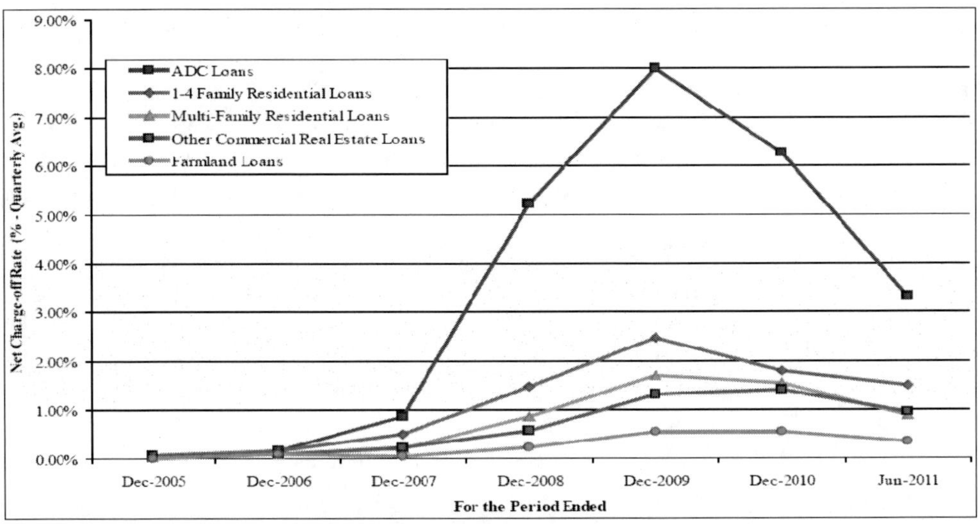

Source: OIG analysis of FDIC's Quarterly Banking Profile reports.

Figure 3. Average Net Charge-Off Rates by Real Estate Loan Categories: All FDIC-Insured Institutions.

Finally, Section 38 of the *Federal Deposit Insurance (FDI) Act*, the *Prompt Corrective Action (PCA)* provisions, requires institutions to maintain minimum capital requirements. Generally, an institution is considered *Well Capitalized* if it maintains a *Tier 1 Leverage Capital ratio*[3] of at least 5 percent.[4] As shown in Figure 4, capital levels for failed financial institutions significantly and steadily declined due, in part, to the recognition of increasing amounts of loan losses and increased ALLL provisions.

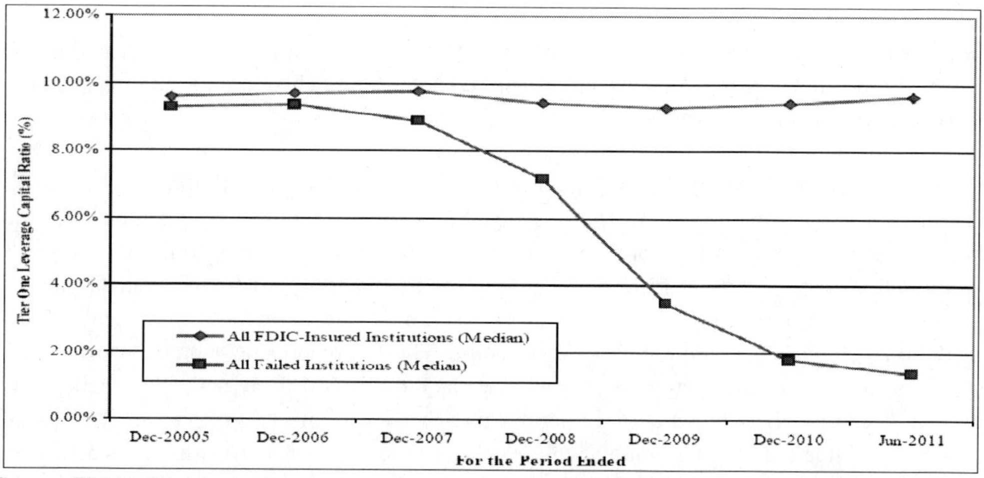

Source: FDIC's Division of Insurance and Research provided medians for all FDIC-insured institutions. OIG analysis of UBPRs determined medians for all failed financial institutions.

Figure 4. Median Tier 1 Leverage Capital Ratio.

Table 1. Average Institutions Supervised and Average Failures by Regulator—2008 through 2011

	FDIC	OCC	FRB
Average Institutions Supervised, 2008-2011	4,838	1,424	840
Average Institution Failures, 2008-2011	63	16	11
Average Percentage of Institutions Supervised	68%	20%	12%
Average Percentage of Institution Failures	70%	18%	12%

Source: OIG Analysis of FDIC's Quarterly Banking Profile and Historical Statistics on Banking data, does not include OTS.

The rapid growth and sudden collapse of the real estate market, and resulting impact on the banking industry, exerted considerable stress on the federal financial regulators (regulators) from both a supervisory and resolution standpoint.[5] The number of problem institutions increased from 76 in 2007 to 702 in 2009, and over 400 institutions with $671 billion in assets failed from 2007 through 2011, resulting in almost $88 billion in losses to the Deposit Insurance Fund (DIF).[6] As shown in Table 1, the average rate of failures during the period 2008 through 2011 was generally proportional to the number of institutions that each regulator supervised.

Overseeing Insured Depository Institutions and Resolving Them When They Fail

The FRB, OCC, and FDIC oversee the nation's insured depository institutions to ensure they operate in a safe and sound manner. The OCC supervises national banks, the FRB supervises state-chartered banks that are members of the Federal Reserve System and bank holding companies, and the FDIC supervises state-chartered banks that are not members of the Federal Reserve System (state nonmember banks). The FDIC also has additional responsibilities for insuring deposits, effectively resolving failed institutions, and maximizing the recovery of receivership assets.

Examining Institutions. The regulators assess the condition of institutions through off-site monitoring and on-site examinations. At each full-scope examination, examiners review the institution's risk exposure on a number of components using the *Uniform Financial Institutions Rating System* (UFIRS). Under this rating system, each financial institution is assigned a composite rating based on an evaluation of six essential components of an institution's financial condition and operations. These component factors address the adequacy of **C**apital, the quality of **A**ssets, the capability of **M**anagement, the quality and level of **E**arnings, the adequacy of **L**iquidity, and the **S**ensitivity to market risk, known as *CAMELS*. Evaluations of the components take into consideration the institution's size and sophistication, the nature and complexity of its activities, and its risk profile. The regulators assign composite and component examination ratings based on a 1 to 5 numerical scale. A "1" indicates the highest rating, strongest performance, excellent *risk management practices*, and least degree of supervisory concern, while a "5" indicates the lowest rating, critically deficient performance, inadequate risk management practices, and the highest degree of supervisory concern.

- **Assessing Asset Quality.** Asset quality is one of the most critical areas in determining the overall condition of a bank and the component rating most relevant to our review. The primary factor affecting overall asset quality is the quality of the loan portfolio and the credit administration program. Loans typically comprise a majority of a bank's assets and carry the greatest amount of risk to their capital. The regulators have longstanding policies for examiners to review an institution's lending and loan review functions and recommend improvements, if needed. Every financial institution must maintain an ALLL, basically a reserve, adequate to absorb estimated credit losses associated with the institution's loan and lease portfolio. During an examination, examiners review a sample of the institution's loan portfolio to determine the adequacy of loan underwriting, credit risk administration, and internal loan review and grading systems as well as adherence to regulatory requirements and institution policy. As a result, examiners identify loans that show undue risk and may not be fully collectible. Institutions are required to categorize such loans as *Substandard*, *Doubtful*, or *Loss*, or some similar classification. If loans are classified as Loss, they are charged off the institution's balance sheet through reductions to the loan balance and ALLL. If examiners disagree with institution's risk rankings or determine that additional loans should be classified, the institution must update its risk rating or classification process. If examiners determine an ALLL is inadequate, the institution must increase its provision sufficiently to restore the ALLL to an adequate level consistent with *generally accepted accounting principles* (GAAP). The related loan loss provision expense directly impacts the institution's capital level.

  Another key aspect of an institution's credit administration is its appraisal program. The December 2010 *Interagency Appraisal and Evaluation Guidelines* (Appraisal

Guidelines) require examiners to consider the size and the nature of an institution's real estate-related activities when assessing the appropriateness of its appraisal program, and assess whether the methods, assumptions, and value conclusions are reasonable when reviewing an appraisal or evaluation for individual transactions. While examiners consider individual appraisals as part of their loan review, loan classification decisions are primarily based on the repayment capability of the borrower, unless the loan is collateral-dependent.

- **Determining Capital Adequacy.** The Capital component rating also plays a prominent role in several of the matters we addressed in our review. Examination policies and procedures require that examiners determine the extent to which a financial institution is maintaining capital commensurate with the nature and extent of risks to the institution and the ability of management to identify, measure, monitor, and control these risks. Regulators are required to impose mandatory corrective actions up to and including closure should institution capital levels fall below regulatory minimums.

Taking Supervisory Action. When regulators identify deficiencies or determine that an institution's risk profile is less than satisfactory, they may take a variety of supervisory actions, including formal and *informal enforcement actions*, to address identified safety and soundness deficiencies. Formal enforcement actions are publicly disclosed by regulators and are used to address more severe deficiencies or when the regulator has limited confidence in an institution's ability to implement changes. The three regulators have somewhat different approaches to enforcement actions and have established policies and procedures that describe the circumstances under which examiners should recommend the use of formal and informal enforcement actions to address identified deficiencies.

Resolving Failed Institutions. Should an institution's condition decline to a point that it becomes *Critically Undercapitalized*, the chartering regulator (a state banking authority or the OCC) is generally required by law to close the institution promptly if it cannot be recapitalized. The FDIC is also required by law to resolve failing institutions in the least costly manner.[7]

- **Shared-Loss Agreements.** Faced with increasing failures, declining asset values, and losses that depleted the DIF, the FDIC reinstituted an approach used in the past crisis of the 1980s and began resolving institution failures using SLAs in November 2008. The FDIC enters into an SLA with a purchaser of failed bank assets, known as the *acquiring institution* (AI), to receive a higher price for, and preserve the value of, the failed bank assets. The SLA guarantees that the FDIC will share in a portion of future asset losses and recoveries for a specific time period. In return, the AI agrees to manage the failed bank assets consistent with its legacy assets, pursue residential loan modifications on qualified loans, and work to minimize losses on those assets. Since loss-sharing began in November 2008, through June 30, 2012, the FDIC used SLAs to resolve 293 of 426 institution failures (69 percent) with $212.7 billion in covered assets.[8]
- ***Private Capital Investment.*** The FDIC was aware of the need for additional capital in the banking system and the contribution that private equity capital could make to

meet this need. To that end, in August 2009, the FDIC Board of Directors issued the FDIC's *Final Statement of Policy on Qualifications for Failed Institution Acquisitions* (PCI SOP), which provided guidance to *private capital investors* (PCI) interested in acquiring or investing in failed institutions. The guidance was aimed at encouraging such investment while ensuring that such PCIs had adequate capital and management expertise, and protections against insider transactions.

P.L. 112-88 Required Matters of Study

Our study addresses matters pertaining to eight areas:

- the impact of SLAs,
- losses at institutions that failed,
- examiner implementation of appraisal guidelines,
- examiner assessment of capital adequacy and private capital investment in failing institutions,
- examiner implementation of CRE loan workout guidance,
- the application and impact of formal enforcement orders,
- the impact of FDIC policies on investments in institutions, and
- the FDIC's handling of *private equity company* investments in institutions.

The legislation included a number of topics under these broad matters, and the report is structured consistent with the order of the legislation.

The legislation also required the U.S. Government Accountability Office (GAO) to study matters related to the causes of institution failures, *fair value accounting*, asset write-downs, the community impact of failures, and the feasibility and impact of SLAs.

Study Results

The financial crisis had devastating impacts on the banking industry, businesses, communities, and consumers. Over 400 institutions have failed and several of the largest institutions have required government intervention to remain solvent. CRE collateral values have fallen by more than 42 percent. Construction starts remain partially complete and continue to detract from the quality of neighborhoods and home values. Trillions of dollars of household wealth have vanished, and almost 18 million loans have faced foreclosure since 2007. Unemployment peaked at 10 percent in October 2009 and remains stubbornly high.

Events leading to the financial crisis and subsequent efforts to resolve it involved the dynamic interplay of laws passed by the Congress, regulatory rules, agency-specific policies and practices, and the real estate and financial markets in ways that are continuing to play out. In that regard, our study indicated the following:

- The markets drove behaviors that were not always prudent. Banks expanded lending to keep pace with rapid growth in construction and real estate development, rising mortgage demands, and increased competition. Many of the banks that failed did so because management relaxed underwriting standards and did not implement adequate oversight and controls. For their part, many borrowers who engaged in commercial or residential lending arrangements did not always have the capacity to repay loans, and pursued construction projects without properly considering the risks involved. Ultimately, these loans created significant losses for the institutions involved and often left the FDIC with the challenge of managing and disposing of troubled assets.

- In response to unprecedented circumstances, the regulators generally fulfilled their supervisory and resolution responsibilities as defined by statutes, regulations, accounting standards, and interagency guidance in place at the time. In addition, the regulators reacted to a rapidly changing economic and financial landscape by establishing and revising supervisory policies and procedures to address key risks facing the industry. While not a focus of this study, our report does acknowledge, however, *Material Loss Review* (MLR)[9] findings that showed the FRB, OCC, and FDIC could have provided earlier and greater supervisory attention to troubled institutions that failed. For its part, among other initiatives associated with resolutions, the FDIC reinstituted use of SLAs with AIs and took steps to promote private capital investments in failing institutions.

Our study identified certain areas for improvement and issues warranting management attention. In the interest of strengthening the effectiveness of certain supervisory activities and helping ensure the success of the FDIC's ongoing resolution efforts, we make seven recommendations in this report. Beyond these specific recommendations, any changes to policies, practices, and approaches discussed in this report would involve the Congress and require continued discussion and deliberation among the regulators and industry representatives. Such dialogue will be critical to sustaining recovery efforts, ensuring stability and confidence in the financial system, and helping prevent future crises.

A high-level presentation of our findings and conclusions on P.L. 112-88's required matters of review follows.

The Impact of Shared-Loss Agreements

Impact on Borrowers of Failed Banks and Surviving Institutions. SLAs kept borrowers in a banking relationship with a healthy, often local, AI.[10] Since the FDIC reintroduced SLAs in November 2008, the FDIC has passed approximately 82 percent of failed bank assets to AIs with and without SLAs, thus keeping those assets in the banking sector. Further, 72 and 73 percent of the failed institutions in Georgia and California, respectively, were acquired by AIs headquartered in those states. Georgia and California were both heavily impacted by the financial crisis. Additionally, AIs paid more for failed bank assets under SLAs than the FDIC would have received without a loss guarantee, and AIs are required to undertake loss mitigation efforts. These factors help to preserve asset values in the markets of surviving institutions.

We surveyed a sample of borrowers in order to gauge their views and satisfaction with AIs. Just over one-half of the borrowers responded that they were satisfied or neutral with regard to their AI, while the remainder indicated that they were dissatisfied with their AI.

Given the narrow scope of the survey and limited response, these responses are not projectable to the population of SLA borrowers or AIs.

The FDIC developed a broad program for managing and monitoring SLAs and established controls to ensure that AIs comply with the SLA terms and conditions, covered assets are managed properly, and losses are minimized. The FDIC established the SLA program quickly in the midst of the financial crisis, and program controls have continued to mature. The legislation required that we study the impact of SLAs on several topics that follow:

- **Impact on Loan Modifications.** The FDIC has established various requirements and controls to ensure AIs comply with SLA terms, including reviewing qualified loans for modifications to minimize incidences of foreclosure, when such actions result in the least loss to the DIF. AI officials predominantly indicated that SLAs either encouraged or had no impact on the rate of loan modifications while officials of institutions without SLAs had mixed views. Our analysis showed that both AIs with and without SLAs increased their level of loan modifications from 2008 through 2011, before leveling off in 2012. Further, AIs with SLAs completed roughly the same number of single-family loan modifications and *short sales* as foreclosures through April 2012.
  SLAs provide a number of incentives for loan modifications, and the FDIC's monitoring program includes a number of controls to increase the probability that AIs will work to keep SLA assets performing[11] and not inappropriately attempt to foreclose on SLA assets in order to collect the loss-share guarantee. However, there is a risk that AIs may be less willing to modify or extend commercial loans as SLAs approach their expiration date for fear of losing loss-share coverage on marginal, but performing, loans. While the Division of Resolutions and Receiverships (DRR) indicated that AIs are interested in extending loans with creditworthy borrowers, DRR could strengthen its monitoring of commercial loan modifications to ensure that AIs continue to make loan modification and extension decisions that result in the least loss for the FDIC.
  It is difficult to determine whether more types of loans could be modified with fewer SLAs or if they could be phased out altogether. AIs without SLAs had a slightly higher loan modification rate than AIs with SLAs. AI officials we interviewed did not believe that more types of loans could be modified with fewer SLAs. Representatives of several of the institutions without SLAs that we interviewed did believe that fewer SLAs would result in more modifications. As markets have improved, fewer resolutions have included SLAs and the FDIC has reduced the level of coverage in later agreements.
- **Impact on Credit Availability.** Our analysis showed that credit availability involves factors other than whether or not an instittion has an SLA. While data limitations impacted our ability to make certain conclusions, we performed analyses that indicated SLAs were not a differentiating factor in loan growth between AIs with and institutions without SLAs. Nationwide, institutions without SLAs experienced a greater decrease in lending than AIs with SLAs. Most bankers we interviewed, with few exceptions, believed that SLAs had a positive-to-neutral impact on lending.

- **Impact on Participation Loans.** It is difficult to quantify the impact that SLAs have on *participation loans*. Participation loans comprised 1 percent of total SLA commercial asset balances, and AIs had a lead, controlling interest in 70 percent of those loans, as of June 30, 2012. This data points to SLAs having limited impact on participations in a broad view. AIs with and institutions without SLAs noted certain challenges with participation loans and in working with participants of such agreements.

SLA Terminations and Asset Sales. The SLAs provide certain controls governing SLA terminations. In addition, the FDIC has issued some guidance related to early terminations and is studying risks that early terminations pose to both the Corporation and the real estate market. The FDIC has terminated some SLAs early but currently is only considering early terminations of SLA portfolios with smaller asset balances. The FDIC could benefit from developing more comprehensive policies and procedures for terminating SLAs when they naturally expire.

The FDIC faces a more immediate risk from potential AI requests to sell commercial SLA assets before shared-loss coverage expires in the fifth year of the agreements, which will occur for most commercial SLAs during 2014 and 2015.[12] During our fieldwork, the FDIC was working to establish a committee to review proposed asset sales and issued guidance to AIs on such proposals. Notwithstanding these ongoing efforts, the FDIC needs to formulate a better strategy and procedures for addressing potential asset sale requests because a significant amount of SLA assets could remain when the commercial SLA coverage periods expire. Further, asset values have not recovered at this point from the financial crisis, although the FDIC noted that there are signs of improvement in even the hardest hit areas of the country.

Reasons for Losses at Failed Institutions

Institutions Failing Due to Write-Downs on Loans that Institutions Considered to be Current. We did not identify any instances of an institution failure caused by significant losses arising from loans for which all payments of principal, interest, and fees were current. Rather, a combination of factors related to institutions' poor credit selection and administration in an environment of declining or reduced real estate values ultimately resulted in asset *write-downs*, often from *non-performing loans* that contributed to most institution failures.

Write-Downs on Loans that Institutions Considered to be Current. We confirmed that institutions recorded as current a significant number of the loans that examiners adversely classified. In almost all cases, however, examiners documented multiple reasons to support their loan classifications, such as inadequate collateral protection, poor performance, and weak borrower cash flow, among others. Those classifications contributed to increased institution loan loss provisions and, to a lesser extent, asset write-downs, both of which ultimately decreased capital. The overall impact on the institution varies widely depending on the institution's size and capital level. In certain circumstances, those capital decreases, combined with classifications of loans that both the institutions and examiners recognized as past due, may have caused institutions' capital levels to drop below minimum PCA capital thresholds, requiring institutions to raise additional capital.

Losses from Fair Value Accounting. We concluded that fair value accounting did not have a significant impact on most institutions' financial statements, especially community banks with total assets of less than $1 billion. Instead, impairment losses on loans recorded at amortized cost, resulting largely from non-performing loans, had a much greater impact on the decline of institutions' regulatory capital levels. These impairment losses led to regulatory action, including closure of many institutions. We identified 13 out of 350 failed institutions for which fair value-related securities losses did significantly contribute to the institution's failure.

Use of Appraisal Procedures on Loans that Institutions Considered to be Current. We found that examiners used appropriate appraisal procedures in classifying loans for which all payments of principal, interest, and fees were current, according to the contractual terms of the loans. Under existing guidance, borrower repayment capacity is the primary consideration for examiner classification decisions. However, in the case of a commercial loan, an appraisal of the loan's collateral, along with a comprehensive analysis of the loan, could lead to an immediate write-down. Under regulatory guidance for classifying residential loans, appraisals typically would not result in an immediate write-down in the value of the loan unless the loan was 180 days or more past due.

Examiner Implementation of Appraisal Procedures and Guidance

Institutions Failing Due to Asset Write-Downs and Examiner Implementation of ALLL Guidance. Multiple contributing factors, such as aggressive growth, asset *concentrations*, poor underwriting, and deficient credit administration practices coupled with declining real estate values caused most institutions to fail. As a result of these factors, institutions experienced elevated non-performing loan levels and ultimately increased asset write-downs and related loan charge-offs. These write-downs and charge-offs depleted institutions' capital and caused them to become insolvent and fail. In that regard, virtually all of the MLRs reported that asset write- downs contributed significantly to the failure of the institution and loss to the DIF. The regulators were often critical of an institution's handling of its credit quality review process, noting that the institution's ALLL provision was not sufficient and its ALLL methodology was inadequate prior to an institution's failure. With respect to ALLL policies and procedures, we found that examiners followed examination policies and procedures for evaluating an institution's ALLL, and routinely reviewed and concluded on an institution's ALLL methodology and sufficiency.

Examiner Implementation of Appraisal Policies. The FRB, FDIC, and OCC each established regulations addressing appraisal requirements and standards. In addition, the Appraisal Guidelines address supervisory matters relating to real estate-related financial transactions and provide guidance to institutions and examiners. Because the regulators use an exception-based process, examination reports and working papers typically do not document institutions' compliance with the Appraisal Guidelines or internal appraisal program requirements. Thus, we could not always determine to what extent examiners actually assessed institutions' compliance with the Appraisal Guidelines because examiners generally only documented identified exceptions. We saw evidence that examiners considered appraisal information in evaluating individual loans for classification purposes in almost all of the loans that we reviewed. However, examiners rarely documented their analysis of individual appraisals' reliability, adherence to appraisal standards, or compliance with appraisal rules and regulations. Moreover, we could not determine to what extent examiners assessed institutions' appraisal programs, which include policies and controls for selecting competent appraisers and monitoring their performance. Still, we found instances in examination reports and working papers where examiners documented non-compliance with the Appraisal Guidelines or exceptions to institutions' appraisal program requirements and policies, consistent with the regulators' exception-based process. Finally, we found examiners did not document their assessment of the adequacy of appraisals within the institution's loan files even when those appraisals were several years old.

FDIC Examiner Implementation of 2010 Appraisal Guidelines. The 2010 Appraisal Guidelines clarified for financial institutions and examiners the supervisory expectations for prudent appraisal and evaluation policies, procedures, and practices. Our review of FDIC examination working papers found limited documentation of FDIC examiners implementing the Appraisal Guidelines. Most of the FDIC examiners that we surveyed indicated the criteria and content of the Appraisal Guidelines had already been incorporated and implemented in the examination process by the time the 2010 guidelines were issued and that the guidelines clarified supervisory expectations and provided criteria for assessing certain areas. We identified differences in how examiners approach assessing institutions' appraisal programs and how they document their assessment. While FDIC procedures call for explicit documentation of an institution's compliance with certain appraisal guidance, FDIC examiners do not consistently follow that guidance.

Capital Adequacy and FDIC Review of Private Capital Investment Applications to Purchase Failed Institutions

Examiner Assessment of Capital Adequacy. Examiners assess an institution's capital adequacy by considering a number of factors, including the institution's financial condition; the nature, trend, and volume of problem assets, and the adequacy of ALLL; earnings and dividends; management's access to additional capital; prospects and plans for growth, as well as past experience in managing growth; access to capital markets and other sources of capital; balance sheet composition and risks associated with nontraditional activities; and risk exposure represented by off-balance-sheet activities. Based on our review of a sample of examinations, we found that, among other relevant factors, examiners considered the quality and risk profile of the insured institution's loan portfolio in nearly all cases included in our sample. Prior MLRs similarly referenced examiner assessment of these factors and often noted that examiners had identified risk in the loan portfolio but could have been more aggressive in ensuring that capital was commensurate with that risk.

PCI Requests Received and Approved by the FDIC. Based on the documentation available to us as of December 31, 2011, we determined that the FDIC received approximately 60 requests from PCIs to bid on insured depository institutions in receivership. The FDIC evaluated those requests based on specific factors spelled out in the PCI SOP, which generally address the capital commitments of the investors and their proposed investment structure. Further, in connection with its deposit insurance and supervisory responsibilities, the FDIC applies statutory and regulatory criteria as well as policy considerations to proposals by PCIs to use either a newly chartered institution or an existing institution to acquire a failed bank. The statutory and regulatory criteria focus on the institution's capital, management, and risk to the DIF as well as whether the acquisition would produce an unacceptable impact on competition within the bank's community. Of the 60 PCI requests received, the FDIC approved 31 (52 percent). Of the remaining 29 requests, investors withdrew, superseded, or abandoned 23; the FDIC returned 2 incomplete applications; and 4 were under review by the FDIC as of December 31, 2011. FDIC-identified concerns with non-approved requests generally related to capital, management, and business plans.

FDIC Policy for Evaluating PCI Requests. The PCI SOP applies to proposals by private capital investors to acquire *failed* institutions. Private capital investors who invest in *open* banks without intending to use the open bank to acquire failed bank assets do not go through the PCI SOP process, but rather follow standard statutory and regulatory requirements. The FDIC tracks investors who go through the PCI SOP, but the FDIC does not formally track other private investment. The FDIC uses the factors listed in the PCI SOP in determining whether to grant investors clearance to bid on failed institutions. This clearance-to-bid process includes a pre-filing meeting, a review of the PCI's documentation supporting its clearance-to-bid request, and a post clearance-to-bid review. While strongly encouraged, pre- filing meetings are not required by statute or as part of the PCI SOP process; therefore, there are no formal policies and procedures for conducting those meetings and the FDIC does not track such meetings in a centralized manner. We could not verify the number of meetings that occurred or how many private investors declined to invest as a result of those meetings. The FDIC does have procedures for reviewing clearance-to-bid requests. We tested a sample of those requests and concluded that the FDIC followed its policies and procedures.

As for post clearance-to-bid reviews, once a private investor targets a specific failing institution for acquisition, the FDIC generally requires that investors update the information originally submitted with respect to their request for clearance to bid. If the FDIC has concerns with the updated information, it may suspend the investor from bidding on the target institution. The FDIC generally documented the authorization for those suspensions via email. Guidance for the review process evolved over time and was formalized in March 2012.

FDIC Examiner Implementation of CRE Loan Workout Guidance

We determined that examiners successfully implemented three of the four areas outlined in interagency guidance titled, *Policy Statement on Prudent Commercial Real Estate Loan Workouts*. With the exception of a few instances, we confirmed that examiners implemented the workout guidance related to loan-specific workout arrangements, classification of loans, and regulatory reporting and accounting considerations. Since examiners use an exception-based process, we were unable to determine from examination documentation whether examiners implemented the fourth area of the Policy Statement, that is, an institution's risk management elements for loan workout programs. While examiners reviewed broader institution loan policies and procedures, examiners did not document their review of risk management elements specifically associated with institutions' workout programs, such as infrastructure, staffing, and information systems for managing troubled assets.

With few exceptions, examiners also followed the guidelines for the use of appraisals when considering CRE loan workouts. The examination guidance for reviewing loans resulting from residential and commercial workouts is similar and primarily focuses on the repayment capacity of the borrower, though there are risk factors that differentiate residential from CRE loans. We found that examiners applied the relevant guidance with few exceptions. Accordingly, we concluded there are no significant differences in implementation between residential workouts and commercial workouts.

Examiner Issuance and Impact of Formal Enforcement Orders

Uniformity and Fairness of Orders. Each of the regulators has a different philosophy and approach to the application of enforcement actions. The regulators generally apply formal enforcement actions uniformly to *problem banks*, defined as 4- and 5-rated institutions. The OCC also frequently places formal enforcement actions on 3-rated institutions with management concerns, while the FDIC and the FRB usually rely on informal actions for such institutions. We determined that the FDIC, OCC, and FRB have policies, procedures, and other controls in place to help ensure uniformity and consistency with their respective formal enforcement actions. Further, those actions are supported by safety and soundness examination findings. For the actions we reviewed, the provisions were consistent with templates and/or guidance maintained by the regulators, the provisions were generally uniform within each regulatory agency, and safety and soundness concerns identified in examination reports formed the basis of the actions.

We also determined there was a correlation between examination ratings, key financial ratios, and enforcement actions, which, in our view, illustrates that regulators applied actions fairly across the institutions they regulated.

We identified some instances of non-problem banks with enforcement actions, and conversely, problem banks without formal enforcement actions. We found that, generally, there were circumstances surrounding the condition and management of the financial institutions that justified the regulators' decisions regarding the imposition (or lack thereof) of such actions.

Impact of Orders on Institutions' Ability to Raise Capital. Over 50 percent of the FDIC- supervised financial institutions with informal or formal actions received material capital injections within the period 2008-2011. In addition, 829 of the 1,515 insured financial institutions (55 percent) with enforcement actions raised capital in the year the enforcement actions were issued and/or in subsequent years. This rate of capital injection compares favorably to all active institutions over the same period. Further, according to investment professionals we interviewed, a depository institution's ability to obtain additional capital depends more on the institution's financial condition, including factors such as earnings performance, asset quality, and growth prospects, rather than the issuance of an enforcement action.

Whether Orders Affect Credit Availability. We did not identify any enforcement actions that directly limited credit to existing borrowers that were current on their loans, or to new borrowers when the financial institution applied prudent underwriting and credit administration practices. We did identify some enforcement action provisions that may have limited lending indirectly. However, in all cases, these provisions responded to an underlying safety and soundness concern. Further, while some bankers and the GAO have indicated that regulatory scrutiny has a negative impact on lending, the prevailing view was that the economy, competition, and lack of loan demand from creditworthy borrowers were bigger factors.

Termination of Orders. We determined that, in general, the FDIC, OCC, and FRB terminated their respective actions uniformly and appropriately across the insured depository institutions and in accordance with their respective policies and procedures. The policies and procedures include the condition that, for an action to be terminated, the financial institution is in material compliance with the provisions of the action, and the financial institution has improved sufficiently so that the action is no longer needed. With few exceptions, we concluded that regulators appropriately terminated enforcement actions when an institution's condition improved and retained actions when institutions continued to present safety and soundness risk.

Impact of FDIC Policy on Investment in Troubled Institutions

FDIC Policies on Capital Investment in Institutions. The FDIC has policies in place to protect the DIF and to ensure the character and fitness of potential investors. By their nature, such policies are going to have an impact on investments in institutions. The FDIC approved the majority of applications that it received for *mergers* and *changes-in-control* of insured institutions—those being common forms of investments in existing institutions. Approval rates for change-in-control and merger applications for states such as California, Florida, Illinois, Nevada, and Washington, which experienced 10 or more failures, were lower than the nationwide average from 2008 through 2011. Other states with 10 or more failures had the same or a greater average approval rate for such applications. The underlying reasons for the non- approval of applications generally related to FDIC concerns with potential investors' proposed business plans, capital and/or financial resources, or management background and experience.

Investors take into consideration a number of factors beyond FDIC policies, including the asset quality of the investment target and the potential for return on investment. We also learned that some investors believed that they could secure a better price and return on assets after a bank failed, particularly if it was likely there would be an SLA loss guarantee. In addition, as required by law,[13] the FDIC must determine that an investment in a troubled bank represents the least possible long-term loss to the DIF. Finally, investment professionals also told us that the implementation of the FDIC's PCI SOP negatively impacted financial institution efforts to raise capital because a number of investors chose not to pursue that means of investment as they were concerned about the associated regulatory requirements. In that regard, the PCI SOP sought to balance the regulatory obligations imposed on investors with the FDIC's duty to protect the safety and soundness of insured institutions and the DIF.

FDIC Examiner Application of Capital Standards When an Institution Successfully Raises Capital. We found that examiners fairly and consistently applied capital adequacy and PCA capital standards when an institution was successful in raising capital. Examiners routinely identified recent capital increases and incorporated those financial results into the examination's analysis of the institution's capital adequacy and capital component rating. While an institution might be successful in raising capital and examiners might view that capital favorably, the capital increase was not always sufficient to mitigate the level of risk and financial deterioration within the institution. We found a close correlation between the CAMELS composite rating and an institution's capital level, which indicates that examiners were assessing capital adequacy consistently. The PCA capital designations are set by law and are tied to the institution's regulatory capital ratios. We found that examiners appropriately considered the need for continued mandatory PCA restrictions when an institution's PCA capital designation increased to *Well Capitalized.*

Whether FDIC Steers Away Potential Investment in Troubled Institutions. We did not identify any instances where the FDIC steered potential investors away from troubled institutions. As discussed previously, the FDIC approved the majority of change-in-control and merger applications from 2008 through 2011. The FDIC indicated that it has also incorporated provisions in its enforcement actions that require institutions to seek merger partners as part of their capital plans, which has been successful in averting failures. Historically, 16 percent of problem banks merged without failing while 22 percent of problem banks ultimately failed. In making decisions on proposed investments in troubled banks, the FDIC considers whether the investment or merger will result in a safe and sound institution and whether the proposed investment presents the least loss option to the DIF. We identified five examples where the FDIC did not accept proposed open bank investments and instead closed the institution. However, in each case we found that, in keeping with its policies, the FDIC identified concerns with the proposed investment related to safety and soundness issues, proposed management, or proposed business plans or determined that the proposed transaction would not present the least loss option to the DIF.

Private Equity Acquisitions of Failed Banks

Between August 26, 2009 and March 31, 2012, 19 PCIs submitted bids on 60 failed institutions.[14] Based on our research, it appears that all 19 PCIs had one or more private equity investors. Of the 19 PCIs, 13 were successful in acquiring 36 failed institutions with total assets of $19.3 billion. PCIs were unsuccessful in acquiring the other 24 failed institutions. PCI acquisitions accounted for about 10 percent of the total failed bank asset acquisitions during that timeframe. In general, the primary reason for PCIs being rejected in their attempts to acquire institutions was their bids were not the least costly bid that the FDIC received.

Reader's Guide to Matters and Supplemental Materials

Public Law 112-88 is comprised of eight Matters to be studied under Section 1, subsection (c), which address the following topics:

Matter 1—Shared-Loss Agreements
Matter 2—Losses
Matter 3—Appraisals
Matter 4—Capital
Matter 5—Workouts
Matter 6—Orders
Matter 7—FDIC Policy
Matter 8—Private Equity Companies

To facilitate reading, the Matters are presented as follows:

- Legislative provision
- Brief context
- Subtopic and summary conclusion
- Detailed discussion and recommendation(s), as applicable

An evaluation of comments received from the FDIC, OCC, and FRB is presented following the Matters.

Multiple Appendices, along with the written responses from the regulators, are included in the final section of the report.

MATTER 1. SHARED-LOSS AGREEMENTS

P.L. 112-88 requires the OIG to study the effect of SLAs, including:

(A) the impact of loss-sharing on the insured depository institutions that survive and the borrowers of insured depository institutions that fail, including:
   (i) the impact on the rate of loan modifications and adjustments;
   (ii) whether more types of loans (such as commercial (including land development and 1-4 family residential and commercial construction loans), residential, or small business loans) could be modified with fewer Loss-Sharing Agreements (LSA),[15] or if LSAs could be phased out altogether;
   (iii) the FDIC's policies and procedures for monitoring LSAs, including those designed to ensure institutions are not imprudently selling assets at a depressed value;
   (iv) the impact on the availability of credit; and
   (v) the impact on loans with participation agreements outstanding with other insured depository institutions;

(B) the FDIC's policies and procedures for terminating LSAs and mitigating the risk of AIs having substantial assets remaining in their portfolio when the LSAs are due to expire;
(C) the extent to which LSAs provide incentives for loan modifications and other means of increasing the probability of commercial assets being considered "performing;"
(D) the nature and extent of differences for modifying residential assets and working out CRE under LSAs; and
(E) methods of ensuring the orderly end of expiring LSAs to prevent any adverse impact on borrowing, real estate industry and the Deposit Insurance Fund.

Faced with increasing failures, declining asset values, and losses that depleted the DIF, the FDIC reinstituted the use of SLAs for resolving bank failures in November 2008. The FDIC has reported that turmoil in the economy and significant uncertainty about future loan performance and collateral values necessitated the use of loss sharing, especially early in the crisis, because potential buyers of failing institutions were unwilling to take on the credit risk associated with failed bank assets, without some form of loss protection. Since loss-sharing began in November 2008, through June 30, 2012, the FDIC used SLAs to resolve 293 of 426 failures (69 percent) with $212.7 billion in covered assets.[16]

Under loss share, the FDIC agrees to absorb a significant portion of the losses—typically 80 percent—on a specified pool of assets that it sold to an AI,[17] and the AI is responsible for absorbing the remainder of the losses. The FDIC provides shared-loss coverage for single-family and non-single-family (commercial, securities, and other) assets:

Single-Family SLAs. These SLAs typically cover a 10-year period. The FDIC provides coverage for losses associated with the following single-family mortgage events: (1) modification, (2) short sale, (3) sale of foreclosed property, and (4) charge-offs pertaining to some second lien loans.

Commercial SLAs. These SLAs typically cover an 8-year period with the first 5 years for losses and recoveries and the final 3 years for recoveries only. Loss coverage also applies to loan sales, provided that prior approval of the sale was obtained from the FDIC.

The FDIC covers credit losses as well as certain types of expenses associated with troubled assets (such as advances for taxes and insurance, sales expenses, and foreclosure costs). For single-family loans, the AI is paid when the loan is modified or the property is sold. For commercial loans, the AI is paid when the assets are written down according to established regulatory guidance or when the assets are sold. AIs are required to remit a portion of any recoveries on previously charged-off assets back to the FDIC. Recoveries on loans that experience loss events are split, in most instances, with 20 percent of the recovery going to the AI and 80 percent to the FDIC. Table 2 provides a snapshot of the SLA program.

As of June 30, 2012, the FDIC's single-family SLA assets totaled $46.7 billion and commercial SLA assets (including securities) totaled $73.8 billion. Approximately 34 percent of the decline in assets subject to loss sharing was from principal write-downs and charge-offs, while 66 percent of the decline was from principal pay-downs.

P.L. 112-88 (1)(A)

The effect of loss-sharing agreements, including the impact of loss-sharing on the insured depository institutions that survive and the borrowers of insured depository institutions that fail.

SLAs kept borrowers in a banking relationship with healthy, often local, AIs. Since the FDIC reintroduced SLAs in November 2008, the FDIC has passed approximately 82 percent of failed bank assets to AIs with and without SLAs, thus keeping those assets in the banking sector. Further, 72 and 73 percent of the failed institutions in Georgia and California, respectively, were acquired by AIs headquartered in those states. Georgia and California were both heavily impacted by the financial crisis. Additionally, AIs paid more for failed bank assets under SLAs than the FDIC would have received without a loss guarantee, and AIs are required to undertake loss mitigation efforts. These factors help to preserve asset values in the markets of surviving institutions.

We surveyed a sample of borrowers in order to gauge their views and satisfaction with AIs. Just over one-half of the borrowers responded that they were satisfied or neutral with regard to their AI, while the remainder indicated that they were dissatisfied with their AI. Given the narrow scope of the survey and limited number of responses, these responses are not projectable to the population of SLA borrowers or AIs.

Effects of SLAs

Based on our prior reviews of the SLA program, and various FDIC literature, guidance, and Congressional testimony, SLAs provide a number of benefits to the FDIC, AIs, and borrowers from failed banks. Of these benefits, keeping assets in the private sector, placing failed bank assets with local acquirers, and preserving asset values while reducing resolution costs can have the greatest program-level impact on borrowers of failed institutions and surviving institutions.

Table 2. SLA Statistics at a Glance—as of June 30, 2012 (in billions)

Category	
Number of Failed Institutions Under SLAs	290*
Initial Assets Subject to Loss Sharing	$212.7B
Current Remaining Assets Subject to Loss Sharing	$120.4B
FDIC Loss Estimate (FDIC's Share) Over the Full Term of SLAs	$43.4B
Actual FDIC Losses at this Point in Term of SLAs (Loss Payments to AIs net of $1.3 billion in recoveries from AIs)	$20.3B

Source: Loss Share Summary Report, June 30, 2012.

* This figure includes IndyMac Bank and excludes SLAs from three failed institutions with initial covered assets totaling $254.7 million. These SLAs were terminated prior to June 30, 2012.

Keeping Failed Bank Assets in the Banking Sector

Any bank failure is disruptive for failed bank borrowers. Either the FDIC sells their loans at closing to an AI or retains them temporarily until the FDIC can determine a disposition strategy to maximize recoveries. As a result, the loan officer and bank that made the loan in the first place are replaced and borrowers have to establish a new banking relationship. An AI—versus the FDIC or an investor—has a greater incentive to work with the borrowers to restructure problem credits or to advance additional funding when prudent, in order to establish an ongoing relationship with the borrower and have a performing asset. With regard to institutions that survived, SLAs can soften the effect of bank failures on the local market by keeping more of the failed bank's borrowers in a banking environment. Without SLAs to attract potential acquirers of failing institutions, the FDIC would have been forced to take ownership of the failed institution's assets and liquidated those assets, which has historically resulted in greater disruption to local markets and been more costly.

We analyzed bank failure data during the most recent crisis and determined that since the FDIC reintroduced SLAs in November 2008, the FDIC has passed approximately 82 percent of the failed bank assets to AIs with and without SLAs, thus keeping those assets in the banking sector.

Keeping Failed Bank Assets with Local Acquirers

When the FDIC markets a failing institution, it typically identifies sound financial institutions in the geographic proximity of the failing institution as potential bidders.[18] We evaluated the failed bank acquisition activity for Georgia and California—two of the states heavily impacted by the financial crisis. We found that 72 percent of failed Georgia institutions and 73 percent of failed California institutions were acquired by AIs that were headquartered in those states.

Analysis of Georgia Institutions. There were 60 institutions in Georgia that failed from November 1, 2008 through March 31, 2012 that were acquired by financial institutions using SLAs. Of these 60 institutions, 43 were acquired by other financial institutions within Georgia and 17 were acquired by out-of-state institutions. We reviewed documentation for 8 of the 17 failed institutions that were acquired by financial institutions outside of Georgia and determined that the FDIC selected the least costly resolution in all 8 instances, as required by the FDI Act.

In some cases, a limited number of Georgia institutions submitted bids for failed institutions because few met the criteria for acquiring a failed bank. Most Georgia institutions are smaller community institutions (89 percent had total assets of less than $500 million as of August 23, 2012) and thus could not absorb the size of the failed institutions. Further, half of the institutions in Georgia had composite CAMELS ratings that generally made them ineligible to purchase a failed bank.

Analysis of California Institutions. There were 26 institutions in California that failed from November 1, 2008 through March 31, 2012 that were acquired by financial institutions using SLAs.[19] Of these 26 institutions, 21 were acquired by other California institutions and seven were acquired by out-of-state institutions. We reviewed documentation for all seven of the failed institutions that were acquired by institutions outside of California and determined the FDIC selected the least costly resolution in all seven instances.

The number of institutions on the bid list varied for each failure, primarily due to the asset size of the failing institution, with larger failing institutions tending to have a smaller number of institutions on the bid list because fewer AIs had sufficient capital to be viable bidders. The small size and impaired financial condition of many California institutions resulted in instances where a limited number of California institutions were qualified to bid. Approximately 68 percent of California institutions had total assets of less than $500 million, and one-third of the institutions within California had a CAMELS composite rating that generally made them ineligible to purchase a failed bank.

Preserving Asset Values and Minimizing the Cost of Failures

During the crisis, SLAs helped to preserve asset values and reduce the FDIC's resolution costs. Asset prices were low and investors were demanding steep liquidity and risk discounts when bidding on failed bank assets. In such circumstances, loss-sharing guarantees enabled the FDIC to sell failed bank assets at prices closer to their intrinsic value[20] instead of accepting depressed prices.

Preserving asset values should, in turn, minimize the impact that failed bank assets have on local markets. AIs are required to undertake loss mitigation efforts and to use their best efforts to maximize collections from assets, which helps support collateral values in the failed bank's market. Mortgage loans that are managed well, and held for a period of time, may perform better with the improvement in the overall economy. As a result, the AI and the FDIC may receive a better return on the loans than foreclosures in the current real estate market.

Finally, the FDIC estimates that SLAs reduce resolution costs to the DIF, which is funded by assessments on insured depository institutions. Interested bidders may submit resolution bids with or without a loss-sharing feature. The FDIC performs an LCT of all of the bids and is required to select the least costly form of resolution. The LCT considers all expected losses on the assets covered in an SLA over the life of the agreement.

The FDIC studied the use of SLAs between 1991 and 1993 and found that an AI's purchase of failed bank assets with an SLA was less costly for the FDIC than a purchase without an SLA.[21] For the current financial crisis, as of June 2012, the FDIC estimated that SLAs are projected to save approximately $41 billion over the liquidation scenario.[22] DRR also determined that the average loss rate (estimated losses from failure divided by the failed bank's total assets) for SLA resolutions has been 21.3 percent compared with loss rates of 26.1 percent for failed institution acquisitions without loss share, and 35.6 percent for a payout.[23]

Borrower Satisfaction Survey

In order to gauge SLA borrower views and satisfaction with AIs, we sent surveys to a sample of 130 commercial borrowers and 130 single-family borrowers of failed banks that were acquired by AIs. As of November 27, 2012, we received a total of 49 surveys (32 commercial and 17 single-family). The 49 borrowers indicated that the status of their loans was as follows: performing (32); paid off (10); delinquent (3); and foreclosed (4).[24] Overall, the commercial and single-family borrowers responded similarly:

- Twenty-four borrowers were dissatisfied with their AI, 16 were satisfied and 10 were neutral.[25] The primary reasons for the dissatisfaction related the reasonableness of loan terms offered by the AI and the AIs' level of customer service.
- Compared to their failed bank, 25 borrowers were less satisfied with their AI, 4 were more satisfied with their AI, and 20 were equally satisfied with their AI and failed bank.
- Forty-three borrowers indicated that they contacted their AIs with inquiries or questions about their loans. Twenty-four were dissatisfied with the AIs' level of responsiveness, 14 were satisfied, and 5 were neutral.
- Twenty-seven commercial borrowers indicated that they discussed loan renewals with their AI.[26] Fifteen borrowers were dissatisfied with the AIs' efforts to renew loans, seven were satisfied, and five were neutral.
- Twenty-two borrowers responded that they discussed loan modifications with their AI. Seventeen were dissatisfied with the AIs' loan modification efforts, four were satisfied, and one was neutral.
- Twenty borrowers responded that they requested or obtained additional loans or credit from their AIs. Fourteen were dissatisfied with the AIs' lending efforts, three were satisfied, and three were neutral.
- Six borrowers responded that they contacted the FDIC with a complaint or inquiry about their AIs. Four were dissatisfied with the FDIC's responsiveness, and two were neutral.

Given the narrow scope of the survey and limited response from borrowers, these responses are not projectable to the population of SLA borrowers or AIs.

P.L. 112-88 (1)(A)(i)

The impact of SLAs on the rate of loan modifications and adjustments.

The FDIC has established various requirements and controls to ensure AIs comply with SLA terms, including reviewing qualified loans for modifications to minimize incidences of foreclosure, when such actions result in the least loss to the DIF. AI officials predominantly indicated that SLAs either encouraged or had no impact on the rate of loan modifications, while officials of institutions without SLAs had mixed views. Our analysis showed that both AIs with and without SLAs increased their level of loan modifications from 2008 through 2011, before leveling off in 2012. Further, AIs with SLAs completed roughly the same number of single-family loan modifications and short sales as foreclosures through April 2012.

Residential Mortgage Modification Requirements. Single-family SLAs require the AI to implement a loan modification program, such as the *Home Affordable Modification Program* (HAMP) or the FDIC Loan Modification Program, to modify loans that improve borrower affordability, increase the probability of performance, and allow borrowers to remain in their homes.

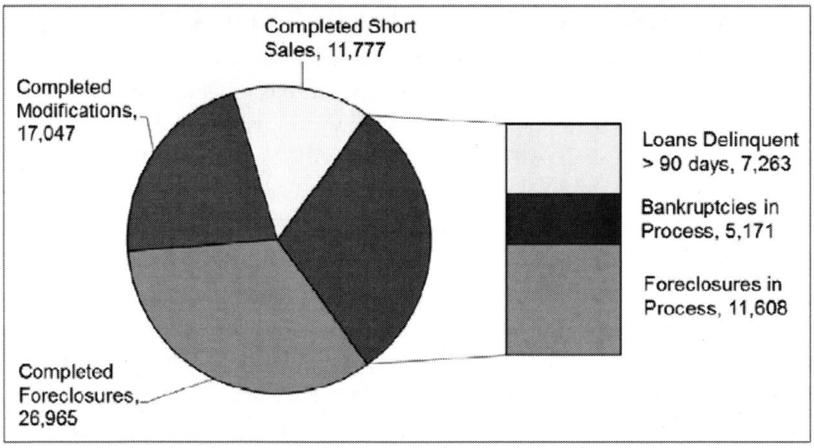

Source: Data provided by DRR.

Figure 5. SLA Single-Family Loss Mitigation Efforts (January 2009 through April 2012).

For single-family mortgage loans, the AI is required to perform and document a least loss evaluation when assessing the feasibility of modifying a single-family mortgage loan. If a qualified borrower accepts the modification offer, the AI can submit a shared-loss claim to the FDIC. The other option for submitting a claim for a residential mortgage loan occurs after all loss mitigation options have been pursued and the real estate owned property is sold after a foreclosure.

AIs had modified 17,047 single-family loans and completed 11,777 short sales under SLA programs through April 2012. As discussed in Matter (1)(A)(ii), we found that both AIs with and without SLAs reported an increasing level of loan modifications from 2008 through 2011. Figure 5 presents cumulative information for completed modifications, foreclosures, and short sales and in-process information for delinquent loans and loans in bankruptcy or in the process of foreclosure. It is possible that loans in the process of being foreclosed could be modified.

Commercial Real Estate Loan Restructuring Requirements. Commercial loan restructurings are designed to convert a non-performing loan, or a loan that is on the verge of becoming non-performing, to performing status consistent with the ability of the borrower to repay the debt. Loan modifications can reduce the loan payment for a period of 2 to 4 years and may permanently alter some conditions of the loan, including extension of the term of the loan, interest rate reduction, and principal forbearance or forgiveness which may be adjusted in any sequence. The commercial SLA requires the AI to seek to maximize recoveries on CRE loans. In addition, AIs may want to develop and expand business relationships with commercial borrowers in these communities. Restructuring loans at risk can turn these loans into interest- earning assets while keeping the protection of loss-share coverage during the 5-year coverage period. It also provides an opportunity for borrowers to improve their business conditions. Nonetheless, both borrowers and lenders must recognize the near-term challenges posed by an oversupply of construction and development projects in many communities.

On December 17, 2010, the FDIC issued *Commercial Loss Mitigation Guidance on Commercial Real Estate (CRE) Loans* to AIs, which notes that AIs should conduct a review of the loan portfolio to identify shared-loss CRE loans that are candidates for modification. A loan modification should be offered if the evaluation indicates that it will minimize the loss to the FDIC and the AI on that shared-loss CRE loan. The evaluation and analysis of shared-loss CRE loans should be consistent with the AI's current underwriting practices for non-shared-loss loans.

The guidance also encourages AIs to pursue disposition strategies other than foreclosure when loan modifications do not present the best net present value (NPV) alternative or are not otherwise feasible. For commercial loans, the AI is reimbursed for claims based on a loan or portion of a loan that is categorized as a loss under supervisory examination criteria. Therefore, an AI may file a shared-loss claim on a commercial loan restructure as a result of a principal reduction, as well as a result of a foreclosure.

The FDIC began tracking commercial loan modifications in December 2011. As of September 30, 2012, AIs reported to DRR that 30,218 SLA loans were more than 90 days delinquent and that AIs had modified 14,182 commercial loans. Further, AIs had completed at least 15,265 foreclosures[27] and an additional 4,428 foreclosures were in process.

Public Inquiries and Bankers' Views on the Impact of SLAs on Loan Modifications

As of August 27, 2012, DRR had received 146 inquiries pertaining to AI residential and commercial loan modifications and responded to 142 of those inquiries.[28] The inquiries generally pertained to borrowers' inability to obtain a loan modification from the AI, obtain more favorable loan modification terms, or renew an existing loan; alleged that AIs wrongfully pursued foreclosure actions and did not adequately consider borrowers' single-family loan modification requests under an approved program such as HAMP; and requested assistance on obtaining a loan modification.

In order to obtain bankers' views on the impact of SLAs on loan modifications, we selected a sample of 12 AIs from states that experienced a large number of bank failures. The 12 AIs collectively acquired 73 failed institutions with initial SLA assets totaling $44.8 billion, representing 25 percent of failed institutions under SLAs and 21 percent of initial assets subject to loss share.

We also selected 12 institutions without SLAs from the same states that were similar in size and location to some of the failed institutions that the 12 AIs in our sample had acquired. However, six of the institutions elected not to participate in our study because they had no involvement with, or opinions regarding, SLAs. Of the remaining six institutions that participated in our study, only two had business dealings with AIs.

Eight of the 12 AIs that we interviewed indicated that SLAs had a positive impact on residential loan modifications and that they were performing more loan modifications as a result of the SLAs. Two of the AIs indicated that SLAs had little or no impact on residential loan modifications. Seven AIs reported that SLAs have little impact on commercial loan modifications and that AIs treat SLA assets similarly to their non-SLA (legacy) assets. One AI responded that the short-term nature of commercial SLAs had a negative impact on an AI's willingness to make commercial loan modifications.

With respect to the six institution officials that we interviewed that did not have SLAs, three of the officials believed that SLAs do not affect an institution's ability to pursue either residential or commercial loan modifications. Two believed that SLAs negatively impact an institution's ability to pursue either residential or commercial loan modifications because the institution is more interested in collecting the SLA loss guarantee rather than continuing to rely on the repayment ability of the borrower. One official believed that an institution's ability or willingness to pursue a loan modification was enhanced by an SLA, because the SLA provides an opportunity for the AI to identify the inherent risks involved in purchasing an asset while allowing those identified risks to be mitigated through modifying or restructuring commercial loan transactions during the SLA period.

We also participated in a panel discussion about the impact of SLAs with the FDIC's Advisory Committee on Community Banking.[29] The Advisory Committee is comprised of community bankers representing various states. Two of the committee members whose institutions were also AIs indicated that SLAs provided an incentive for their institutions to modify loans. Two committee members whose institutions did not have SLAs expressed their belief that the loss- sharing guarantee did not provide an incentive for AIs to modify loans and instead incentivized AIs to foreclose and collect on the loss-share guarantee.

P.L. 112-88 (1)(A)(ii)

Whether more types of loans could be modified with fewer LSAs, or if LSAs could be phased out altogether.

It is difficult to determine whether more types[30] of loans could be modified with fewer SLAs or if they could be phased out altogether. AIs without SLAs had a slightly higher loan modification rate than AIs with SLAs. We found that both AIs with and without SLAs reported an increasing level of loan modifications from 2008 through 2011, before the loan modification rate leveled off in 2012. AI officials we interviewed did not believe that more types of loans could be modified with fewer SLAs. Officials at several of the institutions without SLAs that we interviewed did believe that fewer SLAs would result in more modifications. As markets have improved, fewer resolutions have included SLAs, and the FDIC has reduced the level of coverage in later agreements. Loss coverage for most of the commercial SLAs will naturally expire in 2014 and 2015 and for the single-family SLAs from 2019 through 2021.

Loan Modifications for AIs and Institutions Without SLAs. It is difficult to fairly compare loan modification activity between AIs with SLAs and institutions without SLAs because AI loan portfolios include failed bank assets. A more relevant comparison may be between AIs with and without SLAs. However, the FDIC does not reimburse AIs for losses on assets acquired without SLAs and does not collect loan modification statistics for AIs without SLAs.

The nature of individual loan portfolios is also a major factor in how successful an institution is in modifying loans. Single-family portfolios comprised of *Alt-A loans*[31] with negatively amortizing characteristics are difficult to modify because the proposed loan modification frequently cannot pass the *NPV test* (i.e., the loan modification is less costly than a foreclosure). Likewise, AIs that acquired assets from failed institutions with CRE portfolios concentrated in distressed areas such as Georgia or Nevada may find it more difficult to modify loans because collateral values have fallen so drastically.

Although the FDIC does not collect modification statistics for AIs without SLAs, in order to gauge SLAs' impact on loan modifications, we analyzed *Call Report* data on *troubled debt restructuring* (TDR) activity for AIs with and without SLAs. Loan modifications should be reported as TDRs if the borrower is experiencing financial hardship and if the institution grants some form of concession on the loan.

AIs without SLAs had a slightly higher average loan modification rate than AIs with SLAs. Both AIs with and without SLAs showed an increasing level of loan modifications from 2008 through 2011, before the loan modification rate[32] leveled off in 2012 as shown in Figure 6.

The higher loan modification rate for the AIs without SLAs was influenced by the modification rates of three large institutions. As of June 30, 2012, these institutions accounted for 43 percent of the total loans for AIs without SLAs and had modification rates of 5.9 percent, 3.7 percent, and 3.5 percent. Excluding the three large institutions, the June 2012 loan modification rate for AIs without SLAs would drop from 2.8 to 1.7 percent, in line with the SLA modification rate.

On an individual institution basis, loan modification rates as of June 30, 2012 varied for both AIs with and without SLAs. The rate for AIs without SLAs ranged from zero to 8.6 percent and the rate for AIs with SLAs ranged from zero to 11.3 percent. Additionally, the existence of an SLA did not prevent an institution from having one of the higher loan modification rates. As indicated in Table 3 below, both AIs with and without SLAs had approximately the same percentage of institutions that exceeded a 4-percent loan modification rate.

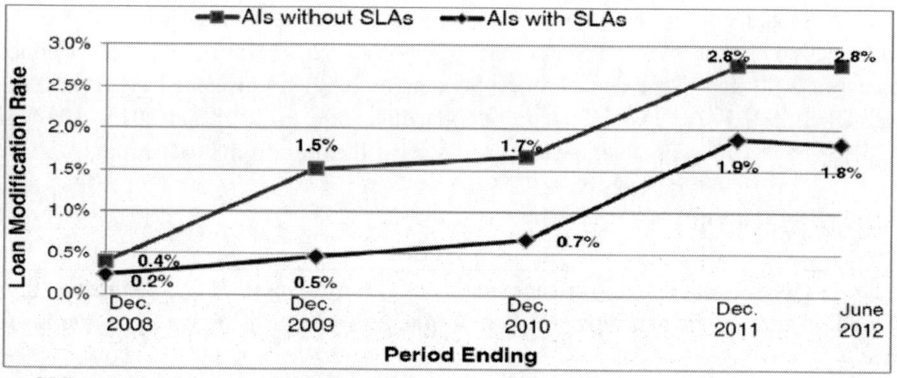

Source: OIG analysis of data provided by the Division of Risk Management Supervision (RMS).

Figure 6. Average Loan Modification Rates for AIs with and without SLAs.

Table 3. Modification Rates for AIs as of June 30, 2012

	AIs without SLAs		AIs with SLAs	
	Number	Percent	Number	Percent
Loan Modification Rate > 4%	9	12%	20	14%
Loan Modification Rate 1% to 4%	28	38%	73	49%
Loan Modification Rate < 1%	37	50%	55	37%
Total	74	100%	148	100%

Source: OIG analysis of Call Report data.

Bankers' Views. We asked officials from our sample of AIs and institutions without SLAs about their views on whether more loans could be modified with fewer SLAs:

- None of the officials of the 12 AIs that we interviewed believed that more types of loans could be modified with fewer SLAs. Six of them indicated that they perform more modifications because of SLA coverage than they would otherwise. One said that without an SLA, the institution would modify fewer loans and would have to make loan termination decisions earlier.
- Officials at four of the six institutions without SLAs believed that more loans could be modified with fewer SLAs or if SLAs were eliminated. This opinion is based on the belief that AIs will not modify loans because they might lose SLA coverage, that it is easier to just collect the loss-share guarantee, and the AIs do not have an incentive to resolve problem loans. One official believed that AIs are more experienced and better staffed to resolve problem assets. Another institution official stated that AIs had already evaluated the loan portfolios, including those which might be eligible for loan modification, when they prepared their bid to acquire failed bank assets.

With respect to whether SLAs could be phased out altogether, as the market has improved, fewer resolutions have resulted in SLAs. Further, the FDIC has been reducing the percentage of loss- share coverage in more recent SLAs, with some agreements requiring AIs to share in 50 percent of the losses. DRR reported that the annual percentage of bank resolution activities that involved SLAs rose to a high of 82 percent in 2010 and declined to 63 percent in 2011 and 42 percent through September 2012. As discussed later, most of the commercial SLAs' 5-year loss coverage period will expire in 2014 and 2015. The single-family SLAs have a 10-year coverage term and most will expire from 2019 through 2021.

P.L. 112-88 (1)(A)(iii)

The FDIC's policies and procedures for monitoring SLAs, including those designed to ensure institutions are not imprudently selling assets at a depressed value.

The FDIC developed a broad program for managing and monitoring SLAs and established controls to ensure that AIs comply with the SLA terms and conditions, covered assets are managed properly, and losses are minimized. The FDIC established the SLA program quickly in the midst of the financial crisis, and program controls have continued to mature.

Key SLA Program Controls

The FDIC has established a number of controls and processes to monitor SLAs and ensure that AIs comply with the terms and conditions of the SLAs, covered assets are managed properly, and losses are minimized, including the following:

- The loss-sharing percentage is intended to provide the AI with an incentive to minimize losses.
- AIs are required to pursue the least loss strategy in managing and disposing of covered assets.
- AIs are required to manage covered assets consistent with their legacy assets.
- AIs are required to implement a loan modification program acceptable to the FDIC and review qualified residential loans for modification.
- Compliance monitoring contractors (CMC) and FDIC staff perform on-site visitations and testing of submitted claims.
- FDIC examiners in RMS review AIs' compliance with SLA terms, including consistent management of covered and non-covered assets and proper accounting treatment.
- SLAs limit AIs' ability to sell covered assets without the FDIC's prior approval.
- A "True-up" provision requires AIs to reimburse the FDIC after the termination of an SLA, if losses are less than anticipated.

These controls are discussed in more detail in Appendix 3 of this report. Further, DRR identified these additional SLA controls:

- An FDIC specialist is assigned to each AI to monitor AI compliance with the SLAs and facilitate communication between the AI and the FDIC.
- The FDIC created a system to track the resolution of compliance review findings and implemented a secondary review to ensure the resolution of material findings over $75,000.
- The FDIC established a Compliance Review Committee to ensure that every failed institution is reviewed annually in accordance with FDIC established guidelines.
- The FDIC has policies in place to escalate AI non-compliance with SLAs and distributes a monthly Watch List report to DRR management and other regulators, which identifies non-compliant AIs.
- DRR distributes all compliance reviews done by CMCs and DRR to RMS where the FDIC is the primary federal regulator of the AI and to the FRB and OCC, upon request.

P.L. 112-88 (1)(A)(iv)

SLAs' impact on the availability of credit.

Our analysis showed that credit availability involves factors other than whether or not an institution has an SLA. While data limitations impacted our ability to make certain conclusions, we performed an analysis that indicated SLAs were not a differentiating factor in loan growth between AIs with and institutions without SLAs. Nationwide, institutions without SLAs experienced a greater decrease in lending than AIs with SLAs. Most bankers we interviewed, with few exceptions, believed that SLAs had a positive-to-neutral impact on lending.

Given the magnitude of the SLA program, we performed a comprehensive evaluation of the FDIC's program for monitoring SLAs. The primary objective of the evaluation was to evaluate DRR's overall efforts to monitor and ensure compliance with the terms of conditions of the SLAs. We also performed individual audits of seven AIs to evaluate each AI's compliance with the SLA terms. Our evaluation and audit efforts are discussed in more detail in Appendix 3.

To assess availability of credit, we evaluated loan growth from the beginning of 2008 through the end of 2011 for all AIs with SLAs and the total population of all institutions that did not have SLAs. We used an analysis similar to that which the FDIC uses to estimate lending activity. As described below, this analysis has limitations. The loan amounts that we analyzed were adjusted for mergers and acquisitions, which helped ensure that changes in loan amounts were due to lending rather than the acquisition of another institution's loans.

Nationwide Changes in Total Loan Balances for AIs with SLAs and Institutions without SLAs

Both AIs with SLAs and institutions without SLAs experienced an overall decrease in lending over this period. Based on aggregate dollar volume, institutions without SLAs had a greater overall decrease in lending (-6.2 percent) than institutions with SLAs (-2.0 percent). However, the overall decline in loan balances for institutions without SLAs was heavily impacted by lending declines in the five largest institutions over the 4-year period.

Proportionately, the number of institutions without SLAs that had loan growth from the beginning of 2008 to the end of 2011 exceeded the number of AIs with SLAs that had loan growth during this period. A total of 4,298 out of 7,212 (60 percent) of institutions without SLAs had increases in total loans. Only 39 out of 145 (27 percent) of AIs with SLAs had increases in total loans.

One weakness with this analysis is that it simply measures changes in an institution's total loan balance during two financial reporting periods. The analysis does not consider balance changes due to borrower pay-down of loans or loan charge-offs. DRR reported that total SLA loan balances decreased by $93.4 billion due to borrower pay-downs and principal write-downs. Thus, adding SLA loan pay-downs and write-downs back to total AI loan balances yields a lending increase of 7.2 percent (versus a decrease of -2.0 percent) from 2008 through 2011. Data was not available to perform a similar analysis for institutions without SLAs.

SLA Terms that May Impact Credit

The commercial SLAs contain the following two provisions that one could interpret as limiting the availability of credit.

- **Permitted Amendments.** Initially, AIs were not allowed to extend the term of a covered loan beyond the term of the SLA without risking losing SLA coverage on the loan. The FDIC relaxed this provision in December 2011.
- **Permitted Advances.** The AI may advance a borrower up to an additional 10 percent of the book value of the loan. The AI will lose loss-share coverage on the entire loan for advances in excess of 10 percent.

These provisions are intended to minimize losses and are supposed to prevent the AIs from "throwing good money after bad" and thereby exposing the DIF to additional loss claims. The FDIC has processes and a loan review committee for considering AI-proposed exceptions to these provisions, and the FDIC will approve exceptions on a case-by-case basis if they result in a least loss outcome for the asset in question.

Inquiries from the Public

From June 2010 through August 27, 2012, the FDIC received 14 inquiries from the public, which stated that the borrowers were unable to obtain additional credit. The FDIC assigned a specialist and had provided written responses to 12 of the inquirers and was in the process of responding to the remaining two inquirers as of August 27, 2012. The inquiries pertained to borrowers' inability to obtain additional funds to complete construction projects. One complaint stated that the AI was refusing to accept partial payments from the borrower because the institution was demanding payment in full. In addition to these inquiries, the FDIC received several others that discussed borrowers' inability to renew or extend existing loans. These inquiries also pertained to loan modifications and are addressed earlier in Matter (1)(A)(i).

Institution Views on How SLAs Impact Credit Availability

We asked officials of the 12 AIs and 6 institutions without SLAs that we interviewed about what impact they believed the SLAs had on their ability to extend credit to borrowers. A summary of those responses is provided below.

- Officials from five of the AIs stated that the SLAs had a positive impact on their ability to make credit available to borrowers because the SLAs provided the institutions with new customers. Two officials said that the SLAs have a negative impact because the FDIC's review process slows down their approval process and it takes substantial

  resources to manage SLAs, making it harder to build new business. Officials from eight AIs said there was no impact. Several officials said that they are looking to make loans to any creditworthy borrowers and use the same criteria to determine when to extend new credit to all customers.
- Seven AI officials said that they experienced an increase in lending since entering into their SLAs.
- Nine AI officials said that the SLAs do not limit or impair their ability to extend additional credit to creditworthy borrowers. Three said they are reluctant to extend additional credit to borrowers whose loans are covered in an SLA if the additional credit would be backed by the same collateral that secures the SLA assets. In such instances, the new loan is subordinated to the SLA-covered loan with respect to the underlying collateral.
- Seven officials said that they had received complaints from borrowers regarding their limited access to credit. The AI officials said that these borrowers had poor credit histories.

With respect to the six institutions that do not have SLAs:

- Officials at three of the institutions believed that SLAs could have a negative effect on an AI's ability to make credit available because the institution is focused on the short term and administering the SLA.
- Officials at two institutions expected a positive effect because the SLA assists in protecting an institution's potential loss and in turn allows the AI to continue providing loans.
- One institution's officials did not feel the existence of the SLA would have an effect on credit availability in general.

We inquired about SLAs' impact on credit availability during the June 2012 meeting of the FDIC Advisory Committee on Community Banking. None of the committee members expressed a concern that SLAs impact credit availability.

Participations are generally large loans involving multiple institutions. The participating institutions may have either a lead (decision-making) or downstream (non-decision-making) interest in a participation loan. It is difficult to quantify the impact that SLAs have on such loans. However, participation loans comprise 1 percent of total commercial SLA assets. Participation loans can present risks to institutions because downstream participants often rely on the lead participant to perform adequate underwriting and credit administration, and the terms of the participation agreement may not adequately protect the interests of downstream participants. Loan participations were often noted as a contributing factor to an institution's failure in MLRs.

P.L. 112-88 (1)(A)(v)

SLAs' impact on loans with participation agreements outstanding with other insured depository institutions.

It is difficult to quantify the impact that SLAs have on participation loans. Participation loans comprised 1 percent of total SLA commercial asset balances, and AIs had a lead, controlling interest in 70 percent of those loans, as of June 30, 2012. This data points to SLAs having limited impact on participations in a broad view. Officials from AIs with and institutions without SLAs noted certain challenges with participation loans and in working with participants of such agreements.

FDIC SLA Guidance on Loan Participations

DRR issued Risk Sharing Asset Management Guidance (RSAM-2011-15), *FDIC Commercial Loss Mitigation Guidance for Loan Participations*, dated June 24, 2011, to AIs regarding the administration of commercial SLA loans that are not wholly-owned by the AI, including participations. The guidance provides that AIs should conduct a review of their commercial SLA portfolio as soon as possible to identify participations with priority given to SLA loans when imminent monetary default is probable. The AI's evaluation should include a comprehensive legal review of the participation agreement and all related loan documents to determine the AI's rights, responsibilities, recourse, and risks and to identify potential conflicts with the terms of the commercial SLA.

Table 4. Active Loan Participations in Commercial SLAs (in millions)

Participation Interest	Initial Balance	Current Loans	June 30, 2012 Balance
Lead Interest	$645.8 (55%)	862 (76%)	$501.9 (70%)
Downstream Interest	$533.4 (45%)	269 (24%)	$218.5 (30%)
Total	$1,179.2	1,131	$720.4

Source: DRR information request to AIs.

AI interests in participation loans totaled $720.4 million or 1 percent of the SLA commercial asset balances as of June 30, 2012.[33] AIs had a lead interest in 70 percent of the covered participation loans, as of June 30, 2012, as shown in Table 4.

Further, 29 percent of the covered participation loans have some form of government guarantee, such as a Small Business Administration loan guarantee, according to data that the AIs provided to the FDIC as of June 30, 2012. Assuming that the lead participant complies with the terms of the government guarantee program, this guarantee reduces this risk of loss to the participants and to the FDIC.

As of August 27, 2012, the FDIC had received seven inquiries regarding participation loans in the SLA program since DRR began recording inquiries in June 2010. All of the inquiries were from non-SLA institutions that were downstream participants. Four of the inquiries related to downstream participating institutions' questions regarding the terms of shared-loss coverage, two inquiries related to a request for the FDIC to facilitate proposed transactions involving the loan participation, and one inquiry related to litigation filed by the downstream institution against the AI. The FDIC reported that it has responded to all seven inquiries.

Banking Industry Views on Participations

Bankers that we interviewed offered differing viewpoints regarding whether SLAs had an impact on participation loans. In general, AI officials indicated that the shared-loss guarantee does not impact their treatment of participation loans. They noted though that institutions without SLAs that have participation interests tend to delay and avoid writing down participation loans. Some stated that their SLA often impacted negotiations with participant institutions because the participating institution did not understand the terms of the SLA and believed that they should share in loss coverage. AI officials also reported that the time required to get approval from the FDIC hampers the AI's ability to work directly with the other participants.

P.L. 112-88 (1)(B)

FDIC's policies and procedures for terminating LSAs and mitigating the risk of acquiring institutions having substantial assets remaining in their portfolios when the LSAs are due to expire.

The SLAs provide certain controls governing SLA terminations. In addition, the FDIC has issued some guidance related to early terminations and is studying risks that early terminations pose to both the Corporation and the real estate market.

The FDIC could benefit from developing more comprehensive policies and procedures for terminating SLAs when they naturally expire. The FDIC faces a more immediate risk from potential AI requests to sell commercial SLA assets before shared-loss coverage expires in the fifth year of the agreements, which will occur for most commercial SLAs during 2014 and 2015. During our fieldwork, the FDIC was establishing a committee to review proposed asset sales and issued guidance to AIs on such proposals. Notwithstanding these ongoing efforts, the FDIC needs to formulate a better strategy and procedures for addressing potential asset sale requests because a significant amount of SLA assets could remain when the commercial SLA coverage periods expire. Further, asset values have not recovered at this point from the financial crisis, although the FDIC noted that there are signs of improvement in even the hardest hit areas of the country.

Institutions without SLAs, on the other hand, indicated that the AIs with lead participation interests are influenced by the shared-loss guarantee and tend to foreclose without regard for downstream participants. Both officials at AIs and at institutions without SLAs agreed that participation loans were problematic, and stated that, in the future, they would likely avoid participation loans.

Policies and Procedures Related to Terminations

The FDIC has developed procedures, in the form of job aids, for processing the early termination of SLAs. However, DRR has not developed policies or procedures for handling terminations that expire naturally according to the SLA. As discussed later in this report, because many of the commercial SLAs' loss coverage will expire in 2014 and 2015, it is important that DRR establish procedures for staff to follow when processing SLA terminations.

SLA Provisions Pertaining to Loan Sales

Generally, the FDIC discourages loan and note sales during the life of an SLA, preferring to let the agreement run its course. The FDIC can, however, grant permission for such sales on an exception basis if the AI is able to provide documentation that the sales result in the least loss. AIs may request to sell SLA assets as part of a group or individually. DRR generally refers to portfolio sales as the sale of 10 or more unrelated assets. Note sales involve the sale of an individual note or several notes to the same purchaser. The AIs must sell SLA assets to unaffiliated parties through a competitive bid process.

After approximately 4.25 years under the commercial SLA or at any time during the single- family SLA, the vast majority of the SLAs explicitly state that the AIs may request the FDIC's concurrence to sell all or a portion of the SLA assets. The AIs may sell SLA assets without the FDIC's approval but would lose SLA coverage associated with any losses on the sold assets. The FDIC can also repurchase SLA assets from an AI or require an AI to sell assets if the AI is not properly managing the assets. Finally, DRR can withhold SLA payments, remove certain SLA assets from coverage, or terminate an AI's participation in the program all together if an AI is not properly managing the assets. During our fieldwork, DRR was taking steps to address issues involving SLA asset sales. It was establishing a loan sale review committee to review AI requests for note and portfolio sales. The committee is expected to ensure consistency in the FDIC's review and approval of SLA asset sales and should be established by the end of 2012. In October 2012, DRR also sent a letter to the AIs reiterating the SLA requirement that AIs seek to maximize recoveries. The letter stated that the FDIC will consider all proposals for portfolio sales but will only provide its concurrence or consent if the AI has clearly demonstrated to the FDIC that the proposed sale maximizes collections on an asset-by-asset basis and otherwise satisfies the requirements in the SLA pertaining to the sale of assets. The letter also states that AIs should continue to use their best efforts to maximize collections and should not rely on asset sales as the primary resolution strategy for SLA assets. Further, during a conference that DRR held for AIs in October 2012, DRR reiterated that it would approve portfolio sale requests if the AIs could show that the sales represented the least loss alternative. DRR informed the AIs that they should provide the FDIC with the following documentation when requesting concurrence or consent to sell SLA assets:

- a cost justification such as an internal credit memorandum outlining the proposed sale that was approved by the AI's Board,
- evidence that the AI considered and/or attempted other alternatives and determined that a portfolio sale was the least loss resolution, and
- an NPV analysis and documents such as current appraisals to support the AI's valuation of the assets.

DRR stated that commercial loan portfolio sale requests could theoretically be as high as \$63.0 billion should AIs request approval to sell all of the projected remaining commercial SLA assets when these assets reach the 4.25 year mark. However, as discussed below, the FDIC does not expect the volume of sale requests to be as high as \$63.0 billion. About \$49.9 billion of these assets (or 79 percent) will reach the 4.25 year mark from July 2014 through June 2015. DRR has not made projections regarding probable future loan sale requests but does maintain information showing the geographic areas where remaining SLA assets are concentrated. Also, around March 2012, the FDIC began aggregating data on portfolio sale requests and approvals. As of June 30, 2012, DRR reported that AIs sold \$885.5 million of commercial SLA assets through six portfolio sale transactions, of which \$605.4 million (68.4 percent) was charged off, and the FDIC authorized one single-family sale of 13 loans valued at \$1.2 million. The FDIC was not tracking individual note sale requests and approvals at the time of our fieldwork.

Institution Views on SLA Asset Sales

Five of the officials at 12 AIs that we interviewed stated that they would like more clarity and guidance from the FDIC regarding their rights to sell SLA assets.[34] Further, four AI officials believed that note and portfolio sales would have a negative impact on the real estate industry and the economy. These officials indicated that portfolio sales would result in a large supply of SLA assets with limited demand, which would depress real estate prices. These officials noted that as the commercial SLA coverage period ends, AIs will want to sell SLA assets to reduce losses. Two AI officials believed that there would be little impact on local economies because the damage from real estate devaluations has already occurred and because the AIs can take write-downs on commercial assets during the 5-year coverage period. Thus, the overall impact at the end of the SLA coverage period will be minimal.

Officials at the AIs and at institutions without SLAs provided the following additional comments.

- Four AI officials stated that they expect to have substantial assets remaining at the end of the SLA, and are concerned about the need for write-downs and portfolio sales at the end of the SLA. One said that ADC loans pose the biggest problems and the market is not likely to improve soon.
- Six AI officials said that as SLA termination dates come closer, there will be an increased incentive for AIs to collect loss claims. Five AIs said that if an institution is doing its job correctly, it charges loan balances down and claims losses as necessary throughout the SLA coverage period.
- Six AI officials said they would identify the good and bad assets, liquidate bad assets through pay-offs and charge-offs; move good assets to their legacy loan portfolios; and conduct portfolio sales when possible.
- Five AI officials suggested that the FDIC should extend the coverage period for commercial SLA assets in hopes that real estate markets continue to improve. The FDIC has discussed this internally but is not inclined to extend SLA coverage periods.
- Of the officials at the six institutions without SLAs that we interviewed, four said that a pending SLA termination provides an incentive for an AI to collect loss claims as opposed to working to keep the assets performing.

As the commercial SLAs approach their termination date, there is a possibility that the AIs will have a greater incentive to dispose of non-performing SLA assets in order to collect the FDIC loss guarantee before coverage expires. DRR noted that the 5-year coverage period of the commercial SLAs was determined when SLAs were first used in 1991. Since the terms of most commercial loan agreements typically do not exceed 5 years, the FDIC chose a 5-year term for the coverage period for commercial SLAs during the last crisis. At the time the FDIC entered into these shared-loss transactions in 1991, the expectation was that 5 years out, the economy would be on the path to a sustained recovery. The FDIC patterned its agreements for the current crisis after the agreements used in the last crisis, including the length of the agreement. DRR noted that given the depth of the recession in the current crisis, at least in some of the hardest hit real estate markets, the recovery has been muted to date. However, DRR also noted that there are signs that the long-awaited upturn is happening in even the hardest hit areas. Finally, DRR noted that given that the SLA coverage period on all but one of the commercial shared-loss agreements does not expire until 2014 at the earliest and assuming the recovery continues, there is reason to believe the impact of the coverage period expiration for covered assets on local real estate markets may not be that pronounced.

Although the SLAs require the FDIC's concurrence to sell SLA assets, the portfolio sale clause may create an expectation on the part of the AI that the FDIC will allow the AI to sell assets at the 4.25 year mark. A concentration of portfolio sales could present risk to the FDIC in the form of substantially increased SLA loss claims and to local real estate markets based on the sale of a number of SLA CRE assets at a discount. During our fieldwork, DRR was establishing a committee to study these risks, identify possible solutions, and consolidate the approval of SLA asset sales in DRR headquarters. DRR also provided additional guidance to AIs on SLA asset sales. Still, we concluded that the FDIC needs to better formulate its strategy for mitigating the risks associated with portfolio asset sales and SLA terminations. DRR will also need to develop procedures and ensure adequate and correct resources are assigned to implement this strategy and to address the potentially high volume of terminating SLAs and requests for asset sales.

Recommendation

We recommend that the Director, DRR:

1. Develop a strategy for mitigating the impact of impending portfolio sales and SLA terminations on the DIF and ensure that procedures, processes, and resources are sufficient to address the volume of terminations and potential requests for asset sales.

SLA Incentives to Promote Loan Modifications

AIs are required to modify single-family loans and to pursue other loss mitigation efforts to minimize foreclosures, when possible. The commercial SLA does not prescribe specific criteria outlining when an AI is required to modify a commercial loan. However, the FDIC has encouraged AIs to modify commercial loans when doing so represents the least loss alternative for the FDIC. The FDIC has identified the following factors as incentives for AIs to pursue loan modifications and restructures:

- The loss-sharing percentage provides an incentive for the AI to modify loans because the AIs are responsible for a portion of the losses.
- A performing, interest-earning asset is of more value to the AI than the FDIC's loss coverage on a foreclosed asset.
- Commercial restructures provide the AI the opportunity to develop and expand business/borrower relationships.
- The residential foreclosure process can be lengthy and difficult in some states.

P.L. 112-88 (1)(C)

Extent to which SLAs provide incentives for loan modifications and other means of increasing the probability of commercial assets being considered "performing."

SLAs provide a number of incentives for loan modifications, and the FDIC's monitoring program includes a number of controls to increase the probability that AIs will work to keep SLA assets performing and not inappropriately attempt to foreclose on SLA assets in order to collect the loss-share guarantee. However, there is a risk that AIs may be less willing to modify or extend commercial loans as SLAs approach their expiration date for fear of losing loss-share coverage on marginal, but performing, loans. While DRR indicated that AIs are interested in extending loans with creditworthy borrowers, the division could strengthen its monitoring of commercial loan modifications to ensure that AIs continue to make loan modification and extension decisions that result in the least loss for the FDIC.

We also asked our sample of officials at AIs and institutions without SLAs about their views on whether SLAs increase the probability of commercial assets becoming performing:

- Ten of the 12 AI officials believed that SLAs have a neutral effect on the probability of non-performing assets becoming performing and that cash flow and the repayment ability of the borrower are the determining factors. Two AI officials responded that SLAs may have a positive effect because the SLA provides the AI with more time to work with marginal borrowers and AIs want to develop long-term customer relationships.
- Officials from three of the six institutions without SLAs believed that SLAs do not increase the probability that non-performing commercial assets will become performing. This view was based primarily on the belief that SLA institutions would rather collect on the shared-loss guarantee than expend the time and effort to improve loan performance.

SLA Incentives for Extending Commercial Loans

Many SLA commercial loans are 3-to 5-year, interest-only loans with principal due as a balloon payment at the end of the loan. Borrowers often attempt to extend the term of those loans instead of paying the balloon amount, especially in times of economic distress.

We determined that a risk pertaining to the SLA program is that as an SLA approaches maturity, the AI may have a greater incentive to not extend maturing commercial loans. If the AI does not extend a loan and the borrower cannot immediately pay the full amount of the loan, the loan may become non-performing, providing an incentive for the AI to foreclose and collect on the loan while losses are still covered under the SLA. DRR officials stated that AIs decide on loan extensions on a case-by-case basis and that it is in an AI's best interest to extend the term of *performing loans* with creditworthy borrowers.

In making modification or extension decisions, institutions may be unable to change the terms of the underlying loans, as is often requested by the borrowers. Institutions are required to maintain minimum *loan-to-value (LTV) ratios*. When collateral values decrease, as they have in many geographic areas, banks may be required to request principal repayments in order to meet LTV requirements.

DRR staff informed us that DRR does not currently track loan extensions. DRR could mitigate risks of AIs not reasonably extending commercial loans by adding additional controls to its SLA monitoring program. For example, DRR could:

- communicate to AIs DRR's expectation that AIs should be working to maximize collections when making loan extension decisions,
- have CMCs review a sample of AI loan extension decisions during CMC on-site visits, and
- collect and monitor trend information on extensions across AIs to identify AIs with lower rates of loan extensions for further analysis.

Recommendation

We recommend that the Director, DRR:

2. Research risks presented by commercial loan extension decisions and determine whether DRR should develop additional controls for monitoring AIs' efforts to extend the term of commercial loans.

P.L. 112-88 (1)(D)

Nature and extent of differences for modifying residential assets and working out commercial real estate under LSAs.

There are a number of similarities between residential and commercial loan modification efforts. Most notably, both residential and commercial modification efforts have to result in the least loss alternative to the FDIC and DIF. One key difference between residential and commercial modifications is that AIs are required to implement a residential loan modification program, while AIs are encouraged to modify troubled CRE loans.

Table 5 presents the key features of residential and commercial loan modifications. Other than AIs being required (versus encouraged) to implement a residential loan modification program, the table illustrates how the efforts are similar.

Table 5. Key Features of Residential and Commercial Loan Modification Efforts

Key Feature	Residential Modification	Commercial Modification
SLA Requirement for a Loan Modification Program	AIs are required to implement a loan modification program acceptable to the FDIC.	The AI is required to seek to maximize recoveries and encouraged to modify loans.
Solicitation of Potential Candidates	AIs should solicit borrowers in default or in danger of imminent default for modifications.	The AI should conduct a review of the SLA loan portfolio to identify commercial SLA loans that are candidates for modification.
Underwriting	The AI must verify borrower income and occupancy status and other underwriting requirements.	The AI must conduct a global cash flow analysis, evaluate guarantors, and assess collateral values.
Loan Adjustment Options	The AI applies a "waterfall" analysis to adjust the borrower's mortgage terms to achieve a 31-percent *debt-to-income ratio* by first reducing the loan interest rate, then extending the loan term, and, where necessary, offering forbearance of principal.	The modification may include extending the term of the loan, an interest rate reduction, or principal forgiveness or forbearance.
Least Loss Analysis	AIs conduct an NPV test (i.e., the NPV of the modification must exceed the NPV of a foreclosure).	The modification is subject to the NPV test (i.e., the NPV of the modification must exceed the NPV of the foreclosed collateral, discounted payoff (DPO), or short sale alternatives).
Alternatives to Modification	If the NPV test is negative, the AI should consider the borrower for a short sale or deed-in-lieu program before pursuing foreclosure.	If the loan does not qualify for a modification, other alternatives such as a short sale or a DPO may be considered if one of those alternatives minimizes loss to the FDIC.

Source: OIG-developed from SLA and other FDIC documents.

P.L. 112-88 (1)(E)

Methods of ensuring the orderly end of expiring SLAs to prevent any adverse impact on borrowing, the real estate industry, and the Deposit Insurance Fund.

As discussed earlier, the FDIC does not have a formal strategy for ensuring the orderly end of expiring SLAs and mitigating the risk that terminating SLAs will negatively impact local real estate economies because asset values have not recovered. The FDIC and the AI may agree to terminate an SLA early or allow it to run its natural course. The FDIC has terminated some SLAs early but currently is only considering early terminations of SLA portfolios with smaller balances. The 5-year loss coverage for most commercial SLAs will expire in 2014 and 2015, and the 10-year loss coverage for most single-family SLAs will expire from 2019 through 2021.

Early SLA Terminations

As the dollar amount of the remaining covered assets declines over the life of the SLA, an AI may have an incentive to terminate an SLA with the FDIC to reduce or eliminate future compliance costs and discontinue the level of FDIC oversight. In making such requests, an AI asks the FDIC to terminate its SLA early for a certain amount of money, or the FDIC reaches out to the AI. The FDIC may also have an incentive to accept an early termination offer if doing so results in the least loss to the DIF.

In early 2012, the FDIC put further consideration of early termination offers from AIs on hold because it was concerned that early terminations may not maximize value to the DIF and that AIs might use their in-depth knowledge of the true value of their SLA assets to disadvantage the FDIC. In mid-2012, however, the FDIC began a pilot program that consisted of offering AIs with single-family SLA portfolios under $1.5 million the opportunity to terminate those portfolios in exchange for a cash payout from the FDIC. In determining a cash payout amount, the FDIC performs an asset valuation review to derive an acceptable payout price. As of October 5, 2012, DRR had terminated seven SLAs, four of which were through the pilot program.

Prior to the early termination of an SLA, the FDIC performs a review to ensure that the AI has resolved all outstanding issues, including an AI's payment of any questioned costs resulting from CMC or OIG compliance audits to the FDIC. RMS staff in headquarters and the field as well as the AI's primary federal regulator must also approve the early termination. The FDIC's Legal Division prepares the early termination agreement, which is signed by the AI and the FDIC.

Natural SLA Expirations

The SLA loss reimbursement period is 5 years for the commercial SLAs and 10 years for single- family SLAs. The SLAs detail the AIs' responsibilities to assist the FDIC in unwinding SLAs when they naturally expire; that is, when they reach the expiration date contained in the SLA. The AIs are required to provide requested data to the FDIC, cooperate with the FDIC to facilitate the termination, and perform requested services.

DRR estimates that when the commercial and single-family SLA coverage expires, as much as $108.7 billion in assets will lose SLA coverage and remain in the institutions' portfolios assuming AIs do not sell SLA assets before the SLA coverage periods end.[35] According to DRR, as much as $62.4 billion in commercial SLA assets could theoretically remain in AIs' portfolios when SLA loss coverage expires, as shown in Figure 7.

DRR performed analyses over a 42-month period through June 30, 2012, to estimate the rates of decline in commercial SLA asset balances. DRR reported that commercial SLA assets were declining at an average rate of 1.9 percent per month. Further, DRR data showed that covered commercial assets were 53 percent of their inception balances as of June 30, 2012.

DRR stated that theoretically, as much as $46.3 billion in single-family assets could remain in AIs' portfolios when SLA loss coverage expires. DRR also analyzed the rate of decline in single-family assets.

According to this analysis, as of June 30, 2012, single-family assets were declining at an average rate of 1.4 percent per month. DRR reported that this decline will slow as the age of each SLA increases. DRR also reported that covered single-family assets were 62 percent of their inception balances as of June 30, 2012.

As discussed earlier, we are recommending that DRR develop a strategy for mitigating the impact of impending portfolio sales and SLA terminations.

MATTER 2. LOSSES

P.L. 112-88 requires the OIG to study the significance of losses, including–

(A) the number of insured depository institutions that have been placed into receivership or conservatorship due to significant losses arising from loans for which all payments of principal, interest, and fees were current, according to the contractual terms of the loans;

(B) the impact of significant losses arising from loans for which all payments of principal, interest, and fees were current, according to the contractual terms of the loans, on the ability of insured depository institutions to raise additional capital;

(C) the effect of changes in the application of fair value accounting rules and other accounting standards, including the ALLL methodology, on insured depository institutions, specifically the degree to which fair value accounting rules and other accounting standards have led to regulatory action against institutions, including consent orders and closure of the institution; and

(D) whether field examiners are using appropriate appraisal procedures with respect to losses arising from loans for which all payments of principal, interest, and fees were current, according to the contractual terms of the loans, and whether the application of appraisals leads to immediate write-downs on the value of the underlying asset.

The primary factor leading to loan losses is a borrower's unwillingness or inability to repay outstanding debt. When an institution or an examiner considers a loan (or a portion of a loan) uncollectible and of such little value that its continuance as a bankable asset is not warranted, then that amount is required to be promptly charged off. The losses on charged-off loans, in turn, can ultimately deplete an institution's capital.

The performance of individual loans and the deterioration of a financial institution's condition, however, can be concealed by loan underwriting structures or liberal use of extensions, renewals, or interest reserves that mask loan weaknesses and obscure a borrower's repayment capacity or ability to meet reasonable repayment terms.

GAAP and supervisory guidance require each institution to maintain an ALLL at a level that is appropriate to absorb estimated credit losses associated with the held-for-investment (HFI) loan and lease portfolio. The ALLL is an estimate of uncollectible amounts that is used to reduce the book value of *loans and leases held for investment* by the amount of probable incurred losses as of the balance sheet date. This valuation allowance is established by the institution and maintained by charges against the institution's operating income. Although in establishing its ALLL, an institution considers the probable incurred losses in individual loans and categories of similar loans, the ALLL is a general allowance available to absorb all charge-offs in the portfolio; no part of the allowance is segregated for, or allocated to, any particular asset or group of assets.

The regulators do not retain information about losses from loans that institutions consider to be current. Accordingly, available financial data did not allow us to specifically determine the extent of losses occurring from loans that the institution considered to be current. However, to assess whether institutions failed as a result of losses associated with current loans, we first reviewed 131 MLRs, covering 142 failures, to identify the causes of institutions' failures. Next, we analyzed Quarterly Banking Profile reports and UBPR data to determine which factors ultimately resulted in asset write-downs that contributed to most institution failures.

Lastly, we reviewed a *non-statistical sample* of 42 institutions that failed with low levels of non-current loans at the time of failure to determine to what extent losses associated with current loans contributed to the institutions' failure. We reviewed institutions with the lowest levels of non-current loans to identify situations where examiner-required write-downs may have had a greater impact on the institution's financial condition.

P.L. 112-88 (2)(A)

The number of insured depository institutions that have been placed into receivership or conservatorship due to significant losses arising from loans for which all payments of principal, interest, and fees were current, according to the contractual terms of the loans.

We did not identify any instance of an institution failure caused by significant losses arising from loans for which all payments of principal, interest, and fees were current. Rather, a combination of factors related to institutions' poor credit selection and administration in an environment of declining or reduced real estate values ultimately resulted in asset write-downs, often from non-performing loans, that contributed to most institution failures.

Review of MLR-Identified Causes of Failure

None of the MLR reports indicated that an institution was placed into receivership or conservatorship due to significant losses arising from loans for which payments of principal, interest, and fees were current, according to the contractual terms of the loans. The most commonly reported causes of the 142 failures studied by the Inspectors General for the Treasury, FRB, and FDIC were the institutions' management strategy of aggressive growth that concentrated assets in CRE and ADC loans, often coupled with inadequate *risk management practices* for loan underwriting, credit administration, and credit quality review. The extent that these conditions contributed to material loss failures is shown in Table 6.

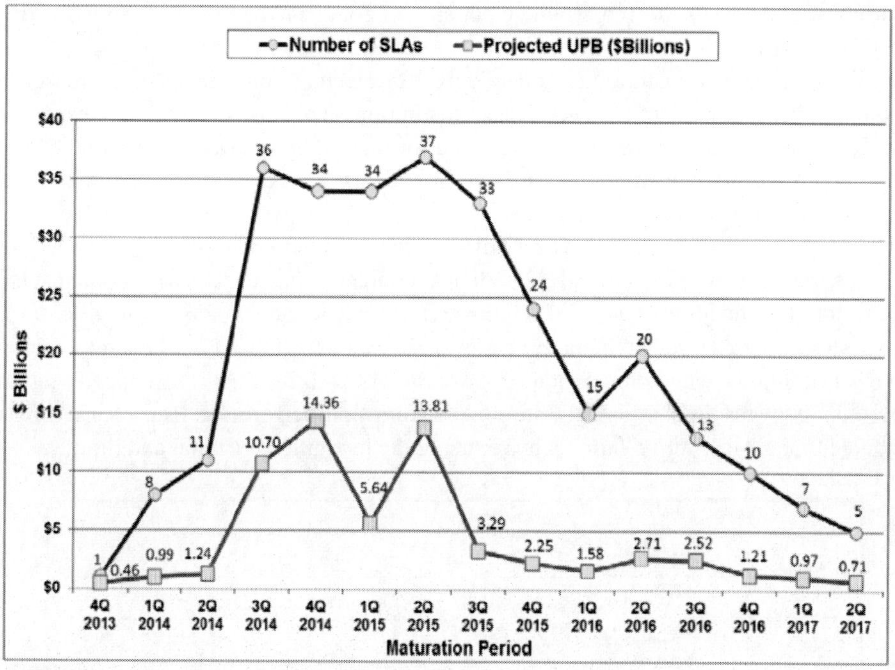

Source: DRR.

Figure 7. Natural Expiration of Commercial SLA Coverage.

Table 6. Most Common Contributing Causes of Material Loss Failures

	FDIC	OCC	FRB
High ADC or CRE Concentrations	95%	86%	100%
Rapid Asset Growth	69%	82%	82%
Relying on Volatile Funding Sources to Support Growth	55%	27%	14%
Inadequate Loan Underwriting	70%	50%	23%
Inadequate Credit Administration Practices	71%	55%	27%
Inadequate Credit Risk Management	76%	77%	73%

Source: OIG analysis of 131 MLR reports for 142 institutions that failed from January 2007 through September 2011.

Analysis of Loan Charge-Offs

Financial institutions report their current financial condition and results of operations in Call Reports, filed quarterly with the FDIC. Call Reports do not specifically capture data on charge- offs and related losses from loans that institutions considered to be paying as agreed. However, loans are classified as Loss and charged off when they are considered uncollectible and of such little value that their continuance as bankable assets is not warranted. Thus, it is unlikely that an examiner would require an institution to completely charge off a loan that was genuinely paying as agreed under reasonable terms. Moreover, even if all or some portion of such a loan were written off, the impact on the institution's financial condition likely would be temporary and limited because payments would increase interest income and net earnings, and the institution would recognize ongoing payments as a recovery for the charged-off items.

While all financial institutions collectively experienced some level of increased loan charge-offs during the recent financial crisis, institutions that failed collectively experienced greater levels of loss. As shown in Figure 8, on average, the *net real estate loan charge-off* rate for failed financial institutions rose faster and higher than the rate for the financial institutions that did not fail.

Of note, in the case of failed institutions, the management strategy of aggressive growth that concentrated assets in CRE and ADC loans, coupled with inadequate risk management practices for loan underwriting, loan administration, and credit quality review, resulted in average rates of net charge-offs remaining elevated, even after those rates began to decline in surviving institutions. The combination of those factors with declining or reduced real estate values ultimately resulted in asset write-downs from non-performing loan charge-offs that contributed to most institution failures by reducing the institutions' capital and liquidity.

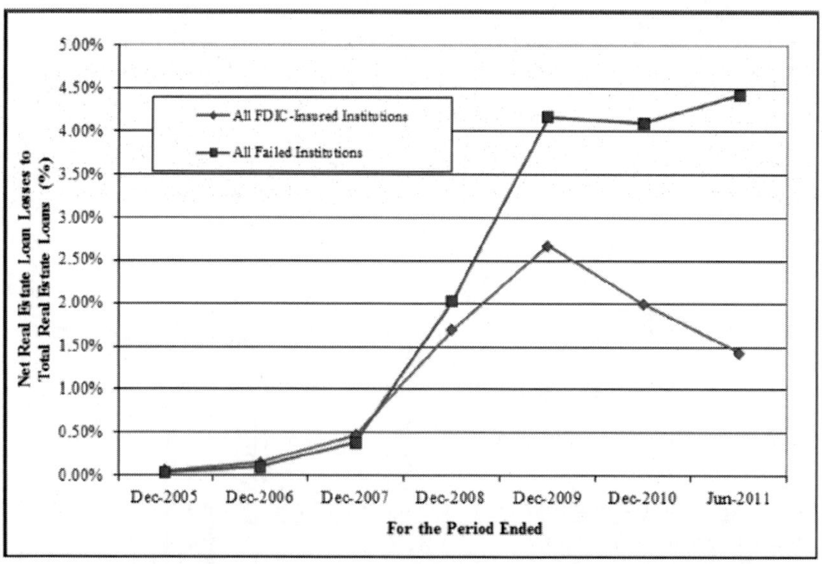

Source: OIG analysis of the FDIC's Quarterly Banking Profile reports and UBPRs for failed financial institutions.

Figure 8. Net Real Estate Loan Charge-Off Rate.

We found that losses on 1-4 family residential loans represented the greatest dollar amount of loan losses among various types of real estate-secured loans. ADC loans also contributed significantly to the level of losses incurred, and these losses represented a significantly higher portion of net charge-offs, as a percentage of its portfolio segment, than the non-1-4 family residential loan categories. The 1-4 family residential loan losses led to declines in interest income; diminished profits or net operating losses; declines in liquidity; capital depletion; and ultimately, for some, the financial institutions' failure.

In total, the 350 FDIC-insured institutions that failed from January 2007 through September 2011 recognized approximately $21.8 billion in loan loss provisions and $15.0 billion in net credit losses (write-offs less recoveries).[36] On average, these net credit losses represented 83.0 percent of Tier 1 Capital.[37] Such credit losses, coupled with declining interest income and increasing loan loss provision expenses, depleted capital and were a significant contributing factor in these institutions' failures. In addition, the DIF recognized an additional $56.9 billion in losses after these institutions failed, likely due to those institutions not fully recognizing potential losses within their loan portfolios.

Analysis of Non-Current Loan Rates

We looked more closely at failed institutions' level of non-performing loans and determined that 79.1 percent of failed institutions had elevated levels for a sustained period of time. Such non- performing loans are often a precursor to loan charge-offs. The volume of a financial institution's loan portfolio that is reported as non-performing, or non-current, is measured, in part, by the *non-current loan ratio*. This ratio measures the level of loans and leases past due over 90 days and still accruing interest and loans the institution has placed on non-accrual status, as a percentage of total loans. While the net loan charge-off rate measures the level of net loan losses recognized by an institution, the non-current loan ratio provides an indication of the potential level of remaining problem assets and future loan losses not yet recognized.

A significant level of non-performing loans ultimately would reduce interest income and potentially lower retained earnings. Coupled with write-downs and other loss recognition, significant non-performing loans increase an institution's risk of failure. Figure 9 illustrates that non-current loans, on average, were significantly higher over an extended period of time for failed financial institutions than for financial institutions that did not fail. This trend supports the view that non-current loans were a significant contributing factor to institutions' failures.

As shown in Figure 10, to assess non-current loan ratios for failed institutions in more detail, we averaged their non-current loan ratios over the final nine quarterly reporting periods of their existence, and then stratified the results to identify those institutions that failed with lower average levels of non-performing loans. We found that for almost 80 percent of the failed financial institutions, non-current loans averaged 5 percent or more of total loans for 2 years before they failed. This finding indicates that these institutions were subject to a prolonged period of financial distress due to higher levels of non-performing loans, and likely experienced higher rates of loan charge-offs from such loans.

Based on the above analysis, we examined more closely a non-statistical sample of 42 insured financial institutions that failed between January 2007 and September 2011. These institutions had low average levels of non-current loans.[38] We determined that 21 of the 42 institutions failed for reasons other than write-downs on current loans, such as fraudulent or other questionable activity or losses related to the devaluation of securities.

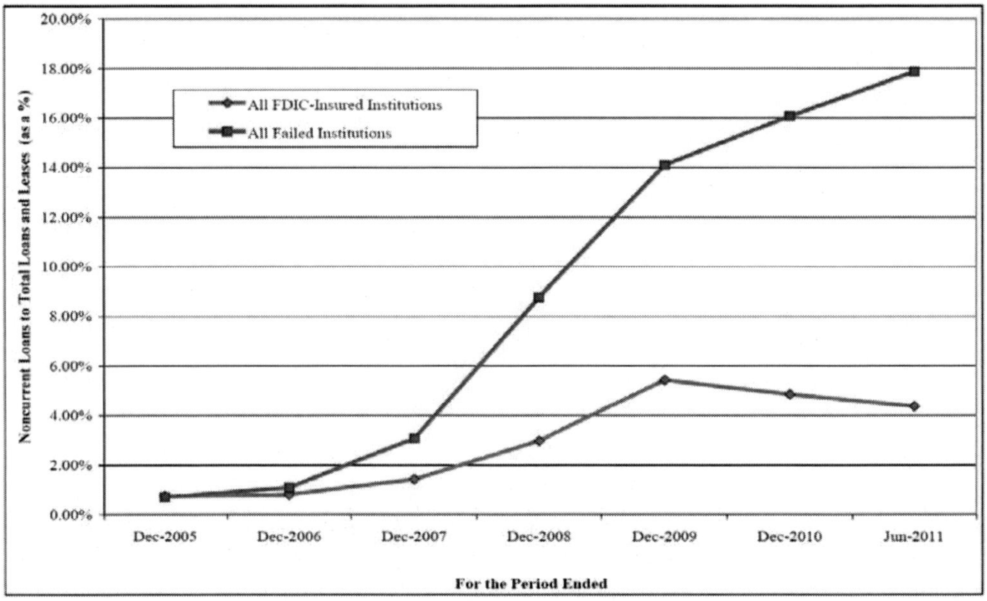

Source: OIG analysis of the FDIC's Quarterly Banking Profile reports and UBPRs for failed financial institutions.

Figure 9. Non-Current Loans and Leases to Total Loans and Leases.

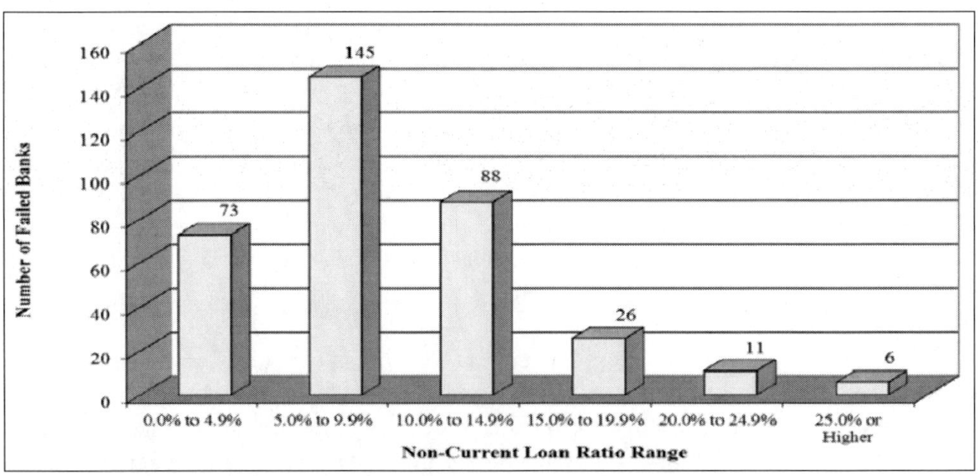

Source: OIG analysis of UBPR non-current loan ratios.

Note: The figure excludes one financial institution whose non-current loan ratios were not recorded within the UBPRs, for a total of 349 failed financial institutions.

Figure 10. Failed Institutions' 9-Quarter Average Non-Current Loan Ratio.

For the remaining 21 institutions, we performed a detailed analysis of the examination working papers to determine whether examiners required asset write-downs on loans that were considered current by the institution and, if so, the extent of such write-downs. Our review of the remaining failed institutions, discussed in the next section of this report, indicates that asset write-downs on loans that were current were not a significant contributing factor in the institutions' failures. Further, we did not identify, from our analysis, any institutions that failed due to losses from loans that were current.

P.L. 112-88 (2)(B)

The impact of significant losses arising from loans for which all payments of principal, interest, and fees were current, according to the contractual terms of the loans, on the ability of insured depository institutions to raise additional capital.

We confirmed that institutions recorded as current a significant number of the loans that examiners adversely classified. In almost all cases, however, examiners documented multiple reasons to support their loan classifications, such as inadequate collateral protection, poor performance, and weak borrower cash flow, among others. Those classifications contributed to increased institution loan loss provisions and, to a lesser extent, asset write-downs, both of which ultimately decreased capital. The overall impact on the institution varies widely depending on the institution's size and capital level. In certain circumstances, those capital decreases, combined with classifications of loans that both the institutions and examiners recognized as past due, may have caused institutions' capital levels to drop below minimum PCA capital thresholds.

Loan Analysis and Classifications

As discussed further in Matter (3)(A), an institution's board of directors and management are responsible for reviewing and risk-rating loans and maintaining an ALLL for probable incurred credit losses. Examiners review a sample of loans during the examination to confirm that the institution's loan review and grading process identified relevant credit quality issues and appropriately reflected those concerns in management's computation of the ALLL.

Examiners review loans based on a risk assessment of the "5 Cs" of credit: Character, Capacity, Capital, Collateral, and Condition. The FDIC's *Risk Management Manual of Examination Policies* instructs examiners to consider the risk involved in the character and capacity of the borrower; the borrower's financial responsibility, position, and history (Capital); the nature and degree of collateral security; and the financed project, feasibility, and probability of a loan's orderly liquidation in accordance with specified terms (Condition). A borrower's willingness and ability to perform as agreed remain the primary measures of a loan's risk.

Loans are classified as Substandard, Doubtful, or Loss based on risk of nonpayment. A June 2004 interagency policy titled, *Uniform Agreement on the Classification of Assets and Appraisal of Securities Held by Banks and Thrifts,* defined these classifications as follows:

- **Substandard.** Loans classified Substandard are inadequately protected by the current sound worth and paying capacity of the obligor or of the collateral pledged, if any. Such loans must have a well-defined weakness or weaknesses that jeopardize the liquidation of the debt. They are characterized by the distinct possibility that the institution will sustain some loss if the deficiencies are not corrected.
- **Doubtful.** Loans classified Doubtful have all the weaknesses inherent in those classified Substandard with the added characteristic that the weaknesses make collection or liquidation in full, on the basis of currently known facts, conditions, and values, highly questionable and improbable.
- **Loss.** Loans classified Loss are considered uncollectible and of such little value that their continuance as bankable assets is not warranted. This classification does not mean that the loan has absolutely no recovery or salvage value, but rather it is not practical or desirable to defer writing off the asset even though partial recovery might occur in the future.

The classification of a loan as Loss requires the institution to charge off the classified amount. Substandard and Doubtful classifications require the institution to reserve for potential future loss through additions to the ALLL. Both charge-offs and increases in reserves reduce Tier 1 Capital.

Examiner Classification of Loans Reported by the Institution as Current

We reviewed 19 failed institutions whose records showed that 44.7 percent of the total value of loans examiners adversely classified were, in the institution's view, current. However, 10.2 percent of the classified loans that the institutions considered to be current were in non- accrual status,[39] and 29.4 percent were part of loan relationships with borrowers that had other delinquent, non-accrual, or restructured troubled debt.[40] In virtually all cases, examiners documented multiple reasons supporting their classifications.

Loss Classifications. As shown in Table 7, these institutions reported as current 24.0 percent of the value of all loans that examiners classified Loss, though they also showed 23.1 percent of those loans were in non-accrual status, and 33.3 percent as part of loan relationships with borrowers that had other loans that were delinquent, non-accrual, or restructured troubled debt. On average, the loans examiners classified as Loss that the institutions reported as current represented only 0.3 percent of total loans, so Loss classifications did not materially impact the institutions' capital levels or overall financial condition.

Substandard and Doubtful Classifications. Although classified less severely, the volume of loans examiners classified as Substandard or Doubtful had a greater impact on the 19 institutions' capital levels and financial condition than loans classified as Loss because the institutions had to increase their loan loss reserves. The institutions reported 46.6 percent of the value of all loans examiners classified Substandard as current, and those represented an average of 6.0 percent of total loans. The institutions reported 45.6 percent of the value of all loans examiners classified Doubtful as current, and those represented only 0.2 percent of their total loans.

Table 7. Adversely Classified Current Loans for 19 Failed Institutions (in thousands)[a]

	Substandard	Doubtful	Loss
Classified Current Loans (current according to the institution)	$516,980	$19,892	$25,830
Total Classified Loans	$1,109,894	$43,645	$107,692
Classified Current Loans to Total Classified Loans	46.6%	45.6%	24.0%
Average Potential ALLL Provision or Charge-Off[b]	13.1%	1.3%	3.3%

Source: OIG analysis of the last examination prior to an institution's failure.

[a] In performing our ratio analysis, we used financial data derived from the previous quarter of the examination's "As of Date" to eliminate potential errors in double-counting derived from examination adjustments and Call Report amendments incorporated into the institution's financial statements.

[b] Potential ALLL provision based on OIG-assumed reserve factors of 20 percent for Substandard classifications, 50 percent for Doubtful classifications, and 100 percent for Loss classifications.

Reasons for Examiner Loan Classifications

Our review of the 19 failed financial institutions identified 277 loans that examiners adversely classified that institutions had designated as current. We identified a total of 723 reasons examiners cited to support their classifications, with examiners presenting multiple classification reasons for most loans. Examiners most frequently supported loan charge-offs on current loans for conditions such as lack of performance and lack of guarantor support (35 percent of the classification reasons), repayment capacity such as inadequate cash flow or unknown ability to service debt (32 percent of the classification reasons), or weak or inadequate collateral or collateral-dependent loans (25 percent of the classification reasons).

Impact of Classifications

On average, we estimated that examiner-required classifications would have reduced a sampled institution's capital by 3.3 percent for Loss classifications, 1.3 percent for Doubtful classifications, and 13.1 percent for Substandard classifications, assuming the ALLL provision reserve factors noted in Table 7. However, we noted that there is a wide range of potential impact depending on the proportion of such loans that examiners classify at individual institutions and the institution's size and amount of capital.

To illustrate the potential impact of the average classifications shown in Table 7, we calculated the following:

- For an institution with an 8.0 percent Tier 1 Leverage Capital ratio, examiner classifications of 6 percent of an institution's loan portfolio as Substandard, 0.2 percent as Doubtful, and 0.3 percent as Loss and the assumption of additional provision expense would lower the institution's Tier 1 Leverage Capital ratio to 6.7 percent, still *Well Capitalized* for PCA purposes.
- For an institution with a Tier 1 Leverage Capital ratio of 5 percent, the classifications, and the assumption of additional provision expense discussed above, would reduce the institution's Tier 1 Leverage Capital ratio to 4.15 percent, below the minimum capital requirements.

Thus, for institutions with lower capital levels, examiner-required classifications, combined with the institution's voluntary classifications, could cause the institution's capital levels to drop below minimum PCA capital thresholds for a *Well Capitalized* institution.

During the course of our study, we identified one of the 19 institutions that was particularly impacted by examiner-required classifications of loans the institution recorded as current. At that institution, nearly 40 percent of all loans examiners classified as Loss were loans the institution recorded as current. Specifically, examiners classified as Loss $3.4 million of loans recorded as current by management and required the institution to make an additional ALLL provision of $4.6 million to restore the ALLL to an appropriate level. Examiners attributed the classifications to the unknown ability of borrowers to service their debt, weak or inadequate collateral protection, and lack of borrowers' actual performance. The institution's Tier 1 Leverage Capital ratio declined from 7.8 percent to negative 5.1 percent. The institution dropped from *Well Capitalized* to *Critically Undercapitalized*[41] and failed. The report of examination (ROE) reported problems with the ALLL methodology, appraisal valuations, and impairment analysis and concluded that critically deficient asset quality and resulting losses resulted in unacceptable earnings and negative capital levels. The ROE stated that the overall condition of the institution was a direct result of ineffective management and Board supervision and noted that all of the losses identified during the examination resulted from loans made by the institution president, who lacked the experience, capability, and skills necessary to manage the loan portfolio.

P.L. 112-88 (2)(C)

(2)(C) The effect of changes in the application of fair value accounting rules and other accounting standards, including the allowance for loan and lease loss methodology, on insured depository institutions, specifically the degree to which fair value accounting rules and other accounting standards have led to regulatory action against banks, including consent orders and closure of the institution.

We concluded that fair value accounting did not have a significant impact on most institutions' financial statements, especially community banks with total assets of less than $1 billion. Instead, impairment losses on loans recorded at amortized (historical) cost, resulting largely from non-performing loans, had a much greater impact on the decline of institutions' regulatory capital levels. These impairment losses led to regulatory action, including closure of many institutions. We identified 13 out of 350 failed institutions for which fair value-related securities losses did significantly contribute to the institution's failure.

Fair Value and Impairment Accounting Standards

To address this topic, it is first important to discuss the differences between fair value accounting and *impairment accounting standards*.

Fair Value Accounting

According to a December 2011 study by the Federal Reserve Bank of Boston,[42] in the 1980s, accounting standard setters began to shift away from a revenue/expense approach, where the income statement is the primary focus and historical cost is considered to be the most appropriate basis for measurement and reporting. This shift was due, in part, to concerns that the combination of historical cost and delayed loss recognition were producing financial results disconnected from economic reality. Historical cost accounting was also criticized for providing managers with the means to smooth profits through hidden, excess reserves and selective sales of securities. During this period, a number of other factors also influenced accounting standard setters. Historical cost was proving to be a poor measurement approach in inflationary markets. In addition, financial instruments and markets were becoming more complex. New financial products such as derivatives and structured investments simply could not be measured in a meaningful way using traditional approaches.

> **Fair value** is defined as the price that would be received to sell an asset or paid to transfer a liability in an orderly transaction between market participants at the measurement date. FDIC-insured institutions most often apply fair value measurements to record changes in the value of securities. Changes in the value of debt securities held for trading purposes are recorded as losses or gains in net income regardless of whether or not the security has been sold. Most community banks, however, classify debt securities as *available for sale* (AFS). These debt securities are also recorded at fair value, but any unrealized gains and losses are reflected in other *comprehensive income* (OCI) and aggregated in accumulated other comprehensive income (AOCI), a separate category within shareholders' equity that does not, under current banking regulations, impact regulatory capital.

Partially in response to these issues, the Financial Accounting Standards Board (FASB) began to increase the use of fair value measurement in accounting standards. The earliest standards to incorporate fair value measurement more broadly were limited to footnote disclosures and had no balance sheet or income statement impact. Subsequently, fair value was applied to defined sets of instruments or transaction types. Most significantly, investment securities and derivative contracts were required to be measured at fair value.

Specifically, under *Financial Accounting Standard* (FAS) No. 115, *Accounting for Certain Investments in Debt and Equity Securities*, issued May 1993,[43] investment securities designated as held for trading or AFS must be measured at fair value each reporting period. Changes in fair value each period are recognized in net income for trading securities and in OCI for AFS securities. Debt securities can also be designated as held to maturity (HTM) and measured at historical (amortized) cost. FAS No. 133, *Accounting for Derivative Instruments and Hedging Activities*, issued June 1998,[44] requires that all freestanding and certain embedded derivatives be measured at fair value each reporting period, with changes in fair value recorded in net income (unless a derivative is designated as and qualifies as a cash flow hedge). These two standards continue to be the principal drivers of recurring fair value measurements on the balance sheets of financial institutions.

FAS No. 157, *Fair Value Measurements*, issued in 2006,[45] provided a definition of fair value, along with a measurement framework and disclosure requirements, but did not require any new fair value measurements. Appendix 4 presents a listing of these and other fair value-related accounting pronouncements.

Studies and white papers have reported that the recent financial crisis and resulting credit crunch created challenges for fair value accounting.[46] The markets for subprime and other asset and liability positions were severely illiquid and disorderly, making it difficult for financial entities to identify representative fair values for their assets. These difficulties led to a heated debate about the merits and limitations of fair value accounting.

Impairment Accounting

Accounting standards addressing asset impairment have also been in place for decades. FAS 5, *Accounting for Contingencies*, issued in 1975,[47] established standards of financial accounting and reporting for loss contingencies, and FAS 114, *Accounting by Creditors for Impairment of a Loan*, issued in 1993,[48] addressed the accounting by creditors for impairment of individual loans. FAS 5 and 114 comprise the basis that financial institutions use to determine the ALLL. Appendix 5 presents a listing of impairment-related accounting pronouncements.

> **Impairment accounting** standards are applied to adjust the carrying value of a security when a decline in the fair value of the security represents an *other-than-temporary impairment* (OTTI). Impairment accounting standards are applied to loans and leases HFI, which typically represent the largest asset class for community banks when a credit loss is determined to be probable and reasonably estimable. Such loans and leases are measured at amortized cost, with a separate valuation allowance (the ALLL) recorded to measure any impairment amount. The measurement of impairment is based on probable incurred losses, and not the fair value of the loans except in limited circumstances. The provision expense to establish or increase the ALLL directly affects net income and, consequently, regulatory capital levels.

As noted in a 2008 Securities and Exchange Commission (SEC) report,[49] accounting for impairment of financial assets, except those subject to fair value accounting with changes in fair value recognized in net income, has developed over many years and differs depending upon the characteristics, form, and intended use of the financial asset. In the context of community banks, the most relevant financial assets to which impairment accounting applies are loans and leases HFI. Impairment accounting also applies to non-financial assets related to loans such as collateral obtained through foreclosure.

Under GAAP, loans and leases HFI are recorded at amortized cost less an allowance for probable losses incurred as of the balance sheet date. Based on the type of loan, the nature of impairment, and how the portfolio is managed, the allowance is determined on a pool or an individual loan basis.

Typically, a pool basis is used for large portfolios of small, homogeneous or highly similar loans, such as mortgage loans or other consumer loans as required by FAS 5/ASC 450. When analyzing loans on a pool basis, generally the ALLL is not based on the fair value of the underlying loans, but is instead based on historical loss percentages, adjusted for current environmental factors. This general principle has been refined over the years, but has not been significantly changed since first promulgated by the FASB in 1975.

Large, individually significant loans often are analyzed on an individual basis as prescribed in FAS 114/ASC 310. Community banks may also track mortgage or consumer loans on an individual basis once they have specifically identified particular loans as impaired. While the objective for determining the ALLL is the same whether or not it is evaluated as part of a pool or individually, there are differences in measurement techniques. In particular, if an institution has determined that the likely recovery of its investment in an individually evaluated and imparied loan is limited to the value of underlying collateral, then it will estimate the ALLL for the loan based on the value of the collateral. This is not a new principle, but has been used by institutions for many years, and was formally codified into GAAP in 1993.

Use and Impact of Fair Value and Impairment Accounting on Failed and Open Institutions

We engaged KPMG LLP to assist us in analyzing the impact of fair value and impairment accounting on FDIC-insured depository institutions. We analyzed Call Report data for the period 2007 through 2011 to measure the extent of use and impact of fair value and impairment accounting on failed and open national, state member, and state nonmember banks.[50] We segmented our analysis by community banks with assets of less than $1 billion, mid-size institutions with assets between $1 and $10 billion, and large institutions with assets over $10 billion. We evaluated Call Report data for an average of 6,910 open institutions over the period January 1, 2008 through December 31, 2011 and 378 failed institutions over the period January 1, 2007 through December 31, 2011. We present relevant results of our analysis pertaining mostly to community banks with assets totaling less than $1 billion below.

Accounting Basis and Impact for Selected Balance Sheet Elements

The typical balance sheet of FDIC-insured institutions includes assets and liabilities recorded using different accounting classifications depending on the nature and purpose of the asset or liability. AFS securities, loans and leases HFI, and other real estate owned (OREO) represent the greatest percentage of assets for institutions with assets less than $1 billion. Appendix 6 presents how various balance sheet accounts are affected by fair value and impairment accounting and presents a more detailed analysis of the impact of AFS securities, loans and leases HFI, and OREO.

AFS Securities. AFS Securities represented 18 and 9 percent of total assets for open and closed institutions, respectively, and is the balance sheet account most impacted by fair value accounting for community banks. While securities are recorded at their fair value, changes in fair value do not impact regulatory capital unless an OTTI occurs or if the security is sold.[51] These changes are referred to as unrealized gains or losses. Any positive or negative changes in value are recorded in OCI, and aggregated in the AOCI component of stockholders equity. Currently, AOCI associated with AFS debt securities is removed from the Tier 1 Capital calculation when determining an institution's regulatory capital levels.

Loans and Leases HFI. Total loans and leases HFI represented on average two-thirds of total assets. If the institution has the intent and ability to hold the loan or lease for the foreseeable future or until maturity or payoff, it is typically classified as HFI. Loans and leases HFI are recorded at amortized cost less an ALLL for the estimated amount of loans and leases it is probable the institution will be unable to collect. Quarterly loan loss provisions and loan charge- offs represented a significant percentage of institution losses, especially for failed institutions. In 2009, losses associated with loans and leases HFI exceeded more than 300 percent of net interest income (NII) for failed institutions.[52]

OREO. OREO represented 0.65 and 4.15 percent of total assets for open and closed institutions, respectively. OREO usually includes assets repossessed through a foreclosure process for defaulted loans. When an institution receives the real estate asset, this asset is generally categorized as HFS and the institution initially recognizes the asset at its fair value less cost to sell. The estimate of fair value less cost to sell is continuously updated for further declines (and recoveries of previously recognized declines), which must be charged (credited) to expense, although increases in fair value less costs to sell to an amount in excess of the foreclosed asset's initial fair value less cost to sell are not recognized until the asset is subsequently sold. OREO losses were higher for failed institutions and grew throughout the industry over time as institutions had to foreclose on assets that were declining in value.

Overall Impact of Fair Value and Impairment-Related Losses

Figure 11 presents an analysis of the impact on NII of the balance sheet accounts most affected by fair value and impairment-related accounting. As shown, charge-offs on loans recorded at amortized cost were the largest category of losses as a percentage of NII, especially for institutions that failed. Failed institutions also experienced unrealized losses related to fair value changes in AFS debt securities during 2008 and 2009, but such losses did not impact net income or regulatory capital. Open institutions experienced unrealized gains on AFS securities starting in 2009. Finally, beginning in 2008, failed institutions reported moderate losses from repossessed OREO following foreclosures.

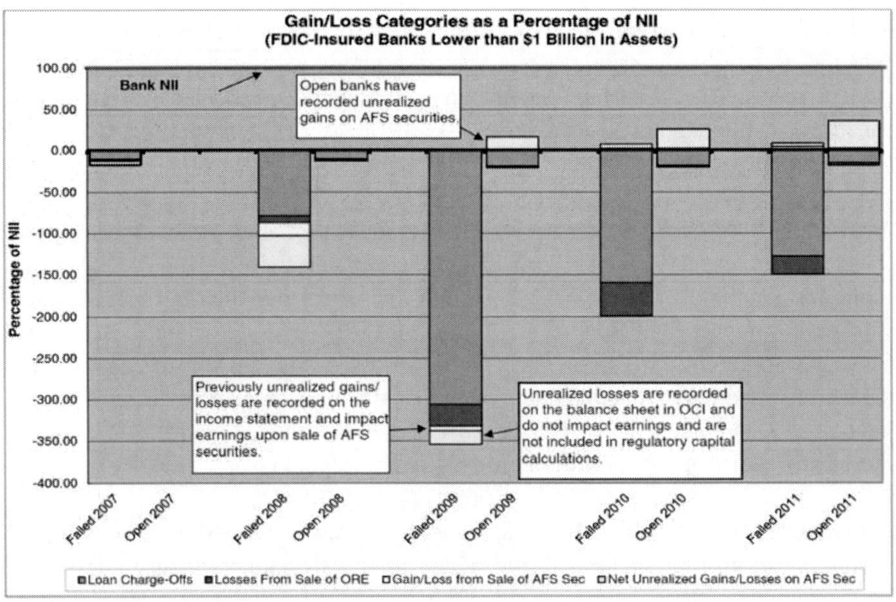

Source: OIG and KPMG analysis of Call Report Information.

Figure 11. Balance Sheet Impact of Fair Value and Impairment Accounting.

Institutions Failing as a Result of Fair Value or Impairment Accounting Standards

We determined that failures related to fair value accounting issues were uncommon. As discussed earlier in this report, our analysis of failed financial institutions with low levels of non-performing loans identified 13 institutions that failed related to fair value accounting issues. Eleven of the 13 were part of two banking organizations. Four of the 13 institutions failed primarily as a result of *collateralized debt obligations* or securities losses. Nine institutions failed largely due to the U.S. Government placing *Fannie Mae and Freddie Mac* in conservatorship. In addition, we identified another 12 institutions where MLRs noted issues related to fair value accounting as a contributing cause of failure.

As discussed throughout this report, many institutions failed as a result of impairment-related losses. Also as discussed later in this report, the regulators have issued numerous enforcement actions with provisions related to improving institutions' ALLL methodology and allowance levels.

Our study corroborates the conclusion of prior studies from the SEC and the Federal Reserve Bank of Boston that fair value accounting did not appear to have a significant impact on the financial statements of financial institutions, especially institutions with total assets of less than $1 billion. In addition, our analysis of Call Report data from 2007 through 2011 found that assets recorded at fair value had limited negative impact on institutions' regulatory capital levels that could lead to regulatory action against institutions, including consent orders and closure of the institution.

P.L. 112-88 (2)(D)

Whether field examiners are using appropriate appraisal procedures with respect to losses arising from loans for which all payments of principal, interest, and fees were current, according to the contractual terms of the loans, and whether the application of appraisals leads to immediate write-downs on the value of the underlying asset.

We found that examiners used appropriate appraisal procedures in classifying loans for which all payments of principal, interest, and fees were current, according to the contractual terms of the loans. Under existing guidance, borrower repayment capacity is the primary consideration for examiner classification decisions. However, in the case of a CRE loan, an appraisal of the loan's collateral, along with a comprehensive analysis of the loan, could lead to an immediate write-down. Under regulatory guidance for classifying residential loans, appraisals typically would not result in an immediate write-down in the value of the loan unless the loan was 180 days or more past due.

According to the *Interagency Appraisal and Evaluation Guidelines*, dated October 27, 1994 (subsequently revised on December 2, 2010), a borrower's ability to repay a real estate loan according to reasonable terms remains the primary consideration in the lending decision.

However, as institutions make lending decisions and examiners analyze individual transactions, they must consider the value of the underlying real estate collateral in accordance with the agencies' appraisal regulations. When analyzing individual transactions, examiners should review the appraisal or evaluation to determine whether the methods, assumptions, and value conclusions are reasonable; whether the appraisal or evaluation complies with the agencies' appraisal regulations; and whether the appraisal is consistent with supervisory guidance and the institution's policies. Also, the FDIC's RD Memorandum titled, *Re-appraising/Re-evaluating Real Property*, dated March 18, 2009, notes that the lack of a reliable or accurate appraisal will not preclude examiners from adversely classifying an asset or relieve the institution from the responsibility of maintaining an appropriate ALLL.

Application of Appraisal Procedures on Examiner Loan Classifications

Our review of MLR reports found that the supervisory agencies frequently identified deficiencies or weaknesses in failed institutions' appraisal programs. In cases where MLRs criticized the regulatory supervision of an institution's appraisals and appraisal program, the reports mentioned the need for a stronger and earlier supervisory response to the identified operational weaknesses. Reports did not identify as a concern examiners' failure to comply with regulatory guidance on appraisals.

Our review of examination documentation from a sample of 19 failed institutions found that examiners reviewed a loan's collateral and its appraised value in addition to a loan's terms, purpose, repayment sources, and payment history and status (delinquent or current). We found that examiners reviewed the most recent appraisal for the value of the loan's collateral and compared it with the loan's book balance when determining a Loss classification or when computing a loan write-down. Examiners also subtracted the collateral's appraised value less cost to sell from the loan's outstanding book balance to determine the amount classified as Loss.

We concluded that examiners used the appropriate appraisal procedures in recognizing losses on loans that institutions reported to be current. As discussed earlier, examiners cited collateral along with other reasons for adversely classifying loans. Of the $26 million of loans examiners classified as Loss that the institution reported as current, 56.4 percent (22 of 39 loans) were either in non-accrual status or were related to other loans that were delinquent, non-accrual, or a TDR. Examiners classified only 2.6 percent (1 of 39) of the current loans based solely on collateral deficiencies. This specific loan was related to another loan that was severely delinquent.

Examiners noted various other credit quality reasons in addition to collateral deficiencies for 69.2 percent (27 of 39) of the current loans. In those cases, examiners typically noted the loans exhibited one or more of the following credit quality concerns:

- Borrowers did not have sufficient financial support or cash flow to repay the debt.
- Unknown ability of borrower to service debt.
- Lack of actual performance.
- Guarantors provided little financial support.
- Projects lacked adequate performance to generate proceeds to repay the debt, in some cases due to the downturn in the economy.

Examiners also classified 15.4 percent (6 of 39) of the current loans as Loss to reflect an institution's earlier charge-off or settlement with the borrower. Examiners did not provide clearly documented explanations for another 12.8 percent (5 of 39 loans) of the current loans classified as Loss.

Appraisals that Could Result in Loan Write-Downs

Under the agencies' appraisal regulations and guidelines, the application and use of appraisals in conjunction with a comprehensive analysis of a CRE loan could result in an immediate write- down of the loan depending on the circumstances of the individual loan. Appraisals or evaluations frequently help to establish the level of support that collateral provides to a loan. New appraisals, evaluations, or adjusted values of collateral securing loans help examiners determine whether classification is necessary. If the collateral's value has declined below the outstanding loan amount, an examiner may adversely classify the credit. However, a loan that has demonstrated continuing and committed performance with the original terms of the loan generally would not be subjected to a Loss classification. Any portion classified as Loss would need to meet the regulatory standard of being an amount that is "considered uncollectible and of such little value that their continuance as bankable assets is not warranted."[53] Institutions are expected to promptly eliminate from their books all amounts classified as Loss. When it is probable that a creditor will be unable to collect all principal and interest due according to a loan's contractual terms, the loan is considered impaired.[54] The level of impairment is measured based on one of three available measurement methods: (1) present value of expected future cash flows, (2) fair value of collateral if the loan is collateral-dependent, or (3) observable market price of the loan. For regulatory reporting purposes, institutions are required to measure impairment on impaired collateral-dependent loans using the fair value of collateral method. An institution should consider the appraised value of the collateral as the starting point for determining its fair value, though it should also consider other factors and events in its environment that may affect the current fair value of the collateral since the appraisal was performed. Ultimately, an institution's or an examiner's review and analysis of an appraisal could lead to the immediate write-down of a CRE loan beyond the initial market value assigned within the appraisal, especially if the appraisal is outdated and the economic environment has deteriorated. Assuming that no required charge-off was identified on an impaired collateral-dependent loan, the outstanding amounts owed by the borrower less the fair value of the loan's collateral value would then be the required allowance.

Appraisals under the Uniform Retail Credit Classification and Account Management Policy

For classifying retail credits, which includes open- and closed-end 1-4 family residential loans, the Interagency *Uniform Retail Credit Classification and Account Management Policy* indicates that appraisals would not typically result in an immediate write-down in the value of the institution's recorded loan balance unless the credit was delinquent 180 days or more. Further, if an institution can clearly document that a past-due loan is well secured and in the process of collection, then the loan does not need to be adversely classified regardless of the loan's delinquency status. However, actual credit losses on individual retail credits should be recorded when the institution becomes aware of the loss.

MATTER 3. APPRAISALS

P.L. 112-88 requires the OIG to study appraisals, including:

(A) the number of insured depository institutions placed into receivership or conservatorship due to asset write-downs and the policies and procedures for evaluating the adequacy of an insured depository institution's ALLL;
(B) the policies and procedures examiners use for evaluating the appraised values of property securing real estate loans and the extent to which those policies and procedures are followed; and
(C) FDIC field examiner implementation of guidance issued December 2, 2010, titled "Agencies Issue Final Appraisal and Evaluation Guidelines."[55]

P.L. 112-88 (3)(A)

The number of insured depository institutions placed into receivership or conservatorship due to asset write-downs and the policies and procedures for evaluating the adequacy of an insured depository institution's ALLL.

Multiple contributing factors, such as aggressive growth, asset concentrations, poor underwriting, and deficient credit administration practices, coupled with declining real estate values, caused most institutions to fail. As a result of these factors, institutions experienced elevated non-performing loan levels and ultimately increased asset write-downs and related loan charge-offs. These write-downs and charge-offs depleted institutions' capital and caused them to become insolvent and fail. In that regard, virtually all of the MLRs reported that asset write-downs contributed significantly to the failure of the institution and loss to the DIF. The regulators were often critical of an institution's handling of its credit quality review process, noting that the institution's ALLL provision was not sufficient and its ALLL methodology was inadequate prior to an institution's failure. With respect to ALLL policies and procedures, we found that examiners followed examination policies and procedures for evaluating an institution's ALLL and routinely reviewed and concluded on an institution's ALLL methodology and sufficiency.

While borrowers' ability to repay real estate loans according to reasonable terms remains the primary consideration in lending decisions, institutions and examiners also must consider the value of the underlying real estate collateral in accordance with the agencies' appraisal regulations and real estate lending standards. Appraisals are professional judgments of the market value of real property, and professional appraisers use three basic valuation approaches in estimating the market value of real property: cost, market data or direct sales comparison, and income. Examiners consider the size and the nature of an institution's real estate-related activities when assessing the appropriateness of its appraisal program and assess whether the appraisal methods, assumptions, and value conclusions associated with collateral are reasonable when reviewing individual transactions. As discussed previously in Matter 2—Losses, institutions are required to maintain an ALLL at a level that is appropriate to absorb estimated credit losses associated with the HFI loan and lease portfolio. The regulators have longstanding policies that require examiners to assess an institution's ALLL. If examiners determine an ALLL is inadequate, the institution must increase its *provision for loan and lease losses* (PLLL) sufficiently to restore the ALLL to an appropriate level consistent with GAAP. The provision is an expense that reduces net income and available capital.

Number of Insured Depository Institutions Placed into Receivership or Conservatorship due to Asset Write-Downs

As discussed throughout our report, several factors contributed to most institution failures. These factors included management practices such as aggressive growth, high CRE and ADC asset concentrations, and poor underwriting and credit administration practices. Failing institutions experienced elevated non-performing loan levels that led to increased asset write- downs and loan charge-offs. In fact, in the 2½ years from mid-2008 through 2010, institutions reported net charge-offs on ADC loans that were more than three times greater than those reported over the prior 17 years. These write-downs and charge-offs ultimately depleted institutions' capital and caused hundreds of institutions to become insolvent and fail. As discussed in Matter (2)(A), MLR reports have outlined a number of factors that led to institutions' failures. CRE and ADC concentrations and rapid asset growth were listed as contributing causes of failure more than 93 and 77 percent of the time, respectively, and we found that more than 80 percent of the failures involved elevated rates of non-performing loans that led to asset write-downs and loan charge-offs. Virtually all of the MLRs reported that asset write-downs contributed significantly to the failure of the institution and loss to the DIF. Further, the MLR reports indicated that the regulators often cited supervisory concerns related to the sufficiency of an institution's ALLL provision and its ALLL methodology.

ALLL Policies and Procedures

An institution's board of directors and management are responsible for maintaining the ALLL at an appropriate level consistent with GAAP, and for developing, maintaining, and documenting a comprehensive, systematic, and consistently applied process for determining the ALLL and provision expense. The relevant supervisory guidance for doing so includes the following:

- *Interagency Policy Statement on the Allowance for Loan and Lease Losses*, dated December 13, 2006 (December 2006 Interagency ALLL Policy), and
- *Policy Statement on Allowance for Loan and Lease Losses Methodologies and Documentation for Banks and Savings Institutions*, dated July 25, 2001 (July 2001 Interagency ALLL Policy).

In carrying out its responsibilities, an institution's management is expected to:

- Establish and maintain a loan review system that identifies, monitors, and addresses asset quality problems in a timely manner.
- Ensure the prompt charge-off of loans, or portions of loans, deemed uncollectible.
- Ensure that the process for determining an adequate allowance level is based on comprehensive, adequately documented, and consistently applied analysis.

With respect to the examiner's role, the December 2006 Interagency ALLL Policy provides that examiners should assess the credit quality of an institution's loan portfolio, the appropriateness of its ALLL methodology and documentation, and the appropriateness of the reported ALLL in the institution's regulatory reports. In their review and classification or grading of the loan portfolio, examiners should consider all significant factors that affect the collectability of the portfolio, including the value of any collateral. Following a quality assessment of the loan and lease portfolio, loan review system, and lending policies, examiners determine whether the ALLL adequately addresses the interagency ALLL standards and policies and is consistent with GAAP.

If the examiner does not consider the institution's ALLL level as appropriate on the date of the evaluation, or finds the institution's ALLL evaluation process is deficient, examiners will recommend in the ROE that the institution correct these problems. Additionally, when examiners determine that an institution's ALLL level is inadequate, institution management is required to increase the PLLL expense sufficiently to restore the ALLL to an adequate level consistent with GAAP. Appendix 7 provides a series of process maps for evaluating the ALLL and implementing corresponding accounting guidance.

Examiner Practices and Findings Related to the ALLL

Because the ALLL analysis is critical in determining the appropriate allowance level, write- downs, and charge-offs, we reviewed examiners' evaluation of institutions' ALLL. For the 19 closed institutions sampled, examiners found that 78.9 percent (15 of 19) did not have sufficient ALLL reserve balances and had inadequate ALLL methodologies. With only one exception, the examination reports specifically documented the level of the institution's ALLL deficiency. In 73.3 percent (11 of 15) of those examinations, examiners also cited the institution for an apparent contravention of the December 2006 Interagency ALLL Policy or noted additional work was needed to bring the ALLL methodology into full compliance with that policy. For institutions with an inadequate ALLL methodology, examiners found in the majority of cases that the institutions did not follow GAAP: ASC 450-20 (formerly FAS 5) and ASC 310-10-35 (formerly FAS 114).

We also reviewed the most recent full-scope examination available for 136 open financial institutions and found that examiners routinely reviewed and concluded on an institution's ALLL methodology and allowance sufficiency. However, we found a few instances where examiners did not fully document an assessment of the institution's ALLL methodology or did not determine the appropriate level for the ALLL balance. We also noted that all of the examinations included a review of the institution's loan portfolio; however, in a few instances, we did not find evidence of the examiner's assessment of the institution's internal loan review function and credit grading system.

Overall, in the case of the 136 open institutions, 26.5 percent of the examination reports that we reviewed stated that they did not have sufficient ALLL balances. Although some examination reports specifically documented the level of the institution's ALLL deficiency, the reports generally noted that the ALLL was deficient and, in some instances, instructed the institution to make certain corrections and to determine the needed reserve. In addition, examiners noted in 64 reports (or 47.0 percent) that the institutions had an inadequate ALLL methodology. Of those 64 examinations, 23.4 percent cited the institution for an apparent contravention of the December 2006 Interagency ALLL Policy. In some cases, examiners also reported weaknesses in the institution's credit grading system resulting in inaccurate internal loan risk ratings and identified loan administration weaknesses related to the institution's failure to obtain updated financial statements, both of which would delay the timely recognition of loss or loan portfolio weaknesses.

P.L. 112-88 (3)(B)

The policies and procedures examiners use for evaluating the appraised values of property securing real estate loans and the extent to which those policies and procedures are followed.

The FDIC, OCC, and FRB each established regulations addressing appraisal requirements and standards. In addition, the Appraisal Guidelines address supervisory matters relating to real estate-related financial transactions and provide guidance to institutions and examiners.

Because the regulators use an exception-based process, examination reports and working papers typically do not document institutions' compliance with the Appraisal Guidelines or internal appraisal program requirements. Thus, we could not always determine to what extent examiners actually assessed institutions' compliance with the Appraisal Guidelines because examiners generally only documented identified exceptions. We saw evidence that examiners considered appraisal information in evaluating individual loans for classification purposes in almost all of the loans that we reviewed.

However, examiners rarely documented their analysis of individual appraisals' reliability, adherence to appraisal standards, or compliance with appraisal rules and regulations.

Moreover, we could not determine to what extent examiners assessed institutions' appraisal programs, which include policies and controls for selecting competent appraisers and monitoring their performance. Still, we found instances in examination reports and working papers where examiners documented non-compliance with the Appraisal Guidelines or exceptions to institutions' appraisal program requirements and policies, consistent with the regulators' exception-based process.

Finally, we found examiners did not document their assessment of the adequacy of appraisals within the institution's loan files even when those appraisals were several years old.

Table 8. Examination Coverage of the ALLL

	FDIC	OCC	FRB
Examinations Reviewed	56	42	38
Percent of examinations documenting the following:			
Methodology: We saw evidence that examiners assessed the institution's ALLL methodology, including management's assumptions, analysis of qualitative and environmental factors, and process for making credit loss estimates.	94.6%	100.0%	97.4%
Adequacy: We saw evidence that examiners reviewed the appropriateness and reasonableness of the overall level of the ALLL.	96.4%	100.0%	100.0%
Policies and Procedures: We saw evidence that examiners evaluated whether ALLL policies and procedures provided for a comprehensive, well-documented, and consistently applied analysis of the institution's loan portfolio, an effective loan classification or credit grading system, and prompt charge-off of loans, or portions of loans, that available information confirmed to be uncollectible.	91.1%	100.0%	94.7%

Source: OIG analysis of a non-statistical sample of examinations and corresponding working papers.

Table 8 details some of the areas examiners documented in their review of 136 open financial institutions' ALLL methodology, adequacy, and policies and procedures, as required by the December 2006 Interagency ALLL Policy.

We concluded that examiners generally followed examination policies and procedures for evaluating an institution's ALLL, and routinely reviewed and concluded on an institution's ALLL methodology and allowance sufficiency.

Policies and Procedures Used for Evaluating Appraised Values of Property Securing Real Estate Loans

The FDIC, OCC, and FRB have issued regulations[56] pursuant to Title XI of the Financial Institutions Reform, Recovery, and Enforcement Act of 1989, P.L. 101-73, as amended, that identify which real estate-related transactions require an appraisal by a certified or licensed appraiser, establish minimum standards for performing appraisals, discuss appraiser independence and competency requirements, and highlight potential supervisory enforcement actions as a result of non-compliance. Among other things, these regulations require appraisals to conform to the generally accepted appraisal standards as evidenced by the *Uniform Standards of Professional Appraisal Practice* (USPAP) promulgated by the *Appraisal Standards Board of the Appraisal Foundation*.[57]

The *Interagency Appraisal and Evaluation Guidelines* (Appraisal Guidelines), dated December 2, 2010, updated and rescinded an earlier October 27, 1994, version and reflect developments concerning appraisals and evaluations, as well as changes in appraisal standards and advancements in regulated institutions' collateral valuation methods. The Appraisal Guidelines also clarify the regulators' longstanding expectations for an institution's appraisal and evaluation program to conduct real estate lending in a safe and sound manner, and the guidelines promote consistency in the application and enforcement of the regulators' appraisal regulations and safe and sound banking practices. In particular, an institution is required to incorporate an effective appraisal and evaluation program into its policies and procedures.

Examiner responsibilities under the Appraisal Guidelines are two-fold. First, during an examination, examiners consider appraisals when reviewing individual transactions. Second, they are required to review the institution's appraisal program.

When analyzing individual transactions, examiners should:

- review the appraisal or evaluation[58] to determine whether methods, assumptions, and value conclusions are reasonable;
- determine whether the appraisal or evaluation complies with the agencies' appraisal regulations and is consistent with supervisory guidance as well as the institution's policies; and
- review the steps taken by an institution to ensure that the persons who perform the institution's appraisals and evaluations are qualified, competent, and are not subject to conflicts of interest.

When reviewing the institution's appraisal program, among other things examiners should:

- verify that that the bank's policies and procedures establish an effective real estate appraisal and evaluation program;
- review steps taken by the institution to ensure that appraisers are qualified, competent, and free of conflicts of interest;
- assess the institution's established criteria for selecting, evaluating, and monitoring the performance of appraisers; and
- ensure that policies sufficiently address appraisal and evaluation reviews, including reviewer qualifications.

The regulators have issued their own examination policies to implement the appraisal regulations and 2010 Appraisal Guidelines. In addition, the FDIC and FRB developed an interagency *Real Estate Appraisal Program* Examination Documentation (ED) Module that incorporates the tenets of the 2010 Appraisal Guidelines as a tool for examiners to use in documenting their work.

Examiner Compliance with Appraisal-Related Examination Policies

Because the agencies use an exception-based process to document examination findings, examination reports and working papers typically do not document institutions' compliance with the Appraisal Guidelines or internal appraisal program requirements. Therefore, we could not fully determine to what extent examiners assessed institutions' compliance with the 2010 Appraisal Guidelines. Our review noted that examiners cited weaknesses or instances of non- compliance; however, the ROE or examination working papers generally contained no information about the extent of examination procedures performed to assess the reliability of individual appraisals or the sufficiency of the institution's appraisal program.

We reviewed 136 full-scope examinations of open institutions, including 753 loans totaling $2.3 billion that examiners reviewed at those examinations. In most cases, examiner implementation of the 2010 Appraisal Guidelines was only apparent when they cited a violation of a law or regulation or a contravention of a statement of policy. When discussed within the examination report, examiners' concerns centered around the institution's failure to obtain a required appraisal or evaluation or the validity of appraisals and evaluations.

Examiner review of individual transactions. We confirmed that examiners routinely considered appraisal information in evaluating individual loans for classification purposes. Specifically, examiners routinely identified and documented within the examination working papers the appraised value, the date of the appraisal or evaluation, and resulting LTV ratio supporting almost all individual loans that we reviewed. In addition, we noted that examiners identified instances when an institution did not obtain an appraisal or evaluation and cited apparent violations. Table 9 details the number of instances in which examiners cited an apparent violation with an appraisal regulation, and the cited area of concern.

We could not confirm that examiners followed other parts of the guidelines because we found limited documentation in examiner working papers concerning the reliability of individual appraisals and evaluations, including documentation of examiners' review of the cost, income, and market approach to value or the highest and best use of the property; the appraisals' adherence to minimum appraisal standards; potential deficiencies in appraisals and evaluations; and compliance with the agencies' rules and regulations on appraisals.

Examiner review of the institution's appraisal program. We noted that examiners did not always provide an overall conclusion on the adequacy of institution's appraisal program. When an examiner provided an overall conclusion, it generally was supported by the examiner's observation of an ineffective appraisal and evaluation program or program noncompliance. We discuss this issue further in the following section regarding FDIC field examiner implementation of the guidance.

The regulators have differing guidance with respect to documenting examination findings and examination procedures performed. The FDIC and FRB developed the ED Modules to define common objectives for reviewing important activities within institutions and to assist in documenting examination work. However, use of the ED modules is not always mandatory, and examiners generally have the discretion to document their work through other means.

Table 9. Appraisal Violations Cited

	FDIC	OCC	FRB
Examinations Reviewed	56	42	38
Examinations Impacted by Violations	18	4	4
Loans or Loan Relationships Reviewed	346	178	229
Total Violations Cited	29	5	5
Specific Violations Cited:			
• Failure to Obtain Required Appraisal/Evaluation	66%	100%	80%
• Failure to Achieve Minimum Appraisal Standards	10%	0%	20%
• Failure to Obtain Appraiser with Required Independence or Competency	24%	0%	0%

Source: OIG analysis of a sample of safety and soundness examinations and corresponding working papers.

The FDIC provides that use of the ED Modules is discretionary and should be tailored to the characteristics of each institution based on its size, complexity, and risk profile. FDIC guidance states that when an ED Module is not used, examiners should provide documentation of their findings through a combination of brief summaries, source documents, report comments, and other working papers that clearly describe financial conditions, management practices, and examination conclusions. Documentation should generally describe key audit/risk scoping decisions, core source documents reviewed, and general examination procedures performed.

The FRB requires that primary ED modules be used at full-scope examinations and that any use of supplemental ED modules, such as the *Real Estate Appraisal Program* module, be discussed in the examination scoping memorandum.

The OCC does not use ED modules and instead typically uses standard electronic examination work programs to document examination procedures performed. OCC examination policies require examiners to prepare working papers to document which examination procedures were performed and whether they were performed fully or partially.

Recommendation

The adequacy of an institution's appraisal program, and the extent to which appraisals supporting loans are current and reliable, are key factors in assessing the risk that exists in an institution's loan portfolio. More robust documentation of examination procedures and conclusions in this area may help assure agency management that examiners are consistently assessing institutions' compliance with relevant guidance and may facilitate subsequent examination planning efforts.

We recommend that the FDIC, OCC, and FRB:

3. Strengthen examiner documentation requirements related to examination methodologies and examination procedures performed to assess an institution's appraisal program.

Examiner Reassessment of Appraised Values

Agency guidance instructs examiners to use their judgment to determine if appraisals or evaluations are providing reliable collateral values based on current market conditions. Within that determination, an examiner should conclude if the assumptions reflected in the appraisal accurately identify and monitor changing market conditions. Appendix 8 provides examples of supervisory expectations for updated valuations of real property collateral.

We found only four instances among the 416 adversely classified loans ($1.2 million of $1.2 billion) that we reviewed where examiners either adjusted the market value approach by reducing the appraised value considering current market deterioration or by using an on-line retail database. In all other cases, examiners appeared to have accepted the collateral value within the appraisal or evaluation contained in the institution's loan files.

We noted at least 51 appraisals that were 3 or more years old. Out-of-date appraisals might not reflect current market values, which could limit the effectiveness of examiners' analyses of loan credit quality and collateral protection. We decided to review examiners' documentation for seven loans that had appraisals dated prior to the 2007 financial crisis. We confirmed the appraisals related to those loans had one or more of the following characteristics that could warrant a current assessment of collateral value: account delinquency, bankruptcy of primary repayment source, deterioration of the property's available cash flow to service debt, reliance on collateral sale for repayment, or modified loan terms. We found that examiners noted that a few of the appraisals were stale, but in six of the seven instances appeared to accept the dated appraised values without documenting additional analysis of current value. In the seventh instance, the institution estimated an updated value of the property and detailed some of the estimate's key assumptions, but the examiners did not document an assessment of the adequacy of the institution's assumptions.

As discussed in Matter (3)(C), we interviewed and surveyed 51 FDIC examiners-in-charge about several matters pertaining to appraisals. We discussed with examiners instances in which they might be influenced to reassess the collateral value supporting loans under review or request that an institution obtain a new appraisal. The examiners told us that each situation is handled based on the unique circumstances involved. However, the performance of the loan is generally a key consideration, such as when an existing real estate loan is not paying as agreed, has been internally downgraded by the institution, or has gone through a modification or workout. Some examiners indicated that they refrain from reassessing values because they are not appraisers. Instead, they explain to institution management why a new appraisal or assessment of value may be necessary. Two examiners stated that they may be more likely to cite an appraisal violation and classify the loan, but they will not necessarily request the institution to obtain a new appraisal or evaluation. A few other examiners reported that appraisal specialists have been made available to examination teams in the past and used to assist in the review of an institution's policies, loans, and appraisals.

P.L. 112-88 (3)(C)

FDIC field examiner implementation of guidance issued December 2, 2010, titled "Agencies Issue Final Appraisal and Evaluation Guidelines."

The 2010 Appraisal Guidelines clarified for financial institutions and examiners the supervisory expectations for prudent appraisal and evaluation policies, procedures, and practices. Our review of FDIC examination working papers found limited documentation of FDIC examiners implementing the Appraisal Guidelines. Most of the FDIC examiners that we surveyed indicated the criteria and content of the 2010 Appraisal Guidelines had already been incorporated and implemented in the examination process by the time the 2010 guidelines were issued and that the guidelines clarified supervisory expectations and provided criteria for assessing certain areas. We identified differences in how examiners approach assessing institutions' appraisal programs and how they document their assessment. While FDIC procedures call for explicit documentation of an institution's compliance with certain appraisal guidance, FDIC examiners do not consistently follow that guidance.

We contracted with KPMG LLP to advise and assist OIG staff in planning the work associated with this area of study and presenting the results of testing.

The 2010 Appraisal and Evaluation Guidelines

The FDIC adopted appraisal standards in *Part 323–Appraisals of the FDIC Rules and Regulations* (Part 323), effective September 19, 1990. Part 323, as amended, identifies which real estate-related financial transactions require the services of an appraiser, prescribes which categories of federally related transactions must be appraised by a state certified appraiser and which by a state licensed appraiser, and prescribes minimum standards for the performance of real estate appraisals in connection with federally related transactions under FDIC supervision.

The December 2010 Appraisal Guidelines superseded the 1994 guidelines and addressed changes in appraisal practices and advancements in institutions' collateral valuation methods. The 2010 Appraisal Guidelines continued to incorporate the USPAP to set minimum standards that apply in all appraisal, appraisal review, and appraisal consulting assignments.

In conjunction with the issuance of the 2010 Appraisal Guidelines, the RMS Director issued RD Memorandum 2010-036, *Procedures for the Interagency Appraisal and Evaluation Guidelines*. This memorandum provides guidance and updates examination and regional office procedures relative to the 2010 Appraisal Guidelines. The RD Memorandum states that when reviewing an institution's real estate lending activities, examiners should determine whether the institution's policies and procedures establish an effective appraisal and evaluation program and consider the size and nature of an institution's real estate-related activities when assessing the appropriateness of its program. Notably, the RD Memorandum requires that examiners briefly document their assessment regarding the reliability of appraisals and evaluations supporting the real estate loans that were reviewed, including the minimum appraisal standards. If examiners find no deficiencies relative to the institution's compliance with Part 323 or appraisal-related guidance, and the ED module is not used to document the examination's findings, then examiners should include the following statement (or something similar), in the examination working papers:

> Based on the review conducted during the examination, the institution has implemented adequate procedures to assure that appraisals and evaluations for real estate loans conform to the minimum standards outlined in Part 323.

FDIC Field Examiner Implementation of the 2010 Appraisal Guidelines

As discussed in the previous section, we found limited documentation of examiners' review and analysis of institutions' appraisal programs and compliance with the 2010 Appraisal Guidelines in our review of 136 full-scope examinations of open institutions. Among the 56 full-scope FDIC examinations in our sample, documentation showed that FDIC examiners were reviewing for, and noting deficiencies with, an institution's individual appraisals, the institution's appraisal program, or both. However, we found few instances where FDIC examiners provided a statement of positive assurance that an institution was in compliance with Part 323. Specifically, examiners:

- cited 18 institutions for an apparent violation of Part 323 or an apparent contravention of the 2010 Appraisal Guidelines;
- reported 17 institutions for various deficiencies in their appraisal practices that were not formally cited as an apparent regulatory violation or policy contravention; and

- used in 4 examinations either the Loan Portfolio or the Appraisal ED modules, or both, in lieu of providing the statement of positive assurance.

The remaining 15 examinations did not include in the examination working papers the required statement of positive assurance concerning the institution's conformance to the minimum appraisal standards.

Survey of Examiners Related to Their Implementation of the 2010 Appraisal Guidelines

Due to the limited documentation within examination working papers, we expanded our review to interview and survey 51 FDIC examiners-in-charge to determine how they implemented the 2010 Appraisal Guidelines. We focused our survey questions on the following topics.

Impact of the 2010 Appraisal Guidelines. The examiners we surveyed generally noted that the issuance of the 2010 Appraisal Guidelines did not have a major impact on the review and assessment of an institution's appraisal and evaluation program because the overall tenets of the 2010 Appraisal Guidelines had already been incorporated in the examination process. For example, 35 percent of examiners said the guidelines had "little" or "no" impact, and 47 percent of examiners considered there to be "some" impact on examination procedures. Examiners said that the 2010 Appraisal Guidelines clarified the supervisory expectations for prudent appraisal and evaluation policies, procedures, and practices, which benefited examiners when applying examination procedures. The 2010 Appraisal Guidelines also provided additional supervisory criteria and clarification for certain areas, including the use of discounts and deductions in appraisals and when a new appraisal should be obtained by an institution, specifically in cases of loan modifications and workouts.

Examiner approach to assessing an institution's appraisal program. Surveyed examiners stated that the examination process typically incorporates assessing an institution's appraisal and evaluation program through the review of the institution's policies and procedures, as well as through an asset quality review of loan files. Among other things, examiners stated that an appraiser list approved by the board of directors and effective internal controls for reviewing valuations are key aspects of the policy review. That said, we found there was inconsistency in how examiners addressed reviewing an institution's appraisal and evaluation policy, as follows:

- Sixty-two percent of our survey respondents noted that the institution's policy is reviewed separately and thoroughly, and the institution's adherence to the policy is fully assessed.
- Half as many–31 percent of respondents–noted that an institution's policy is only reviewed when a specific loan appraisal weakness is noted during the credit review process. Examiners would expand their procedures to address the weakness that corresponds to the policy statement, such as failure to obtain appraisals as required by guidance, nonconformance with USPAP, or outdated appraisals in instances of obvious market changes.

- The remaining seven percent of respondents only routinely review and assess adherence to certain segments of an institution's policy. In those cases, some examples of specific policy items reviewed include appraiser selection, approval, and ordering; re-appraisal guidelines; and the use of *automated valuation models*.

According to examiners, the depth of the review performed is determined using a risk-focused approach that depends on, among other things, the financial condition and rating of the institution, and might be addressed from either a top-down or bottom-up approach. For example, if the examiner responsible for reviewing the appraisal and evaluation program identifies certain weaknesses or gaps in the policy, that examiner would notify the examiners who were reviewing loans files and instruct them to review the loan file appraisals for such weaknesses or gaps (top-down approach). Alternatively, if examiners identify recurring appraisal issues in the loan file review, they may conduct a broader analysis of potential global and systemic weaknesses in the overall appraisal and evaluation program (bottom-up approach).

Documenting examination procedures related to appraisals. Among surveyed examiners, 37 percent noted that their examination working papers include a summary paragraph that specifically references and discusses the 2010 Appraisal Guidelines, and 33 percent noted that their examination working papers include certain institution documents that examiners would annotate in their review of the appraisal program, which typically include the loan policy and any documents with identified weaknesses or issues. However, 26 percent noted that the examination report and working papers would not specifically reference the 2010 Appraisal Guidelines.

Many examiners interviewed stated that they rely upon their experience and knowledge of prudent appraisal and evaluation standards in performing their review during examinations rather than the *Real Estate Appraisal Program* ED Module. Twenty-nine percent of the examiners interviewed stated that they use the ED Module or a similar field office or regional checklist to document their review of an institution's real estate appraisal program.

We found that examiners do not regularly and consistently follow the RD Memorandum 2010-036 requirement to document when no deficiencies are noted relative to the institution's compliance with Part 323 or appraisal-related guidance. Sixty-five percent of examiners surveyed noted that such a statement is not always included in the examination working papers in instances where no deficiencies are noted. A few examiners added, though, that an examination report may include language noting the sufficiency and adequacy of an institution's credit administration practices, which they said would be inclusive of the appraisal and evaluation review.

Recommendations

To ensure consistency among the examination procedures that examiners perform to assess an institution's appraisal and evaluation program, we recommend that the Director, RMS:

4. Clarify supervisory expectations related to examiners' review of the institution's appraisal program and whether that review should include all program elements in

the 2010 Appraisal Guidelines or be limited to appraisal program areas of concern resulting from the examiner loan file review.

To ensure that supervisory examiners comply with established policies and procedures, we recommend that the Director, RMS:

5. Reiterate that examiners should be including a positive assurance statement in the ROE or examination working papers in situations where examiners conclude that the institution has implemented adequate procedures over appraisals and evaluations, and develop an RMS internal review control to periodically verify examiner compliance.

MATTER 4. CAPITAL

P.L. 112-88 requires the OIG to study capital adequacy and private capital investments in failing institutions, including:

(A) the factors that examiners use to assess the adequacy of capital at insured depository institutions, including the extent to which the quality and risk profile of the insured institution's loan portfolio is considered in the examiners' assessment;
(B) the number of applications received by the FDIC from PCIs to acquire insured depository institutions in receivership, the factors used by the FDIC in evaluating the applications, and the number of applications that have been approved or not approved, including the reasons pertaining thereto; and
(C) the policies and procedures associated with the evaluation of potential private investments in insured depository institutions and the extent to which those policies and procedures are followed.

A financial institution's capital performs several important functions, including, but not limited to, the absorption of losses, promotion of public confidence, restriction of excessive asset growth, and protection to depositors and the DIF. According to interagency guidelines, as presented within the UFIRS, a financial institution is expected to maintain capital commensurate with the nature and extent of risks to the institution and the ability of management to identify, measure, monitor, and control these risks. The types and quantity of risk inherent in an institution's activities will determine the extent to which it may be necessary to maintain capital at levels above required regulatory minimums to properly reflect the potentially adverse consequences that these risks may have on the institution's capital.

As it relates to capital investment in failed financial institutions, in August 2009, the FDIC Board of Directors issued the FDIC's PCI SOP, which provided guidance to PCIs interested in acquiring or investing in failed institutions. Proposed capital investments in open insured depository financial institutions that require FDIC approval are governed by the FDI Act and are submitted for FDIC review using various types of applications, such as those for a change-in- control or a merger, among others. The FDIC reviews these applications for the applicable statutory factors, including risk that the proposed transaction presents to the DIF.

P.L. 112-88 (4)(A)

The factors that examiners use to assess the adequacy of capital at insured depository institutions, including the extent to which the quality and risk profile of the insured institution's loan portfolio is considered in the examiners' assessment.

Examiners assess an institution's capital adequacy by considering a number of factors, including the institution's financial condition; the nature, trend, and volume of problem assets, and the adequacy of ALLL; earnings and dividends; management's access to additional capital; prospects and plans for growth, as well as past experience in managing growth; access to capital markets and other sources of capital; balance sheet composition and risks associated with nontraditional activities; and risk exposure represented by off-balance-sheet activities.

Based on our review of a sample of examinations, we found that, among other relevant factors, examiners considered the quality and risk profile of the insured institution's loan portfolio in nearly all cases included in our sample. Prior MLRs similarly referenced examiner assessment of these factors and often noted that examiners had identified risk in the loan portfolio but could have been more aggressive in ensuring that capital was commensurate with that risk.

Factors Examiners Use to Assess Capital Adequacy

Capital adequacy is one of the elements that must be evaluated to arrive at a composite rating. When assigning ratings, examiners are instructed to consider an institution's size and sophistication, the nature and complexity of its activities, and its general risk profile. As stated in the UFIRS, among other things, an institution's capital is rated based upon assessing the following factors:

- The level and quality of capital and the overall financial condition of the institution.
- The nature, trend, and volume of problem assets, and the adequacy of ALLL and other valuation reserves.
- The quality and strength of earnings, and the reasonableness of dividends.
- The ability of management to address emerging needs for additional capital.
- Prospects and plans for growth, as well as past experience in managing growth.
- Access to capital markets and other sources of capital, including support provided by a parent holding company.
- Balance sheet composition, including the nature and amount of intangible assets, market risk, concentration risk, and risks associated with nontraditional activities.
- Risk exposure represented by off-balance-sheet activities.

Examiners are also expected to consider internal controls such as policies, risk limits, and practices; audit functions and independent reviews; information and communication systems surrounding capital preservation; and accuracy of capital accounts.

Examiner Assessment of Capital Adequacy

Based on our review of 136 full-scope examinations of open institutions, we found evidence that, with the exception of assessing an institution's balance sheet composition and risk exposure of off-balance-sheet activities, examiners considered and assessed the factors outlined in the UFIRS. With respect to the exceptions, these factors may have been immaterial to the institution's overall risk profile in some cases.

Examiners are not required to quantify an institution's level of capital deficiency during the examination process and generally did not do so. Also, in those cases where an institution had a capital plan or was actively engaged in capital raising efforts, examiners often did not discuss the sufficiency of the capital plan and/or capital raising efforts unless the institution was subject to an enforcement action.

We generally found less documented coverage of internal controls such as policies, risk limits, and information systems. We attributed that finding to the regulators' general practice of documenting examination results on an exception basis, as described earlier in our report.

Our review of prior MLR reports further evidenced that examiners evaluated the adequacy of banks' capital consistent with the factors outlined in the UFIRS. These MLRs noted that examiners often reported significant deterioration in asset quality due to the volume of problem assets, significant decline or a lack of earnings, an inability to raise sufficient capital, and insufficient capital given the institution's risk profile. The MLR reports often concluded that examiners could have been more aggressive in requiring the institution to increase capital commensurate with risk, even if doing so required capital levels to be above the minimum PCA thresholds for a *Well Capitalized* institution.

The term "private capital investor" (PCI) is used but not defined in the PCI SOP, as the FDIC found "it exceedingly difficult to use precisely defined terms to deal with the relatively new phenomenon of private capital funds joining together to purchase the assets and liabilities of failed banks and thrifts where the investors all are less than 24.9 percent owners but supply almost all of the capital to capitalize the new depository institution."[59] For purposes of our study, we defined PCI to refer to an entity or group of entities that raises capital from private rather than public sources in order to acquire a failed institution. In order to make those acquisitions, PCIs first invest in an existing or new institution (we refer to those as a *PCI institution*) and use that PCI institution as a vehicle to submit a bid for failed institution assets and deposits.

P.L. 112-88 (4)(B)

The number of applications received by the FDIC from private capital investors to acquire insured depository institutions in receivership, factors used by the FDIC in evaluating the applications, and the number of applications that have been approved or not approved, including the reasons pertaining thereto.

Based on the documentation available to us as of December 31, 2011, we determined that the FDIC received approximately 60 requests from PCIs to bid on insured depository institutions in receivership. The FDIC evaluated those requests based on specific factors spelled out in the PCI SOP, which generally address the capital commitments of the investors and their proposed investment structure.

Further, in connection with its deposit insurance and supervisory responsibilities, the FDIC applies statutory and regulatory criteria as well as policy considerations to proposals by PCIs to use either a newly chartered institution or an existing institution to acquire a failed bank. The statutory and regulatory criteria focus on the institution's capital, management, and risk to the DIF as well as whether the acquisition would produce an unacceptable impact on competition within the bank's community. Of the 60 PCI requests received, the FDIC approved 31 (52 percent). Of the remaining 29 requests, investors withdrew, superseded, or abandoned 23; the FDIC returned 2 incomplete applications; and 4 were under review by the FDIC as of December 31, 2011. FDIC-identified concerns with non-approved requests generally related to capital, management, and business plans.

Requests Received by the FDIC to Acquire Financial Institutions in Receivership

FDIC personnel informed us that the FDIC received and processed 60 PCI requests for clearance-to-bid on financial institutions in receivership from August 26, 2009 (i.e., the effective date of the PCI SOP) through December 31, 2011. There is no specific form to be completed by private investors to commence the PCI SOP process, but requests for clearance-to-bid on failed banks typically included applications for deposit insurance, change-in-control, merger, or business plan changes.

Those requests and related applications were evaluated by the FDIC using the factors described below.

Factors Used by the FDIC in Evaluating Requests

The PCI SOP provides guidance to PCIs interested in acquiring or investing in failed insured depository institutions, including the terms and conditions that PCIs are expected to satisfy to obtain bidding eligibility for a proposed acquisition structure. With certain exceptions, the SOP applies to:

- Private investors in a company, including any company acquired to facilitate bidding on failed banks or thrifts that is proposing to, directly or indirectly, assume deposit liabilities, or such liabilities and assets, from the resolution of a failed insured depository institution; and
- Applicants for insurance in the case of *de novo*[60] charters issued in connection with the resolution of failed insured depository institutions.

Among other things, the PCI SOP generally provides that (1) for 3 years following the acquisition, the PCI institution hold a greater minimum level of capital than the level required of non-PCI institutions, (2) the PCI may not sell its shares in the bank without prior FDIC approval for 3 years following the acquisition, and (3) the PCI must provide the FDIC with any information considered necessary to assure compliance with the PCI SOP.

PCIs may make a written request for clearance to bid on future resolutions. The FDIC's RMS, in coordination with the Legal Division (Legal), processes clearance-to-bid requests. Those requests may be processed by the FDIC as either a shelf charter or an inflatable charter depending on the circumstances of the proposed acquisition.

- **Shelf Charter.** In the shelf charter process, the PCIs propose to establish a new insured depository institution to be used as a vehicle to acquire failed banks or thrifts. In these cases, the clearance-to-bid request is accompanied by an Interagency Charter and Federal Deposit Insurance Application (deposit insurance application) to the FDIC and to the designated chartering authority for the proposed new depository institution. RMS and Legal process the deposit insurance application in conjunction with the clearance-to-bid request, in consultation with the designated chartering authority.
- **Inflatable Charter.** In the inflatable charter process, the PCIs may file an Interagency Bank Merger Act Application (merger application) or an Interagency Notice of Acquisition of Control (change-in-control application) with the primary federal regulator for an existing institution[61] in conjunction with a request for clearance to bid from the FDIC. If the existing institution is still in its *de novo* period,[62] the clearance-to-bid request may be accompanied by a change in business plan application. For state nonmember institutions, RMS and Legal process the merger, change-in-control, or change in business plan application in conjunction with the clearance-to-bid request. For other than state nonmember institutions, RMS and Legal process the clearance-to-bid request in consultation with the primary federal regulator.

If the PCI investors are deemed qualified based on the Legal and RMS reviews, the PCIs and related PCI institution receive a clearance-to-bid letter from the FDIC advising that RMS has qualified them to bid on one or more failing insured depository institutions. The clearance-to-bid letter includes any limits on the PCI's asset and deposit acquisition amounts, as well as any restrictions on the geographic areas for PCI bids.

In some instances, the letter requires that additional information be provided to the FDIC before a bid can be submitted on a specific institution, and notes that any material changes in the information, representations, or commitments provided to the FDIC could alter the FDIC's decision to qualify the PCI institution to bid.

Further, the letter includes a notification to the PCIs that the submission of a bid will be deemed to constitute agreement to abide by the PCI SOP. PCIs submit a signed copy of the clearance-to-bid letter before the PCI institution will be permitted to bid on a failing institution.

RMS and Legal jointly review PCI clearance-to-bid requests. Concurrently with Legal, RMS assesses any applications for deposit insurance (for shelf charters) or for change-in-control, merger, or material changes in business plans, as applicable (for inflatable charters).

Clearance-to-Bid Requests. When Legal reviews a clearance-to-bid request, it makes a threshold determination as to whether the PCI SOP is applicable. The attorney will typically conclude, subject to certain exceptions,[63] that the PCI SOP applies if the proposed transaction includes the acquisition of a failed bank or thrift by an institution that has, either directly or through its holding company, raised capital from private investors in contemplation of such an acquisition.

If the PCI SOP is applicable, the attorney is required to review whether the PCI and the proposed transaction address the following requirements outlined in the PCI SOP:

(1) **Capital Commitments.** The resulting depository institution must maintain a ratio of Tier 1 common equity to total assets of at least 10 percent for the first 3 years of operation and remain *Well Capitalized* for purposes of the PCA provisions.
(2) **Cross Support.** If two or more insured depository institutions are at least 80-percent owned by the same investor(s), those investor(s) must pledge their stock in the commonly owned institutions to the FDIC against loss.
(3) **Transactions with Affiliates.** Insured depository institutions acquired by investors may not extend credit to investors, their investment funds, and any affiliates.
(4) **Secrecy Law Jurisdictions.** Investors using organizational structures domiciled in bank secrecy jurisdictions[64] are not eligible to bid on insured depository institutions unless the investors are subsidiaries of companies subject to comprehensive consolidated supervision as recognized by the FRB and they agree to certain additional requirements.
(5) **Continuity of Ownership.** Certain investors are prohibited from selling or transferring their securities for 3 years following the acquisition, absent prior FDIC approval.
(6) **Prohibited Structures.** Complex and functionally opaque ownership structures in which beneficial ownership cannot be ascertained, responsible decision-making parties are not clearly defined, and/or ownership and controls are separated are not appropriate for approval as bidders of insured depository institutions.
(7) **Required Disclosure.** Investors subject to the PCI SOP are expected to submit to the FDIC information about the investors and all entities in the ownership structure.

The FDIC reviews other applications submitted with the clearance-to-bid request for compliance with regulatory requirements, as described below.

Shelf Charters. For all shelf charters, the FDIC evaluates the deposit insurance application, using the following seven factors from Section 6 of the FDI Act:[65]

1. The financial history and condition of the proposed depository institution.
2. The adequacy of the proposed depository institution's capital structure.
3. The proposed depository institution's future earnings prospects.
4. The general character and fitness of the depository institution's management.
5. The convenience and needs of the community to be served by the depository institution.
6. The risk presented by such depository institution to the DIF.
7. Whether the proposed institution's corporate powers are consistent with the purposes of the FDI Act.

Inflatable Charters. For inflatable charters, the FDIC evaluates the change-in-control application using the following six factors from Section 7(j)(7) of the FDI Act:[66]

1. If the proposed acquisition of control would result in a monopoly.
2. If the effect of the proposed acquisition of control in any section of the country may be substantially to lessen competition or to tend to create a monopoly, or would in any other manner be in restraint of trade.
3. If the financial condition of the acquiring person is such that it might jeopardize the financial stability of the bank or prejudice the interests of the depositors of the bank.
4. If the competence, experience, or integrity of any acquiring person or of any of the proposed management indicates that it would not be in the interest of the depositors of the bank or in the interest of the public to permit such person to control the bank.
5. If any acquiring party neglects, fails, or refuses to furnish all the information required by the FDIC.
6. If the transaction would have an adverse effect on the DIF.

In the event of a merger, the FDIC evaluates the merger application using the following eight factors from Section 18(c) of the FDI Act:[67]

1. Whether the proposed merger would result in a monopoly.
2. Whether the effect of the proposed merger in any section of the country may be substantially to lessen competition or to tend to create a monopoly, or would in any other manner be in restraint of trade.
3. The financial and managerial resources of the existing and proposed institutions.
4. The future prospects of the existing and proposed institutions.
5. The convenience and needs of the community to be served.
6. The effectiveness of any insured depository institution involved in the proposed merger in combating money laundering activities, including in overseas branches.
7. The risk presented to the stability of the United States banking or financial system.
8. For interstate mergers that do not involve one or more insured depository institutions in default or in danger of default, whether the resulting institution will control more than 10 percent of the total amount of deposits of insured depository institutions in the U.S.

For inflatable charters that require FDIC review of a change in business plan application, the FDIC evaluates the application using the same seven factors used to evaluate a deposit insurance application.

Requests Approved and Not Approved by the FDIC

The FDIC approved 31 (52 percent) of the 60 PCI requests received and the remaining 29 requests were not approved as of December 31, 2011.[68]

Table 10 below provides an overall summary of the 60 requests received.

Table 10. Status of PCI Requests for Clearance to Bid as of December 31, 2011 (for requests received August 26, 2009 through December 31, 2011)

Status	Total
Approved	31
Not Approved:	
Under Review	4
Superseded	2
Returned	2
Abandoned	2
Withdrawn	19
Total PCI Requests	**60**

Source: OIG analysis of RMS files.

The reasons for the 29 requests that were not approved as of December 31, 2011 follow.

- *Under Review:* The FDIC was still in the process of evaluating four requests. In general, these requests had been in process for less than 9 months, but we noted that one request had been in process for 2 years. FDIC records indicate that critical information missing for the request included, among other things, a stock purchase agreement that conforms to the PCI SOP and a business plan for proposed acquisition transactions.[69]
- *Superseded:* In two cases, the PCIs elected to pursue a new request in lieu of the initial request. In both cases, the subsequent request was approved and is reflected in the 31 approved requests.
- *Returned:* The FDIC returned the materials to two PCIs and closed their files because the requests submitted were substantially incomplete and the PCIs did not respond to requests for additional information. In particular, for both requests, the FDIC determined that information about the proposed capital, management, and business plan was inadequate.
- *Abandoned:* In two cases, correspondence from the PCIs indicated that the request was no longer being pursued by the PCIs, but a formal withdrawal letter was never sent by the PCIs to the FDIC. For both requests, the FDIC identified concerns related to whether sufficient capital would be available to implement the proposed business plan, and for one of the requests, there was an additional concern about the acceptability of proposed management and compensation plans.
- *Withdrawn:* Nineteen PCIs submitted letters to the FDIC withdrawing their applications before FDIC processing was complete. In most cases, the withdrawal letters did not indicate a reason for withdrawal.

Based on our review, for a majority of the withdrawn requests, the FDIC had identified concerns with the request prior to the receipt of the withdrawal letter, and those concerns may have had an impact on applicants' decisions to withdraw. FDIC concerns with investor requests fell into the following general categories: capital, management, and business plans. Examples of capital concerns included investors raising less capital than anticipated, or capital-related agreements or permits terminating before the PCIs were able to complete the request for clearance process. Concerns with management included, among others, unacceptable background investigation results and inadequate relevant banking experience. Finally, the FDIC also noted concerns with the feasibility of certain investors' business plans.

P.L. 112-88 (4)(C)

The policies and procedures associated with the evaluation of potential private investments in insured depository institutions and the extent to which those policies and procedures are followed.

The PCI SOP applies to proposals by private capital investors to acquire *failed* institutions. Private capital investors who invest in *open* banks without intending to use the open bank to acquire failed bank assets do not go through the PCI SOP process, but rather follow standard statutory and regulatory requirements. The FDIC tracks investors who go through the PCI SOP, but the FDIC does not formally track other private investment. The FDIC uses the factors listed in the PCI SOP in determining whether to grant investors clearance to bid on failed institutions. This clearance-to-bid process includes a pre-filing meeting, a review of the PCI's documentation supporting its clearance-to-bid request, and a post clearance-to-bid review. While strongly encouraged, pre-filing meetings are not required by statute or as part of the PCI SOP process; therefore, there are no formal policies and procedures for conducting those meetings and the FDIC does not track such meetings in a centralized manner. We could not verify the number of meetings that occurred or how many private investors declined to invest as a result of those meetings. The FDIC does have procedures for reviewing clearance-to-bid requests. We tested a sample of those requests and concluded that the FDIC followed its policies and procedures.

As for post clearance-to-bid reviews, once a private investor targets a specific failing institution for acquisition, the FDIC generally requires that investors update the information originally submitted with respect to their request for clearance to bid. If the FDIC has concerns with the updated information, it may suspend the investor from bidding on the target institution. The FDIC generally documented the authorization for those suspensions via email. Guidance for the review process evolved over time and was formalized in March 2012.

FDIC's Evaluation of Potential Private Investments

As discussed in connection with Matter (4)(B) above, any PCI interested in bidding on failed banks must receive clearance to bid on such banks consistent with the process and factors discussed in the prior topic. This clearance-to-bid process includes a pre-filing meeting, a review of the PCI's clearance-to-bid documentation, and a post clearance-to-bid review as discussed below.

Pre-Filing Meeting. These meetings are generally attended by the investors, FDIC regional or headquarters RMS and Legal staff, and the chartering authority, if applicable. The

FDIC strongly encourages a pre-filing meeting prior to potential investors filing a request in order to ensure that all parties understand filing requirements and expectations, and so that issues or problems with a proposal can be identified early. While strongly encouraged, pre-filing meetings are not required by statute or as part of the PCI process; therefore, the FDIC does not have formal policies and procedures for conducting the pre-filing meetings and does not track the number of meetings held.[70] We could not verify the number of meetings that occurred or the results of those meetings. FDIC management told us that they generally apply the relevant statutory and PCI SOP criteria to the facts and circumstances presented at the pre-filing meetings in order to give the investors an idea of the strength and weakness of their proposals. Further, FDIC officials indicated that some investors who attended these meetings decided not to pursue investment in failed institutions.

We confirmed with RMS that headquarters RMS officials generally attend pre-filing meetings— in person or by phone—to ensure consistency and that the FDIC does not make approval decisions pertaining to PCI proposals at those pre-filing meetings.

Clearance-to-Bid Documentation Review. As discussed in greater detail in response to Matter (4)(B), when the FDIC receives a request for clearance to bid, RMS and Legal jointly review it to determine whether the investors are subject to the PCI SOP, as that policy requires that private investors agree to various conditions before the FDIC will provide a clearance-to-bid letter. RMS reviews any deposit insurance, change-in-control, merger, or change in business plan applications/requests that may have been submitted concurrently with the request for clearance to bid. RMS documents the results of the RMS and Legal review in a Summary Memorandum or requests additional information from the PCI if needed. If the PCI investors are deemed qualified based on the Legal and RMS reviews, the PCI and the PCI institution receives a clearance-to-bid letter from the FDIC indicating that the PCI institution may bid on one or more failed institutions.

In addition to the evaluation factors described in response to Matter (4)(B), the FDIC's *Risk Management Manual of Examination Policies* and *Case Manager Procedures Manual* describe how applications for deposit insurance, merger, change-in-control, and change in business plan should be processed by the FDIC. Further, Legal has internal procedures for analyzing investor transactions under the requirements of the PCI SOP that were formally documented on March 27, 2012.

As noted in Matter (4)(B), the FDIC approved 31 (52 percent) of the 60 PCI requests it received. As part of a 2011 audit that we performed of the PCI process (2011 Audit),[71] we selected a non- statistical sample of 10 requests submitted by PCIs that were cleared to bid on failing institutions to verify whether the requests received appropriate internal approvals. We found evidence demonstrating FDIC review for all 10 requests, but the manner in which approvals were evidenced and the extent and organization of documentation supporting approvals varied.

The 2011 Audit also included a detailed review of five requests and found that the FDIC staff members who reviewed the requests were knowledgeable of the circumstances regarding each request, considered the requirements of the PCI SOP and the FDI Act, and were generally able to locate documentation to support their decisions. In some instances, however, we found that the FDIC had not fully documented the analysis performed to support decisions made on requests reviewed. For example, the summary memoranda for two of the five requests did not include a clear recommendation regarding whether the investor was in compliance with the PCI SOP. At the time of our 2011 Audit, the FDIC's implementation of procedures for processing clearance-to-bid requests in effect from 2009 through April 2011 did not result in consistent documentation of the FDIC's rationale for issuing or not issuing clearance-to-bid letters. Subsequent to our 2011 Audit, and consistent with our audit recommendations, the FDIC enhanced and expanded its written procedures for processing and documenting review of clearance-to-bid requests. FDIC management told us that since the PCI SOP was a newly adopted policy, FDIC staff monitored its implementation and looked for ways to improve it. As a result, the process evolved over time.

Post Clearance-to-Bid Review. If a PCI receives a clearance-to-bid letter, the PCI institution must go through a post clearance-to-bid review process before it is permitted to submit a bid to acquire a target institution. At that time, the FDIC generally requires that the PCI provide, among other things, a description of the proposed transaction; updated information with respect to its initial submission, including any changes to the proposed organizational structure, capitalization, management, or material aspects in light of size, scope, complexity, or other attributes of the target institution; and a comprehensive customized business plan covering the first 3 years of operation.

If the FDIC has concerns with the submission during this post clearance-to-bid process, the PCI would be suspended from bidding on the target institution. Guidance for this aspect of the review process is in the form of a question-and-answer document, and FDIC management told us the process has evolved over time and decisions are generally documented via email. Generally, a request for suspension is communicated from RMS to DRR. We noted that the question-and- answer document includes specific criteria that reviewers should use in making a determination to suspend a previously cleared PCI institution from bidding. The FDIC formally tracks the dates that the institution is suspended from the lists of *eligible bidders*. DRR and RMS personnel identified 14 of the 26 PCI institutions that had been cleared to bid and were subject to the PCI SOP, that had been suspended from the lists of eligible bidders one or more times during the years 2010 through 2011.[72] Those suspensions generally occurred because the FDIC determined that the PCI institution needed a waiting period to effectively integrate prior bank acquisitions before placing new bids to initiate additional failed bank acquisitions. The 14 PCI institutions were suspended from bidding for the following reasons:

- Seven PCI institutions were suspended as a result of the FDIC implementing a waiting period due to prior bank acquisitions.
- One PCI institution was suspended at one point to implement a waiting period and at another point for failure to submit an integration plan for a targeted failed bank acquisition.
- One PCI institution was suspended at one point to implement a waiting period and at another point because the PCI institution's compliance examination rating was less than satisfactory, indicating a need to improve the PCI institution's compliance program.
- One PCI institution was suspended when its capital commitments expired.
- Four related PCI institutions were suspended pending review of a change in the proposed board and management.

MATTER 5. WORKOUTS

P.L. 112-88 requires the OIG to study the success of FDIC field examiners in implementing FDIC guidelines titled, *Policy Statement on Prudent Commercial Real Estate Loan Workouts*, dated October 31, 2009, regarding workouts of CRE, including:

(A) whether field examiners are using the correct appraisals; and
(B) whether there is any difference in implementation between residential workouts and commercial (including land development and 1-4 family residential and commercial construction loans) workouts.

P.L. 112-88 (5)

> **The success of FDIC field examiners in implementing FDIC guidelines titled "Policy Statement on Prudent Commercial Real Estate Loan Workouts" (October 31, 2009) regarding workouts of commercial real estate.**
>
> We determined that examiners successfully implemented three of the four areas outlined in interagency guidance titled, *Policy Statement on Prudent Commercial Real Estate Loan Workouts*. With the exception of a few instances, we confirmed that examiners implemented the workout guidance related to loan-specific workout arrangements, classification of loans, and regulatory reporting and accounting considerations. Since examiners use an exception-based process, we were unable to determine from examination documentation whether examiners implemented the fourth area of the Policy Statement, that is, an institution's risk management elements for loan workout programs. While examiners reviewed broader institution loan policies and procedures, examiners did not document their review of risk management elements specifically associated with institutions' workout programs, such as infrastructure, staffing, and information systems for managing troubled assets.

CRE lending has traditionally been risky for financial institutions. Real estate markets are cyclical, so that even the most well-conceived and soundly underwritten projects can become troubled during periodic overbuilding cycles.[73] During such periods, financial institutions may face challenges when working with troubled CRE borrowers. While CRE borrowers may experience deteriorating financial condition, many continue to be creditworthy customers who have the willingness and capacity to repay. Institutions may find that loan workouts are mutually beneficial for such borrowers. Loan workouts can take many forms, including a renewal or extension of loan terms, extension of additional credit, or a reduction in the loan interest rate. Recognizing increased CRE concentrations and risks at institutions, the regulators issued CRE- related guidance from 2006 to 2010, including the *Policy Statement on Prudent Commercial Real Estate Loan Workouts* (guidance) in October 2009.

We contracted with KPMG to advise and assist OIG staff in planning the work, conducting necessary testing, and analyzing and presenting testing results. For purposes of our review, we defined "successful" implementation of the guidance as examiners complying with its provisions. Our scope was limited to FDIC-supervised insured depository institutions.

FDIC Supervisory Expectations, Dissemination, and Training Related to the Workout Guidance

The interagency workout guidance took effect upon issuance and provides direction to examiners on evaluating an institution's efforts to renew and restructure loans to creditworthy borrowers who are experiencing diminished operating cash flows, depreciated collateral values, or prolonged delays in selling or renting commercial properties. Essentially, it updated and replaced existing supervisory guidance[74] to promote supervisory consistency, enhance the transparency of CRE workout transactions, and ensure that supervisory policies and actions do not inadvertently curtail the availability of credit to sound borrowers. Key features of the guidance include the following:

- The regulators recognize that reasonable and prudent workouts are often in the best interest of institutions and creditworthy CRE borrowers.
- Examiners are expected to take a balanced and consistent approach in their review of institutions' workout activity.
- The primary focus of an examiner's review of a commercial loan is an assessment of the borrower's ability to repay the loan.
- Prudent workouts will not be subject to examiner criticism even if the restructured loan is adversely classified.
- A restructured loan will not be adversely classified solely because the value of the underlying collateral has declined to an amount that is less than the loan balance.
- Workout programs should be well conceived and maximize the institution's collection of principal and interest and not simply be restructured to mask underlying weaknesses.

The guidance promotes prudent CRE loan workouts at institutions, the goal of which is to maximize recovery potential versus maintaining a credit relationship. It reiterates existing guidelines and incorporates the components of effective workout programs. It also includes references and materials related to regulatory reporting, but it does not change existing regulatory reporting guidance provided in relevant interagency statements issued by the regulators or accounting requirements under GAAP.

The FDIC disseminated the guidance to examiners and the industry; developed a related ED Module, *Troubled Debt Restructuring*, in September 2011; and discussed the guidance at industry conferences.

FDIC Examiner Implementation of Guidance

The October 2009 guidance is divided into four distinct areas: (1) an institution's risk management elements for loan workout programs, (2) loan-specific workout arrangements, (3) loan classifications, and (4) regulatory reporting and accounting considerations, each of which highlights elements for the institutions and examiners to consider. To determine whether examiners successfully implemented the guidance, we reviewed ROEs and examination documentation for the elements within each of the four areas.

Risk Management Elements for Loan Workout Programs

According to the guidance, an institution's risk management practices for renewing and restructuring[75] CRE loans should be appropriate for the complexity and nature of its lending activity and should be consistent with safe and sound lending practices and relevant regulatory reporting requirements. Institutions should have the following controls in place:

- Management infrastructure to identify, control, and manage the volume and complexity of the workout activity.
- Documentation standards to verify the borrower's financial condition and collateral values.
- Adequate management information systems and internal controls to identify and track loan performance and risk, including concentration risk.
- Capability to produce regulatory reports that are consistent with regulatory reporting requirements (including GAAP) and supervisory guidance.
- Effective loan collection procedures.
- Adherence to statutory, regulatory and internal lending limits.
- Collateral administration to ensure proper lien perfection of the institution's collateral interests for both real and personal property.
- An ongoing credit review function.

We reviewed ROEs and examiner working papers for evidence that examiners performed procedures to assess whether institutions implemented the guidance for risk management elements for loan workout programs. We found evidence indicating that, for all 48 of the sampled institutions, examiners reviewed institutions' implementation of risk management elements associated with overall loan policy and guidelines. However, we were unable to locate evidence for any of the institutions that examiners had reviewed the institution's implementation of the risk management elements listed in the guidance specific to loan workout programs. As discussed in the workout guidance, in order to work out troubled assets effectively, institutions should ensure they have adequate infrastructure and staffing, such as a special assets or workout department, information, and documentation standards. For their part, examiners should assess/review these workout program elements. An RMS official expressed confidence based on experience working with examination staff and participating in regional examinations that examiners were doing what was required under the guidance.

Loan-Specific Workout Arrangements

According to the guidance, loan workouts can take many forms, and institutions should consider loan workouts after analyzing a borrower's repayment capacity, evaluating the support provided by guarantors, and assessing the value of the collateral pledged on the debt. Workouts need to be designed to help ensure that the institution maximizes its recovery potential. While institutions may enter into restructurings with borrowers that result in an adverse classification, an institution will not be criticized for engaging in loan workout arrangements so long as management has the following:

- A prudent workout policy that establishes appropriate loan terms and amortization schedules and that permits the institution to modify the workout plan if sustained repayment performance is not demonstrated or if collateral values do not stabilize.
- An analysis of the borrower's *global debt service* that reflects a realistic projection of the borrower's and guarantor's expenses.[76]
- The ability to monitor the ongoing performance of the borrower and guarantor under the terms of the workout.
- An internal loan grading system that accurately and consistently reflects the risk in the workout arrangement.
- An ALLL methodology that covers estimated credit losses in the restructured loan, measured in accordance with GAAP, and recognizes credit losses in a timely manner through provisions and charge-offs, as appropriate.[77]

The guidance further provides that an examiner's review of a commercial loan should focus on the following factors.

- Repayment capacity of the borrower(s): the character, overall financial condition, resources, and payment record of the borrower; global cash flow analysis to consider the borrower's total debt obligations; and market conditions that influence repayment capacity.
- Evaluation of support provided by guarantors: a willingness to fulfill all current and previous obligations, economic incentive to fulfill investment obligations, and investment in the project to serve as an incentive to fulfill obligations.
- Evaluation of collateral values: analysis of appraisals and internal evaluation, confirmation of use of market values, review of the appropriateness of the major facts, identification of weaknesses, and the institution ability/inability to address the deficiencies in a timely manner.

With few exceptions, examination documentation showed that examiners appropriately applied guidance related to loan workout arrangements and reviewed the factors listed above. The most frequent exceptions were 16 instances among the 390 CRE line sheets tested that related to evaluating collateral values. For example, we found a loan where the appraisal value on the line sheet was different from the appraisal value found in the institution's credit file, and we could not determine the source of the field examiner's appraisal value. In another case, an examiner used an appraisal from 2001, while the examination report date was January 25, 2010. In addition, we found several examples of line sheets that did not adequately document the appropriateness of the major facts, assumptions, and valuation approaches in the collateral valuation. We found an additional five exceptions related to aspects of examiners' analyses of borrowers' repayment capacity and evaluation of guarantors.

Loan Classifications

According to the guidance, loans that are adequately protected by the current sound worth and debt service capacity of the borrower, guarantor, or the underlying collateral generally are not adversely classified. Similarly, loans to sound borrowers that are renewed or restructured in accordance with prudent underwriting standards should not be adversely classified or criticized unless well-defined weaknesses exist that jeopardize repayment. Further, loans should not be adversely classified solely because the borrower is associated with a particular industry that is experiencing financial difficulties. When an institution's restructurings are not supported by adequate analysis and documentation, examiners are expected to exercise reasonable judgment in reviewing and determining loan classifications until the institution is able to provide information to support management's conclusions and internal loan grades.

To assess the success of the examiner's implementation of the guidance related to loan classifications, we reviewed the loan sample for evidence that examiners had appropriately classified loans based on performance, renewals/restructurings, sale of collateral for repayment, and partial charge-off. Specifically, we reviewed examiner documentation and ROEs related to the following.

- *Loan performance assessment for classification purposes.* The impact on classification from declining collateral values and repayment capacity, and classification of loans that are being kept current with an interest reserve or some other below-market means.
- *Classification of renewals or restructurings of maturing loans.* The reasonableness of restructure and classification based on repayment of the loan.
- *Classification of troubled CRE loans dependent on the sale of collateral for repayment.* If loan repayment is dependent on sale of collateral, classification of the loan balance should be based on the appraised value of the collateral.
- *Classification and accrual treatment of restructured loans with a partial charge-off.* When well-defined weaknesses exist and a partial charge-off has been taken, the remaining recorded balance for the restructured loan generally should be classified no more severely than substandard unless the loss exposure cannot be reasonably determined.

With few exceptions, we concluded that examiners appropriately applied the above guidance related to loan classifications. The most frequent exceptions were 16 instances among the 390 CRE line sheets tested where examiners did not appropriately review troubled CRE loans. For example, we found loans that examiners classified that lacked adequate documentation, or where the examiner specifically did not document whether repayment of the loan was dependent on the sale of collateral. We also found loans where the examiner did not determine the portion of the loan balance exceeding the market value of the collateral less cost to sell. We also found exceptions related to examiners' assessment of loan performance for classification purposes, and examiners' classification of renewals and restructurings of maturing loans or partial charge-offs.

Regulatory Reporting and Accounting Considerations

According to the guidance, institution management is responsible for preparing regulatory reports in accordance with GAAP and regulatory reporting requirements and supervisory guidance. Management also is responsible for establishing and maintaining an appropriate governance and internal control structure over the preparation of regulatory reports. Management should ensure that loan workout staff appropriately communicates with the accounting and regulatory reporting staff concerning the institution's loan restructurings and that the reporting consequences of restructurings are presented accurately in regulatory reports.

For their part, in addition to evaluating credit risk management processes and validating the accuracy of internal credit grades, examiners are responsible for reviewing management's processes related to accounting and regulatory reporting. The guidance states that examiners need to have a clear understanding of the differences between the credit risk management and accounting and regulatory reporting concepts (such as accrual status, restructurings, and the ALLL) when assessing the adequacy of the institution's reporting practices.[78]

To assess the success of examiners' application of the guidance related to regulatory reporting and accounting considerations, we reviewed examiner documentation in the loan sample for evidence that field examiners applied regulatory and accounting considerations in their review of interest accruals, TDR status,[79] and ALLL calculations. With few exceptions, we found that examiners appropriately applied guidance related to regulatory reporting and accounting considerations. The most frequent exceptions were 18 instances among the 390 CRE line sheets tested related to examiners' assessment of TDRs for ALLL purposes. For example, we found loans where it appeared that the examiner did not assess or did not document an assessment of TDRs for ALLL purposes or properly determine the need for a valuation allowance, or where there was no evidence of ALLL calculations. We found another nine exceptions related to correctly recording TDRs or determining interest accrual status.

Recommendation

The Policy Statement was intended, in part, to promote supervisory consistency and ensure that institutions have an effective program for managing loan workout activity. Greater documentation of examination procedures performed would provide the FDIC with assurance that those objectives are being met. Accordingly, we recommend that the Director, RMS:

6. Reiterate or strengthen examiner documentation requirements related to examination methodologies and examination procedures performed to assess the risk management elements of an institution's workout program.

P.L. 112-88 (5)(A)

Whether field examiners are using the correct appraisals.
With few exceptions, examiners followed the guidelines for use of appraisals in the October 2009 guidance.

For purposes of our review, we defined "correct appraisals" to be those that examiners confirmed were appropriate for their intended use with a particular asset. Such a confirmation would include determining whether appraisals reflected appropriate market values, facts, assumptions, and weaknesses, and verifying that institutions addressed appraisal deficiencies timely. To address this requirement, we assessed whether examiners were applying the loan workout appraisal guidance as part of their review of loan workouts. For CRE loans involved in a workout situation, the guidance notes that examiners should ensure that a new or updated appraisal or evaluation, as appropriate, addresses current project plans and market conditions that were considered in the development of the workout plan.

Use of Correct Appraisals

We reviewed examiner documentation in our sample and concluded that examiners generally followed the guidance when assessing collateral values. Table 11 presents relevant aspects of the guidance and the results of our testing.

To provide perspective on the exceptions, in one instance, there was no indication on the loan line sheet that an appraisal was performed for the examiner to analyze collateral values. In another instance, there was an outdated appraisal in the institution's supporting documentation and no indication in the working papers that the examiner directed the institution to address the need for an updated appraisal.

Table 11. Examiner Use of Appraisals

Of 48 institutions tested, did FDIC Examiners:	Yes	No
1. Analyze collateral values based on the institution's original appraisal or internal evaluation, any subsequent updates, additional information, and relevant market conditions?	44	4
2. Confirm that the institution used the market value conclusion (and not the fair value) that corresponds to the workout plan and the loan commitment?	47	1
3. Review the appropriateness of the major facts, assumptions, and valuation approaches in the collateral valuation and in the institution's internal credit review and impairment analysis?	46	2
4. Identify any weaknesses in the institution's supporting documentation or appraisal evaluation review process? If so, did the examiner direct the institution to address the weaknesses?	46	2
5. If the institution was unable or unwilling to address the deficiencies in a timely manner, did the examiner assess the degree of protection that the collateral affords?	48	0

Source: OIG/KPMG analysis.

P.L. 112-88 (5)(B)

Whether there is any difference in implementation between residential workouts and commercial (including land development and 1-4 family residential and commercial construction loans) workouts.

The examination guidance for reviewing loans resulting from residential and commercial workouts is similar and primarily focuses on the repayment capacity of the borrower, though there are risk factors that differentiate residential from CRE loans. We found that examiners applied the relevant guidance with few exceptions. Accordingly, we concluded there are no significant differences in implementation between residential workouts and commercial workouts.

We reviewed examiner documentation in our sample (described previously in this section of the report) to determine whether examiners applied workout guidance for the two types of workouts differently. Specifically, we reviewed the use of the *debt service coverage ratios*[80] for CRE loans and debt-to-income ratios[81] for residential loans and residential loan resets to fixed terms at renewal. Those ratios are indicators of the borrower's ability to service the debt.

Commercial versus Residential Workouts

As described in previous sections, when reviewing CRE loans that resulted from workouts, examiners should consider the repayment capacity of the borrower, guarantors, and collateral value. With respect to reviewing residential workout loans, under interagency *Uniform Retail Credit Classification and Account Management Policy* guidelines, examiners are primarily concerned about the borrower's repayment performance. However, if the loan is past due, then examiners would consider additional risk factors, similar to those for CRE loan workouts, such as whether the loan was dependent on the sale of collateral for repayment.

There are some differences with respect to the factors that examiners consider in deciding whether to classify commercial or residential workout loans. In the case of commercial workouts, the cash flow from CRE could negatively impact commercial borrowers' repayment capacity. In the case of residential loan workouts, a particular risk to borrowers' repayment capacity is adjustable rates on mortgages, especially when the borrowers were qualified based on a low introductory payment. Under both circumstances, there is increased probability of adverse loan classifications.

We reviewed documentation related to 20 sampled residential loans in the FDIC's New York, Atlanta, and San Francisco Regional Offices for evidence of how examiners evaluated loan specific workout arrangements, classified loans, and considered institutions' regulatory and accounting procedures and controls. We found examiners applied relevant guidance with limited exceptions, just as they had for commercial workouts as summarized above; thus, we concluded there were no significant differences in implementation between the two types of workouts.

MATTER 6. ORDERS

P.L. 112-88 requires the OIG to assess the application and impact of consent orders and *cease and desist orders*, including:

(A) whether such orders have been applied uniformly and fairly across all insured depository institutions;
(B) the reasons for failing to apply such orders uniformly and fairly when such failure occurs;
(C) the impact of such orders on the ability of insured depository institutions to raise capital;

(D) the impact of such orders on the ability of insured depository institutions to extend or modify credit to existing and new borrowers; and
(E) whether individual insured depository institutions have improved enough to have orders removed.

When the FDIC, the OCC, and the FRB identify deficiencies or determine that a financial institution's condition is less than satisfactory, they may take a variety of supervisory actions, including informal and formal enforcement actions, to address identified deficiencies and generally have discretion in deciding which type of action to take. Informal actions generally are used to address less severe deficiencies and when the regulator has confidence that the institution is willing and able to implement changes. The most commonly used informal actions are *memorandums of understanding* (MOU), *bank board resolutions* used by the FDIC, *board resolutions* used by the FRB, *commitment letters* used by the OCC and FRB, individual minimum capital requirements used by the OCC, and *safety and soundness plans* used by the OCC and the FDIC.

Formal enforcement actions are publicly disclosed by regulators and are used to address more severe deficiencies or when the regulator has limited confidence in an institution's ability to implement changes. Formal enforcement actions against a financial institution include cease and desist orders, consent orders, and *formal written agreements*.[82] Such enforcement actions are intended to accomplish several things, including bringing about alterations in the practices that caused the problems, and in some cases stabilizing the institutions, and averting potential losses to the DIF.

Orders. Section 8 of the FDI Act (12 U.S.C. § 1818) authorizes the agencies to issue formal orders, which include consent orders, cease and desist orders, and *temporary cease and desist orders*. Orders may be issued to stop violations of law, rule, or regulation or unsafe or unsound practices, as well as to require affirmative action to correct any conditions resulting from such violations or practices. Orders are public and enforceable by law. Orders may be issued after notice and hearing (cease and desist orders) or after stipulation by the institution or *institution-affiliated party* (consent orders).

A temporary cease and desist order is an interim order issued to impose measures that are needed immediately pending resolution of a final cease and desist order. Such orders are typically used only when immediately necessary to protect the financial institution against ongoing or expected harm. A temporary cease and desist order may be challenged in U.S. district court within 10 days of issuance but is effective upon issuance and remains effective unless overturned by the court or until a final order is in place.

Formal Written Agreements. The OCC and the FRB also use formal written agreements, which are bilateral documents signed by the board of directors on behalf of the financial institution and an authorized agency official. Like a consent order, the provisions in formal written agreements are set out in article-by-article form and prescribe those restrictions and corrective and remedial measures necessary to correct deficiencies or violations in the financial institution and return it to a safe and sound condition. Formal written agreements are legally recognized documents issued pursuant to the OCC and FRB's enforcement authority under 12 U.S.C. § 1818(b). Violations of a formal written agreement can provide the legal basis for assessing civil money penalties against the financial institution and its directors, officers, and other institution-affiliated parties. An important difference between a formal written agreement issued by the OCC and a consent order is that willful violation of a consent order may be used by the OCC as grounds for appointment of the FDIC as receiver while a violation of a formal written agreement may not.[83]

Collectively, the FDIC, the OCC, and the FRB issued 1,515 formal enforcement actions during our review period, 2008-2011. Each of the regulators has developed its own process and approach for issuing formal enforcement actions. Table 12 below shows the number and types of formal enforcement actions issued by the FDIC, the OCC, and the FRB during 2008-2011. These statistics are for informational purposes only, and we did not evaluate the effectiveness of the extent or types of enforcement actions used by one regulator versus another.

P.L. 112-88 (6)(A)

Whether such orders have been applied uniformly and fairly across all insured depository institutions.

Each of the regulators has a different philosophy and approach to the application of enforcement actions. The regulators generally apply formal enforcement actions uniformly to problem banks, defined as 4- and 5-rated institutions. The OCC also frequently places formal enforcement actions on 3-rated institutions with management concerns, while the FDIC and the FRB usually rely on informal actions for such institutions. We determined that the FDIC, OCC, and FRB have policies, procedures, and other controls in place to help ensure uniformity and consistency with their respective formal enforcement actions. Further, those actions are supported by safety and soundness examination findings. For the actions we reviewed, the provisions were consistent with templates and/or guidance maintained by the regulators, the provisions were generally uniform within each regulatory agency, and safety and soundness concerns identified in examination reports formed the basis of the actions. We also determined there was a correlation between examination ratings, key financial ratios, and enforcement actions, which, in our view, illustrates that regulators applied actions fairly across the institutions they regulated.

Table 12. FDIC, OCC, and FRB Safety and Soundness Formal Enforcement Actions Issued—2008 through 2011

Type of Order	FDIC	OCC	FRB	Total
Consent Order/Cease and Desist Order	885	159	8	1,052
Temporary Cease and Desist Order	4	0	0	4
Formal Written Agreement	0	312	147	459
Total	**889**	**471**	**155**	**1,515**
Percentage of Problem Banks (CAMELS Composite 4-, and 5-Rated Institutions) with Formal Enforcement Actions	97%	92%	89%	95%

Source: OIG analysis of FDIC, OCC, and FRB data.

Policies, Procedures, and Other Controls for Enforcement Actions

The FDIC, OCC, and FRB each have policies and procedures governing the use of formal enforcement actions. Each regulator has a differing philosophy and approach with respect to the type of actions they use and at what point they issue an action. The FDIC has adopted a policy that presumes a formal or informal action will be taken on financial institutions with composite ratings of 3, 4, or 5, and the FDIC's position is that financial institutions with composite ratings of 4 or 5 by definition have problems of sufficient severity to warrant formal action. The OCC's formal enforcement actions for 3-, 4-, and 5-rated financial institutions include cease and desist orders or formal written agreements. Most of the OCC's informal actions are imposed on 2- and 3-rated institutions. The FRB generally issues formal enforcement actions, typically formal written agreements, for 4- or 5-rated financial institutions and informal enforcement actions on CAMELS 3-rated and higher, to address safety and soundness concerns relating to the financial condition of the bank. Despite these noted differences, we determined that each regulator has policies, procedures, and controls in place to help ensure (1) uniformity and consistency of its respective formal enforcement actions and (2) that actions are supported by safety and soundness examination findings. For example, regulators' legal officials review the recommended provisions, draft the actions, and approve the provisions included in the actions. The FDIC and the OCC maintain electronic enforcement action templates in varying degrees of detail that help to ensure enforcement action consistency and uniformity. Enforcement actions are drafted in Washington, D.C. (FRB) or in a regional or district office (FDIC and OCC) to help ensure consistency. Regulator management and legal officials meet with the financial institution's board of directors and management to discuss the provisions and the actions. Regulators monitor financial institution compliance with provisions in the actions through bank-submitted progress reports and on-site visitations and examinations of the institutions. Finally, each of the regulators terminates actions based on the financial institutions' improvement and compliance with provisions of the actions. Appendix 9 contains a detailed description of the formal enforcement action processes for each of the regulators.

Uniformity of Enforcement Actions

To assess whether the regulators applied enforcement actions uniformly to the institutions within their jurisdictions, we reviewed a sample of 119 formal enforcement actions—60 FDIC, 37 OCC, and 22 FRB—and confirmed that the enforcement action provisions were:

- generally uniform within each regulatory agency,
- generally supported by examination findings in the safety and soundness examination that was the basis for the enforcement action, and
- still appropriately in place based on findings from the most recent safety and soundness examination.

For each of the 119 sampled actions, we:

- Reviewed all provisions in each action for a total of 2,379 provisions.
- Ensured there was a safety and soundness concern (finding) identified in the ROE that was the basis for the action to document support for the provisions.

- Determined the reasons for terminating the action or reviewed the most recent ROE to understand the basis for keeping the action open.

Table 13 below shows the number and types of provisions, linked to the CAMELS rating components, included in our 119 sampled actions – 60 FDIC, 37 OCC, and 22 FRB actions. For the 119 actions we reviewed, we determined that the provisions were consistent with the enforcement action provisions outlined in the templates and/or guidance maintained by the regulators, and the provisions were generally uniform within each regulatory agency. We determined that the basis for all 2,379 provisions was safety and soundness concerns that each regulator had identified in ROEs. In addition, for the 68 actions still active as of June 30, 2012, we concluded that, based on the findings in the most recent ROEs, it was appropriate for the actions to still be in place. For 12 of the 60 FDIC actions, we also tested the following controls:

- Reviewed the written recommendations for initiating the actions that were prepared by the examiner-in-charge (EIC) of the respective safety and soundness examination to prompt the enforcement action.
- Ensured the recommendations for the actions were submitted to FDIC management for approval.
- Determined that the actions were discussed with FDIC legal officials.
- Identified the extent to which the FDIC coordinated the issuance of the action with respective State regulatory agencies, when applicable.
- Ascertained that FDIC supervision and legal officials met with financial institution management and its board of directors to discuss the actions and the provisions in the actions.

With the exception of maintaining documentation of the written recommendations for actions prepared by the safety and soundness EIC and/or the case manager,[84] we determined that all of the controls were consistently implemented. We noted that for 7 of the 12 actions we reviewed, FDIC regional correspondence files did not contain the written recommendations for initiating the actions and identifying the provisions to be included in the actions. FDIC officials explained that there were occasions where the communications between the case manager and the EIC would not always be documented in the files, but they added that recommendation memoranda and other forms of communication, such as records of telephone calls, would be documented in examination working papers.

Fairness of Enforcement Actions

To assess whether regulators applied enforcement actions fairly, we analyzed the extent to which there was a correlation between examination ratings and enforcement actions, and in turn, key financial ratios used by regulators to assess the safety and soundness of financial institutions. As described below, the results of our view showed that the regulators applied enforcement actions fairly across insured depository institutions that they regulate. We first analyzed examination rating and enforcement action data and determined that the FDIC and FRB generally issued formal enforcement actions when a financial institution reached problem status (i.e., assigned a 4 or 5 CAMELS composite rating). In a small number of cases, the FDIC and FRB issued formal actions on 3-rated financial institutions—usually when management was deficient. OCC frequently issued formal actions on 3-rated institutions with management issues, as well as 4- and 5-rated institutions. Table 14 shows the percentage of CAMELS 2-, 3-, 4-, and 5-rated FDIC, OCC, and FRB financial institutions with formal enforcement actions. Table 14 shows that OCC issued formal enforcement actions (usually in the form of formal written agreements) 57 percent of time that institutions were 3-rated compared to FRB (4 percent) and the FDIC (3 percent). However, a large percentage of the time, FRB and FDIC 3-rated financial institutions were subject to an MOU or some other form of an informal enforcement action. Specifically, during 2008-2011, the FDIC, FRB, and OCC had imposed informal enforcement actions on 92, 73, and 64 percent of their 3-rated institutions, respectively. We next performed an analysis of key financial ratios, namely, *return on assets* (ROA), Tier 1 Leverage Capital, and *adversely classified assets* that impact CAMELS ratings and, in turn, enforcement actions.

- The ROA ratio represents annualized net income expressed as a percentage of average total assets. The ROA ratio is a basic measure of a financial institution's profitability and an indication of how efficiently the assets are being used. We found that non-problem banks (i.e., those assigned a composite rating of 1, 2, or 3) had statistically significant higher ROA ratios than problem banks (i.e., those assigned a composite rating of 4 or 5) and that the ratios were largely consistent among the regulators.
- The Tier 1 Leverage Capital ratio represents Tier 1 Capital (the core measure of a bank's financial strength from a regulator's point of view) divided by total assets. We found that non-problem banks had statistically significant higher Tier 1 Leverage Capital ratios than problem banks and that the ratios were largely consistent among the regulators.
- Finally, adversely classified assets are assets that are subject to criticism and/or comment in a safety and soundness examination report and allocated on the basis of risk (lowest to highest) in three categories—Substandard, Doubtful, and Loss. A high level of adversely classified assets places a financial institution's capital at risk, and when adverse classifications are significant, an institution has increased risk of loss, thus requiring the financial institution to maintain a higher level of capital to offset risk. We found that non-problem banks had statistically significant lower total *adversely classified assets ratios* than problem banks and that the ratios were largely consistent between the regulators.

Table 13. OIG Review of Enforcement Action Provisions

Provision Type	FDIC	OCC	FRB
Capital Adequacy-Related	242 (18%)	136 (23%)	60 (15%)
Asset Quality-Related	415 (30%)	260 (43%)	162 (40%)
Management-Related	415 (30%)	86 (14%)	95 (23%)
Earnings-Related	169 (12%)	38 (6%)	55 (14%)
Liquidity-Related	112 (8%)	80 (13%)	34 (8%)
Sensitivity to Market Risk- Related	18 (1%)	1 (<1%)	1 (<1%)
TOTAL PROVISIONS	**1,371**	**601**	**407**

Source: FDIC OIG analysis.

Note: Percentages may not add to 100 percent due to rounding.

Table 14. Percentage of Examinations Resulting in Formal Enforcement Actions—2008 through 2011[a]

CAMELS Rating	FDIC	OCC	FRB[b]
Percentage of Institutions with Cease and Desist or Consent Orders			
2	<1%	<1%	0%
3	3%	3%	<1%
4	96%	37%	4%
5	99%	39%	7%
Percentage of Institutions with Formal Written Agreements			
2	0%	<1%	<1%
3	0%	53%	4%
4	0%	54%	80%
5	0%	54%	90%
Total Percentage of Institutions with Formal Enforcement Actions			
2	<1%	1%	<1%
3	3%	57%	4%
4	96%	91%	84%
5	99%	93%	97%

Source: OIG analysis of FDIC, OCC, and FRB data.

[a] The percentages in Table 14 represent individual examinations resulting in an enforcement action or an examination while a financial institution was under an enforcement action. Most institutions had multiple examinations during the analysis period (2008 through 2011). If an enforcement action was initiated but not executed, due to bank failure, merger, or other reason, it was not counted.

[b] FRB enforcement actions were included in Table 14 if the examination leading to the enforcement action had a "start date" in 2008-2011, and if the enforcement action was "initiated" (recommended) and "effective" (signed by the parties) in 2008-2011.

We also performed analyses of the same key financial ratios for financial institutions with and without enforcement actions. Again, we found that institutions without enforcement actions had statistically significant higher ROA and Tier 1 Leverage Capital ratios and statistically significant lower total adversely classified assets ratios than institutions with enforcement actions. Specifically,

- ROA ratios were 2 to 2.5 percentage points higher,[85] on average, for financial institutions without enforcement actions.
- Tier 1 Leverage Capital ratios were 3.1 to 4.2 percentage points higher, on average, for institutions without enforcement actions.
- Total adversely classified assets ratios were 6 to 9.2 percentage points lower, on average, for financial institutions without enforcement actions.

Based on our analysis, we determined there was a correlation between examination ratings, key financial ratios, and enforcement actions, which, in our view, illustrates that regulators applied actions fairly across the institutions they regulated.

P.L. 112-88 (6)(B)

The reasons for failing to apply such orders uniformly and fairly when such failure occurs.

We identified some instances of non-problem banks with enforcement actions, and conversely, problem banks without formal enforcement actions. We found that, generally, there were circumstances surrounding the condition and management of the financial institutions that justified the regulators' decisions regarding the imposition (or lack thereof) of such actions.

Non-Problem Banks with Enforcement Actions

We identified 28 non-problem banks that were subject to formal enforcement actions.[86] For the purpose of this analysis, we identified non-problem banks as composite 1-, 2-, and 3-rated banks for the FDIC and FRB and composite 1- and 2-rated banks for the OCC. In 10 cases, the basis for the enforcement action was that the institution had safety and soundness weaknesses coupled with Bank Secrecy Act or consumer compliance concerns. In other cases, institutions had failed to comply with previously issued informal enforcement actions. Several actions were related to servicing and foreclosure deficiencies.

Problem Banks without Enforcement Actions

We reviewed problem banks (defined as 4- or 5-rated) for the period 2008-2011 and identified 95 cases where the banks were not subject to formal enforcement actions (of these 71 were 4- rated and 24 were 5-rated). In approximately 70 percent of these cases, the banks were already operating under an informal action. We found 41 instances where the FDIC was in the process of pursuing a formal enforcement action on an institution, but the actions were withdrawn for various reasons, including: the institution failed before the action could be completed, the financial institution received a capital injection, or the institution was in the process of merging with a healthy institution precluding the need for an enforcement action. With respect to all of the 5-rated institutions without a formal action, we found that those banks generally experienced a precipitous decline to a point where they were no longer viable. In those cases, regulators typically did not pursue consent orders because institution failure was imminent or the institution was in the process of merging with another institution. We noted that five FDIC-regulated institutions without a consent order were subject to other formal actions such as a PCA directive.

P.L. 112-88 (6)(C)

The impact of such orders on the ability of insured depository institutions to raise capital.

Over 50 percent of the FDIC-supervised financial institutions with informal or formal actions received material capital injections within the period 2008-2011. In addition, 829 of the 1,515 insured financial institutions (55 percent) with enforcement actions raised capital in the year the enforcement actions were issued and/or in subsequent years.

This rate of capital injection compares favorably to all active institutions over the same period. Further, according to investors we interviewed, a depository institution's ability to obtain additional capital depends more on the institution's financial condition, including factors such as earnings performance, asset quality, and growth prospects.

Results of Analyses on Material Capital Injections

We reviewed an April 2012 internal FDIC study titled, *Material Capital Injections, Banks with Assets under $1 Billion (2008-2011)*. We found that over 50 percent of the FDIC-supervised financial institutions with informal or formal actions received material aggregate capital injections within the period 2008-2011. The average aggregate capital injection per institution was $6.6 million and represented roughly 38 percent of average Tier 1 Capital. The extent of capital injections for these institutions compares favorably to all active financial institutions over that same period. Specifically, according to the FDIC study, nearly 30 percent of all active financial institutions received capital injections during the period 2008-2011. The average injection was about $7 million and represented approximately 40 percent of Tier 1 Capital. We also obtained material capital raise information[87] from RMS for all financial institutions for the period 2008 through 2011 and determined that 829 of the 1,515 insured institutions (55 percent) with enforcement actions raised capital in the year the enforcement actions were issued and/or in subsequent years. Of the 1,515 insured institutions, 889 are FDIC-supervised, 471 are OCC-supervised, and 155 are FRB-supervised. The percentage of institutions that were able to raise capital while being subject to enforcement actions are: FDIC – 51 percent, OCC – 58 percent, and FRB – 61 percent.

Results of Interviews with Investment Professionals and Regulators

Based on our interviews with representatives from three investment companies, we learned that investors tend to focus on the financial condition and franchise value versus the presence of an enforcement action when deciding whether to invest in a troubled bank. Representatives from these companies noted that it was common for financial institutions to have enforcement actions during 2009 through 2011, and investors were not dissuaded from making investments in financial institutions simply because they were subject to actions. A representative from one company said that one of the company's clients wanted and obtained reassurances from the bank's regulator that the enforcement action would remain in place after the investment was made. FDIC, OCC, and FRB officials told us that they do not believe that enforcement actions limit banks' efforts to raise capital. Rather, these officials think that generally a bank's financial condition and investment opportunities in general are the main reasons why investors choose to invest in a financial institution.

P.L. 112-88 (6)(D)

The impact of formal orders on the ability of insured depository institutions to extend or modify credit to existing and new borrowers.

We did not identify any enforcement actions that directly limited credit to existing borrowers that were current on their loans, or to new borrowers when the financial institution applied prudent underwriting and credit administration practices.

We did identify some enforcement action provisions that may have limited lending indirectly. However, in all cases, these provisions responded to an underlying safety and soundness concern. Further, while some bankers and the GAO have indicated that regulatory scrutiny has a negative impact on lending, the prevailing view was that the economy, competition, and lack of loan demand from creditworthy borrowers were bigger factors.

Analysis of Provisions that Could Restrict Lending

We identified all provisions in enforcement actions that could restrict lending included in a sample of 60 FDIC actions, 37 OCC actions, and 22 FRB actions issued from January 1, 2008 through December 31, 2011.

Each lending provision type is discussed in greater detail below, and we provide examples of the provisions to illustrate how they impact lending and are supported by safety and soundness concerns.

Classified Assets. For most of the enforcement actions we reviewed, the action limited the financial institution from extending, renewing, or granting new credit to borrowers with criticized loans.[88] The provision restricted the institution's ability to extend or modify credit to borrowers with *criticized assets* until the debt was paid, or until interest owed was paid—unless the bank's board of directors documented that extending or modifying the credit was in the best interest of the institution. OCC's actions tended to limit this restriction by a threshold based on the credit's value. If the criticized credit exceeded a certain dollar amount, the restriction would apply. The dollar amounts ranged from $50,000 to $1,000,000, with the majority at $500,000.

One FDIC action required the financial institution to obtain approval from the regulator prior to extending or modifying credit to a borrower whose credit was classified as Loss.

Concentrations. Another provision we identified that indirectly impacted credit to existing and new borrowers was the requirement to reduce concentrations. Some of the actions required financial institutions to reduce concentrations, which could impact credits in a particular loan type. The reduction in concentrations has the potential of limiting an institution from making new loans in the concentrated type of loans (e.g., CRE or ADC loans). However, the financial institution would still have the ability to originate other types of loans. In about half of the FRB actions reviewed, FRB required the institutions to reduce concentrations, and a majority of those actions specifically cited CRE concentrations. As the CRE loans were reduced by payments or charge-offs or the capital in the institution increased, the financial institution would have the ability to make new loans up to the concentration limits established by the bank. We verified that the regulators cited high concentrations in the ROEs to support the provisions imposed.

Loan Growth. Similar to reductions in concentrations, some actions contained growth limitations that could restrict lending until the bank's assets, including loans, were reduced or capital was increased. Approximately 20 percent of the FDIC actions contained limitations on asset growth. Approximately half were restricted to 5 percent, and the other half were restricted to 10 percent per year. In one FDIC action, the financial institution was restricted from establishing any new branches without the approval of the regulators. One FRB action required the financial institution to obtain the regulator's written approval for any aggregate increase in the institution's loan portfolio until the institution submitted to the federal and state regulators and implemented (1) acceptable plans to reduce concentrations, manage credit risk, improve assets, and manage liquidity; (2) a revised ALLL program; and (3) policies and procedures for these areas.

Underwriting. Several of the enforcement actions required the financial institutions to implement prudent underwriting standards, which could potentially impact the institution with respect to extending or modifying credit to existing and new borrowers. The OCC used this provision most frequently among the regulators (60 percent of the 37 OCC actions that we reviewed). As underwriting tightens, the pool of creditworthy borrowers decreases. Tightening underwriting standards suggests that borrowers who previously were considered creditworthy might not meet the higher underwriting standards. However, this provision does not impact the bank's ability to make prudent loans to creditworthy borrowers. Four of the 37 OCC actions stated that the bank may not grant, extend, renew, alter, or restructure any loan or other extension of credit without first documenting in writing the purpose, identifying the source of repayment, assessing the borrower's global debt, and making other determinations to ensure the repayment of the loan. In all cases, the regulators had rated each financial institution as seriously deficient (Asset Quality Component rating of "4" or "5") and reported high levels of problem loans and serious credit administration weaknesses. One FRB action required the financial institution to obtain the regulator's approval prior to originating or underwriting any residential mortgage until the financial institution developed and implemented appropriate internal controls over its residential mortgage lending program.

Capital Requirement. Finally, although many factors influence a bank's lending decisions, the amount of capital a financial institution holds is a key factor. Capital provides a cushion against losses, but if a financial institution needs to increase it, the cost of raising capital can raise the cost of providing loans. For example, if a financial institution needs to increase its capital ratio without a capital injection, then the financial institution may have to reduce its loans to increase the capital ratio. The majority of actions we reviewed contained a capital provision. All of the 60 FDIC actions that we reviewed contained a specific minimum capital ratio requirement. Sixty percent of the OCC actions and 5 percent of the FRB actions contained a capital requirement. Most of the FRB and OCC enforcement actions required the institution to develop a capital plan.

Industry and Regulator Views on Credit Availability

In 2011, the FDIC conducted a survey at each examination about credit availability. The survey asked the Chief Executive Officer or Chief Lending Officer about obstacles in the bank's lending markets, regulatory process interference in originating or restructuring loans, and suggestions for regulators to promote credit availability. The bankers stated that the biggest obstacles to extending or modifying credit to existing or new borrowers were economic factors, competition, and lack of loan demand from creditworthy borrowers. Fifty-one percent of the bankers interviewed stated that the regulatory process has not interfered with their ability to prudently originate and restructure loans. The other 49 percent who stated that the regulatory process had interfered specifically cited consumer compliance regulations and related disclosures. Also, 29 percent of surveyed bankers said that regulators were not responsible for promoting credit availability.

Additionally, in a 2011 credit underwriting survey conducted by the OCC, only about 13 percent of the bankers cited regulatory practices as the reason for tightening underwriting standards.

According to the regulators, enforcement actions do not impact the bank's ability to make prudent loans to creditworthy borrowers. The bank's financial condition, capital level, and strategic plans impact the bank's lending activity. The regulators told us that the economy played a major role in the financial crisis, including the credit crunch. Typically, when a financial institution reaches problem bank status, the bank's focus tends to be on improving the bank's condition and working out problem loans, rather than on creating new loans.

P.L. 112-88 (6)(E)

Whether individual insured depository institutions have improved enough to have such orders removed.

We determined that, in general, the FDIC, OCC, and FRB terminated their respective actions uniformly and appropriately across the insured depository institutions and in accordance with their respective policies and procedures. The policies and procedures include the condition that, for an action to be terminated, the financial institution is in material compliance with the provisions of the action, and the financial institution has improved sufficiently so that the action is no longer needed. With few exceptions, we concluded that regulators appropriately terminated enforcement actions when an institution's condition improved and retained actions when institutions continued to present safety and soundness risk.

In a GAO report on CRE lending,[89] some bankers stated that examiners were impeding the bank's ability to make new loans, especially if the financial institution already had high CRE concentrations. However, according to the report, other bankers noted that CRE loan demand from creditworthy borrowers was down significantly and, therefore, was inhibiting loan growth.

GAO noted that although the economic research is limited, increased regulatory scrutiny during credit downturns can have a small impact on overall lending. Increases in capital requirements can raise the cost of providing loans, which, in turn, could lead to higher interest rates for borrowers, tighter credit terms, or reduced lending. When regulators increase capital requirements at the same time that losses from an economic downturn decrease a bank's capital, the financial institution may be less able to lend while it seeks to rapidly raise additional capital. Importantly, GAO notes that loan demand from borrowers also has an impact on the amount of credit that financial institutions may extend, and loan demand often declines during an economic downturn.

Policies and Procedures for Terminating Enforcement Actions

Procedures for termination are similar to those for initiating a formal enforcement action. Generally, the decision to terminate an enforcement action is based on the regulator's assessment of a financial institution's compliance with the action's provisions determined through a safety and soundness examination or visitation. The examiners will recommend that an action be removed in circumstances where: the financial institution has adopted, implemented, and adhered to the provisions set forth in the action; the corrective actions are effective in addressing the institution's problems; and examiners have verified corrective actions through the examination process. Section 8(b) actions may be terminated under the following conditions:

- The financial institution is in material compliance with the provisions of the action.
- Deterioration or lack of compliance leads to issuance of a new or revised formal action.
- The financial institution merges or is closed.
- The financial institution's condition has improved sufficiently, and the action is no longer needed.
- The provisions of the action have been partially met, and a new formal or informal action has been issued to address the outstanding provisions.
- Other changes render the action unnecessary.

Table 15. Terminations of Actions—2008 through 2011

Reason for Termination	FDIC	OCC	FRB
Bank Failed	223 (60%)	63 (25%)	37 (77%)
Bank Merged or Was Acquired Prior to Failure	41 (11%)	30 (12%)	11(23%)
Action Was Replaced with Another Enforcement Action or Financial Institution Condition Relapsed	27 (7%)	64 (25%)	
Financial Institution Condition Improved	76 (21%)	90 (35%)	
Financial Institution Changed Charter	1 (<1%)	5 (2%)	
Financial Institution Voluntarily Closed	2 (<1%)	3 (1%)	
Total	**370**	**255**	**48**

Source: OIG analysis of the FDIC's *Virtual Supervisory Information on the Net* (ViSION) system and FRB and OCC information.

If a revised action is being recommended, the original action generally remains in effect until the new action is issued and effective. The regulators are required by law to publicly disclose all final actions and terminations of actions. The FDIC, OCC, and FRB disclose their actions and terminations of actions on their respective Websites.

Analysis of Terminated Actions

We determined that the FDIC, OCC, and FRB reported that they terminated a total of 673 actions during the period 2008 through 2011. Table 15 captures the reasons provided by the regulators for terminating the respective actions. In many cases, actions were terminated due to bank failure or merger. For those actions where the financial institution's condition improved, we confirmed that in nearly every case, the financial institution's condition had improved as reflected in better CAMELS ratings. We noted that the OCC experienced a higher rate of terminations due to the financial institution's condition improving (35 percent). We confirmed that the OCC imposed 66 of the 90 actions we reviewed when the financial institution was 3-rated. We observed that OCC's practice of issuing actions on 3-rated financial institutions, before the institutions deteriorated to problem bank status, may have contributed to the higher rate of terminations due to improvement. However, our analysis was limited and may not have been sufficiently broad to serve as the basis for conclusions regarding the effectiveness of one approach over the others. For example, our analysis did not review the rate of improvements on 3-rated institutions with informal actions.

Analysis of Active Actions Where Bank Condition Had Improved

We identified 98 institutions with improved conditions that remained under an action as of December 31, 2011. During the course of our field work, we found that many actions had been terminated during 2012 due to improved conditions and because the financial institutions were in material compliance with the actions. The regulators terminated 61 actions during our fieldwork. Thirty-seven actions remained in place even though the institutions' composite ratings had improved since the action was issued. We reviewed these banks to determine whether there was support for not terminating the action. In two instances, we could not determine why the order remained in place. For the remaining 35 banks, examination report information sufficiently documented the reasons for not terminating the actions. In general, regulators noted that some provisions had not been sufficiently addressed, even though the bank's condition had improved. Based on our review, we concluded that the regulators properly retained enforcement actions in the 35 cases.

Recommendation

While each regulator imposed formal enforcement actions uniformly and fairly across their regulated institutions, we noted differences in the types of actions that the regulators use (i.e., consent orders and formal written agreements) and in the timing of actions (i.e., when a bank is 3-rated or once a bank becomes 4- or 5-rated). We recommend that the FDIC, OCC, and FRB:

7. Study these differences to determine whether there are certain approaches that have proven to be more effective in mitigating risk and correcting deficiencies that should be implemented by all three agencies.

MATTER 7. FDIC POLICY

P.L. 112-88 requires the OIG to study the application and impact of FDIC policies, including:

(A) the impact of FDIC policies on the investment in insured depository institutions, especially in states where more than 10 such institutions have failed since 2008;
(B) whether the FDIC fairly and consistently applies capital standards when an insured depository institution is successful in raising private capital; and
(C) whether the FDIC steers potential investors away from insured depository institutions that may be in danger of being placed in receivership or conservatorship.

The primary statutes governing how the FDIC must review potential investments in insured institutions, evaluate insured institution capital, and assess potential resolutions for failing institutions are the FDI Act and the *FDIC Improvement Act of 1991* (P.L. 102-242) (FDICIA). In general, those statutes provide criteria to be used by the FDIC and other regulators to assess investments in, and the capital of, insured institutions in order to promote the safety and soundness of insured institutions and the protection of the DIF. The FDIC has issued regulations based on those statutory requirements and has developed policies and internal procedures to govern their implementation.

FDIC Policies on Investment

There are multiple ways in which an entity may invest in an insured depository institution, some of which would be within the power of another federal regulator or a state authority to approve or deny. We identified five types of applications that are filed with the FDIC and that could have an impact on a proposed investment in an insured institution. The two most common are a change-in-control application[90] and a merger application. Applications for *mutual-to-stock conversions* may also involve additional investment in an institution but are not as common. Other applications that may have an impact on an insured institution's attempts to raise capital include applications for a change in business plan for *de novo* institutions and applications for approval of a material transaction by a bank that is *Critically Undercapitalized* according to the PCA regulations implementing Section 38 of the FDI Act.[91] The FDIC has policies in place to protect the DIF and to ensure the character and fitness of potential investors. By their nature, such policies will have an impact on investments in institutions. The primary FDIC Statements of Policy relevant to such investments include:

- *Statement of Policy—Applications for Deposit Insurance*, effective date: October 1, 1998.
- *Statement of Policy—Bank Merger Transactions*, effective date: August 20, 1998.
- *Statement of Policy—Regarding Use of Offering Circulars in Connection With Public Distribution of Bank Securities*, dated August 13, 1996 (i.e., for mutual-to-stock conversions).
- *Statement of Policy—Qualifications for Failed Bank Acquisitions*, effective date: September 2, 2009.

P.L. 112-88 (7)(A)

The impact of FDIC policies on the investment in insured depository institutions, especially in states where more than 10 such institutions have failed since 2008.

The FDIC has policies in place to protect the DIF and to ensure the character and fitness of potential investors. By their nature, such policies are going to have an impact on investments in institutions.

The FDIC approved the majority of applications that it received for mergers and changes-in-control of insured institutions—those being common forms of investments in existing institutions. Approval rates for change-in-control and merger applications for states such as California, Florida, Illinois, Nevada, and Washington, which experienced 10 or more failures, were lower than the nationwide average from 2008 through 2011. Other states with 10 or more failures had the same or a greater average approval rate for such applications. The underlying reasons for the non- approval of applications generally related to FDIC concerns with potential investors' proposed business plans, capital and/or financial resources, or management background and experience.

Investors take into consideration a number of factors beyond FDIC policies, including the asset quality of the investment target and the potential for return on investment. We also learned that some investors believed that they could secure a better price and return on assets after a bank failed, particularly if it was likely there would be an SLA loss guarantee. In addition, as required by law, the FDIC must determine that an investment in a troubled bank represents the least possible long-term loss to the DIF. Finally, investment professionals also told us that the implementation of the FDIC's PCI SOP negatively impacted financial institution efforts to raise capital because a number of investors chose not to pursue that means of investment as they were concerned about the associated regulatory requirements. In that regard, the PCI SOP sought to balance the regulatory obligations imposed on investors with the FDIC's duty to protect the safety and soundness of insured institutions and the DIF.

FDIC procedures for implementing these policies are reflected in the FDIC *Case Manager Procedures Manual*, the FDIC *Risk Management Manual of Examination Policies*, various FDIC circulars, and other procedural guidance. Our study did not test whether the FDIC properly implemented these policies and procedures, or assess the adequacy of actions taken or not taken by the FDIC in reviewing potential investments in insured depository institutions. Our study was limited to identifying the outcome of proposed investment-related transactions and inferring the impact of FDIC policies from those outcomes.

Review of Applications

Based upon our testing, we found that the FDIC approved the majority of change-in-control and merger applications during 2008 through 2011. The overall reasons for the non-approval of investment-related applications during that time related to FDIC concerns with potential investors' proposed business plans, capital and/or financial resources, or management background and experience. FDIC concerns with business plans ranged from the overall feasibility of the plan to the lack of significant information in the plan. FDIC concerns with capital and/or financial resources included the financial condition of the applicant(s) and whether investors had the ability to raise sufficient funds. FDIC concerns with management focused on the background and experience of proposed management, the proposed management structure, and management's ability to address risk management or compliance issues. In some instances, the investment target institution failed during the application process. In other instances, the application was on track for approval, but the applicant withdrew the application due to a change in business strategy.

Change-in-Control Applications. Table 16 below provides the statistics on actions taken by the FDIC on change-in-control applications during the period from January 1, 2008 through December 31, 2011.

The table shows a nationwide approval rate of 60 percent for change-in- control applications during that period. Looking at the states with 10 or more failures, the approval rates for California, Florida, Illinois, Nevada, and Washington were all lower than the nationwide rate, with Florida being the most significant. Other states, however, had higher approval rates. The FDIC did not deny any applications, but applications were returned to or withdrawn by investors. In many cases, however, investors were aware of FDIC concerns at the time they withdrew their applications.

We judgmentally sampled 27 withdrawn or returned change-in-control applications for California, Florida, Georgia, Illinois, Missouri, Nevada, and Washington to understand why they were withdrawn or returned. For Florida, a majority (7) of the 12 applications that were withdrawn or returned were filed in 2009. We reviewed five of the seven applications and determined the FDIC had concerns with proposed management's experience in the banking industry, business plan comprehensiveness, and the investor's ability to obtain capital. For example, applicants were not able to provide support for their ability to contribute capital, background checks showed problems related to an investor's character and pending civil actions, and investor wealth could not be substantiated with appropriate financial statements. One Florida institution in our sample whose change-in-control application was not approved, subsequently failed.

The statistics for California were heavily impacted by seven change-in-control applications that were filed for one institution within a 1-year period from October 16, 2009 through October 13, 2010. The FDIC returned all seven applications because proposed management lacked adequate experience and the business plan was missing significant information. The seventh application requested immediate approval because investors had $6 million in escrow to invest, but capital commitments were set to expire. The bank failed during the last application review process. Excluding these seven applications from state totals increases California's approval rate to 48 percent.

Merger Applications. Table 17 below provides the statistics on actions taken by the FDIC on merger applications during the period January 1, 2008 through December 31, 2011. As shown, the FDIC had a nationwide 87-percent approval rate for merger requests during this time period.

While half of the states had approval rates near or greater than the nationwide average, the approval rates for California, Florida, Georgia, Illinois, Minnesota, Nevada, and Washington were all lower than the nationwide rate.

We judgmentally sampled 15 withdrawn or returned merger applications from those states and found that FDIC concerns centered on the adequacy or feasibility of proposed business plans and the financial condition of the applicant or target institution and the ability to raise needed capital. We noted that merger applications for three target institutions in our sample (one each in the states of California, Florida, and Minnesota) were either withdrawn or returned, and that those institutions subsequently failed.

Table 16. FDIC Change-in-Control Application Approval Rates—2008 through 2011

	Total	Approved	Withdrawn	Returned	Approval Rate
Nationwide	**171**	**102**	**38**	**31**	**60%**
Arizona	2	2	0	0	100%
California	36	14	10	12	39%
Florida	19	4	7	8	21%
Georgia	8	6	2	0	75%
Illinois	7	3	3	1	43%
Michigan	2	2	0	0	100%
Minnesota	2	2	0	0	100%
Missouri	3	2	1	0	67%
Nevada	3	1	2	0	33%
Washington	6	3	1	2	50%

Source: OIG analysis of application information in ViSION.

Table 17. FDIC Merger Application Approval Rates—2008 through 2011

	Total	Approved	Withdrawn	Returned	Approval Rate
Nationwide	**400**	**347**	**43**	**10**	**87%**
Arizona	4	4	0	0	100%
California	28	23	3	2	82%
Florida	16	11	5	0	69%
Georgia	11	8	2	1	73%
Illinois	20	17	3	0	85%
Michigan	3	3	0	0	100%
Minnesota	15	11	3	1	73%
Missouri	21	21	0	0	100%
Nevada	1	0	0	1	0%
Washington	3	2	1	0	67%

Source: OIG analysis of application information in ViSION.

Other Investment-Related Applications. We also tested 12 other applications that had been withdrawn by the applicant or returned or denied by the FDIC and involved a potential increase in capital. These applications included four proposed mutual-to-stock conversions, four requests for change in business plan, and four proposed material transactions, primarily related to banks in the 10 states with 10 or more failures. FDIC concerns related to these applications again included the inadequacy or feasibility of the proposed business plan, the ability to raise needed capital, and the potential impact of the transaction on the financial condition of the applicant. The latter concern led the FDIC to deny one material transaction application that included a proposed sale of assets and transfer of deposits. The applicant institution subsequently failed.

Two applicants withdrew their change in business plan applications to submit updated applications, which were later approved by the FDIC.

Case Study Review

We also tried to measure the impact of FDIC policies on investment in insured institutions in states with 10 or more failures by conducting a case study of 20 troubled banks located in those states. Specifically, we looked at the reasons that 10 of those banks did not receive capital and failed, while the other 10 received capital and survived. Our goal was to understand whether FDIC policies or other factors impacted potential investment in a bank.

Based on the documentation for our sampled institutions, we concluded that SLAs and the PCA provisions could impact potential investments in troubled institutions. First, SLAs offered by the FDIC appear to have influenced some investors to wait to invest in institutions until after failure in the hopes that the FDIC would agree to share some of the losses. Second, the PCA provisions of the FDI Act require the FDIC to resolve the problems of the insured depository institutions at the least possible long-term loss to the DIF, which could impact the FDIC's consideration of potential capital investments in troubled institutions.[92] Specifically, the FDIC sometimes determined that closing a troubled bank would result in lower losses to the DIF than allowing it to remain open through an investment of capital when the investment of capital was not sufficient in amount to return the bank to viability but only to delay failure.

We concluded from our case studies that, notwithstanding FDIC policies, institutions that received capital had management that took quick action to obtain capital while the bank was *Well Capitalized*. Those institutions that did not receive capital had management that either waited to obtain capital until the bank was no longer *Well Capitalized* or waited to look for capital from sources outside of existing bank directors and shareholders. For 7 of the 10 banks in our sample that received capital, management actively looked for capital while the bank was *Well Capitalized*, and 4 of those 7 banks never fell below the *Well Capitalized* threshold.

Investment Professional Interviews

Finally, our third way to measure the impact of FDIC policies on investments in states with 10 or more failures was to ask investment professionals who facilitated investment in banks whether FDIC policies influenced investor decisions. We requested interviews with eight investment professionals and held discussions with three. These investment professionals confirmed the notion that it was difficult for banks that were not *Well Capitalized* to obtain capital investment. Investment professionals explained that a decision to invest or not invest in a bank is based on bottom line numbers and key questions—how big are the losses at the bank, how much capital is on hand to cover those losses, and how much capital will an investor need to supply to fill that gap and receive a future return on the investment?

Investment professionals also told us that they were aware of potential investors performing due diligence on open banks but then waiting until they were in receivership to receive a better deal on the assets, including an SLA. Reduction in asset values at failure as well as the SLA loss guarantee influence the amount of capital an investor needs to contribute in order to provide a return on investment. Finally, investment professionals also mentioned that some investors chose not to invest in failed banks after the FDIC initiated the PCI SOP, as they were concerned about what they referred to as "the bureaucratic process" and other regulatory requirements for such investments. In implementing the PCI SOP, the FDIC sought to balance regulatory obligations imposed on investors with the FDIC's duty to protect the safety and soundness of insured institutions and the DIF.

P.L. 112-88 (7)(B)

Whether the FDIC fairly and consistently applies capital standards when an insured depository institution is successful in raising private capital.

We found that examiners fairly and consistently applied capital adequacy and PCA capital standards when an institution was successful in raising capital. Examiners routinely identified recent capital increases and incorporated those financial results into the examination's analysis of the institution's capital adequacy and capital component ratings. While an institution might be successful in raising capital and examiners might view that capital favorably, the capital increase was not always sufficient to mitigate the level of risk and financial deterioration within the institution. We found a close correlation between the CAMELS composite rating and an institution's capital level, which indicates that examiners were assessing capital adequacy consistently. The PCA capital designations are set by law and are tied to the institution's regulatory capital ratios. We found that examiners appropriately considered the need for continued mandatory PCA restrictions when an institution's PCA capital designation increased to *Well Capitalized.*

FDIC Guidance

A financial institution is expected to maintain capital commensurate with the nature and extent of risks to the institution and the ability of management to identify, measure, monitor, and control those risks. The FDIC *Risk Management Manual of Examination Policies* notes that what is adequate capital for safety and soundness purposes may differ significantly from minimum leverage and *risk-based capital standards* and the *Well Capitalized* and *Adequately Capitalized* definitions that are used in the PCA regulations and other capital-based rules. The minimum levels set forth in the leverage and risk-based capital standards apply to sound, well-run institutions. Most institutions maintain capital levels above the minimums, based on the institution's particular risk profile.

Capital adequacy is influenced by several factors. One factor that examiners consider to evaluate capital adequacy is the institution's access to capital markets, including holding company support. If management has ample access to capital on reasonable terms, the institution may be able to operate safely with less capital than an institution without such access. Also, the strength of a holding company will factor into capital requirements. For example, if a holding company previously borrowed funds to purchase newly issued stock of a subsidiary financial institution (a process referred to as "double leverage"), the holding company may be unable to provide additional capital in the future. The examiner would need to consider more than ratio analysis of the institution to assess management's continuing access to capital sources in such cases.

Examiner Consideration of Capital Increases in Assessing Capital Adequacy and Minimum PCA Capital Standards

Based on our review of 56 full-scope FDIC ROEs and corresponding working papers,[93] we identified 29 institutions (52 percent) that raised capital. Examiners routinely identified and discussed within the ROE the nature and source of the institution's recent capital increases.

We also found that 66 percent of the ROEs concluded on whether the capital increase was sufficient to meet the financial needs of the institution. Examiners determined in 24 percent of the ROEs that the capital increase was insufficient to mitigate the level of risk and financial deterioration within the institution. Of those institutions that increased capital, 69 percent maintained and 21 percent improved their CAMELS capital component rating. Despite the capital increase, the FDIC rated 86 percent of those institutions less than satisfactory (capital component rating of 3, 4, or 5). Examiners cited the following capital adequacy weaknesses:

- elevated risk within the loan portfolio,
- high CRE/ADC concentrations,
- continued asset quality deterioration, and
- deficient net income and/or depleted earnings.

As discussed in Matter (6)(A), we determined there was a statistically significant correlation between the composite CAMELS ratings and institutions' Tier 1 Leverage ratios, which indicates that examiners were assessing capital adequacy consistently. For PCA capital purposes, the PCA capital designation remained unchanged for 21 of the institutions raising capital (72 percent).

- Sixteen of the 21 institutions maintained the highest PCA capital category designation of *Well Capitalized.*
- Five institutions remained less than *Well Capitalized* following the capital increase.

Five institutions improved their PCA capital category designation from *Adequately Capitalized* to *Well Capitalized*. We researched the five institutions to assess how the FDIC considered and treated PCA capital restrictions on brokered and high-rate deposits. We found that the FDIC continued to fairly and consistently apply, as needed, PCA capital restrictions when an institution's PCA capital category improved. In particular, we noted that four of the institutions were still technically considered *Adequately Capitalized* for PCA capital designation purposes due to outstanding enforcement actions with minimum capital requirements. Three of those actions contained a provision that restricted non-core funding, and the two remaining institutions did not appear to have brokered or high-rate deposits—which appears to have mitigated any potential regulatory concern or action. We concluded that the examiners fairly applied the capital standards to these five institutions.

P.L. 112-88 (7)(C)

Whether the FDIC steers potential investors away from insured depository institutions that may be in danger of being placed in receivership or conservatorship.

We did not identify any instances where the FDIC steered potential investors away from troubled institutions. As discussed in Matter (7)(A), the FDIC approved the majority of change-in-control and merger applications from 2008 through 2011.

The FDIC indicated that it has also incorporated provisions in its enforcement actions that require institutions to seek merger partners as part of their capital plans, which has been successful in averting failures. Historically, 16 percent of problem banks merged without failing while 22 percent of problem banks ultimately failed.[94] In making decisions on proposed investments in troubled banks, the FDIC considers whether the investment or merger will result in a safe and sound institution and whether the proposed investment presents the least loss option to the DIF. We identified five examples where the FDIC did not accept proposed open bank investments and instead closed the institution.
However, in each case we found that, in keeping with its policies, the FDIC identified concerns with the proposed investment related to safety and soundness issues, proposed management, or proposed business plans or determined that the proposed transaction would not present the least loss option to the DIF.

P.L. 112-88 does not define the term "steer" as it is used in this question. We interpreted the term to mean that an investor was ready to invest in an insured institution that was in danger of being placed in receivership or conservatorship, but some action on the part of the FDIC, inconsistent with its policies, caused the investor not to invest in the bank. The FDIC does not specifically identify or track actions that could be interpreted as steering away investors from insured institutions in danger of being placed in receivership, so we took a number of steps to try to identify examples. Specifically, we: (1) used our case study analysis and review of investment-related applications performed for Matter (7)(A) to identify examples where FDIC did not approve proposed open bank transactions; (2) noted examples of the FDIC not approving proposed investments in troubled institutions from our MLRs; and (3) interviewed investment professionals for examples of the FDIC not approving proposed capital investments.

Examples Where the FDIC Did Not Approve Proposed Capital Investments in Troubled Institutions

We identified several examples of FDIC actions, and actions of other regulators, that impacted proposed investments in insured depository institutions that were in danger of being placed in receivership or conservatorship. In all cases, we found that the FDIC had identified one or more concerns about the business plan, capital, or management for the proposed investment-related transaction or that the FDIC determined that the proposed transaction would not present the least loss option to the DIF. In most cases, the applicant withdrew from the investment after receiving feedback information from the FDIC or other regulators.

We identified the following examples as a result of our work. They do not represent a comprehensive list of situations where the FDIC did not approve proposed capital investments in troubled institutions, but they illustrate the types of factors the FDIC considers during the approval process.

- *Example One:* The first example involved both the FRB and the FDIC. An affiliate of a troubled Midwest bank applied to the FRB to form a holding company to acquire the shares of the Midwest bank. A change-in-control application was also filed with the FDIC, as the Midwest bank was supervised by the FDIC. The FDIC and the FRB performed a joint visitation of the affiliate and found significant underwriting and administration concerns with consumer regulations as well as poor management supervision. The change-in-control application was subsequently amended to have the two principals of the affiliate acquire control of the bank. The potential investors proposed to invest $6 million into the bank initially, with additional investments to be provided as needed. The FDIC communicated various concerns about the application to the investors, including inconsistency in the amount of capital to be provided and how that capital would be provided, the need for additional financial and background information on the proposed investors, and detail in the business plan. The investors subsequently withdrew the change-in-control application. The bank was closed by the FDIC 3 months later at an estimated cost to the DIF of $18.1 million.

- *Example Two:* The second example involved a troubled bank that requested approval of a *PCA-related material transaction* to sell 16 branches and related loans and fixed assets, as well as to transfer certain deposits in those branches to another insured institution. The bank's primary federal regulator was the FRB. Continuous losses from deteriorating asset quality severely depleted capital, and the bank fell to *Critically Undercapitalized.*

  The bank filed applications for approval of the transaction with the state banking department, the FRB, and the FDIC. The intended purchaser also filed an application for approval of the transaction with the OCC. Section 38(i)(2)(A) of the FDI Act requires that the FDIC must approve any material transactions of *Critically Undercapitalized* institutions. Material transactions are those other than in the usual course of business, and include any investment, expansion, acquisition, sale of assets, or other similar action with respect to which the depository institution is required to provide notice to the appropriate federal banking agency. Documentation indicates that the state banking department and the OCC approved the sales transaction, but the FDIC did not approve the transaction.

  The FDIC's analysis indicated that even after the sale of the assets and transfer of the deposits, the bank would have had a high-risk profile, inadequate capital, a large concentration of problem assets, and deficient earnings. Further, the FDIC found that the transaction would significantly diminish the value of the resulting institution and increase the risk to the DIF. The FDIC concluded that the bank would fail even if the transaction was approved and that the estimated loss to the DIF after the branch sale would significantly exceed the loss associated with liquidating the bank without the branch sale. Thus, the FDIC notified the bank that its application was denied. The FRB subsequently appointed the FDIC as receiver of the bank, and the bank failed at an estimated cost to the DIF of $225 million.
- *Example Three:* The third example involved a troubled bank for which, as a result of the bank's deteriorating condition, bank management signed a merger and acquisition agreement with a private equity entity. The merger transaction contemplated the injection of approximately $440 million into the bank by the PCI through the formation of a Special Purpose Acquisition Corporation (SPAC). The SPAC was chartered to invest in one or more companies before October 10, 2009 or all capital was to be returned to the investors. In order for the SPAC to invest in the

bank, it was required to submit an application to become a bank holding company to the FRB. The FRB requested comments on the application from the FDIC as is customary among bank regulators. The FDIC drafted a letter to the FRB outlining concerns with the lead private investor, given prior experience with the investor in another institution as well as how that investor would influence the bank's future business plans and management. Internal FDIC documents indicate the FRB was also concerned with investor group control, proposed management, and the bank's business plan. Those regulatory concerns were not resolved before the October 2009 expiration of the private investor's capital commitments. The institution failed at an estimated cost to the DIF of about $1.27 billion.

- *Example Four:* The fourth example involved a troubled bank into which a potential investor proposed to invest $11 million and placed $8 million in escrow in anticipation of the transaction. However, at the time of the change-in-control application, the potential investor also served as non-executive Chairman of the Board of another troubled financial institution. The FDIC therefore returned the application and advised the potential investor to fulfill the fiduciary responsibility to improve the financial condition of the bank currently controlled before the FDIC would favorably consider a proposed acquisition of an unaffiliated institution. Shortly thereafter, the targeted bank failed at an estimated cost to the DIF of about $25.6 million.
- *Example Five:* The fifth example involved a troubled bank into which two potential investors proposed to invest $7.5 million and placed $6 million in escrow in anticipation of the transaction. The FDIC communicated its concerns about the proposed transaction to the potential investors in 2010. Subsequently, the FDIC indicated that the potential investors did not address its concerns related to the experience of proposed management, inadequately supported financial projection assumptions, and an inadequately supported business plan, among other concerns. In addition, the FDIC concluded that the bank's capital level would remain less than satisfactory following the proposed capital injection because of the level of adversely classified assets and the institution's overall risk profile. The institution failed at an estimated cost to the DIF of about $9.6 million.

MATTER 8. PRIVATE EQUITY COMPANIES

P.L. 112-88 requires the OIG to study the FDIC's handling of potential investments from private equity companies in insured depository institutions, including:

(A) the number of insured depository institutions that have been approved to receive private equity investment by the FDIC;
(B) the number of insured depository institutions that have been rejected from receiving private equity investment by the FDIC; and
(C) the reasons for rejection of private equity investment when such rejection occurs.

Section (1)(b)(2) of P.L. 112-88 defines the term private equity company as having the meaning given the terms "hedge fund" and "private equity fund" in section 13(h)(2) of the Bank Holding Company Act of 1956 (12 U.S.C. 1851(h)(2)) to include any issuer that is exempt from SEC registration under the Investment Company Act of 1940 (15 U.S.C. § 80a-1–80a-64) based on Section 3(c)(1) (100 or fewer beneficial owners) or Section 3(c)(7) (qualified purchasers). It also would include any "similar fund" determined by the regulators.

Private equity companies fall within the broader definition of entities covered by the PCI SOP. FDIC personnel informed us that PCIs may have one or more private equity companies as investors. The FDIC tracks information for PCI closed bank investment efforts but does not separately track information for private equity company closed bank investment efforts.

As discussed in Matter (4), PCI capital investments in open institutions requiring FDIC approval are governed by the FDI Act. The FDIC reviews applications for change-in-control or bank mergers for a number of statutory factors, including risk that the proposed transaction presents to the DIF. The FDIC does not consider it feasible or necessary to specifically identify and track all potential private capital or private equity investments in open insured depository institutions. Accordingly, we focused our evaluation efforts on potential investments in failing institutions by PCIs that are subject to the PCI SOP.

P.L. 112-88 (8)

Private Equity Companies – the FDIC's handling of potential investment from private equity companies in insured depository institutions including (A) the number of insured depository institutions that have been approved to receive private equity investment by the FDIC; (B) the number of insured depository institutions that have been rejected from receiving private equity investment by the FDIC; (C) and the reasons for rejection of private equity investment when such rejection occurs.

Between August 26, 2009 and March 31, 2012, 19 PCIs submitted bids on 60 failed institutions. Based on our research, it appears that all 19 PCIs had one or more private equity investors. Of the 19 PCIs, 13 were successful in acquiring 36 failed institutions with total assets of $19.3 billion. PCIs were unsuccessful in acquiring the other 24 failed institutions. PCI acquisitions accounted for about 10 percent of the total failed bank asset acquisitions during that timeframe. In general, the primary reason for PCIs being rejected in their attempts to acquire institutions was that their bids were not the least costly bid that the FDIC received.

Failed Depository Institutions Receiving Private Capital Investments

As noted in Table 18 below, the FDIC reported that PCIs, through their respective PCI institutions, acquired about 11 percent of the total number of failed institutions from the August 26, 2009 issuance of the PCI SOP through March 31, 2012, representing about 10 percent of the total failed bank assets acquired. Most failed institution and their associated assets were purchased by non-PCI acquirers. The FDIC was unable to find buyers for about 5 percent of the failed banks and had to pay out deposits to failed bank depositors. PCI bid activity has declined significantly since 2011. We found that the 19 PCIs submitted 73 bids[95] to acquire 60 failed institutions. In a number of cases, multiple PCIs submitted a bid for the same failed institution. We researched the "covered investors" for the 19 PCIs to determine whether those investors were private equity investors. Covered investors are generally those investors in a PCI structure that hold more than 5 percent of the voting equity and are thus subject to the PCI SOP. Based on our research, all 19 PCIs had one or more covered investors that appear to be private equity investors.[96] Those investors included, among others, private equity firms, investment management firms, and hedge fund managers. Ultimately, 13 PCIs acquired a total of 36 failed institutions with assets of $19.3 billion, while 24 failed institutions were not acquired by PCIs.[97] PCIs were unsuccessful in acquiring the 24 failed institutions for the following reasons:

- For one failed bank, the sole PCI bid was disqualified due to a less than satisfactory compliance examination rating for the PCI institution.
- For a second failed bank, the sole PCI bid was disqualified because the PCI did not address FDIC concerns about the bidder's ability to effectively integrate the failed bank into its operations.
- For a third failed bank for which two PCI bids were received, one PCI bid was disqualified due to a less than satisfactory compliance examination rating for the PCI institution. The other PCI bid was not determined to be the least costly resolution alternative, based on the results of the FDIC's LCT, which is described below.
- For the remaining 21 failed banks, the PCI bids were not determined to be the least costly resolution alternative.

As referenced above, the LCT addresses the statutory requirement of FDICIA to use the least costly method to the DIF when resolving failed institutions. The FDIC uses the LCT Model to determine the liquidation value of a failing institution and to evaluate bids submitted to purchase a failing institution. The LCT calculates the FDIC's cost of liquidating a failing institution and the cost to the FDIC of each bid submitted. A comparison can then be made of all possible resolution transactions. The winning transaction is the resolution transaction that is the least costly resolution transaction to the DIF. We reviewed documentation related to a non-statistical sample of three of the 22 failed institutions that did not receive private capital investment because of the LCT. In each instance, we found that there was a bid from another bank that the FDIC determined was less costly to the DIF than the bid or bids from PCIs.

Table 18. Comparison of PCI Acquisition Efforts to Non-PCI Acquisition Efforts—August 26, 2009 through March 31, 2012

Results of Bid Efforts	PCI Institutions	Non-PCIs	Payouts/ Other
Failed Banks Acquired	36	272	16
Percentage of Total Failed Banks Acquired	11%	84%	5%
Failed Bank Assets Acquired	$19.3B	$169B	$6.2B
Percentage of Total Failed Bank Assets Acquired	10%	87%	3%

Source: May 29, 2012 FDIC Board Case.

REGULATOR COMMENTS AND OIG EVALUATION

We provided a draft of this report to the FDIC, OCC, and FRB for review and comment. The regulators provided technical comments, which we incorporated into the final report, where appropriate. The regulators also provided written comments that we have included in their entirety in Appendix 12. Collectively, the regulators' responses and planned actions adequately address the intent of our recommendations.

FDIC Response

The FDIC concurred with the seven recommendations in this report. With respect to SLAs (Recommendation 1), the FDIC indicated that it will review its existing strategies for mitigating the impact of portfolio sales; the loan sale review committee process for considering portfolio sale requests; the SLA monitoring program to ensure resources are appropriate to enforce the agreement through the 3-year recovery period; and the early termination program, to include a review of the results of the program to date, to ensure that the program mitigates the impact on the DIF. The FDIC indicated that it will formally assess the sufficiency of its procedures, processes, and resources for the anticipated volume of portfolio sales and SLA terminations and will deliver its conclusions to the OIG by September 30, 2013.

In order to ensure that AIs are making the best efforts to maximize recoveries and achieve modifications when prudent (Recommendation 2), the FDIC agreed to:

- reinforce previous communications to AIs regarding the FDIC's expectation that AIs should use best efforts to maximize recoveries when making loan modification decisions;
- require the CMCs to review a sample of AI loan modification decisions for maturing loans during CMC on-site visits; and
- analyze the costs and benefits of collecting and monitoring trend information on commercial loan modifications across AIs to identify AIs with lower rates of modifications for further analysis. If deemed cost beneficial, the FDIC will begin collecting such information from AIs when operationally feasible.

The FDIC indicated that it will implement the three action items above and complete an assessment of the benefits and risks presented by commercial loan modifications for loans covered under SLAs, and will deliver its conclusions to the OIG by September 30, 2013.

With regard to the appraisal and workout-related recommendations (Recommendations 3, 4, 5, and 6), the FDIC indicated that it will clarify its expectations for examiners' review of an institution's appraisal program and will remind examiners that working papers should document the extent of reviews, including positive assurance statements where required by separate guidance. This reminder will include references both to the Appraisal Guidelines and to the four elements required by the interagency *Policy Statement on Prudent Commercial Real Estate Loan Workouts*. The FDIC noted that the reminder will reinforce to examiners the importance of complete working paper documentation, particularly given the exception-based nature of comments in ROEs. The FDIC also indicated that it would coordinate with the FRB and the OCC to review the Appraisal Guidelines and determine the most appropriate way to strengthen examination documentation requirements.

Finally, with respect to enforcement actions (Recommendation 7), the FDIC indicated that it plans to conduct an internal study in 2013 on the approach utilized for informal and formal enforcement actions to determine whether an alternative approach to mitigate risk and correct deficiencies may be more effective. The FDIC will coordinate with the FRB and OCC to consider and discuss the various approaches taken with respect to enforcement matters.

OCC Response

The OCC concurred with the two recommendations that were directed to all three regulators. With respect to strengthening appraisal program examiner documentation requirements (Recommendation 3), the OCC indicated that while it believes that its existing supervisory examination strategy and core assessment processes satisfy the recommendation, the OCC has plans to improve its guidance by including a section specific to appraisals in the CRE and mortgage handbooks that are currently undergoing revision.

With respect to enforcement actions (Recommendation 7), the OCC indicated that it welcomed the opportunity to enter into dialogue with the FDIC and FRB to compare the relative effectiveness of the regulators' respective enforcement policies and practices.

FRB Response

The FRB concurred with the two recommendations that were directed to all three regulators. With respect to strengthening appraisal program examiner documentation requirements (Recommendation 3), the FRB noted that it requires that the use of supplemental modules such as the *Real Estate Appraisal Module* be discussed in the examination scoping memorandum. The FRB noted that it is continually looking for ways to improve its examination processes, including ways to improve documentation procedures, as suggested in this recommendation.

With respect to enforcement actions (Recommendation 7), the FRB agreed to work with the FDIC and OCC to discuss the various approaches taken with respect to enforcement matters.

APPENDIX 1. OBJECTIVE, SCOPE, AND METHODOLOGY

Objective

The overall objective of this evaluation was to conduct a comprehensive study on the impact of the failure of insured depository institutions.

Scope and Methodology

The scope and methodology pertaining to all of the P.L. 112-88 Matters generally included reviewing applicable FDIC, OCC, and FRB policies, procedures, and other documentation, and interviewing staff from these agencies. We performed field work at:

- FDIC, OCC, and FRB offices in Washington, DC; and Arlington, Virginia.
- FDIC Regional Offices in Atlanta, Georgia; San Francisco, California; New York, New York; and Dallas, Texas.
- FRB Reserve Banks in Richmond, Virginia; Atlanta, Georgia; San Francisco, California; Philadelphia, Pennsylvania; Minneapolis, Minnesota; New York, New York; Kansas City, Missouri; and Chicago, Illinois.
- Selected state banking agencies, as needed.

We relied on data from a number of interagency and individual regulator information systems, such as the Central Data Repository, which houses Call Report and UBPR information, and internal systems such as the FDIC's ViSION system. In assessing the reliability of data, we relied on our knowledge of these systems based on past OIG reviews and also corroborated select data obtained from systems through our analysis of information from various sources, including ROEs, examiner working papers, and testimonial evidence. We concluded that the information was sufficiently reliable for this review. We also relied on certain DRR management reports and attempted to independently validate their reliability.

We conducted our evaluation from January 2012 through October 2012 in accordance with the Council of the Inspectors General on Integrity and Efficiency's *Quality Standards for Inspection and Evaluation*. Specific work steps pertaining to each Matter are described below.

Matter 1—SLAs

To address this Matter, we performed the following:

- Relied on our February 2012 evaluation, titled: *FDIC's Monitoring of Shared-Loss Agreements.*[98] This report contained an overview of the FDIC's oversight of SLAs. We also relied on the results from seven OIG audits of individual SLAs issued from May 2010 through March 2012. These reports tested seven AIs' compliance with their respective SLAs.
- Reviewed FDIC policies and procedures related to commercial loan modifications, administration of participation loans, portfolio and note sales, and examination of AIs.
- Interviewed officials from 12 AIs and 6 banks without SLAs regarding SLA impact;[99] FDIC, OCC, and FRB examiners; and CMC representatives.
- Participated in an FDIC Advisory Committee on Community Banking meeting to obtain perspectives on the use of SLAs from AIs and banks without SLAs.

- Reviewed examiner and CMC working papers for a sample of SLAs to confirm consistent treatment of SLA and legacy assets.
- Documented FDIC policies and controls for monitoring AIs and SLA terminations.
- Gathered information and statistics regarding the impact of SLAs on loan modifications, extensions of credit by AIs, and participation loans covered by SLAs.
- Analyzed Call Report data for AIs and banks without SLAs pertaining to lending levels.
- Analyzed Call Report data for AIs with and without SLAs pertaining to loan modification activity.
- Analyzed the number of bank failures in California and Georgia from November 1, 2008 through March 31, 2012 that were acquired by in-state and out-of-state AIs[100] using SLAs and the FDIC's associated marketing efforts.
- Mailed surveys to 260 single-family and commercial SLA borrowers to gauge their experiences and level of satisfaction with AIs.
- Compiled information from DRR showing when SLAs will expire, estimated covered assets remaining, and portfolio and individual loan sales of SLA assets.
- Observed two training events held by DRR for CMCs and DRR staff.

Matter 2—Losses

To address this Matter, we performed the following:

- Analyzed Quarterly Banking Profile reports and UBPRs for all FRB-, FDIC-, and OCC- supervised failed financial institutions from December 2005 through June 2011 to understand non-performing loan and loan charge-off trends.
- Reviewed 131 MLR reports covering 142 institutions[101] that failed from January 2007 through September 2011.
- Identified and reviewed FRB, FDIC, and OCC policies and procedures and the extent to which examiners use them for assigning adverse loan classifications, evaluating an institution's ALLL, and examining a financial institution's appraisal programs.
- Selected and studied a non-statistical sample of 42 institutions that failed from January 2007 through September 2011, consisting of 14 institutions supervised by each of the FRB, FDIC, and OCC with the lowest levels of average non-current loans for a 9-quarter period prior to failure. We readily determined that 21 of the 42 institutions failed for reasons other than write-downs on loans that the institution considered to be paying as agreed. We analyzed the final examination and related working papers for 19 of the remaining 21 institutions[102] to understand the extent to which examiners classified loans that the institution considered to be paying as agreed.
- Contracted with KPMG LLP to advise and assist OIG staff in planning the assessment in Matter (2)(C) and conducting and presenting the results of testing, which included:
    - Analyzing relevant accounting standards and interviewing the chief accountants for the FRB, FDIC, OCC, and SEC.

- Considering and updating an SEC report to Congress dated December 30, 2008 by the Office of the Chief Accountant of the SEC titled, *Report and Recommendations Pursuant to Section 133 of the Emergency Economic Stabilization Act of 2008: Study on Mark-To-Market Accounting* (SEC Report), and other fair value-related studies.
- Analyzing Call Report data for the period 2007 through 2011 to measure the extent of use and impact of fair value and impairment accounting on failed and open institutions.

Matter 3—Appraisals

To address this Matter, we performed the following:

- Identified and reviewed FRB, FDIC, and OCC policies and procedures and the extent to which examiners use them to evaluate the adequacy of an institution's ALLL.
- Determined the extent to which asset write-downs contributed to the failure of 350 financial institutions from January 2007 to September 2011.
- Determined from 131 MLR reports covering 142 institutions that failed from January 2007 through September 2011 the contributing causes of failure and OIG conclusions on supervision.
- Reviewed the most recent full-scope examination and related working papers for a non- statistical sample of 136 open financial institutions with a CAMELS composite 3, 4, or 5 rating to assess examination coverage of the ALLL.
- Selected and reviewed a non-statistical sample of 753 adversely classified and non-classified loans that examiners reviewed as part of those 136 examinations from four loan types: 1-4 family ADC loans, other ADC loans, other CRE loans, and 1-4 family residential loans.
- Determined the policies and procedures that examiners use for evaluating the appraised values of property securing real estate loans and the extent to which examiners follow these policies and procedures.
- Identified and reviewed FDIC policies and procedures for examining a financial institution's appraisal program and procedures and the extent to which examiners follow these procedures.
- Contracted with KPMG LLP to advise and assist OIG staff in planning the assessment in Matter (3)(C) and conducting and presenting the results of testing which consisted of interviewing a non-statistical sample of 51 FDIC examiners (in charge of the examinations of the FDIC-supervised institutions selected for the sample of open financial institutions mentioned above), to obtain their views, understanding, and practices related to the *Interagency Appraisal and Evaluation Guidelines* and corresponding implementing guidance.

Matter 4—Capital

To address this Matter, we performed the following:

- Identified and reviewed relevant statutes, regulations, policy statements, and examination procedures related to determining capital adequacy.
- Selected and reviewed the most recent full-scope examination and related working papers for a non-statistical sample of 136 open financial institutions with a CAMELS composite 3, 4, or 5 rating to determine examiner compliance with components of examination policies and procedures that are applicable to assessing capital adequacy.
- Reviewed 131 MLR reports covering 142 institutions that failed from January 2007 through September 2011 to determine trends in findings associated with examiner assessment of capital adequacy.
- Identified FDIC policies, procedures, and guidelines related to private capital investments in insured depository institutions.
- Updated the results of the OIG's audit report titled, *The FDIC's Qualification Process for Private Capital Investors Interested in Acquiring or Investing in Failed Insured Depository Institutions* (AUD-12-004), and reviewed RMS and Legal responses to the recommendations in that report.
- Interviewed RMS, Legal, and DRR officials to gain an understanding of the current PCI clearance-to-bid process and the status of selected PCI requests for clearance to bid on insured depository institutions in receivership.
- Identified a population of 60 PCI requests for clearance to bid that were received by RMS from August 26, 2009 through December 31, 2011.
- Reviewed and summarized shelf and inflatable charter filing reports that indicated the status of PCI requests for clearance to bid.
- Identified statutory factors to be considered by the FDIC when reviewing PCI requests for clearance to bid on insured depository institutions in receivership.
- Reviewed PCI charter file documents and related file summaries to determine the rationale for approving or not approving each PCI request, and identified common reasons why PCI requests were not approved.

Matter 5—Workouts

To address this Matter, we performed the following:

- Reviewed applicable FDIC policies, procedures, guidelines, and other communications related to CRE and residential loan workouts.
- Contracted with KPMG LLP to advise and assist OIG staff in planning the assessment of this Matter, and conducting and presenting the results of testing, which included:
    - Reviewing and summarizing the most recent full-scope ROE for a non-statistical sample of 48 open FDIC-supervised financial institutions.

- Assessing FDIC examiners' implementation of the *Policy Statement on Prudent Commercial Real Estate Loan Workouts*, dated October 31, 2009, associated with the sample of 48 open institutions and from a non-statistical sample of 410 loan line sheets for restructured CRE and residential loans.
- Reviewing examiner documentation for the 48 institutions to determine whether examiners used correct appraisals with respect to analysis of original appraisals, use of market values, consideration of appropriate major facts, identification of appraisal weaknesses, and disposition of appraisal deficiencies.
- Assessing differences in examiner implementation of commercial and residential workout guidelines.

Matter 6—Orders

To address this Matter, we performed the following:

- Gathered information and statistics regarding the use of enforcement actions at the FDIC, OCC, and FRB during the period 2008 through 2011.
- Conducted interviews with senior supervision and legal officials at the FDIC, OCC, and FRB to discuss their respective enforcement action processes.
- Reviewed applicable laws, rules, and regulations pertaining to enforcement actions.
- Reviewed examination reports, orders, problem bank memoranda, and other supervisory records for a sample of orders to determine whether each regulator handled orders consistently.
- Reviewed and documented FDIC, OCC, and FRB policies, procedures, and controls for initiating, monitoring, and terminating enforcement actions.
- Gathered information and statistics regarding terminations of orders, along with researching reasons for terminating orders or not terminating orders when a bank's condition had improved.
- Reviewed examiner guidance at the FDIC, OCC, and FRB issued to address enforcement actions.
- With assistance from the FDIC's Division of Insurance and Research, calculated and analyzed key bank performance financial ratios for all banks supervised by the FDIC, FRB, and OCC to determine the correlation of the ratios with the banks' CAMELS ratings and the correlation of ratios between banks with and without enforcement actions.
- Collected information and analyzed the extent of capital raises obtained or acquired during the period 2008 through 2011 for all insured institutions.
- Interviewed agency officials and private investment professionals to obtain their experience and views regarding the impact of formal orders on a bank's ability to raise capital.
- Interviewed agency officials to obtain their views regarding the impact of formal orders on a bank's ability to lend.
- Considered various regulator studies pertaining to credit availability.
- Considered the impact of orders issued by state regulators.

Matter 7—FDIC Policy

To address this Matter, we performed the following:

- Identified and reviewed relevant statutes, regulations, policy statements, and examination procedures related to determining capital adequacy.
- Analyzed a non-statistical sample of 56 open FDIC-supervised financial institutions with composite 3, 4, and 5 ratings to determine examiner compliance with components of examination policies and procedures that are applicable to capital adequacy.
- Reviewed 131 MLR reports covering 142 institutions that failed from January 2007 through September 2011 to determine trends in findings associated with examiner assessment of capital adequacy.
- Identified FDIC policies and procedures related to investment in insured depository institutions.
- Studied a non-statistical sample of 10 banks that failed during the period January 1, 2009 through December 31, 2011 to determine why the banks were unable to receive sufficient capital.
- Studied a non-statistical sample of 10 banks with unsatisfactory ratings during the period January 1, 2009 through December 31, 2011 that received capital, to determine why the banks were able to obtain capital.
- Captured key information about the sampled failed and open banks' capital-related activities, such as capital ratios over time, dates and content of capital restoration plans, dates and content of merger or reorganization applications submitted, and dates and content of FDIC responses to applications submitted.
- Interviewed RMS case managers for the 20 non-statistically sampled banks to determine the reasons why the sampled banks did or did not receive capital.
- Reviewed a non-statistical sample of 54 investment-related applications filed with the FDIC that were not approved by the FDIC, to determine why the applications were not approved.
- Captured FDIC ViSION system comments and other RMS correspondence for the sampled applications to determine the reasons why those applications had been withdrawn by the applicant or returned by the FDIC.
- Analyzed historical approval rates for change-in-control and merger applications filed with the FDIC.
  The analysis compared the nationwide approval rate with the approval rate for the 10 states with 10 or more failures since 2008.
- Interviewed selected investment professionals involved with companies that invested in one or more financial institutions or with companies that provided investment-related advisory, banking, or other services to financial institutions to obtain their views on the impact of FDIC policies on proposed investments in insured depository institutions.

Matter 8—Private Equity Companies

To address this Matter, we performed the following:

- Identified FDIC policies, procedures, and guidelines related to private capital investments in insured depository institutions.
- Interviewed RMS, Legal, and DRR personnel to gain an understanding of the process for determining PCIs that are to be suspended from bidding on failed institutions, and for qualifying bids received from PCIs.
- Reviewed DRR investor activity reports to identify the number of bids from PCIs to acquire failed institutions during the period August 26, 2009 through March 30, 2012, the number of failed institutions receiving bids from PCIs during that time period, and the number of failed institutions acquired by PCIs.
- Interviewed DRR personnel to determine why certain PCI bids on failed institutions were not successful.
- Reviewed bid-related documents for a non-statistical sample of five failed institutions that received bids from one or more PCIs, but for which the PCI bids were not successful, to determine the reasons why the PCI bids were not successful.
- Reviewed the DRR list of all PCIs that had been cleared to bid but had been suspended from bidding one or more times during the period August 26, 2009 through September 30, 2012.
- Interviewed RMS personnel to determine the reasons why PCIs that were cleared to bid had been suspended from bidding.

APPENDIX 2. SAMPLING METHODOLOGY

This appendix describes how we judgmentally and randomly selected samples associated with the eight Matters that we studied.

Matter 1—SLAs

Our analysis of SLAs included the selection of four judgmental samples.

Selection of 12 AIs. We judgmentally selected 12 AIs at which to conduct interviews, each of which had experience managing SLAs. We selected the AIs from a total listing of 131 as of March 2, 2011. As of June 30, 2012, the 12 AIs selected managed $44.8 billion assets (21 percent of the assets subject to SLAs) from 73 failed banks (25 percent of the failed banks acquired with SLA loss coverage).

We used the following criteria to select each AI:

- Six AIs whose primary regulator was the FDIC, three AIs whose primary regulator was the OCC, and three AIs whose primary regulator was the FRB.
- AIs that had purchased assets from at least two failed banks with SLA loss coverage.

- The AIs and/or the failed banks the AIs acquired had their main offices in Georgia, Florida, California, Nevada, or Illinois. While we also selected AIs that were located in other states, we wanted to ensure coverage of the listed states because they have experienced a large number of bank failures.

Selection of 12 Institutions Without SLAs. We judgmentally selected 12 institutions without SLAs for the purpose of interviewing bank officials. We selected these institutions from a universe of approximately 7,500 institutions that filed Call Report data as of December 31, 2011. We selected institutions in the same geographic areas as failed banks that our sample of 12 AIs acquired.

We used the following criteria to select each non-SLA institution.

- Six institutions whose primary regulator was the FDIC, three whose primary regulator was the OCC, and three whose primary regulator was the FRB.
- Six institutions with assets above $1 billion as of December 31, 2011, to correspond with the size of some of the AIs selected for interviews.
- Six institutions with assets below $1 billion based on feedback that we received from March 2012 briefings with Congressional staff. During those briefings we confirmed that

Congressional staff were concerned about the impact of SLAs on small community banks.

Marketing of Failed Banks in Georgia and California. We performed analyses to determine the extent to which the FDIC marketed banks that failed in Georgia and California and were acquired by out-of-state AIs. We judgmentally selected these states due to the large number of bank failures in these states. Our selection criteria follows.

- Sixty Georgia institutions failed from November 1, 2008 through March 31, 2012 and were acquired by an AI with SLA coverage, according to DRR's records. Forty-three were acquired by other institutions in Georgia, and 17 were acquired by out-of-state institutions. We judgmentally selected 8 of the 17 out-of-state AIs that had acquired failed Georgia banks.
- Twenty-six California institutions failed from November 1, 2008 through March 31, 2012 and were acquired by an AI with SLA coverage, according to DRR's records. Nineteen were acquired by other institutions in California and seven were acquired by out-of-state institutions. We selected all seven out-of-state AIs that had acquired failed California banks.

Borrower Survey. On September 19, 2012, we mailed surveys to 260 SLA borrowers from failed banks to assess their experiences with AIs. Our selection of 260 loans represented 6.34 percent of the universe of 4,098 loans that met our sampling criteria (260/4,098). Our sample was non-statistical and cannot be projected to the universe of borrowers. We mailed surveys to 130 single-family borrowers and 130 commercial borrowers. The surveys consisted of questions asking borrowers to rate their level of satisfaction with their AI in several areas. We received 47 surveys back as of November 13, 2012. Our selection methodology and criteria were as follows:

- Our starting point was the 12 AIs that we selected for interviews plus one additional AI because a borrower from that AI contacted our office to discuss concerns regarding SLAs.
- From the 13 AIs, we selected one or two failed banks that were purchased by each AI, for a total of 14 failed banks.
- Using FDIC data that contained lists of borrowers, their loan amounts, the types of loans they acquired, and the associated failed banks and AIs, we identified loans that met our sampling criteria, which consisted of single-family and commercial loans with UPBs greater than $250,000 and $500,000, respectively. We identified 1,825 single-family and 2,273 commercial loans that met this criteria, for a total universe of 4,098 loans.
- Using statistical software, we generated random numbers and selected corresponding loans, generally, 20 loans per AI. In cases where an AI had fewer than 20 loans meeting our selection criteria, we expanded our criteria to include lower dollar loans.
- As of October 17, 2012 we had received 14 residential surveys back due to invalid addresses. These surveys pertained to nine AIs. We mailed 14 additional residential surveys to different borrowers who banked with the same nine AIs.

Matters 2 and 3—Losses and Appraisals

We conducted our analyses of Losses and Appraisals jointly. As such, our analyses of these Matters included the selection of two non-statistical samples. Because the samples were non- statistical, our analyses applied only to the institutions tested and could not be projected across the universe of financial institutions.

Our specific selection methodology and criteria follows:

- For closed financial institutions, we selected a sample of 42 institutions to review from all institutions supervised by the FDIC, OCC, and FRB that failed between January 2007 and September 2011 that had a low average non-current loan ratio over 2 years (9 quarterly reporting periods) prior to the institution's failure. We selected 14 state member banks, 14 state nonmember banks, and 14 national banks.

  After determining from MLR reports, Board cases, or both, that 21 of those 42 institutions failed for reasons other than asset quality issues, we attempted to obtain reports of examination and related working paper documentation for further review of the remaining institutions' final supervisory examination. We excluded from our sample and did not replace two institutions for which we were unable to obtain or access sufficient examination documentation and completed testing on the remaining 19 institutions.
- For open institutions, we judgmentally selected the FDIC's Atlanta, San Francisco, and New York regions from which to identify financial institutions for testing. This included two geographic areas that had been significantly affected by the latest

downturn in real estate values (Atlanta and San Francisco), and one that was among the least affected (New York).

- For open institutions, we selected in January 2012 a non-statistical sample of 136 FDIC- insured financial institutions supervised by the FDIC, OCC, and FRB from all open institutions that (1) received a composite CAMELS rating of 3, 4, or 5 at the institution's most recent full-scope examination and (2) had the highest percentage of loans and at least 10 percent of their loan portfolio in four real estate loan categories: 1-4 Family ADC Loans, Other ADC Loans, 1-4 Family Residential Loans, and Non-Owner Occupied CRE Loans.
  We then selected from the examination working papers a non-statistical sample of 753 adversely classified and non-adversely classified loans that examiners reviewed from the four targeted real estate loan categories in order to assess examiners' review and analysis of appraisals, appraisal programs, and ALLL.
- With regards to Matter 3 – Appraisals, to supplement our analysis of documentation, we selected, interviewed, and surveyed a non-statistical sample of 51 of the FDIC examiners- in-charge of the FDIC-led examinations in the open-institutions sample above.

Matter 4—Capital

Our analysis of examiner assessment of capital adequacy included the review of examination documentation of the non-statistical sample of 136 financial institutions selected and analyzed for Matter 2—Losses and Matter 3—Appraisals. Because the sample is non-statistical, our analysis applies only to the institutions tested and cannot be projected across any population of financial institutions.

Matter 5—Workouts

Our analysis of workouts included the selection of a non-statistical sample of open FDIC-supervised financial institutions to assess FDIC examiners' implementation of the FDIC guidelines titled, *Policy Statement on Prudent Commercial Real Estate Loan Workouts*. Because the sample is non-statistical, our analysis applies only to the institutions tested and cannot be projected across any population of financial institutions.

Consistent with our sample selection for Matter 2—Losses, and Matter 3—Appraisals, we selected a non-statistical sample as follows:

- We judgmentally selected the FDIC's Atlanta, San Francisco, and New York regions from which to identify financial institutions for testing. These included two geographic areas that had been significantly affected by the latest downturn in real estate values, and one that was among the least affected.
- We analyzed ViSION data to identify financial institutions that received a composite CAMELS rating of 3, 4, or 5 at the institution's last full-scope examination completed prior to September 30, 2011. Choosing institutions with a composite

CAMELS rating of 3, 4 or 5 provided greater probability of finding more relevant workout information for testing.

- We determined, based on analysis of UBPR or Call Report data, the 20 institutions within each of the selected regions that had the highest mean ratio of current and noncurrent restructured loans to gross loans and leases based on a 2-year average (9 quarterly reporting periods) on the basis that those institutions would have the greatest probability of instances where examiners may have had to review CRE loan workouts.
- We removed from the sample (and did not replace) institutions that were closed, merged, or acquired by another institution, or were no longer doing business under the same bank certification number.
- Finally, from the latest, finalized examination for each sampled institution, we judgmentally selected 10 loans, or as many that we could identify if we could not identify 10, from the field examiner's sample of loans reviewed that were CRE with TDRs or appeared to have had a workout after October 2009, or that were residential loan workouts or modifications that occurred after October 2009.

Matter 6—Orders

Uniformity of Orders and Ability of Insured Institutions to Extend or Modify Credit. We judgmentally selected 110 institutions representing 119 orders issued by the FDIC, FRB, and OCC to determine if enforcement actions were applied uniformly for each regulator and to determine the impact on extending and modifying credit. We selected these institutions from a universe of approximately 1,500 orders that were issued to institutions between 2008 and 2011. Selection criteria included (1) institutions from all regions of the country representing over 30 states; (2) obtaining a mix by year of issuance, CAMELS rating, and asset size; and (3) assessing both open and closed institutions.

Matter 7—FDIC Policy

Impact of FDIC Policies on Investment in Institutions. Our analysis of the impact of FDIC policies on financial institutions' ability to acquire capital included the selection of samples of financial institutions and samples of investment-related applications filed with the FDIC.

First, we selected a non-statistical sample of 20 FDIC-supervised financial institutions, 10 open and 10 closed as of December 31, 2011, to determine the reasons why some problem banks received capital and survived, while others did not receive capital and failed. We used the following criteria to select the sample of 20 financial institutions.

- Based on the language in Matter 7, we limited our sampling to FDIC-supervised banks in the states with 10 or more failures since 2008. To identify those states, we organized the FDIC list of banks that failed during the period January 1, 2008 through March 15, 2012 by state and counted the number of failures for each state.

We identified the following 10 states with 10 or more failures – Arizona, California, Florida, Georgia, Illinois, Michigan, Minnesota, Missouri, Nevada, and Washington.

- We limited our sampling to banks with $1 billion or less in total assets based on feedback from Congressional representatives who were familiar with the legislation during March 2012 briefings that we held to discuss the study's scope and methodology.
- For selecting the sample of 10 closed banks, we calculated the estimated loss ratio for all of the failed banks in our population, which included dividing the estimated loss as determined by the FDIC by the total assets at failure. Our sample targeted banks with the lower loss ratios, under the presumption that it may have been easier for these banks to raise capital than others.
- For selecting the sample of 10 open banks, we targeted problem banks that had a significant increase in their CAMELS composite and Capital component ratings at some point during the years 2009 through 2011 and where the bank also had a corresponding increase in capital.

Second, we selected a non-statistical sample of 54 investment-related applications that were filed with, but not approved by, the FDIC to determine why the applications were not approved.

- Based on our review of FDIC application-related policies and procedures, and discussion with FDIC personnel, we identified five types of applications that might be used to seek FDIC approval of a potential capital investment in a financial institution. These application types included a change-in-control, a merger, a mutual-to-stock conversion, a request for change in business plan, and a PCA material transaction pursuant to provisions of the FDI Act.
- We generally focused our sampling on applications related to financial institutions in the 10 states with 10 or more failures since 2008. However, two sample applications were related to financial institutions in other states, one from Colorado and one from Ohio.
- For the relevant states, we identified all applications for each of the five application types in the FDIC ViSION system that had an action type of withdrawn, returned, or denied and an action date during the period January 1, 2009 through December 31, 2011.
- Because many change in business plan and PCA material transaction applications were not investment-related, we reviewed ViSION summary information for each withdrawn, returned, or denied application to identify the subset of applications that were investment- related.
- From the population of withdrawn, returned, or denied investment-related applications, for each application type, we selected a majority of the applications by action type for review, targeting at least one application (if applicable) from each of the relevant states.

The final sample of 54 applications included 27 change-in-control applications, 15 merger applications, 4 mutual-to-stock conversion applications, 4 change in business plan applications, and 4 PCA material transaction applications.

Examiner Consideration of Capital Standards. Our analysis of FDIC Policy included the review of examination documentation of the 56 FDIC-supervised institutions in the non-statistical sample of 136 FDIC-insured financial institutions selected and analyzed for Matter 2— Losses and Matter 3—Appraisals. Because the sample is non-statistical, our analysis applies only to the institutions tested and cannot be projected.

From among those 56 FDIC-supervised institutions, we determined that 29 institutions received a capital injection between their second-most recent and most recent supervisory examinations (which typically occurred within a 12-18 month period) and we selected their most recent examination to assess examiners' review and analysis of capital injections. From those 29 FDIC-supervised institutions, we determined that five had improved from *Adequately Capitalized* to *Well Capitalized* and selected their most recent examination to assess how the FDIC considered and treated PCA capital restrictions on brokered and high-rate deposits.

Case Studies of FDIC Not Approving Proposed Investments in Troubled Institutions. We identified five instances where the FDIC did not approve proposed capital investments in troubled institutions that ultimately failed. We judgmentally selected those five institutions based on our past MLR work and analysis of sample items. Those five instances are not intended to be comprehensive or inclusive of all situations where the FDIC may have not accepted proposed investments.

Interviews of Investment Professionals. We obtained from RMS a list of investors who had invested in shelf or inflatable charters that had been cleared to bid by the FDIC. In addition, we identified various investment advisers, investment companies, and potential investors as a result of our case studies of open and closed financial institutions. From this population of investment professionals, we judgmentally selected eight individuals to contact with questions regarding the impact of FDIC policies on investment in insured depository institutions. Our sample was designed to obtain the perspective of investment professionals from locations across the country.

Matter 8—Private Equity Companies

Our analysis of proposed private equity investment in insured depository institutions included the selection of a sample of failed institutions that did not receive private equity investment. We selected a non-statistical sample of five failed financial institutions to assess the reasons why the institution did not receive a proposed investment by a PCI. We used the following criteria to select the sample of five financial institutions:

- We limited the population to financial institutions that failed between August 26, 2009, the date of the PCI SOP, and March 31, 2012.

- We further limited the population to the 24 failed financial institutions that received a bid from one or more PCIs and where the winning bidder was not a PCI.
- For selecting the sample of five banks, we chose two failed institutions where the only PCI bid submitted was disqualified. We then judgmentally selected three additional failed financial institutions, targeting two failed institutions with bids from multiple PCIs and one failed institution with a bid from a PCI that never submitted a successful bid. Our sample included coverage of both shelf and inflatable charter PCIs.

APPENDIX 3. SLA PROGRAM CONTROLS

The FDIC has established a number of controls to manage the SLA program and to monitor AIs to ensure that they comply with SLA terms and conditions, which include the following:

Loss-Sharing Percentage. An important feature of SLAs that is intended to control AI behavior is the loss-sharing percentage—typically an 80- to 20-percent split for most agreements. The FDIC and proponents of SLAs maintain that the AI loss percentage aligns the AI's interests with the FDIC's requiring the AI to have "skin in the game," which incentivizes the AI to minimize losses and manage the covered SLA assets consistent with how AIs manage their own non-covered, legacy assets.

Critics of SLAs maintain that the AI loss percentage is not enough to curb behavior and that the FDIC loss guarantee incentivizes the AIs to foreclose on an asset or not work to keep an asset performing in order to collect the loss-share guarantee.

FDIC officials told us they were not aware of any AIs that were aggressively foreclosing on loans and noted that the CMCs have been put on alert to flag such activity. Moreover, nothing has come to our attention during our SLA audits to suggest that AIs are aggressively pursuing foreclosure without first considering other loss mitigation efforts.

SLA Requirement to Pursue the Least Loss Strategy. AIs are required to administer and undertake loss mitigation efforts prior to taking any foreclosure action and pursue the least loss strategy when deciding whether to foreclose or modify troubled loans. AIs are expected to manage, administer, and collect amounts on the shared-loss loans and assets using usual, prudent business and banking practices as required under customary servicing procedures, as defined in the SLA.

SLA Requirement to Manage Covered Assets Consistently with Legacy Assets. The AI is required to manage and administer each SLA loan in accordance with prudent business and banking practices and the AI's written internal credit policies and usual practices. This includes striving to maximize collections on shared-loss assets and managing and administering shared- loss assets without favorable treatment of any assets owned by the AI or its affiliates that are not shared-loss assets (known as legacy assets).

As part of our study, we reviewed the CMC and RMS examiner efforts for a sample of 12 AIs to verify that the CMCs and examiners were including procedures in their on-site compliance reviews and examinations to confirm that AIs were treating SLA and legacy assets consistently.

We found that both the CMCs and examiners tested samples of SLA and legacy assets to confirm that AIs applied consistent procedures to both types of assets when servicing, evaluating, and performing charge-offs of the loans. Neither the CMCs nor the examiners identified any significant problems in this area.

SLA Requirement to Implement a Loan Modification Program. The FDIC requires that an AI modify qualified single-family loans using the HAMP or an FDIC-approved modification program. Both programs adjust the current loan terms to achieve an affordable payment.

The objectives of loan modification programs are to minimize losses to the AI and the FDIC and maximize the opportunity for qualified homeowners to remain in their homes with affordable mortgage payments.

Compliance Monitoring Contractors. The FDIC monitors SLA compliance through monthly or quarterly reporting by the AI and by performing periodic, on-site reviews of the AI's adherence to the SLA terms. The FDIC has engaged eight CMC firms to oversee the AIs. The CMCs review and analyze AI loss claim certificates and perform annual on-site visitations of the AIs.[103] The FDIC requires the CMCs to develop individual monitoring and visitation plans for each AI. DRR staff monitor the CMC efforts.

The CMCs' on-site compliance monitoring visitation activities include reviewing AI loss claim certificates and supporting documentation, reviewing and analyzing loan files to support claims for covered losses, following up with AI management on corrective actions taken to remediate prior findings, and reviewing AI policies and procedures and shared-loss loan files to ensure that SLA assets are treated in the same manner as the AI's legacy loans. CMCs are required to submit a written visitation report, which includes findings and recommendations for appropriate corrective actions, and to oversee the AI's progress towards making those corrective actions.

The CMCs work with the AIs and DRR to resolve any issues discovered during the monitoring process. DRR and the CMCs completed 441 SLA compliance reviews in 2011. According to DRR, the compliance reviews conducted in 2011 identified 1,890 findings and questioned claims totaling $465.5 million. DRR further reported that all of the 2011 findings have been resolved and AIs paid the FDIC $363.1 million of the questioned claims and subsequently provided documentation to substantiate the remaining $102.4 million in questioned claims.

DRR established a Compliance Review Committee to provide oversight and authority to mitigate risks to its SLA oversight program when the AI fails to comply fully with SLA provisions. Some of the committee's activities include reviewing all final compliance reports, including the AI management responses, and taking corrective action to resolve and mitigate non-compliant business processes.

RMS Examination of SLA Compliance. FDIC bank examiners evaluate AI compliance with SLAs and the impact of SLAs on institutions. Among other things, examinations determine if AIs provide equal treatment of covered and legacy commercial assets, appropriately account for SLA assets, and consider the overall risk mitigation provided by loss sharing in assigning the CAMELS rating. FDIC RD Memorandum 2010-018, *Examinations of Institutions with Assets Covered by Loss-Sharing Agreements*, dated May 6, 2010, notes that the examination asset review scope should include a sufficient sample of commercial assets covered by an SLA.

The review scope should provide the EIC with sufficient information to assess whether the AI applies its loan administration processes, credit risk management policies (including its loan review and credit grading policies), and loss recognition and charge-off standards to covered commercial assets in a manner consistent with its treatment of commercial legacy assets not covered by SLAs.

The FDIC also issued RD Memorandum 2011-023, *Amendment to Memorandum 2010-018: Examinations of Institutions with Assets Covered by Loss-Sharing Agreements*, dated October 14, 2011, to enhance RMS coordination with DRR. The FDIC and FRB developed an ED Module titled, *FDIC-Assisted Transactions,* that includes suggested examination procedures for reviewing an institution's SLA-related activities.

RMS officials told us that, overall, they are finding that AIs are treating their SLA and legacy assets in a similar manner. RMS also told us that coordination with DRR, and with other regulators, has improved markedly.

The FDIC has also participated in examinations of SLA operations at non-FDIC supervised institutions, at the request of the other regulators.

For a sample of 12 AIs, we reviewed examination reports; interviewed FDIC, OCC, and FRB examination staff; and reviewed examination working papers supporting examiners' reviews of SLA activities. We confirmed that examiners performed procedures to ensure that AIs treated covered assets consistently with their legacy loans. Examiners for all 12 AIs concluded that AIs treated SLA and legacy assets consistently.

However, examiners identified problems related to two AIs' accounting treatment of their SLA assets and communicated these concerns to DRR and/or FDIC regional staff. Examiners for 6 of the 12 AIs—4 AIs regulated by the FDIC, 1 by the OCC, and 1 by the FRB—coordinated with DRR staff pertaining to examination work related to the SLAs.

Limitations on AIs' Ability to Sell Covered Assets. The SLAs include several limits on the AIs' ability to sell covered assets. The AI is free to sell SLA loans, but if it does so without the prior approval of the FDIC, it will lose loss coverage on the loan. The FDIC will not approve requests to sell SLA loans unless the AI can demonstrate that the sale represents the least loss alternative.

True-up Provision. Since October 2009, the SLAs have included true-up payment provisions requiring AIs to reimburse the FDIC at the end of the SLA if losses are lower than expected, based on the results of a calculation performed at the expiration of the SLA. If an AI's original bid amount included a discount of 5 percent or more of the purchase price of the assets and the true-up calculation result is positive, the AI must pay the FDIC that amount. If an AI pays the FDIC, it indicates that the institution's SLA bid was discounted too much and did not align with the FDIC's intrinsic loss estimate of the assets.

OIG Audits and Evaluations of the SLA Program and Agreements

Given the magnitude of the SLA program, we performed a comprehensive evaluation of the FDIC's program for monitoring SLAs.

The primary objective of the evaluation was to evaluate DRR's overall efforts to monitor and ensure compliance with the terms and conditions of the SLAs. We determined that the FDIC devoted high-level management attention to the quickly expanding SLA program, including establishing corporate-wide performance goals, convening a Project Management Office task group, and providing quarterly updates to the Chairman and Audit Committee on the findings of its AI compliance reviews and planned corrective actions.

The Corporation also substantially increased staff, engaged contractors, and developed procedures and systems to manage the associated workload and risks.

We also found that the SLA program was continuing to mature, as evidenced by the finalization of policies and procedures, initiation of training programs, strengthened AI compliance monitoring efforts, and implementation of data resources to manage program data. The FDIC was also taking steps to enhance the following:

- information security of its SLA data resources;
- guidance to AIs pertaining to commercial loan modifications and the tracking of such modifications;
- tracking of questioned claims and processes for ensuring corrective action in response to AI reviews; and
- oversight of AIs by implementing a proactive monitoring initiative to more promptly prevent or detect instances of non-compliance.

Notwithstanding, we reported that with any program of this size, there would be emerging issues and risks that require monitoring and attention. In that regard, we made five recommendations, including issuing guidance to better ensure consistent AI monitoring efforts among DRR staff and for evaluating whether AIs are pursuing and reporting recoveries experienced on covered assets. As of October 2012, the FDIC had addressed and closed all five recommendations.

We also conducted audits of seven AIs to evaluate each AI's compliance with the terms of its SLA. The audits specifically focused on evaluating the AI's SLA policies and procedures, compliance with the SLA reporting requirements, and the extent to which the AI maximized returns.

The audits also addressed the FDIC's oversight of the SLAs. The audits have resulted in substantial recoveries to the FDIC and further improvement in SLA controls. The extent and significance of findings have decreased as the FDIC program matured and AIs better understood and implemented processes to comply with SLA terms.

APPENDIX 4. ACCOUNTING STANDARDS RELATED TO FAIR VALUE ACCOUNTING

Matter (2)(C) of P.L. 112-88 pertains to changes in fair value accounting rules. Table 19 presents fair value-related accounting standards and original issuance dates. In June 2009, FASB codified existing GAAP accounting literature (e.g., the FAS) into the ASC.

Table 19. Fair Value Accounting Standards*

Standard / Date Issued
FAS 107, December 1991, *Disclosures about Fair Value of Financial Instruments* Current ASC Topic Reference: ASC 825 *Financial Instruments*
FAS 115, May 1993, *Accounting for Certain Investments in Debt and Equity Securities* Current ASC Topic Reference: ASC 320 Investments – *Debt and Equity Securities*
FAS 133, June 1998, *Accounting for Derivative Instruments and Hedging Activities* Current ASC Topic Reference: ASC 815 *Derivatives and Hedging*
FAS 140, September 2000 (Amendment of FAS 125, June 1996), *Accounting for Transfers and Servicing of Financial Assets and Extinguishments of Liabilities* Current ASC Topic Reference: ASC 860 *Transfers and Servicing*
FAS 141R, December 2007 (Revision of FAS 141 issued June 2001), *Business Combinations* Current ASC Topic Reference: ASC 805 *Business Combinations*
FAS 155, February 2006, *Accounting for Certain Hybrid Financial Instruments* Current ASC Topic Reference: ASC 815 *Derivatives and Hedging*
FAS 156, March 2006, *Accounting for Servicing of Financial Assets* Current ASC Topic Reference: ASC 860 *Transfers and Servicing*
FAS 157, September 2006, *Fair Value Measurements* Current ASC Topic Reference: ASC 820 *Fair Value Measurements and Disclosures*
FAS 159, February 2007, *The Fair Value Option for Financial Assets and Financial Liabilities* Current ASC Topic Reference: ASC 825 *Financial Instruments*
FAS 160, December 2007, *Noncontrolling Interests in Consolidated Financial Statements* Current ASC Topic Reference: ASC 810 *Consolidation*
FAS 166, June 2009, *Accounting for Transfers and Servicing of Financial Assets* Current ASC Topic Reference: ASC 860 *Transfers and Servicing*

Source: KPMG LLP.

* This table is not an all-inclusive presentation of fair value accounting-related standards.

APPENDIX 5. ACCOUNTING STANDARDS RELATED TO IMPAIRMENT ACCOUNTING

Matter (2)(C) of P.L. 112-88 pertains to changes in other accounting standards. We interpreted other accounting standards to be those standards related to accounting for impairments. Table 20 presents impairment-related accounting standards and their original issuance dates.

Table 20. Impairment Accounting Standards*

Standard / Date Issued
FAS 5, March 1975, *Accounting for Contingencies* Current ASC Topic Reference: ASC 450 *Contingencies*
FAS 15, June 1977, *Accounting by Debtors and Creditors for Troubled Debt Restructurings* Current ASC Topic Reference: ASC 310 *Receivables*
FAS 109, February 1992, *Accounting for Income Taxes* Current ASC Topic Reference: ASC 740 *Income Taxes*
FAS 114, May 1993, *Accounting by Creditors for Impairment of a Loan* Current ASC Topic Reference: ASC 310 *Receivables*
FSP FAS 115-2, April 2009 *Recognition and Presentation of Other-Than-Temporary Impairments* Current ASC Topic Reference: ASC 320 *Investments – Debt and Equity Securities*
Emerging Issues Task Force (EITF) Issue No. 99-20, January 2001, *Recognition of Interest Income and Impairment on Purchased Beneficial Interests and Transferor's Beneficial Interests in Securitized Financial Assets Obtained in Transfer Accounted for as a Sale* Current ASC Topic Reference: ASC 325 *Investments – Other*
FSP EITF 99-20-1, January 2009, *Amendments to the Impairment Guidance of EITF Issue No. 99-20* Current ASC Topic Reference: ASC 325 *Investments – Other*
SOP 03-3, December 2003, *Accounting for Certain Loans or Debt Securities Acquired in a Transfer* Current ASC Topic Reference: ASC 310-30 *Loans and Debt Securities Acquired with Deteriorated Credit Quality*
FAS 142, June 2001, *Goodwill and Other Intangible Assets* Current ASC Topic Reference: ASC 350 *Intangibles – Goodwill and Other*

Source: KMPG LLP.

* This table is not an all-inclusive presentation of impairment accounting-related standards.

APPENDIX 6. USE AND IMPACT OF FAIR VALUE ACCOUNTING

Table 21 provides a summary of the more significant balance sheet items and how each of those items is recorded in the financial statements. The table also presents the average percentage that each balance sheet item represented in terms of total assets (TA) or total liabilities (TL) for community banks with assets less than $1 billion during the period 2008 through 2011 for open institutions and 2007 through 2011 for closed institutions.

As shown, AFS securities, loans and leases HFI, and OREO represented the greatest percentage of assets for institutions with assets less than $1 billion. The following sections discuss the impact on net income from fair value and impairment accounting associated with these categories of assets.

AFS Securities

AFS Securities represented an average of 18 and 9 percent of total assets for open and closed institutions, respectively, and is the balance sheet account most impacted by fair value accounting for community banks. The FDI Act restricts the types of equity securities that most banking entities are allowed to purchase and hold, thus institutions mostly hold debt securities. These include obligations of the U.S. Government and U.S. Government agencies, direct obligations of *government-sponsored enterprises* (GSE), obligations of state and local governments, corporate bonds, *mortgage-backed securities* (issued by GSEs or private mortgage lenders), and other *asset-backed securities*. Also included are direct and pooled investments in *trust preferred securities* (TRuPS) of institutions which, although legally structured as *preferred shares*, generally have economic characteristics of, and are accounted for, as debt securities.

While AFS debt securities are reported on the balance sheet at their fair value, changes in fair value do not impact regulatory capital unless OTTI occurs or if the security is sold.[104] These changes are referred to as unrealized gains or losses. Any positive or negative changes in fair value are recorded in OCI and aggregated in AOCI, a component of stockholders equity. Currently, AOCI for AFS debt securities is removed from the Tier 1 Capital calculation when determining an institution's regulatory capital levels.

In order to determine what financial impact fair value changes from AFS securities had for community banks, we calculated net unrealized gains and losses as a percentage of institutions' NII. Table 22 presents the results of our analysis. If the amount was a net unrealized gain, it is reported as a positive value. If the amount is a net unrealized loss, it is reported as a negative value.

Results show that open community banks experienced net unrealized gains during each period, while closed institutions experienced significant losses in 2008 and 2009. While not shown in the table below, our study found that open and failed institutions with assets greater than $10 billion experienced larger net unrealized losses in 2008 and 2009.

In April 2009, the FASB changed how OTTI on debt securities is recognized in response to numerous concerns from the banking industry. Previously, any decline in the fair value of a debt security below its amortized cost that, upon evaluation, was determined to be an OTTI triggered a charge against earnings for the full amount of the fair value decline. After FASB's change, any decline in the fair value of a debt security below its amortized cost basis still requires an impairment assessment, but there are additional criteria for determining whether the entire loss is recorded through net income. If the present value of cash flows expected to be collected on a debt security is less than its amortized cost basis, a credit loss exists. In this situation, if an institution does not intend to sell the security and it is unlikely that the institution will be required to sell the debt security before recovery of its amortized cost basis less any current- period credit loss, an OTTI has occurred. The portion of the total OTTI related to the credit loss must be recognized in earnings, but the portion of the total impairment related to other factors must be recognized in OCI. Table 23 shows total OTTI losses and the breakdown of the portion recognized in OCI and the portion recognized in earnings.

Table 21. Accounting Classification of Balance Sheet Items

Balance Sheet Item	Average Percentage of Balance Sheet	Accounting Classification	Explanation
Assets			
Trading Assets	Open Institutions 0.02% of TA Closed Institutions 0.01% of TA	Fair Value through net income	Securities and other assets held for trading purposes are recorded at fair value, and unrealized gains and losses are recognized through net income.
Derivatives	Open Institutions 0% of TA Closed Institutions 0% of TA	Fair Value through net income unless used for cash flow hedging purposes	Derivatives, whether in an asset (receivable) or liability (payable) position, are usually recorded at fair value with unrealized changes in the value of the derivative instrument affecting net income. An exception is made for derivatives designated as "cash flow hedges" are recorded at fair value, with the effective portion of the change in fair value temporarily recorded through OCI, and later reclassified to net income as the hedged item affects net income, while the ineffective portion of the change in fair value is recognized in net income.
AFS Securities	Open Institutions 18.30% of TA Closed Institutions 9.16% of TA	Fair Value with unrealized gains/losses recorded as OCI; OTTI generally recorded through net income	Securities that are neither trading securities nor HTM are classified as AFS, with changes in fair value recorded in OCI until the investment is ultimately sold, or OTTI occurs. For AFS debt securities, generally only the credit portion of OTTI is recognized in net income if the entity has the intent and ability to hold the security until recovery of its carry-ing amount while the portion of OTTI not res-ulting from credit losses is recorded in OCI.
HTM Securities	Open Institutions 2.85% of TA Closed Institutions 0.72% to TA	Amortized Cost	Debt securities purchased with the intent and ability to hold until maturity are recorded at amortized cost. Only when a decline in the fair value of the security below amortized cost is determined to be an OTTI or the security is sold (which is expected to be rare) does the change in fair value impact net income. As with AFS securities, generally only the credit portion of OTTI is recognized in net income while OTTI not resulting from credit losses is recorded in OCI.
Loans and Leases Held for Sale (HFS)	Open Institutions 0.33% of TA Closed Institutions 0.27% of TA	Lower of Cost or Fair Value	Loans and leases HFS are recorded at the lower of cost or fair value, with declines in fair value recognized in net income. Institutions with an "originate-to-sell" business model typically had greater amounts of loans that were HFS than institutions that held loans for investment.
Loans and Leases HFI	Open Institutions 63.21% of TA	Amortized Cost	Loans and leases HFI are recorded at amortized cost less an allowance for probable incurred

Balance Sheet Item	Average Percentage of Balance Sheet	Accounting Classification	Explanation
	Closed Institutions 73.18% of TA		credit losses. The provision to build the ALLL reduces net income.
OREO	Open Institutions 0.65% of TA Closed Institutions 4.15% of TA	Lower of Cost or Fair Value less Cost to Sell	OREO assets repossessed through foreclosure are valued at the lower of the assets' cost or fair value less cost to sell. Fair value less cost to sell is continuously updated to determine whether there are further declines.
Liabilities			
Derivatives	Open Institutions 0.12% of TL Closed Institutions 0% of TL	Fair Value unless used for cash flow hedging purposes	Same as explanation for derivative assets.

Source: OIG/KPMG LLP Analysis of Call Report Data.

Table 22. Net Unrealized Gains or Losses on AFS Securities as a Percent of NII (institutions with assets less than $1 billion)

Asset Size		2007	2008	2009	2010	2011
Open Institutions	Net Unrealized Gains (Losses)	---	1.43%	14.55%	23.19%	33.13%
Closed Institutions	Net Unrealized Gains (Losses)	-5.12%	-37.98%	-15.57%	5.35%	3.79%

Source: Net unrealized gains and losses on AFS securities comes from Call Report Schedule RC-R.

Table 23. OTTI Losses on HTM and AFS Debt Securities as a Percentage of NII

Asset Size	Description	2008	2009	2010	2011
Open Institutions	Total OTTI Losses	---	---	1.08%	0.52%
Closed Institutions	Total OTTI Losses	---	---	0.87%	0.69%
Open Institutions	OTTI Losses Recognized in OCI	---	---	0.20%	0.14%
Closed Institutions	OTTI Losses Recognized in OCI	---	---	0.18%	0.00%
Open Institutions	OTTI Losses Recognized in Earnings	---	---	0.88%	0.38%
Closed Institutions	OTTI Losses Recognized in Earnings	---	---	0.69%	0.69%

Source: OTTI information comes from Call Report Schedule RI. Note: These Call Report fields were not required until 2010.

As shown, OTTI losses did not represent a significant percentage of NII during 2010 and 2011. We also reviewed a study of fair value accounting during the financial crisis which analyzed OTTI charges.[105] The study found that although OTTI charges reached unprecedented levels during 2008, OTTI charges still represented only a small percentage of institutions' normal earnings and had minimal impact on institutions' Tier 1 Capital levels.

Loans and Leases HFI and Accounted for at Amortized Cost

During the period analyzed, total loans and leases HFI represented on average approximately two-thirds of total assets. If the institution has the intent and ability to hold the loan or lease for the foreseeable future or until maturity or payoff, it is typically classified as HFI. Loans and leases HFI are recorded at cost less an ALLL for the estimated amount of loans and leases it is probable the institution will be unable to collect as prescribed in FAS 114/ASC 310 and FAS 5/ASC 450.

The PLLL represents the amount needed to adjust the ALLL to a level appropriate to absorb estimated probable loan and lease losses incurred to date, based upon management's evaluation of the institution's current loan and lease loss exposures. Institutions generally apply loan review procedures when identifying loans to be individually evaluated for impairment. When an individually evaluated loan is deemed impaired, institutions choose one of three methods to measure impairment: (1) the present value of expected future cash flows discounted at the loan's effective interest rate (i.e., the contractual interest rate adjusted for any net deferred loan fees or costs, premium, or discount existing at the origination or acquisition of the loan), (2) the loan's observable market price, or (3) the fair value of the collateral if the loan is collateral-dependent. However, for regulatory reporting purposes, institutions are required to measure impairment on impaired collateral-dependent loans using the fair value of collateral method. For loans not individually identified as impaired, an allowance is maintained in accordance with FAS 5/ASC 450. This component of the ALLL is based upon objective evidence, such as historical loss experience and current economic conditions, and other environmental factors, which enables the institution to estimate losses that have been incurred but cannot yet be identified to a specific loan.

Charge-offs represent the realization of credit losses that were previously provided for in the ALLL. A charge-off in itself does not affect net income, as it is recorded as a reduction to the loan balance and the ALLL. However, because it evidences the confirmation of a loss event previously recognized, it is a useful indicator of impairment.

Results indicate that quarterly loss provisions and loan charge-offs represented a significant percentage of NII as presented in Table 24. A considerable difference is noted when these percentages are segmented by open and failed institutions. For failed institutions, both the provisions and charge-offs represented a significantly larger portion of NII. When compared to other asset classes it is noted that loan impairment was a considerably larger contributor to institutions' losses. This is a direct result of loans and leases HFI being a much larger share of total assets.

OREO

OREO represented an average of 0.65 and 4.15 percent of total assets for open and closed institutions, respectively. The percentage of OREO to total assets increased during our period of analysis, especially for failed institutions, which is consistent with the real estate industry environment, where many loans backed by real estate assets defaulted and the properties that served as collateral were acquired and reported as assets in institutions' balance sheets.

OREO usually includes assets repossessed through a foreclosure process for defaulted loans. Regulatory reporting instructions presume that OREO is HFS. When an institution receives the real estate asset, this asset is generally categorized as HFS, and the institution initially recognizes the asset at its fair value less cost to sell. This fair value less cost to sell becomes the cost of the foreclosed asset. The amount, if any, by which the recorded amount of the loan exceeds the fair value (less cost to sell) of the asset is a loss charged to the ALLL at the time of foreclosure or repossession.[106] The estimate of fair value less costs to sell is continuously updated for further declines (and recoveries of previously recognized declines), which must be charged (credited) to expense, although increases are not recognized until the asset is subsequently sold.

Gain or losses on the sale of OREO include increases and decreases in the valuation allowance for foreclosed real estate, and write-downs of OREO subsequent to acquisition (or physical possession) charged to expense. Not included within losses on the sale of OREO are declines in the fair value of collateral for collateral-dependent loans previously charged to the ALLL prior to foreclosure of loans secured by real estate. OREO losses were higher for failed institutions and grew throughout the years as institutions had to foreclose on assets that were declining in value throughout the entire period, as shown in Table 25.

Table 24. Median Loss Provision and Charge-offs as a Percentage of NII

Asset Size	Description	2007	2008	2009	2010	2011
Open Institutions	Quarterly Loss Provision (ALLL)	---	15.52%	23.78%	19.48%	12.18%
Closed Institutions	Quarterly Loss Provision (ALLL)	23.47%	128.90%	285.33%	178.25%	115.76%
Open Institutions	Quarterly Charge-offs	---	10.66%	19.42%	18.35%	15.17%
Closed Institutions	Quarterly Charge-offs	10.87%	79.25%	305.88%	159.57%	127.82%

Source: The PLLL and charge-offs come from Call Report Schedule RI-B part II.

Table 25. Net Gains (Losses) on Sales of OREO as a Percentage of NII (institutions with assets less than $1 billion)

Asset Size	Description	2007	2008	2009	2010	2011
Open Institutions	Quarterly Net Gains (Losses) on OREO Sales	--	-0.38%	-0.65%	-1.91%	-2.81%
Closed Institutions	Quarterly Net Gains (Losses) on OREO Sales	-0.38%	-8.22%	-26.11%	-39.39%	-22.90%

Source: Net gain on sales of loans and OREO come from Call Report Schedule RI.

APPENDIX 7. PROCESS MAPS FOR EVALUATING THE ALLL

Examination Steps to Take When Evaluating the ALLL

Step One

An assessment of the institution's ALLL policy, methodology, and controls to determine compliance with supervisory guidance and generally accepted accounting principles (GAAP)

Step 1(a)

Ensure that the board of directors approved the policy and methodology at least annually and when changes were made.

↓

Step 1(b)

Review policy for adequacy based on an understanding of bank's lending risk profile.

↓

Step 1(c)

Determine if ALLL policy and methodology address the standards established in supervisory guidance. If not in writing, ensure management is committed to developing a written policy that includes a description of the methodology within a specified time frame.

↓

Step 1(d)

Determine if the ALLL methodology is consistent with GAAP. Review whether adjustments have been considered and incorporated for qualitative or environmental factors.

↓

Step 1(e)

Determine if management has written documentation that supports its ALLL methodology, including a summary or consolidation of the ALLL balance as well as any periodic adjustments to the ALLL process or balance.

↓

Step 1(f)

Determine the adequacy of controls around the ALLL estimation process by reviewing the appropriate documentation, board oversight, loan grading process, and the independent review and validation process of the ALLL (e.g., internal or external audit and loan review).

Step Two

An assessment of the appropriateness of the recorded level of the ALLL by evaluating the process used to calculate the ALLL estimate.

See summary of the process for determining the loss estimate under FAS 5, FAS 114, and the interaction of FAS 5 and FAS 114. Review for completeness, directionally consistency, red flags, consistency with industry standards, and reasonableness of the ALLL level.

Source: FRB examiner job aids.

Figure 12. Methodology for Evaluating the ALLL.

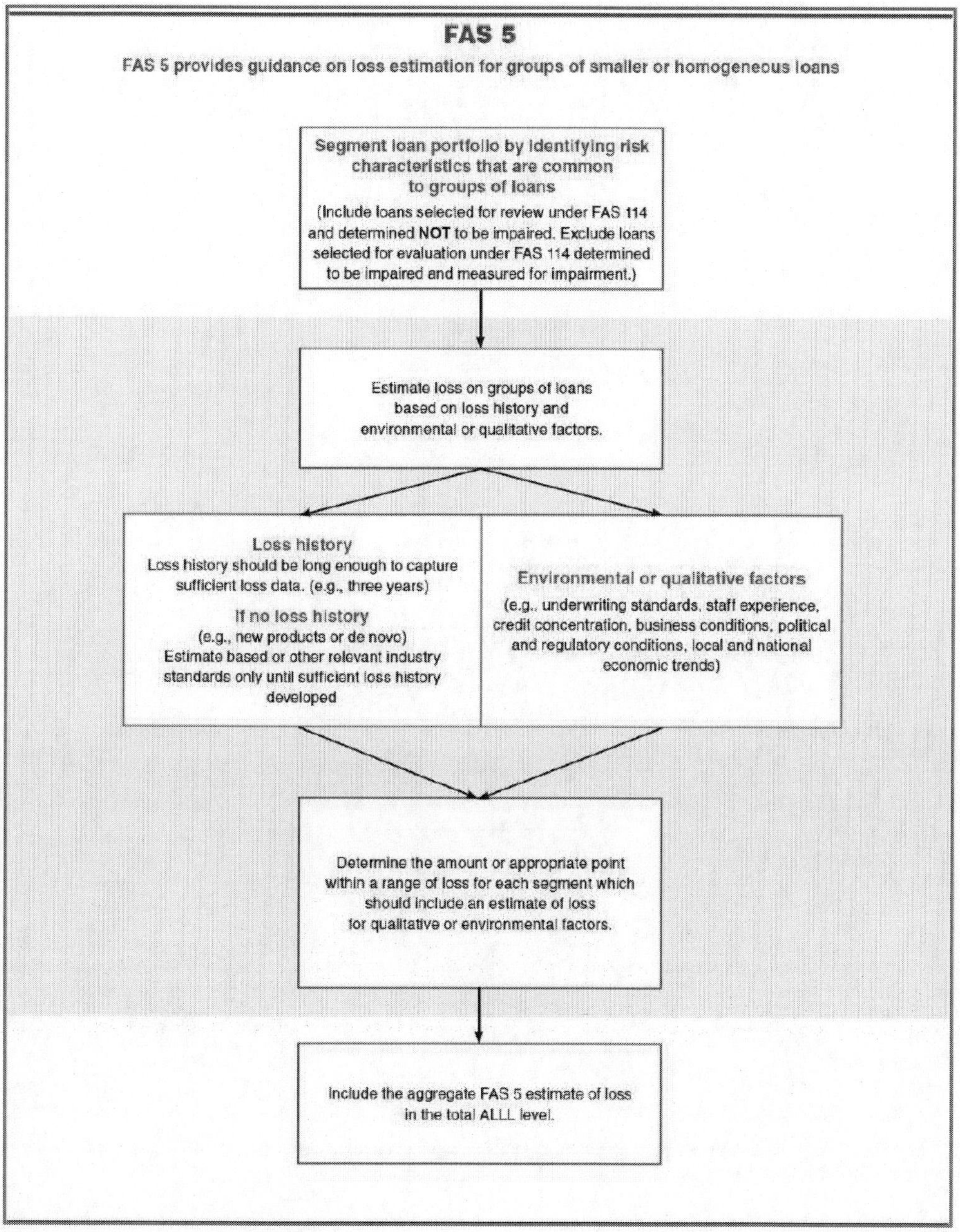

Source: FRB examiner job aids.

Figure 13. Process for Implementation of FAS 5.

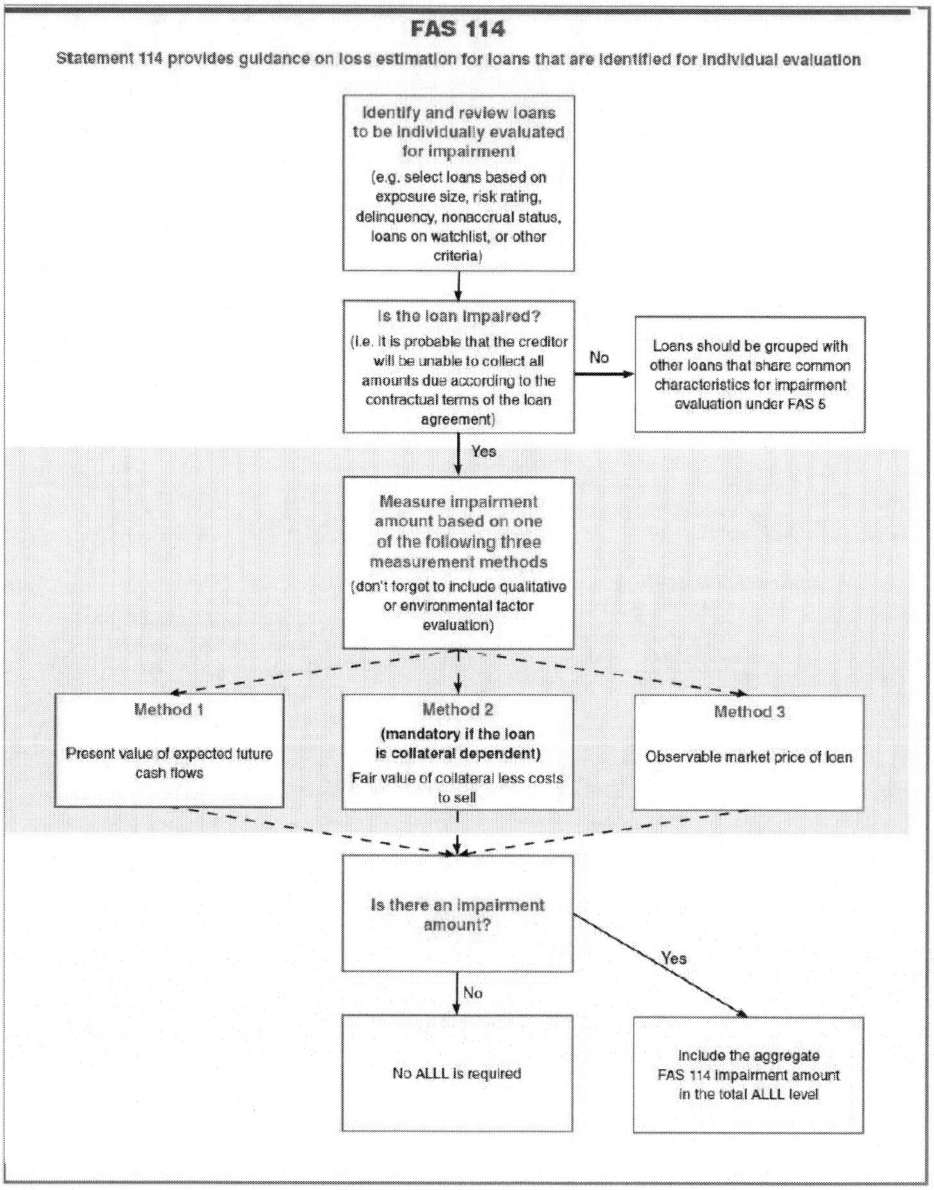

Source: FRB examiner job aids.

Figure 14. Process for Implementation of FAS 114.

APPENDIX 8. RE-APPRAISAL/RE-EVALUATION MATRIX

FDIC RD Memorandum 2009-011, *Re-appraising/Re-evaluating Real Property*, dated March 18, 2009, provides examiners with general supervisory expectations for FDIC-supervised institutions to update real estate appraisals and evaluations as part of their ongoing portfolio review and monitoring process. The RD Memorandum includes the following informational matrix as presented in Figure 15.

<table>
<tr><th colspan="2">Identified Problem Assets</th></tr>
<tr><td>Commercial Real Estate:
• Can use a variety of valuation techniques such as:
  • Updating original appraisal/evaluation,
  • Adjusting original appraisal/evaluation to reflect changes in market conditions or delays in a project's development/ construction for smaller, non-complex credits, or
  • New appraisal/evaluation.
• Need to have implemented a process for obtaining updated values on an ongoing basis.
• Use information to proactively initiate loss mitigation strategy and assess risk exposure.</td><td>Residential Real Estate:
• Updated valuations on open-end and closed-end residential credits are needed before loan is 180 days past due per the Uniform Retail Credit Classification and Account Management Policy (Credit Policy).
• Can use a variety of valuation techniques such as:
  • Automated Valuation Models (AVMs), but must use an alternative method if the AVM does not render a reliable confidence score
  • Broker Price Opinions (BPOs), or
  • Other valuation methods (appraisal/evaluation).</td></tr>
<tr><th colspan="2">Ongoing Portfolio Monitoring of Performing Loans</th></tr>
<tr><td>Commercial Real Estate:
• Unless there is a clear safety and soundness need for a new appraisal/evaluation or an update to an existing appraisal/evaluation, institutions can use generalized valuation methods on different portfolio segments with similar risk characteristics or individual loans such as:
  • Comprehensive market analyses/market trends or
  • Seasoned CRE loans that are paying as agreed.
• Consider obtaining updates to original appraisal/evaluation or new appraisal/evaluation on a property-specific basis on loans that reflect:
  • Large credit exposure,
  • Collateral is a limited or specific use facility,
  • Some history of cash flow/past due problems
  • High LTV (over supervisory LTV threshold),
  • Out-of-territory properties, or
  • Stressed or rapidly declining market.
• Need to establish flexible criteria for obtaining updated valuations on an ongoing basis.
  • Can use evaluations for monitoring purposes even if original loan required an appraisal.</td><td>Residential Real Estate:
• An updated valuation generally is not needed on loans where LTV was 60 percent or less at origination or if LTV has been reduced to no more than 60 percent through payments, which is consistent with the Credit Policy.
• An updated valuation based on an AVM, BPO, or other valuation technique should be obtained according to the institution's monitoring criteria for loans with an LTV greater than 60 percent.</td></tr>
<tr><th colspan="2">Renewals/Refinancings/Modifications</th></tr>
<tr><td colspan="2">In general, renewals and refinancings may be supported by evaluations rather than appraisals per the exemption under Part 323.3(a)(7)(i) and (ii). Modifications do not need an appraisal, as they are not considered new transactions, but the institution does need an updated value to make an informed business decision as to whether a loan modification is more cost-effective than foreclosure.</td></tr>
<tr><th colspan="2">Address Safety & Soundness Concerns</th></tr>
<tr><td colspan="2">After consulting with their Regional Office, examiners should require an institution to obtain a new appraisal/evaluation for credits where the existing value is unreliable, and an accurate valuation is critical to the supervisory review. The lack of a reliable or accurate appraisal will not preclude examiners from adversely classifying an asset or relieve an institution from the responsibility of maintaining the ALLL at an appropriate level.</td></tr>
<tr><th colspan="2">Reducing/Suspending HELOCs</th></tr>
<tr><td colspan="2">Although lenders are not required to obtain an appraisal, institutions should have a factual basis for calculating revised residential property values before reducing/suspending HELOC credit privileges.</td></tr>
</table>

Source: FDIC RD Memorandum 2009-011, *Re-appraising/Re-evaluating Real Property*, dated March 18, 2009.

Figure 15. Re-appraisal/Re-evaluation Matrix.

APPENDIX 9. FDIC, OCC, AND FRB ENFORCEMENT ORDER PROCESSES

The enforcement action process for the FDIC, OCC, and FRB generally begins with examiners performing a bank examination. When deficiencies are identified at the examination, examiners consider a broad range of corrective measures that range from moral suasion to the use of enforcement actions. The severity of action chosen is based on the financial institution's current financial condition, and the type, number, and severity of identified deficiencies or violations of laws and regulations, with consideration given to the cooperation, responsiveness, and capability of the board and management. Enforcement actions fall within two broad categories: informal and formal. The latter is more severe and is generally enforceable by law. Regulators' policies also provide that the selection of specific corrective measures should be tailored to the institution and designed to correct identified deficiencies, improve its overall condition, and return the institution to a safe and sound condition.

Unlike most informal actions, formal enforcement actions are disclosed to the public. Formal enforcement actions include cease and desist/consent orders, formal written agreements, PCA directives, capital directives, safety and soundness orders, termination of FDIC insurance, removal/suspension of institution-affiliated parties, and civil money penalties. Detailed below is a general description of the process used by each regulator for issuing cease and desist/consent orders and formal written agreements.

FDIC

According to FDIC guidance, the ROE generally serves as the FDIC's primary support for proposing an order against an institution. When a formal action against an institution is contemplated, it is mandatory that an examiner consult with the responsible regional office before submitting an ROE containing the basis for a possible order. In preparation of an ROE where the examiner believes an order may be warranted, the following guidelines should be observed:

- Examiners should present their findings on the Examination Conclusions and Comments schedule in the ROE.
- In a separate memorandum to the Regional Director, examiners should detail each specific "Undesirable and Objectionable Practice" regarded as unsafe or unsound, and the facts upon which that conclusion is based should be listed and discussed in the order of importance under appropriately descriptive subheadings and captions.
- Where violations of law or regulations are also present, they should be discussed under a separate subheading. All relevant facts concerning these areas should be addressed, and reference should be made to specific schedules in the report where full details are presented.
- The memorandum should include any statement made by the institution's directors and/or officers either supporting any charge made by the examiner or showing any corrective action.

- This memorandum should also outline incomplete corrective promises of management.

Regional officials (supervision and legal) work together to draft orders. The FDIC also coordinates with state banking authorities. The FDIC uses templates to help draft orders and to ensure consistency. Once an order is drafted, it is sent to the institution for review, and a meeting is scheduled to discuss the order and specific provisions with the board of directors and management. If the institution does not have any exceptions, the order is signed by the institution's board and regulatory officials and subsequently issued. If the institution does not consent to the order, a notice of charges is provided to the institution initiating an administrative hearing process.

To assure greater uniformity of action and to help assure that supervisory efforts are directed to institutions most in need of them, the FDIC has adopted a policy that presumes a formal action will be taken on institutions with composite ratings of 4 or 5, unless specific circumstances argue strongly to the contrary. Institutions with composite ratings of 4 or 5 will, by definition, have problems of sufficient severity to warrant formal action. Exceptions to the policy may be considered when the condition of the institution clearly reflects significant improvement resulting from an effective corrective program or where individual circumstances strongly mitigate the appropriateness or feasibility of an order.

OCC

The ROE documents the OCC's findings and conclusions with respect to its supervisory review of an institution. Generally, the EIC is responsible for initially recommending the use of an enforcement action to address problems and concerns identified during the examination. The OCC's formal actions include formal written agreements, consent orders, and, where necessary, cease and desist orders. The actions an institution takes or agrees to take in response to the ROE are important factors in determining whether the OCC will take enforcement action and the severity of that action. In most cases, the ROE is completed and sent to the institution before an action is formalized, but it is not required.

Problems identified by examiners are discussed with Assistant Deputy Comptrollers, and ROE conclusions are provided to a Supervision Review Committee. The OCC has created a Supervision Review Committee in each of the Districts and a Washington Supervision Review Committee. The purpose of these committees is to help ensure that OCC bank supervision and enforcement policies are applied effectively and consistently. The committee makes a recommendation to the Deputy Comptrollers, who have the final decision. The OCC procedures note that enforcement actions should be drafted using as guidance any standard language provided from time to time by the Director for Enforcement and Compliance, as well as articles used in previous enforcement actions that may be tailored to the specific concerns to be addressed.

Once the order is drafted, the institution is given an opportunity to review the order and discuss the order with the OCC. According to OCC officials we interviewed, the OCC will consider making generally non-substantive changes to the draft order based on discussions with institution officials. Most actions are consented to by the institution. Enforcement action documents should address all substantive supervisory problems.

Under OCC guidance, the presumption for formal action is particularly strong, regardless of an institution's composite CAMELS rating or capital levels, when it is experiencing significant problems or weaknesses in its systems and controls; serious insider abuse; substantial violations of law or serious compliance problems; material noncompliance with prior commitments to take corrective action; or failure to maintain satisfactory books and records or provide examiner access to books and records when, as a result, the OCC is unable to determine the institution's true financial condition.

When an institution becomes composite 3-rated, a determination is made if an action is warranted. If the institution is 3-rated and management is weak, the OCC will begin with the presumption of a formal action. If OCC examiners have confidence in management, they may pursue an informal action. Confidence in management is based on many factors, including a demonstrated ability and willingness to make changes.

The OCC will issue a formal written agreement for 3-rated institutions under 1818(b) of the U.S. Code. If the bank does not comply with the agreement or its condition worsens, the OCC will issue a consent order. OCC guidance notes that formal written agreements can be issued more quickly and have the same overall objective as a cease and desist order. Regarding 4- or 5-rated institutions, OCC guidance notes that because those institutions have serious problems and are more likely to fail, there is a strong presumption in favor of using a cease and desist order or PCA directive, if legally supportable.

FRB

Recommendations for enforcement actions typically originate at the Reserve Banks and are submitted to the Board of Governors in Washington, D.C. According to FRB practices, formal enforcement action referrals should be made where examiners find that the board of directors or management of a financial institution is seriously deficient; the institution has unsatisfactory policies or procedures, or inadequate internal controls or record keeping systems in important areas of operations; and the Reserve Bank staff believes that the institution cannot be operated in a safe or sound manner or in compliance with applicable laws, rules, or regulations. Referrals for formal enforcement actions should also be made where examiners uncover instances of fraud; insider abuse or misconduct; or significant violations of laws, rules, or regulations by the institution or institution-affiliated parties.

To ensure consistency and quality control, attorneys of the Board of Governors prepare the enforcement action after reviewing the ROE, other relevant information, and the recommendations from the Reserve Bank. FRB policies note that when circumstances warrant a less severe form of formal supervisory action, a written agreement may be issued. Depending on the circumstances, the FRB may issue a cease and desist order rather than a Written Agreement. The FRB at times issues a cease and desist order as a follow-up formal enforcement action to a Written Agreement when an institution fails to comply with the requirements of the Written Agreement or significant new deficiencies arise. The FRB coordinates its enforcement actions with state banking authorities. As a matter of practice, the most common form of formal enforcement action issued by the FRB is a Written Agreement.

According to FRB officials, the FRB has standard provisions that are often used in preparing enforcement actions. The FRB typically does not enforce a numeric capital percentage in its enforcement actions but rather includes a capital provision in the enforcement action that requires the institution to provide an acceptable capital plan to the examiners. The FRB prefers to require an acceptable capital plan instead of a fixed numeric capital percentage because use of the capital plan provides the institution and examiners more flexibility in responding to the changing capital needs of the institution.

After an enforcement action is drafted, it is sent from the Board of Governors to the Reserve Bank, who in turn presents it to the financial institution. FRB officials told us that institutions are aware of forthcoming enforcement actions. The enforcement action is then discussed at a formal meeting between regulators and institution management and the board of directors. If the institution does not consent to the order, the FRB would issue a notice of charges, pursue a temporary cease and desist order, and conduct an administrative hearing.

The FRB's *Commercial Bank Examination Manual* states that institutions rated composite 4 or 5 are clearly problem institutions that require close and constant supervisory attention. Unless specific circumstances argue strongly to the contrary, such institutions will be presumed to warrant formal supervisory action, that is, a formal written agreement or cease and desist order.

APPENDIX 10. GLOSSARY

Term	Definition
1-4 Family Residential Loans	Loans secured by residential properties containing 1-4 dwelling units, which includes, but is not limited to, townhouses, condominiums, cooperative housing units, vacation homes, and certain mobile homes. These do not include loans for 1-4 family residential property construction and land development.
Abandoned Private Capital Investor (PCI) Request	A PCI request for clearance to bid that is no longer being pursued by the PCI, and for which the PCI did not submit a formal withdrawal letter to the FDIC.
Accounting Standards Codification (ASC)	FASB's trademarked collection of accounting standards issued by accounting regulators, including FASB, American Institute of Certified Public Accountants, and FASB's EITF. The standards were restructured into one topically organized resource, and technically superseded all previous U.S. GAAP.
Acquiring Institution (AI)	A financial institution that purchases assets from a failed institution. An AI can purchase assets with or without SLA coverage. In this report, an AI refers to an institution with an SLA, unless otherwise noted. The FDIC shares losses and recoveries on SLA assets with the AI, at pre-arranged levels.
Acquisition, Development, and Construction (ADC) Loans	A component of CRE that provides funding for acquiring and developing land for future construction, and that provides interim financing for residential or commercial structures.
Adversely Classified Assets	Assets subject to criticism and/or comment in an examination report. Adversely classified assets are allocated on the basis of risk (lowest to highest) into three categories: Substandard, Doubtful, and Loss.
Total Adversely Classified Assets Ratio	Determines the aggregate level of all assets classified as Substandard, Doubtful, and Loss in relation to total assets.

Allowance for Loan and Lease Losses (ALLL)	An estimate of uncollectible amounts that is used to reduce the book value of loans and leases HFI by the amount of probable incurred losses as of the balance sheet date. It is established to recognize that it is probable that some loans in the institution's overall loan and lease portfolio will not be repaid. Boards of directors are responsible for ensuring that their institutions have controls in place to consistently determine the allowance in accordance with the institutions' stated policies and procedures, GAAP, and supervisory guidance.
Alt-A Loan	Mortgage loan where the borrower's income, assets, or employment are typically not verified. Instead, the loan approval is based primarily on the applicant's credit score.
Amortized Cost	A cost-based measurement that adjusts the historical cost for amortization or other allocations. Amortized cost is calculated as the historical cost amount of the financial asset or financial liability adjusted over time as follows: (1) minus principal repayments, (2) plus or minus the cumulative amortization or accretion of any difference between that initial amount and the maturity amount, (3) plus or minus foreign exchange adjustments, and (4) minus direct write-offs of the principal amount.
Amortized Cost Basis	For an investment, the amount at which the investment is acquired, adjusted for accretion, amortization, collection of cash, previous OTTIs recognized in earnings (less any cumulative-effect adjustments), foreign exchange, and fair value hedge accounting adjustments.
Appraisal Standards Board of the Appraisal Foundation	Six appraisers who are appointed by the Board of Trustees of the Appraisal Foundation to develop, interpret, and amend the USPAP.
Asset-Backed Securities	Bonds or notes backed by financial assets. Typically, these assets consist of receivables other than mortgage loans, such as credit card receivables, auto loans, manufactured-housing contracts, and home-equity loans.
Automated Valuation Model	A computer program that estimates a property's market value based on market, economic, and demographic factors. Hedonic models generally use property characteristics (such as square footage and room count) and methodologies to process information, often based on statistical regression. Index models generally use geographic repeat sales data over time rather than property characteristic data. Blended or hybrid models use elements of both hedonic and index models.
Available-for-Sale (AFS) Securities	One of three accounting categories for securities. AFS securities are those that management has not designated for trading or as held to maturity. AFS securities are reported at fair value, with unrealized gains and losses excluded from earnings and reported in a separate capital component.
Bank Board Resolution	An informal enforcement action constituting a commitment adopted by a financial institution's board of directors that directs the institution to take corrective action regarding specific noted deficiencies. The FDIC uses the term bank board resolution, while the FRB uses the term board resolution to mean the same thing.
Call Report	The Consolidated Reports of Condition and Income, often referred to as the Call Report, include basic financial data for insured institutions in

	the form of a balance sheet, an income statement, and supporting schedules. According to the Federal Financial Institutions Examination Council's (FFIEC) instructions for preparing Call Reports, national banks, state member banks, and insured nonmember banks are required to submit a Call Report to the FFIEC's Central Data Repository (an Internet-based system used for data collection) as of the close of business on the last day of each calendar quarter.
Case Manager Procedures Manual	A manual that addresses the general purpose and the required review procedures and deliverables of FDIC case managers' risk assessment and supervision activities.
Cease and Desist Order	A formal enforcement action issued by a financial institution regulator to a bank or affiliated party to stop an unsafe or unsound practice or a violation of a law or regulation. A cease and desist order may be terminated under certain circumstances, including when the bank's condition has significantly improved and the action is no longer needed or the bank has materially complied with its terms.
Change in Business Plan	An application, submitted by de novo institutions, that proposes changes to business plans during the institutions' first 3 or 7 (state nonmember) years of operations. Newly insured state nonmember institutions are required to obtain FDIC approval before implementing any proposed major change or deviation in their business plans.
Change-in-Control	The acquisition of voting shares of an institution or parent company, if, immediately after the transaction, the acquiring person (or persons acting in concert) will own, control, or hold with power to vote 25 percent or more of any class of voting shares of the institution or its parent company.
Clearance-to-Bid Letter	A written letter, provided by RMS to PCIs, which allows PCIs to bid on failed insured depository institutions. The letter includes any limits on the total assets of the institutions on which the PCIs are cleared to bid, as well as any geographic regions. The letter also requires PCIs to abide by the PCI SOP. All covered investors must return to RMS a signed copy of clearance-to-bid letters before they are permitted to purchase a failed institution.
Collateralized Debt Obligation (CDO)	General terminology for a broad range of structured finance products. CDOs are similar to collateralized mortgage obligations and asset-backed securities in that they are securitized investments that are subdivided into tiers or tranches, and are backed by an underlying collateral pool. Unlike collateralized mortgage obligations and asset-backed securities, the CDO collateral pool can contain a wide variety of less-than-homogeneous assets. In their basic form, CDOs reallocate the risk of the underlying collateral pool to investors based on the investors' risk tolerance levels and investment return objectives. CDOs are most commonly issued by commercial banks, insurance companies, money managers, and investment banks.
Commercial Real Estate (CRE) Loans	Consistent with interagency guidance on Concentrations in Commercial Real Estate Lending, Sound Risk Management Practices (December 2006), CRE loans include loans secured by multi-family property, and nonfarm nonresidential property where the primary source of repayment is derived from rental income associated with the property (that is, loans for which 50 percent or more of the source of repayment

	comes from third-party, nonaffiliated, rental income) or the proceeds of the sale, refinancing, or permanent financing of the property. CRE loans also include land development and construction loans (including 1-4 family residential and commercial construction loans), other land loans, loans to real estate investment trusts, and unsecured loans to developers.
Commitment Letter	An informal enforcement action that is used by the OCC and FRB, which reflects specific written commitments to take corrective actions in response to problems or concerns identified by examiners in the supervision of the financial institution. The document may be written by the regulator or the financial institution and is signed by the institution's board of directors on behalf of the institution and acknowledged by the regulator. A commitment letter is not a binding legal document. However, failure to honor the commitments provides strong evidence of the need for formal action.
Concentration	A significantly large volume of economically related assets that an institution has advanced or committed to a certain industry, person, entity, or affiliated group. These assets may, in the aggregate, present a substantial risk to the safety and soundness of the institution.
Consent Order	A cease and desist order entered into with consent of the parties. A formal enforcement action issued by a financial institution regulator to a bank or affiliated party to stop an unsafe or unsound practice or violation. A consent order may be terminated by a regulator when it has determined that the bank's condition has significantly improved and the action is no longer needed or the bank has materially complied with its terms.
Criticized Assets	Assets adversely classified under the agencies' Uniform Loan Classification Standards risk rating classifications as Substandard, Doubtful, or Loss.
Debt Service Coverage Ratio	A measure of the amount of cash flow available to meet annual interest and principal payments on debt. The ratio is used, in part, to determine if a property will be able to sustain its debt based on cash flow. The ratio is derived by dividing Net Operating Income by Total Debt Service.
De Novo Institution	A newly insured depository institution that is subject to higher capital requirements and more frequent examination activities during its first 3 or 7 (state nonmember) years of operation.
Debt-to-Income Ratio	Represents the percentage of a borrower's income that goes toward all recurring debt payments, including the mortgage payments. The higher the ratio, the greater the risk that the borrower will have cash-flow problems and will miss mortgage payments.
Deposit Insurance Fund (DIF)	A fund that is established by Section 11(a)(4) of the FDI Act, and that is used by the FDIC to carry out the Corporation's insurance purposes in the manner provided by the subsection.
Derivatives	Financial contracts/instruments whose value is based on one or more underlying assets, publically traded securities, interest rates, currency exchange rates, or market indexes. Derivatives are often used to protect assets against changes in value. Financial institutions commonly use derivative instruments for managing (positioning or hedging) their exposures to market risk, cash-flow risk, and/or other risks in their

	operations and for trading. In addition, depository institutions are increasingly employing credit derivatives, which are used to assume or lay off credit risk. The most common types of freestanding derivatives are forwards, futures, swaps, options, caps, floors, and collars.
Discounted Payoff (DPO)	Occurs when a bank charges off a certain portion of an impaired loan and then works with a borrower to close out the loan by collecting as much of the remaining balance as possible.
Doubtful	One of three adversely classified loan (asset) ratings. Loans classified Doubtful have all the weaknesses inherent in those classified Substandard, with the added characteristic that the weaknesses make collection or liquidation in full, on the basis of currently known facts, conditions, and values, highly questionable and improbable.
Eligible Bidder	A depository institution that the FDIC has qualified to submit bids to acquire a failed insured depository institution.
Examination Documentation (ED) Module	An FDIC and FRB examination tool that focuses on risk management and provides guidance on establishing an appropriate examination scope. An ED module, of which there are several, incorporates questions and points of consideration into examination procedures to specifically address an institution's risk management strategies for each of its major business activities. An ED Module also directs examiners to consider areas of potential risk and associated risk control practices, thereby facilitating an effective supervisory program and sets forth standards or "best practices" and the risks associated with not meeting the standards.
Fair Value Accounting	A financial reporting approach in which companies measure and report on an ongoing basis certain assets and liabilities (generally financial instruments) at estimates of the prices they would receive if they were to sell the assets or would pay if they were to transfer the liabilities in an orderly transaction between market participants, at the measurement date. Under fair value accounting, companies report losses when the fair values of their assets decrease or liabilities increase. Those losses reduce companies' reported equity and may also reduce companies' reported income. FDIC-insured institutions most often apply fair value measurements to record changes in the value of AFS securities.
Fannie Mae and Freddie Mac	Shareholder-owned corporations with government charters. These organizations play a critical role in the U.S. home mortgage market by purchasing home mortgages from original lenders, repackaging them as mortgage-backed securities, and either selling or holding them in their investment portfolios.
FDIC Improvement Act of 1991 (FDICIA)	This Act increased the powers and authority of the FDIC. Major provisions recapitalized the Bank Insurance Fund and allowed the FDIC to strengthen the fund by borrowing from the Treasury. The Act mandated a least-cost resolution method and prompt resolution approach to problem and failing banks and ordered the creation of a risk-based deposit insurance assessment scheme. Brokered deposits and the solicitation of deposits were restricted, as were the non-bank activities of insured state banks. FDICIA created new supervisory and regulatory examination standards and put forth new capital requirements for banks. It also expanded prohibitions against insider activities and created new Truth in Savings provisions.

Federal Deposit Insurance (FDI) Act	This Act, established in 1950, revised and consolidated earlier FDIC legislation into one Act that embodied the basic authority of the operation of the FDIC.
Financial Accounting Standards (FAS)	These standards define the accounting, reporting, and disclosure requirements for the FASB, which are rules to be followed by accountants in accumulating financial data and preparing financial statements. The standards are, in effect, generally accepted accounting principles, or GAAP.
Financial Accounting Standards Board (FASB)	Since 1973, FASB has been the private sector's designated organization for establishing standards of financial accounting that govern the preparation of financial reports by nongovernmental entities.
Formal Written Agreement	An agreement used by the OCC and FRB. This document is signed by a financial institution's regulator and the institution's board of directors on behalf of the institution. Its provisions prescribe restrictions and corrective and remedial measures necessary to correct deficiencies or violations in a financial institution and return it to a safe and sound condition.
Generally Acce-pted Accounting Principles (GAAP)	Accounting rules and conventions that define acceptable practices in preparing financial statements.
Global Debt	The aggregate of a borrower's or guarantor's financial obligations, including contingent obligations.
Global Debt Service and/or Global Cash Flow Analysis	A comprehensive evaluation of borrower capacity to perform on a loan. During underwriting, proper global cash flow must thoroughly analyze projected cash flow and guarantor support. Beyond the individual loan, global cash flow analysis must consider all other relevant factors, including: guarantor's related debt at other financial institutions, future economic conditions, and must also include obtaining current and complete operating statements of all related entities. In addition, global cash flow analysis should be routinely conducted as a part of credit administration. The extent and frequency of global cash flow analysis should be commensurate with the amount of risk associated with the particular loan.
Government-Sponsored Enterprise (GSE)	A privately held corporation that was authorized or established by the U.S. Congress to fulfill public purposes in housing, higher education, farming, and the thrift industry. GSEs were created to direct funds to particular sectors of the economy that were believed to be inadequately served by the private credit markets. Presently, GSEs primarily act as financial intermediaries to assist lenders and borrowers in housing and agriculture and include, but are not limited to, the Federal Home Loan Banks, the Federal National Mortgage Association (Fannie Mae), and the Federal Home Loan Mortgage Corporation (Freddie Mac).
Home Affordable Modification Program (HAMP)	A loan modification program designed to reduce delin-quent and at-risk borrowers' monthly mortgage payments. HAMP is effective for mortgages originated on or prior to January 1, 2009, and will expire on December 31, 2013.
Impairment Accounting Standards	These standards are applied to adjust the carrying value of a security when a decline in the fair value of the security represents an OTTI. Impairment accounting standards also are applied to loans and leases

	HFI, which typically represent the largest asset class for community banks, when a credit loss is determined to be probable and reasonably estimable. Such loans and leases are measured at amortized cost, with a separate valuation allowance (the ALLL) recorded to measure any impairment amount. The measurement of impairment is based on probable incurred losses, and not the fair value of the loans except in limited circumstances. The provision expense to establish or increase the ALLL directly affects net income and, consequently, regulatory capital levels.
Inflatable Charter	An existing insured depository institution that is being capitalized or acquired and capitalized with the primary intent of assuming liabilities and purchasing assets of a failed insured depository institution from the FDIC in the agency's capacity as receiver.
Informal Enforcement Action	A voluntary commitment made by the board of directors of a financial institution that is designed to correct identified deficiencies and ensure compliance with federal and state banking laws and regulations. The most common informal enforcement actions include board resolutions, memorandums of understanding, commitment letters, and approved safety and soundness plans. Informal enforcement actions are neither publicly disclosed nor legally enforceable.
Institution-Affiliated Party	Refers to (1) any director, officer, employee, or controlling stockholder (other than a bank holding company or savings and loan holding company) of, or agent for, an insured depository institution; (2) any other person who has filed or is required to file a change-in-control notice with the appropriate federal banking agency; (3) any shareholder (other than a bank holding company or savings and loan holding company), consultant, joint venture partner, and any other person as determined by the appropriate federal banking agency (by regulation or case-by-case) who participates in the conduct of the affairs of an insured depository institution; and (4) any independent contractor (including any attorney, appraiser, or accountant) who knowingly or recklessly participates in (a) any violation of any law or regulation; (b) any breach or fiduciary duty; or (c) any unsafe or unsound practice, which caused or is likely to cause more than a minimal financial loss to, or a significant adverse effect on, the insured depository institution.
Intrinsic Value	The worth inherent in an object, as distinguished from the value for which it can be exchanged at a particular time.
Least Cost Test (LCT)	Shows the calculation of the FDIC's cost of liquidating a failing financial institution in comparison to other possible resolution options. FDICIA requires the FDIC to resolve a failing institution in a manner that results in the least cost to the DIF. The statute requires the FDIC to document its evaluation and the assumptions on which the evaluation is based, and to retain that documentation for at least 5 years.
Liquidity	An institution's ability to fund assets and meet obligations as they become due. Liquidity is essential in all banks to compensate for expected and unexpected balance sheet fluctuations and provide funds for growth.
Loans and Leases Held for Investment (HFI)	Loans that a financial institution has the intention and ability to hold for the foreseeable future or until maturity or payoff.

Loans and Leases Held for Sale (HFS)	Loans and leases that the reporting financial institution does not have the intent and/or ability to hold for the foreseeable future or until maturity (loans not HFI). These loans are reported at the lower of cost or fair value, except for those loans held for sale that the bank has elected to account for at fair value under a fair value option, which should be reported at fair value. For loan and leases held for sale that are reported at the lower of cost or fair value, the amount by which cost exceeds fair value, if any, is accounted for as a separate valuation allowance (not included within the allowance for loan and lease losses).
Loan-to-Value (LTV) Ratio	The total loan amount at origination divided by the market value of the property securing the credit plus any readily marketable collateral or other acceptable collateral.
Loss	One of three adversely classified loan (asset) ratings. Loans classified Loss are considered uncollectible and of such little value that their continuance as bankable assets is not warranted. This classification does not mean that the loan has absolutely no recovery or salvage value but rather that it is not practical or desirable to defer writing off this basically worthless asset even though partial recovery may occur in the future.
Material Loss Review (MLR)	Section 38(k) of the FDI Act, as amended, defines a loss of $25 million to the DIF as material for the time period ending on December 31, 2009; and a loss of $150 million to the DIF as material for the period January 1, 2012 through December 31, 2013. In general, that section provides that if the DIF incurs such loss with respect to an insured depository institution, the Inspector General of the appropriate federal banking agency (which for the OCC is the Inspector General of the Department of the Treasury) shall prepare a report to that agency, reviewing the agency's supervision of the institution.
Memorandum of Understanding	An informal agreement between a regulator and a financial institution, which is signed by both parties.
(MOU)	MOUs are designed to address and correct identified weaknesses in an institution's condition.
Merger	A business combination of two or more institutions with one institution's charter being the survivor.
Mortgage-Backed Securities	Securities representing an undivided interest in a pool of mortgages with similar characteristics. Payments on the underlying mortgages are used to make payments to the security holders.
Multi-family Residential Loan	A real estate-secured loan that includes, but is not limited to, a property with five or more residential units (such as apartment buildings, cooperative buildings, and mixed-use buildings where the primary use is residential with five or more housing units). This type of loan does not include multi-family residential property construction, apartment rehabilitation, and condominium conversion loans.
Mutual-to-Stock Conversion	Conversion of an insured mutual state chartered savings bank to the stock form of ownership.
Net Interest Income (NII)	The difference between the interest income produced by a financial institution's earning assets (loans and investments) and interest that it pays to its depositors.

Net Loan Charge-offs	The gross amount of loans charged off as confirmed losses, less recoveries collected on previously charged-off loans.
Net Present Value (NPV) Test	A standard test that is applied when determining whether to modify a loan. The test results show the expected NPV of modifying past-due loans compared to foreclosure. To modify a loan, the NPV of the loan modification must exceed the NPV of the foreclosed collateral, DPO, or short-sale alternatives. Standard assumptions are used to ensure that a consistent standard of affordability is provided based on a 31-percent borrower mortgage debt-to-income ratio.
Non-accrual Status	The status of an asset, often a loan, on which interest accruals have been suspended for accounting purposes due to financial difficulties of the borrower. Typically, this occurs because full collection of principal or interest is in doubt, or principal or interest payments have not been made for a sustained period of time. Loans with principal or interest unpaid for at least 90 days are generally considered to be in a non-accrual status.
Non-current Loan Ratio	This ratio measures the level of loans and leases past due over 90 days and still accruing interest and loans the institution has placed on non-accrual status, as a percentage of total loans.
Non-performing Loan	Also known as a non-current loan, this includes a non-accrual loan and a loan that is 90 days or more past due on interest or principal repayment.
Non-statistical Sample	A judgmental sample whose results cannot be projected to the population by standard statistical methods.
Other Comprehensive Income (OCI)	Revenues, expenses, gains, and losses that under GAAP are included in comprehensive income but excluded from net income, which includes net unrealized holding gains (losses) on AFS securities.
Other Real Estate Owned (OREO)	Real estate acquired by a lender through foreclosure or otherwise in satisfaction of a debt and held in inventory until sold.
Other-Than-Temporary Impairment (OTTI)	An impairment of a debt security occurs when the fair value of the security is less than its amortized cost basis. According to accounting standards, when the impairment is judged to be OTTI, the carrying value of the individual security must be written down to fair value. If the present value of cash flows expected to be collected on a debt security is less than its amortized cost basis, a credit loss exists. In this situation, if an institution does not intend to sell the security and it is unlikely that the institution will be required to sell the debt security before recovery of its amortized cost basis less any current-period credit loss, an OTTI has occurred. The portion of the total OTTI related to the credit loss must be recognized in earnings, but the portion of the total impairment related to other factors must be recognized in OCI.
Part 323 of the FDIC Rules and Regulations	Part 323 identifies which real estate-related financial trans actions require the services of an appraiser, prescribes which categories of federally related transactions must be appraised by a state-certified appraiser and which by a state-licensed appraiser, and prescribes minimum standards for the performance of real estate appraisals in connection with federally related transactions under FDIC supervision.

Participation Loan	A loan made by multiple lenders to a single borrower. The lead institution typically originates the loan, takes responsibility for servicing the loan, organizes and manages the participation, and deals directly with the borrower. The lead institution sells "participations" in a loan to other institutions to share in the risks associated with the loan.
PCI Institution	An insured depository institution in which the PCI invests, and which will be used to submit a bid on the assets and deposits of a failed insured depository institution.
PCI Request	Any oral or written request by PCIs to RMS for clearance to bid on failed insured depository institutions pursuant to the FDIC's PCI SOP.
Performing Loan	A loan that is less than 90 days past due, has not been placed on non-accrual, or is not in workout status.
Preferred Shares	Equity securities (or stock) having characteristics of both equity and debt instruments. Preferred shares are senior in priority to common shares, but subordinate to bonds. Preferred shares typically do not have voting rights, but the shares often have priority over common shares in the payment of dividends and upon liquidation. Preferred shares may carry a dividend that is paid prior to any dividends to common stockholders.
Private Capital Investment	An investment that is provided by a private entity, exempt from registering with the United States Securities and Exchange Commission, to an existing depository institution for capitalization or for pursuing an acquisition of open or failed bank assets.
Private Capital Investor (PCI)	For purposes of this evaluation, PCI refers to the private entities or a group of entities that raises capital from private rather than public sources to invest in either a newly chartered depository institution or an existing depository institution for the purpose of using that institution to submit a bid on the assets and deposits of a failed insured depository institution.
Private Equity Company	An investment company that has equivalent meaning given the terms "hedge fund" and "private equity fund" in section 13(h)(2) of the Bank Holding Company Act of 1956 (12 U.S.C. 1851(h)(2)).
Problem Bank	Any insured depository institution that has been assigned a composite CAMELS rating of 4 or 5 by its primary federal regulator or by the FDIC if it disagrees with the primary federal regulator's rating.
Prompt Corrective Action (PCA)	The purpose of PCA is to resolve the problems of insured depository institutions at the least possible long-term loss to the DIF. Part 325, subpart B, of the FDIC's Rules and Regulations, 12 CFR, section 325.101, et. seq., implements section 38, *Prompt Corrective Action*, of the FDI Act, 12 U.S.C., section 1831(o), by establishing a framework for taking prompt supervisory actions against insured nonmember banks that are less than adequately capitalized. The following terms are used to describe capital adequacy: (1) *Well Capitalized*, (2) *Adequately Capitalized*, (3) *Undercapitalized*, (4) *Significantly Undercapitalized*, and (5) *Critically Undercapitalized*.
Prompt Corrective Action (PCA) Directive	A formal action that regulators issue to institutions that fail to meet minimum capital requirements. These directives require financial institutions to take one or more specified actions to meet required minimum capital standards. Regulators typically use PCA directives to

	specify corrective actions that need to be taken by significantly and critically undercapitalized institutions.
Prompt Corrective Action (PCA) Related Material Transaction	An activity that is not in the usual course of business. Such activities include any investment, expansion, acquisition, sale of assets, or other similar action for which a financial institution would have to notify the appropriate federal banking agency.
Provision for Loan and Lease Losses (PLLL)	Additions to, or reductions of, the allowance account resulting from evaluations of the collectability of the loan and lease portfolio, to maintain the balance of the allowance at an appropriate level, through charges or credits to the provision in the Report of Income.
Quarterly Banking Profile Reports	Quarterly publications that provide the earliest comprehensive summary of financial results for all FDIC-insured institutions. The reports include, but are not limited to, written analyses, graphs, statistical tables, and time series spreadsheets.
Report of Examination (ROE)	A report summarizing the bank examiners' findings after conducting a thorough examination of the bank's affairs as provided for under the FDI Act.
Returned PCI Request	A PCI request that is sent back to the PCI for being substantially incomplete and that the FDIC considers to be closed after a resubmission period expires.
Return on Assets (ROA) Ratio	A financial institution's annualized net income expressed as a percentage of average total assets. The ROA ratio is a basic measure of a financial institution's profitability and an indication of how efficiently the assets are being used.
Risk-Based Capital Standards	Part 325 of the FDIC Rules and Regulations, which establishes minimum capital requirements, and Appendix A to Part 325—Statement of Policy on Risk-Based Capital, which defines the FDIC's risk-based capital rules. Appendix A states an institution's balance sheet assets and credit equivalent amounts of off-balance-sheet items are assigned to broad risk categories according to the obligor or, if relevant, the guarantor or the nature of the collateral. The aggregate dollar amount in each category is then multiplied by the risk weight assigned to that category. The resulting weighted values from each of the four risk categories are added together, and this sum is the risk-weighted assets total that, as adjusted, comprises the denominator of the risk- based capital ratio. The institution's qualifying total capital base is the numerator of the ratio.
Risk Management Manual of Examination Policies	A manual of FDIC-insured institution examination policies, procedures, and deliverables.
Safety and Soundness Plan	A plan that includes a description of the steps an institution will take to correct identified deficiencies and the time within which these steps will be taken. A financial institution's regulator may require the submission of a safety and soundness plan if it determines that the institu-tion failed to meet certain safety and soundness standards.
Shelf Charter	An insured depository institution that is established after the FDIC's approval of an Interagency Charter and Depo-sit Insurance Application and after assuming liabilities and purchasing assets of a failed

	depository institution from the FDIC in the agency's capacity as receiver.
Short Sale	In general, a short sale is the sale of an asset at a price that is lower than the balance owed on the asset. This type of sale typically occurs when a borrower is facing financial difficulty and the value of the asset drops significantly. In these cases, the financial institution may decide that selling the asset at a loss is better than foreclosure. As it pertains to SLAs, DRR has defined a short sale as the sale of the collateral securing a shared-loss CRE loan to a third party where the AI accepts from the obligor a payoff of an amount that is less than the balance due on the loan and (1) the obligor presents the AI with a secured or unsecured note for all or a portion of the deficiency or (2) the deficiency is forgiven by the AI in whole or in part.
Special Mention Assets	Assets that have potential weaknesses that deserve management's close attention. If left uncorrected, these potential weaknesses may result in deterioration of the repayment prospects for the asset or in the institution's credit position at some future date. Special Mention assets are not adversely classified and do not expose an institution to sufficient risk to warrant adverse classification.
Subprime Loans	Loans to borrowers with weak credit histories at the time of origination or purchase, including, but not limited to, payment delinquencies, charge-offs, judgments and/or bankruptcies. The borrowers may also display reduced repayment capacity as measured by credit scores, debt-to-income ratios, or other criteria that may encompass borrowers with incomplete credit histories. Such loans have a higher risk of default than loans to prime borrowers.
Substandard	One of three adversely classified loan (asset) ratings. Substandard loans are inadequately protected by the current sound worth and paying capacity of the obligor or of the collateral pledged, if any. These loans must have a well-defined weakness or weaknesses that jeopardize the liquidation of the debt. They are characterized by the distinct possibility that a financial institution will sustain a loss if the deficiencies are not corrected.
Superseded PCI Request	A PCI request for clearance to bid that was replaced by another request from the PCI having a different mix of investors.
Temporary Cease and Desist Order	An order that is issued to halt a particularly dangerous practice or condition, pending a formal hearing on a permanent order. A temporary order is typically used only when immediately necessary to protect a financial institution against ongoing or expected harm.
Tier 1 Capital	Defined in Part 325 of the FDIC Rules and Regulations, 12 CFR, section 325.2(v), as: **The sum of:** • Common stockholder's equity (common stock and related surplus, undivided profits, disclosed capital reserves, foreign currency translation adjustments, less net unrealized losses on AFS securities with readily determinable market values); • Non-cumulative perpetual preferred stock; and • Minority interest in consolidated subsidiaries; **Minus:** • Certain intangible assets;

	• Identified losses; • Investments in securities subsidiaries subject to section 337.4; and Deferred tax assets in excess of the limit set forth in section 325.5(g).
Tier 1 Leverage Capital Ratio	An institution's Tier 1 Capital divided by its adjusted average assets, which are an institution's average assets adjusted for ineligible intangible assets used in Tier 1 Capital as well as the unrealized loss on marketable equity securities.
Troubled Debt Restructuring (TDR)	A modified or renewed loan in which an institution, as a creditor, for economic or legal reasons, grants a concession to a borrower experiencing financial difficulties that the institution would not otherwise consider were it not for the borrower's financial difficulties.
Trust Preferred Security (TruPS)	Hybrid instruments possessing characteristics typically associated with debt obligations. Under the basic structure of a TruPS, a corporate issuer, such as a bank holding company, first organizes a business trust or other special purpose entity. This trust issues two classes of securities: common securities, all of which are purchased and held by the corporate issuer, and TruPS, which are sold to investors. The business trust's only assets are deeply subordinated debentures of the corporate issuer, which the trust purchases with the proceeds from the sale of its common and preferred securities. The corporate issuer makes periodic interest payments on the subordinated debentures to the business trust, which uses these payments to pay periodic dividends on the TruPS to the investors. The subordinated debentures have a stated maturity and may be redeemed under other circumstances. Most TruPS are subject to a mandatory redemption upon the repayment of the debentures.
Uniform Bank Performance Report (UBPR)	A compilation of financial data and ratios for a financial institution that includes extensive comparisons to peer group performance. Such reports are produced by the FFIEC for the use of banking supervisors, bankers, and the general public and is produced quarterly from Call Report data submitted by banks.
Uniform Financial Institutions Rating System (UFIRS)	Financial institution regulators and examiners use the UFIRS to evaluate a bank's performance in six components represented by the CAMELS acronym: **C**apital adequacy, **A**sset quality, **M**anagement practices, **E**arnings performance, **L**iquidity position, and **S**ensitivity to market risk. Each component, and an overall composite score, is assigned a rating of 1 through 5, with 1 having the least regulatory concern and 5 having the greatest concern.
Uniform Retail Credit Classification and Account Management Policy	An interagency policy statement that establishes standards for the classification and treatment of retail credit in financial institutions. Retail credit consists of open- and closed-end credit extended to individuals for household, family, and other personal expenditures. Retail credit also includes loans to individuals secured by personal residences, including first mortgage, home equity, and home improvement loans.
Uniform Standards of Professional Appraisal Practice (USPAP)	These standards represent the generally accepted and recognized standards of appraisal practice in the United States. The purpose of the standards is to promote and maintain a high level of public trust in appraisal practice by establishing requirements for appraisers. The

	Appraisal Standards Board of the Appraisal Foundation promulgates these standards for both appraisers and users of appraisal services.
Virtual Supervisory Information on the Net (ViSION)	An FDIC information system that facilitates financial institution supervision activities, which include application processing, examination tracking, offsite analysis and monitoring, formal and informal action tracking, and case management.
Withdrawn PCI Request	A PCI request for clearance to bid that is no longer being processed as a result of a written notification from the PCI.

APPENDIX 11. ACRONYMS AND ABBREVIATIONS

Acronym	**Definition**
ADC	Acquisition, Development, and Construction
AFS	Available for Sale
AI	Acquiring Institution
ALLL	Allowance for Loan and Lease Losses
AOCI	Accumulated Other Comprehensive Income
ASC	Accounting Standards Codification
CAMELS	**C**apital, **A**sset Quality, **M**anagement, **E**arnings, **L**iquidity, and **S**ensitivity to Market Risk
CDO	Collateralized Debt Obligation
CFR	Code of Federal Regulations
CMC	Compliance Monitoring Contractor
CRE	Commercial Real Estate
DIF	Deposit Insurance Fund
DPO	Discounted Payoff
DRR	Division of Resolutions and Receiverships
ED Module	Examination Documentation Module
EIC	Examiner-in-Charge
EITF	Emerging Issues Task Force
FAS	Financial Accounting Standard
FASB	Financial Accounting Standards Board
FDI Act	Federal Deposit Insurance Act
FDIC	Federal Deposit Insurance Corporation
FDICIA	Federal Deposit Insurance Corporation Improvement Act of 1991
FFIEC	Federal Financial Institutions Examination Council
FRB	Board of Governors of the Federal Reserve System
FV	Fair Value
GAAP	Generally Accepted Accounting Principles
GAO	U.S. Government Accountability Office
GSE	Government-Sponsored Enterprise

HAMP	Home Affordable Modification Program
HFI	Held for Investment
HFS	Held for Sale
HTM	Held to Maturity
LCT	Least Cost Test
LTV	Loan-to-Value
MLR	Material Loss Review
MOU	Memorandum of Understanding
NII	Net Interest Income
NPV	Net Present Value
NPV Test	Net Present Value Test
OCC	Office of the Comptroller of the Currency
OCI	Other Comprehensive Income
OIG	Office of Inspector General
OREO	Other Real Estate Owned
OTS	Office of Thrift Supervision
OTTI	Other-Than-Temporary Impairment
PCA	Prompt Corrective Action
PCI	Private Capital Investor
PCI SOP	FDIC's Statement of Policy on Qualifications for Failed Bank Acquisitions
P.L.	Public Law
PLLL	Provision for Loan and Lease Losses
RD Memorandum	Regional Director Memorandum
RMS	Division of Risk Management Supervision
ROA	Return on Assets
ROE	Report of Examination
RSAM	Risk Sharing Asset Management
SEC	Securities and Exchange Commission
SLA or LSA	Shared-Loss Agreement or Loss Sharing Agreement
SPAC	Special Purpose Acquisition Corporation
TA	Total Assets
TDR	Troubled Debt Restructuring
TL	Total Liabilities
TruPS	Trust Preferred Security
UBPR	Uniform Bank Performance Report
UFIRS	Uniform Financial Institutions Rating System
UPB	Unpaid Principal Balance
U.S.C.	United States Code
USPAP	Uniform Standards of Professional Appraisal Practice
ViSION	Virtual Supervisory Information on the Net

APPENDIX 12. REGULATOR COMMENTS

FDIC
Federal Deposit Insurance Corporation
550 17th Street NW, Washington, D.C. 20429-9990

DATE: December 19, 2012

TO: Jon T. Rymer, Inspector General
Office of Inspector General

FROM: Sandra L. Thompson, Director /**Signed**/
Division of Risk Management Supervision

Bret D. Edwards, Director /**Signed**/
Division of Resolutions and Receiverships

SUBJECT: Response to Draft Report Entitled *Comprehensive Study on the Impact of the Failure of Insured Depository Institutions*

The Division of Risk Management Supervision (RMS) and the Division of Resolutions and Receiverships (DRR) have received and considered the draft report *entitled Comprehensive Study on the Impact of the Failure of Insured Depository Institutions* (the Report). The Federal Deposit Insurance Corporation's (FDIC's) Office of Inspector General (OIG), with the assistance of KPMG LLP for certain areas of the review, prepared the Report as required by Public Law 112-88.

The Report finds that bank managements' decisions to engage in aggressive loan growth by relaxing underwriting standards and their failure to implement adequate oversight and controls, coupled with rapidly declining real estate values, caused most of the bank failures that occurred between 2008 and 2011. The Report acknowledges that the FDIC generally fulfilled its supervisory and resolution responsibilities as defined by statutes, regulations, accounting standards, and interagency guidance in place at the time. The Report also acknowledges that the FDIC reacted to a rapidly changing economic and financial landscape by establishing and revising policies and procedures to address key risks facing the industry. In addition the Report makes a number of recommendations aimed at making enhancements in certain resolution and supervisory activities going forward.

The Report recommends that the Director of DRR:

1) Develop a strategy for mitigating the impact of impending portfolio sales and Shared Loss Agreement (SLA) terminations on the Deposit Insurance Fund (DIF) and ensure that procedures, processes, and resources are sufficient to address the volume of terminations and potential requests for asset sales.

2) Research risks presented by commercial loan extension decisions and determine whether DRR should develop additional controls for monitoring AIs' efforts to extend the terms of commercial loans.

DRR concurs with both of these recommendations.

With respect to the first recommendation, DRR notes that the FDIC will review its existing strategies for mitigating the impact of portfolio sales. As part of its review, the FDIC will consider whether it should augment or modify its strategies to mitigate the impact of portfolio sales on the DIF.

SLAs require AIs to receive the FDIC's prior consent for any portfolio sale. An important part of the FDIC's existing strategy to mitigate the impact of potential portfolio sales is that its consent of any sale will be contingent upon evidence that the sale would result in maximizing recoveries on the assets included in the proposed sale. In October 2012, the FDIC clearly communicated in writing its expectations to the AIs that any sales that require consent from the FDIC must, at a minimum, meet the standard of maximizing asset recoveries.

In anticipation of receiving portfolio sales proposals from AIs, the FDIC has created a committee and standard processes to review such requests, particularly to ensure that any approved sale maximizes asset recoveries. The establishment of this committee is an integral part of the FDIC's strategy. The FDIC will review the committee process to ensure that it appropriately mitigates the impact of potential portfolio sales. While the FDIC does not anticipate a significant volume of requests, it will review the committee process to ensure that it has the capacity to thoroughly evaluate each received request and respond in a timely manner, including in the event that the volume of requests exceed the FDIC's expectations.

In the commercial SLAs, after the loss share coverage terminates at the end of year five, the AI can conduct portfolio sales without FDIC approval; however, the AI still must demonstrate that it used its best effort to maximize recoveries on assets through the termination of the agreement at the end of year eight. From the sixth through the eighth years of the agreements, the FDIC shares any recoveries realized by the AIs on assets for which the AI has previously received loss share payments, and, as a result, the FDIC will continue to rigorously enforce the agreements by maintaining a comprehensive oversight and monitoring program. The FDIC will review its monitoring program and ensure that the resources are appropriate to enforce the agreement through the three-year recovery period, including the review of portfolio sales.

The FDIC will review its early termination program, to include a review of the results of the program to date, to ensure that the program mitigates the impact on the DIF. The FDIC's current early termination program for SLAs focuses on portfolios of $20 million or less. Therefore, the small number of SLAs under consideration for early termination combined with the relatively small portfolio size is unlikely to materially impact the DIF. Furthermore, the SLAs fully outline the roles and responsibilities of both the AIs and the FDIC upon expiration of the five-year loss coverage period for commercial loans. The FDIC believes the provisions in the SLAs are adequate to facilitate a smooth transition from the five-year loss sharing period to the three-year recovery period. Additionally, the FDIC maintains a detailed commercial SLA loss sharing expiration schedule and will ensure that it maintains a sound operational plan for dealing with any peaks in the volume of such expirations.

The FDIC will engage in a formal assessment of the sufficiency of its procedures, processes, and resources for the anticipated volume of portfolio sales and SLA terminations, and will deliver its conclusions to the OIG by September 30, 2013.

Regarding the second recommendation, the commercial SLAs require that the AI use its best efforts to maximize recoveries. To satisfy this requirement, we expect the AI to consider every resolution alternative in its analysis, including engaging in loan modifications. When opting for loan modifications, we expect each AI to underwrite each modification request in a prudent manner consistent with normal lending practice and its existing policies and procedures. In order to better assess the extent to which AIs are complying with these requirements, the FDIC will:

- reinforce previous communications to AIs regarding the FDIC's expectation that AIs should use best efforts to maximize recoveries when making loan modification decisions;
- require the FDIC's Compliance Monitoring Contractors (CMCs) to review a sample of AI loan modification decisions for maturing loans during CMC onsite visits; and
- analyze the costs and benefits of collecting and monitoring trend information on commercial loan modifications across AIs to identify AIs with lower rates of modifications for further analysis. If deemed cost beneficial, the FDIC will begin collecting such information from AIs when operationally feasible.

The FDIC will implement the three action items above and complete an assessment of the benefits and risks presented by commercial loan modifications for loans covered under SLAs, and will deliver its conclusions to the OIG by September 30, 2013.

The Report recommends that the Director of RMS:

1) Clarify supervisory expectations related to examiners' review of the institution's appraisal program and whether that review should include all program elements in the 2010 *Interagency Appraisal and Evaluation Guidelines* (Appraisal Guidelines) or be limited to appraisal program areas of concern resulting from the examiner loan file review.

2) Reiterate that examiners should be including a positive assurance statement in the Report of Examination or examination work papers in situations where examiners conclude that the institution has implemented adequate procedures over appraisals and evaluations, and develop an RMS internal review control to periodically verify examiner compliance.

3) Reiterate or strengthen examiner documentation requirements related to examination methodologies and examination procedures performed to assess the risk management elements of an institution's workout program.

The Director of RMS concurs with these recommendations.

RMS' guidance to examiners about the documentation of examination findings is contained in the RMS Manual of Examination Policies, Section 1.1, Basic Examination Concepts and Guidelines, under the heading Examination Workpapers. RMS will clarify its expectations for examiners' review of an institution's appraisal program and will remind examiners that workpapers should document the extent of reviews, including positive assurance statements where required by separate guidance. This reminder will include references both to the Appraisal Guidelines and to the four elements required by the interagency *Policy Statement on Prudent Commercial Real Estate Loan Workouts*. The reminder will reinforce to examiners the importance of complete workpaper documentation, particularly given the exception-based nature of comments in Reports of Examination.

The Report further recommends the FDIC, the Board of Governors of the Federal Reserve System (FRB), and the Office of the Comptroller of the Currency (OCC):

1) Strengthen examiner documentation requirements related to examination methodologies and examination procedures performed to assess an institution's appraisal program.

2) Study differences between the types of enforcement actions that are used by the agencies and the timing of such actions to determine whether there are certain approaches that have proven to be more effective in mitigating risk and correcting deficiencies that should be implemented by all three agencies.

The FDIC concurs with the recommendations.

RMS will coordinate with the FRB and the OCC to review the Appraisal Guidelines and determine the most appropriate way to strengthen examination documentation requirements. Additionally, RMS plans to conduct an internal study in 2013 on the approach utilized for informal and formal enforcement actions to determine whether an alternative approach to mitigate risk and correct deficiencies may be more effective. The FDIC will coordinate with the FRB and OCC to consider and discuss the various approaches taken to enforcement matters.

Thank you for the opportunity to review and comment on the draft Report.

MEMORANDUM

Comptroller of the Currency
Administrator of National Banks

Washington, DC 20219

To: Jon T. Rymer, Inspector General

From: Thomas J. Curry, Comptroller of the Currency /**Signed**/

Date: December 20, 2012

Subject: Response to the Federal Deposit Insurance Corporation's (FDIC) Office of Inspector General's Review of Bank Failures

We have received and reviewed your draft report dated November 19, 2012, on the results of the FDIC's Office of Inspector General's (OIG) study of the impact of the failure of insured depository institutions. It is our understanding that this study was conducted in accordance with Public Law 112-88, which was signed into law on January 3, 2012, and addressed matters pertaining to supervisory or resolution activities at the FDIC, the Office of the Comptroller of the Currency (OCC), and the Board of Governors of the Federal Reserve System (FRB). In accordance with your request, we have included our responses below to recommendations 3 and 7 addressed jointly to the OCC, FDIC, and FRB. You specifically requested our concurrence, partial concurrence, or non-concurrence with these two recommendations from the study.

Strengthen examiner documentation requirements related to examination methodologies and examination procedures performed to assess an institution's appraisal program. We concur with the intent of the FDIC OIG's comments relating to the need for adequate documentation of the evaluation of an institution's real estate appraisal program and the review of individual appraisals as part of an institution's supervisory examination strategy and core assessment. We consider our existing core assessment supervisory process, the real estate loans expanded examination procedures regarding the evaluation of commercial real estate (CRE) appraisal programs, and associated workpaper and report of examination documentation standards to be consistent with this FDIC OIG recommendation. While we believe that our supervisory examination strategy and core assessment processes satisfy this FDIC OIG recommendation, we have plans to improve our guidance by including a section specific to appraisals in the CRE and mortgage handbooks that are currently being revised.

While each regulator imposed formal enforcement actions uniformly and fairly across their regulated institutions, we noted differences in the types of actions that the regulators use (i.e., consent orders and formal written agreements) and in the timing of actions (i.e., when a bank is 3-rated or once a bank becomes 4- or 5-rated). We recommend that the FDIC, OCC, and FRB study these differences to determine whether there are certain approaches that have proven to be more effective in mitigating risk and correcting deficiencies that should be implemented by all three agencies. We concur with your recommendation and welcome the opportunity to enter into dialogue with the FDIC and FRB to compare the relative effectiveness of our respective enforcement policies and practices.

Thank you for the opportunity to review and comment on your draft report. If you have questions or need additional information, please contact Jennifer Kelly, Senior Deputy Comptroller for Midsize and Community Bank Supervision, at (202) 649-5420.

BOARD OF GOVERNORS

OF THE

FEDERAL RESERVE SYSTEM

WASHINGTON, D.C. 20551

December 11, 2012

Mr. Jon T. Rymer
Inspector General
Federal Deposit Insurance Corporation
Arlington, Virginia 22226

Dear Mr. Rymer:

Thank you for the opportunity to review the Federal Deposit Insurance Corporation (FDIC) Office of Inspector General (OIG) draft December 2012 report entitled "Comprehensive Study on the Impact of the Failure of Insured Depository Institutions." Public Law 112-88, signed into law on January 3, 2012, required the FDIC OIG to conduct a study on the impact of the failure of insured depository institutions. The study addressed matters pertaining to supervisory and resolution activities at the FDIC, the Office of the Comptroller of the Currency (OCC), and the Board of Governors of the Federal Reserve System (FRB) (the agencies).

We appreciate the thoroughness of your review and your analysis which found that the agencies effectively carried out their supervisory and resolution responsibilities. The study found that regulators implemented their policies appropriately, and includes seven recommendations to strengthen the effectiveness of certain supervisory activities going forward. Five of the recommendations pertained only to the FDIC. The two recommendations that pertain to all three agencies, identified in the report as Recommendations Three and Recommendation Seven, relate to strengthening the documentation of examination appraisal reviews and improving uniformity in enforcement actions across regulators.

Recommendation Three suggests that the agencies "[s]trengthen examiner documentation requirements related to examination methodologies and examination procedures performed to assess an institution's appraisal program." As the report notes, the FRB has developed Examiner Documentation modules, along with the FDIC, and requires that the use of supplemental modules such as the *Real Estate Appraisal Module* be discussed in the examination scoping memorandum. The FRB is continually looking for ways to improve its examination processes, including ways to improve our documentation procedures as suggested in this recommendation.

Recommendation Seven notes the variation among the agencies regarding the types of enforcement actions the agencies use and the timing of these actions. The report recommends that the agencies "[s]tudy these differences to determine whether there are certain approaches that have proven to be more effective in mitigating risk and correcting deficiencies that should be

Mr. Jon T. Rymer
December 11, 2012
Page 2 of 2

implemented by all three agencies." To address this recommendation, the FRB will work with the FDIC and the OCC to discuss the various approaches taken to enforcement matters.

We would like to thank the OIG team for the professionalism and courtesy that they exhibited throughout the review. We appreciate the opportunity to comment on this report and have provided technical comments on the draft report under separate cover.

Regards,

/Signed/

Michael S. Gibson
Director
Division of Banking Supervision and Regulation
Board of Governors of the Federal Reserve System

End Notes

[1] *Final Report of the National Commission on the Causes of the Financial and Economic Crisis in the United States*, January 2011, issued pursuant to P.L. 111-21.

[2] *Commercial Real Estate Losses and the Risk to Financial Stability*, February 11, 2010. In response to the financial crisis, the Congress created the Congressional Oversight Panel in October 2008 to review the state of financial markets and the regulatory system.

[3] The Tier 1 Leverage Capital ratio is calculated based on an institution's *Tier 1 Capital* divided by adjusted average assets.

[4] Pursuant to Section 38 of the FDI Act (12 U.S.C. § 1831o), the FDIC issued Part 325, Subpart B – Prompt Corrective Action, which defines an institution as *Well Capitalized* if its Leverage ratio is equal or greater than 5.0 percent, Tier 1 Risk-Based Capital ratio is equal or greater than 6 percent, and Total Risk-Based Capital ratio is greater than or equal to 10.0 percent; and it is not subject to any written agreement, order, capital directive, or *PCA directive* to meet and maintain a specific capital level for any capital measure. Regulations issued by the FRB and OCC have similar definitions of *Well Capitalized.*

[5] Unless stated otherwise, for the purposes of this report, the federal financial regulators are the FDIC, FRB, and OCC.

[6] These figures include institutions formerly regulated by the OTS. We generally did not include thrifts in our report analyses because Congress transferred OTS' responsibilities to the OCC, FDIC, and FRB in July 2011.

[7] Section 13(c)(4) of the FDI Act (12 U.S.C. § 1823(c)(4)).

[8] The 293 figure includes IndyMac Bank, which failed in July 2008 and was resolved through a conservatorship. Then in March 2009, using an SLA, the FDIC sold former IndyMac Bank assets to an AI.

[9] Section 38(k) of the FDI Act, as amended, provides that if the DIF incurs a "material loss" with respect to an insured depository institution, the Inspector General of the appropriate regulator (which for the OCC is the Inspector General of the Department of the Treasury) shall prepare a report to that agency, identifying the cause of failure and reviewing the agency's supervision of the institution.

[10] An AI may purchase failed bank assets with or without an SLA. Unless noted otherwise, we use the term AI to refer to a financial institution with an SLA.

[11] For the purposes of this report, we define "performing" to mean a loan for which a borrower is current on all payments or is paying as agreed according to the terms of the loan. We use the terms "performing," "current," and "paying as agreed" interchangeably.

[12] Most single-family SLAs will naturally expire from 2019 through 2021.

[13] Section 38(a)(1) of the FDI Act (12 USC § 1831(o)(a)).

[14] This total excludes 2 PCIs that the FDIC determined were not subject to the PCI SOP.

[15] The FDIC uses the term SLA, and P.L. 112-88 uses the term LSA.

[16] The 293 figure includes IndyMac Bank.

[17] An AI may purchase failed bank assets with or without an SLA. Unless noted otherwise, we use the term AI to refer to a financial institution with an SLA. We also use the term institutions without SLAs, which refers to financial institutions that did not acquire any failed bank assets.

[18] FDIC Circular 6371.1, *Bidders List Preparation and Clearance Process*, governs the preparation of the bid list used in marketing failing institutions and obtaining regulatory approval of bidders. The Circular details criteria, including potential bidders' financial condition and asset size, that DRR uses when developing the bid list.

[19] This analysis does not include IndyMac Bank.

[20] The FDIC uses the term intrinsic value to refer to the price that an asset would be worth in a normally functioning, non-depressed market.

[21] FDIC publication: *Managing the Crisis: The FDIC and RTC Experience 1980-1994*, FDIC, 1998, chapter 7.

[22] If the FDIC is unable to find an acquirer for failed institution assets, the FDIC has to pay off the insured depositors and liquidate the failed institution's assets. This resolution strategy is referred to as a payout and is usually the most costly form of resolution.

[23] We have not performed audit work to validate the FDIC's estimated SLA savings or resolution loss rates.

[24] One borrower declined to indicate the loan status, and one borrower had two loans and indicated that one was a performing loan and one had been paid off.

[25] The borrower that had two loans indicated that he was "dissatisfied" and "neutral" with his AI pertaining to the two loans.

[26] Renewals typically apply to commercial loans and not single-family loans.

[27] AIs reported an additional 11,734 foreclosures as of September 30, 3012. These foreclosures were either performed by a failed institution just prior to closure or by the AI shortly after it assumed the failed institution. These 11,734 foreclosures all occurred in the AIs' first quarter of operations. DRR's data does not distinguish between which of these foreclosures were performed by the failed bank and the AI.

[28] The FDIC receives hard copy and e-mail inquiries from the public, the media, Congress, and the White House and those inquiries are typically received by staff in FDIC headquarters or the FDIC's Consumer Response Center in Kansas City, Missouri. The Consumer Response Center forwards SLA-related complaints to DRR for responses.

[29] On May 29, 2009, the FDIC Board of Directors approved establishing the FDIC Advisory Committee on Community Banking to provide the FDIC with advice and guidance on a broad range of important policy issues impacting small community institutions throughout the country, as well as the local communities they serve, with a focus on rural areas.

[30] For the purposes of this report, we defined "types" of loans as either residential or commercial loans.

[31] Alt-A loans consist of mortgage loans where the borrower's income, assets, or employment are typically not verified. Instead, the loan approval is based primarily on the applicant's credit score.

[32] The loan modification rates were calculated by taking the amount of loans each AI reported in its Reports of Condition and Income as being restructured in TDRs and dividing that amount by the total loans reported by each AI.
[33] DRR reported that assets covered by commercial SLAs totaled $71.6 billion as of June 30, 2012.
[34] Our interviews of the AIs were conducted in April and May 2012. As noted earlier, DRR provided guidance to the AIs on proposed SLA asset sales in October 2012.
[35] DRR calculation based on the estimated unpaid principal balance remaining when each SLA expires.
[36] These figures do not include failed thrifts that were regulated by the OTS.
[37] Tier 1 Capital is defined in Part 325 of the FDIC Rules and Regulations, 12 CFR § 325.2(v). We used the institution's Tier 1 Capital as of December 2005 as the denominator unless the institution had not yet opened. In those cases, we used the most recent year-end data corresponding to the institution's opening. In aggregate, Tier 1 Capital totaled $18.0 billion. This analysis does not include any subsequent capital growth or contributions made prior to an institution's failure.
[38] Only 3 of the 42 institutions in this sample had average non-current loan ratios of 5 percent or more, with 6.0 percent being the highest ratio in the sample.
[39] Non-accrual loans have had their interest accrual suspended because the full collection of principal is in doubt, or interest payments have not been made for a sustained period of time. Institution records may show those loans as zero days past due to distinguish them from other past-due loans that remain in accrual status.
[40] A TDR occurs when an institution grants a concession to a borrower in modifying or renewing a loan that the institution would not otherwise consider if not for the borrower experiencing financial difficulties.
[41] An institution is *Critically Undercapitalized* if its tangible equity capital ratio is less than or equal to 2.0 percent.
[42] Evaluating the Impact of Fair Value Accounting on Financial Institutions: Implications for Accounting Standards Setting and Bank Supervision, Working Paper No. QAU 12-01.
[43] In June 2009 FASB codified existing GAAP accounting literature into the Accounting Standards Codification (ASC). FAS No. 115 was codified into ASC Topic 320, *Investments—Debt and Equity Securities.*
[44] Codified into ASC Topic 815, *Derivatives and Hedging.*
[45] Codified into ASC 820, *Fair Value Measurements and Disclosures.*
[46] *Fair Value Accounting: Understanding the Issues Raised by the Credit Crunch*, dated July 2008, commissioned by the Council of Institutional Investors.
[47] Codified into ASC Topic 450, *Contingencies.*
[48] Codified into ASC Topic 310, *Receivables.*
[49] *Report and Recommendations Pursuant to Section 133 of the Emergency Economic Stabilization Act of 2008: Study on Mark-To-Market Accounting*, dated December 30, 2008, by the Office of the Chief Accountant of the SEC.
[50] KPMG's analysis did not include thrift and savings institutions formerly regulated by the OTS.
[51] For a security, impairment occurs if the fair value of the security falls below its amortized cost basis. In general, the impairment would be an OTTI if recovery of the entire amortized cost basis of the security is not expected.
[52] NII is the difference between the interest income produced by an institution's earning assets (loans and investments) and the interest expense paid on liabilities (deposits and borrowings).
[53] Losses on troubled CRE loans that are collateral-dependent are recognized when advances in excess of calculated current fair value are considered uncollectible and do not warrant continuance as bankable assets, and there is little or no prospect for near-term improvement and no realistic strengthening action of significance pending.
[54] A loan is impaired when, based on current information and events, it is probable that the creditor will be unable to collect all amounts due (principal and interest) according to the zloan's contractual terms.
[55] The legislation refers to a Joint Press Release of the regulators on December 2, 2010 that announced their issuance of *Interagency Appraisal and Evaluation Guidelines.*
[56] FRB – 12 CFR § 208, subpart E, and 12 CFR § 225, subpart G. FDIC – 12 CFR § 323. OCC – 12 CFR § 34, subpart C.
[57] In 1986, nine leading professional appraisal organizations in the United States and Canada formed an Ad Hoc Committee on the USPAP. Agreeing upon a generally accepted set of standards, the eight United States committee members adopted those standards and thereafter established The Appraisal Foundation in 1987 to implement the USPAP.
[58] An evaluation is a valuation permitted by the agencies' appraisal regulations for transactions that qualify for the appraisal threshold exemption, business loan exemption, or subsequent transaction exemption.
[59] Preamble to *Final Statement of Policy on Qualifications for Failed Bank Acquisitions*, 74 Federal Register 45440 at page 45446 (September 2, 2009).
[60] *De novo* is a term used to refer to a recently chartered insured institution.
[61] A PCI may also file a merger or change-in-control application with the FRB if the investment is made at the holding company level.
[62] The deposit insurance order for a *de novo* institution generally requires that for 3 years following the commencement of banking operations, the institution shall obtain approval from the appropriate FDIC Regional Director prior to any major deviation or material change to the business plan before consummation

of the change. In 2009, the FDIC extended this requirement to 7 years for state nonmember banks. A decision to pursue the acquisition of failed financial institutions could be an example of a material change in business plan.

63 These exceptions include: (1) the strong majority interest exception applicable to private investors in a partnership or similar venture with or in a holding company where the investors hold one-third or less of each of the total equity and the voting equity of the partnership post acquisition and the holding company has an established record of successful operation of insured institutions; or (2) the recapitalization exception meaning that within the 18-month period following the recapitalization, the total assets of all of the anticipated failed-bank acquisitions will not exceed 100 percent of the acquiring bank's total assets as of the day before the capital raise.

64 Bank secrecy is a legal principle under which banks are not allowed to provide to authorities personal and account information about their customers unless certain conditions apply. A bank secrecy jurisdiction is a locale that permits bank secrecy.

65 12 U.S.C. § 1816.

66 12 U.S.C. § 1817(j).

67 12 U.S.C. § 1828(c).

68 RMS determined that five of the approved requests were not subject to the PCI SOP because of exceptions related to a "strong majority interest" or "recapitalization."

69 As of September 30, 2012, two of the four requests were withdrawn, one was abandoned, and one was still under review.

70 The FDIC may require pre-filing meetings for applications to acquire control of state savings associations per 12 C.F.R. §390.103.

71 Audit report titled, *The FDIC's Qualification Process for Private Capital Investors Interested in Acquiring or Investing in Failed Insured Depository Institutions*, AUD-12-004, dated December 22, 2011.

72 Two additional PCI institutions were suspended from bidding for the first time in 2012.

73 CRE is defined in the glossary at Appendix 10.

74 This statement replaced the Interagency Policy Statements on the Review and Classification of Commercial Real Estate Loans (November 1991) and Review and Classification of Commercial Real Estate Loans (June 1993).

75 A restructuring involves a formal modification in the loan's terms with written and legally enforceable documentation.

76 *Global debt* represents the aggregate of a borrower's or guarantor's financial obligations, including contingent obligations.

77 Additionally, if applicable, institutions should recognize in other liabilities an allowance for estimated credit losses on off-balance-sheet credit exposures related to restructured loans (e.g., loan commitments) and should reverse interest accruals on loans that are deemed uncollectible.

78 These factors also apply when considering loss estimates for off-balance-sheet credit exposures (e.g., loan commitments).

79 The October 2009 guidance states that a restructured loan is considered a TDR when the institution, for economic or legal reasons related to a borrower's financial difficulties, grants a concession to the borrower in modifying or renewing a loan that the institution would not otherwise consider. To make this determination, the lender assesses whether (a) the borrower is experiencing financial difficulties and (b) the lender has granted a concession.

80 The debt service coverage ratio is the measurement of a property's ability to generate revenueas a percentage of the costof loan payments.

81 The debt-to-income ratio is the borrower's total monthly housing-related payments (principal, interest, taxes, and insurance), as a percentage of the borrower's gross monthly income.

82 Formal enforcement actions also include PCA directives, capital directives, and safety and soundness orders.

83 Unlike the OCC and the FDIC, the FRB does not have authority to appoint the FDIC as receiver based on willful violation of a cease and desist order.

84 The primary goal of the FDIC's Case Manager program is to enhance risk assessment and supervision activities by assigning responsibility and accountability for a caseload of institutions or companies to one individual, regardless of charter and location, and by encouraging a more proactive, but non-intrusive, coordinated supervisory approach. Case Managers, in conjunction with senior management, coordinate and direct RMS' supervisory program using a top-down approach to develop strategies and examination activities for all insured depository institutions in their caseloads.

85 These results are *mean* differences in ratios between the two groups and are statistically significant at the 1 percent significance level.

86 We focused our analysis on safety and soundness-related enforcement actions. We did not include actions that were exclusively related to consumer compliance or Bank Secrecy Act violations.

87 A material capital raise is defined by RMS as the sum of the net stock transactions and net contributions from holding companies. To qualify as a capital raise, the total capital raised for the year must have been at least $100,000 and 0.50 percent of total assets at the end of the year.

[88] Criticized Loans are classified as Loss, Doubtful, and Substandard.

[89] *Banking Regulation: Enhanced Guidance on Commercial Real Estate Risks Needed*, (GAO-11-489), dated May 2011.

[90] The FDIC generally requires a change-in-control application if there is a proposal to acquire voting shares of an insured state non-member bank, if, immediately following the transaction, the acquiring person will own, control or hold the power to vote 25 percent or more of any class of voting shares. The FDIC *Case Manager Procedures Manual* further states if an AI does not hold 25 percent or more, post-transaction, then a voting share of 10 percent or more will constitute an application for acquisition of control. If two or more persons, not acting in concert, each propose to acquire simultaneously equal percentages of 10 percent or more of a class of voting shares of an insured state non-member bank or parent company, each person shall file prior notice with the FDIC. The FDIC will afford any person seeking to rebut a presumption an opportunity to present views in writing or, if appropriate, orally before its designated representatives at an informal conference.

[91] 12 C.F.R. § 325.103.

[92] 12 USC § 1831(o)(a).

[93] These ROEs represented the last full-scope examination completed prior to September 30, 2011 for our sampled institutions.

[94] According to the FDIC's Division of Insurance and Research, from 1985 through 2011, 22 percent of problem banks ultimately failed.

[95] In some cases, a PCI submitted multiple bids for the same failed institution. For the purposes of this study, we are counting the multiple bids as one bid.

[96] We did not have enough information to definitively determine whether those investors met the definition of private equity company as defined in P.L. 112-88. FDIC management indicated that many covered investors were private equity investors, but the FDIC is not required to maintain information on private equity companies.

[97] Between March 31, 2012 and September 30, 2012, three PCIs submitted a total of five bids for five failed institutions. Three of the PCI bids were successful, and two PCIs acquired three failed banks. The other two bids were not successful. The successful bids increased the number of PCIs that acquired one or more failed institutions to 14.

[98] OIG Report No. EVAL-12-002, February 2012.

[99] We contacted representatives from 12 non-SLA banks, but 6 declined our interview request because they had no involvement with, or opinion, of SLAs.

[100] In-state AIs were headquartered in the same states as the failed institutions and out-of-state AIs were headquartered in different states from the failed institutions.

[101] We excluded throughout this report, unless explicitly noted, OTS-supervised institutions because that regulatory agency's authorities and responsibilities transferred to other regulatory agencies effective July 21, 2011, and the OTS ceased to exist effective October 19, 2011.

[102] We were unable to obtain two sets of examination working papers sufficient for our review. One institution was subject to a continuous examination process, so limited loan line sheets were available for review. For the other institution, we were unable to access the examination working papers due to technological constraints.

[103] CMCs perform visitations for AIs with total SLA asset balances greater than $200 million. DRR staff perform oversight of AIs with asset balances less than $200 million.

[104] For a security, impairment occurs if the fair value of the security falls below its amortized cost basis. In general, the impairment would be an OTTI if recovery of the entire amortized cost basis of the security is not expected.

[105] *A Convenient Scapegoat: Fair Value Accounting by Commercial Banks during the Financial Crises*, Brad A. Badertscher, Jeffery J. Burks, and Peter D. Easton, University of Notre Dame. Published in *The Accounting Review*, Vol. 87, No. 1, January 2012. OTTI analysis covered the top 100 institutions ranked by beginning-of-quarter holdings of non-Treasury HTM and AFS securities.

[106] The recorded amount of the loan is the loan balance adjusted for any unamortized premium or discount and unamortized loan fees or costs, less any amount previously charged off, plus recorded accrued interest.

INDEX

A

B

G

H

I

J

L

M

N

O

P

Q

R

S

T